THE LEGACY OF
CHINA

EDITED BY

RAYMOND DAWSON
Fellow of Wadham College, Oxford

OXFORD UNIVERSITY PRESS
LONDON   OXFORD   NEW YORK

Oxford University Press

OXFORD LONDON NEW YORK
GLASGOW TORONTO MELBOURNE WELLINGTON
CAPE TOWN SALISBURY IBADAN NAIROBI DAR ES SALAAM LUSAKA ADDIS ABABA
BOMBAY CALCUTTA MADRAS KARACHI LAHORE DACCA
KUALA LUMPUR SINGAPORE HONG KONG TOKYO

First published by the Clarendon Press 1964
First issued as an Oxford University Press paperback 1971

PRINTED IN GREAT BRITAIN BY
FLETCHER AND SON LTD, NORWICH

CONTENTS

LIST OF PLATES

LIST OF TEXT-FIGURES

CHRONOLOGICAL TABLE

HSIA	legendary		
SHANG	?1523–?1027		
CHOU	?1027–256	Western Chou ?1027–771 Spring and Autumn era 722–481 Warring States era 403–221	Authority divided between virtually independent feudal states
CH'IN	221–206	having annihilated CHOU in 256 and other rival states in the interim	
FORMER HAN	206–A.D. 9		
HSIN	A.D. 9–23	Wang Mang's usurpation	
LATER HAN	25–220		
THREE KINGDOMS		Shu 221–263 (South-west China) Wei 220–265 (North China) Wu 222–280 (South-east China)	
WESTERN CHIN	265–316		
EASTERN CHIN	317–420	controlled only South China. In North China a period of confusion known as the 'Sixteen Kingdoms' (304–439)	
SOUTHERN AND NORTHERN DYNASTIES	420–589 386–581	Liu Sung 420–479 Liang 502–557 Southern Ch'i 479–502 Ch'en 557–589 Northern Wei 386–535 and four minor dynasties	
SUI	589–618	having controlled North China since 581	
T'ANG	618–907		
FIVE DYNASTIES AND TEN KINGDOMS	907–960	Five short dynasties in North China and ten independent régimes elsewhere	
SUNG	960–1279	Northern Sung 960–1126 Southern Sung 1127–1279	Part of North China controlled by Liao Dynasty 907–1125 North China under Chin (Tartar) Dynasty 1125–1234
YÜAN (Mongols)	1279–1368	having earlier succeeded the Chin Dynasty in North China	

MING	1368–1644	
CH'ING (Manchus)	1644–1912	
REPUBLIC	1912–	(People's Republic 1949–)

INTRODUCTION

IT is now more than forty years since the first volume in this series appeared, *The Legacy of Greece.* It was written by men like Sir Richard Livingstone, Gilbert Murray, and Sir Alfred Zimmern, whose very names are redolent of a passionate enthusiasm for the values of Classical antiquity, which now seems slightly old-fashioned but was then one of the dominant patterns on the fabric of our society, while China was seen merely as a decorative silken fringe overhanging the other end of the world. There have since appeared companion volumes devoted to various other civilizations. That this series has so far lacked a book on China may seem almost as strange an anomaly as the non-representation of Peking at the United Nations; but the explanation lies mainly in the fact that the serious study of this ancient civilization is of very recent growth in the West. A generation ago it would not have been possible to produce anything fit to occupy a place on the same shelf as the illustrious first volume of the series.

Very considerable developments have taken place in Chinese studies since the Second World War, for the great increase in the number of those professionally concerned with the subject, both in Europe and in America, has given scope for a much higher degree of specialization than was previously possible. A more balanced view of Chinese achievement is now emerging. To take one example, it is being appreciated for the first time that the Chinese have cultivated the domain of science and technology quite as successfully as other fields of human activity; so if this book had appeared before the results of Dr. Needham's researches had become available, it would have been a very ill-balanced and ephemeral production. Now that Sinology can at last begin to give a soundly based account of Chinese achievement in all the major activities of the human spirit, this seems to be a most appropriate time for the appearance of this contribution to the series.

A second important reason why this book may be regarded as timely is that now for the first time it is possible to speak with some propriety of the legacy of China without doing violence to the meaning of the word 'legacy'. I am not, of course, implying that Chinese civilization is dead: on the contrary it flourishes vigorously. But it is a new kind of Chinese civilization, which has forgotten the dominant Confucian ethos and imperial structure of the old days. What I mean, therefore, is that it is now possible to say that China has finally broken away from her old traditional civilization; so that we can legitimately regard its achievement as an inheritance from something now no longer living. This is neither to deny that much of the old way of life continues nor to underestimate the great interest shown in the traditional arts and literature. Nevertheless it is arguable that, since the Communist government became firmly established, the Chinese state has been basically Western both in its structure and in its culture. The political system is based on a Western doctrine. Education owes much to the West both in organization and in content. In the cities the new international architecture begins to overshadow the traditional Chinese houses, industries develop in Western-style factories, and traditional forms of transport are augmented or replaced by lorries, buses, bicycles, trains, and steamers. In the field of entertainment, although the traditional theatre flourishes, the cinema and Western-style plays vie with it. Western music is performed, and the Chinese attempt to attain to international standards in sports invented in the West. Daily newspapers, radio, television, the telephone, mass political organizations, trade unions, conferences, and a dozen other tools of our modern civilization all introduce a Western style and tempo to life.

Fifteen years ago it might still have been argued that these foreign imports were on too small a scale to have transformed the country's culture, and it was possible for some people to indulge in the comforting belief that China would always be China and that this unchangeable civilization would remain proof against all shocks from the outside world. Now no one is under any illusions about the great changes which have taken place. In the late nineteenth century some Chinese argued that it would be possible to preserve the essential Confucian civilization at the same time as the country was being modernized by the use of Western techniques. Now a stage has been reached where it is the traditional side of the civilization which may even be regarded as unessential and the Western techniques as essential. Many young Chinese intellectuals, particularly those with a modern scientific or technical education, seem to look back on their traditional civilization as a legacy, seeing it rather in the same light as we do Greek civilization. What is traditional is coming to be regarded as the ornamental addition which makes China distinctive among the nations sharing a modern world-civilization. Symbolical of this attitude are the features of traditional architecture used solely for decorative effect on modern international-style buildings. Although much archaism prevails in the arts, with painters continuing to work in the old styles and jade-carvers devoting their skills to figures of the Goddess of Mercy rather than to themes more consonant with an age of socialist construction, we can feel fairly confident that no quite novel work of the human spirit, owing its inspiration purely to Chinese tradition, will be placed before the world. This, then, is the time to take stock of this great tradition and to try to understand what rich gifts we have already received from it and what constitutes its legacy of permanent value to the modern world.

Finally and most obviously, at a time when there is much misunderstanding between China and the West; when genuine knowledge of contemporary conditions is hard to acquire, both because it is difficult to get into the country and because political prejudices warp judgement; and when increasing numbers of people wish to learn about the Chinese, conscious of the important part they are destined to play in the future of the world—any book which sets out seriously to survey our debt to the civilizatory achievements of the Chinese should surely be welcome.

The purpose of this book, then, is to survey the legacy of traditional Chinese civilization. Legacy to whom? It would be convenient if we could simply say 'to world-civilization'; but this would be a patent over-simplification. World-civilization is a concept which has become meaningful to the scientist, despite the fact that a shanty-town dweller would laugh ruefully at the idea that he enjoyed the same fruits of science and technology as an American multi-millionaire; but one must not forget that language differences are stout fences which will continue to keep us in our own back gardens unable to enjoy any but the choicest blooms of neighbouring literatures. Nor must we be betrayed by the example of *The Legacy of Greece*, which naturally thought of modern Western man as the legatee, into forgetting that the main inheritors of the ancient civilization of China are the modern Chinese and other peoples of the Far East. Unfortunately, to do full justice to that aspect of the legacy one would need to write a different book which catered for a different type of reader; so, although something is said about China's modern reaction to her traditional culture, it has only been possible to talk in very general terms about the influence of China on other Far Eastern countries, for it would have been beyond the scope of this book to venture into detailed discussion of such a very different civilization as that of Japan. Inevitably, since this is a book written in English for readers of English, the main emphasis must be on the legacy to the English-speaking world and to Europe, with which the English-speaking world has close cultural ties.

Of course the nature of the legacy and the identity of the legatees must vary from chapter to chapter. It makes no sense to talk of the legacy of Chinese science and technology except as a legacy to modern world-wide scientific and technological development; but on the contrary it would be absurd to talk of the legacy of Chinese poetry except in terms of the possibility of doing it justice in translation into a particular language. There are great differences, too, in the degree to which the outside world has been influenced by Chinese achievements: inventions like paper and printing came to us long ago, but the art of the Chinese historian is almost unknown in the West. Such variations in the nature of the legacy have compelled our contributors to treat their subjects in dissimilar ways. Few general readers have a detailed knowledge of Chinese philosophy, but China has been dominated in an unparalleled manner by philosophical ideas; in order to get the record straight, therefore, our contributors have had to pay considerable attention to the chronological sequence. In the literature section there is some variation of treatment: in a discussion of the art of the novelist, the playwright, and the historian, the development of style and technique is of primary importance and imposes the necessity of chronological treatment; but in the case of poetry the all-important question concerns the relationship between translation and original and this has made it possible to escape from the chronological groove. The nature of Mr. Sullivan's subject has also enabled him to be more discursive; and Dr. Needham has the advantage that the scientific and technological fields he surveys are international and thus less unfamiliar to the general reader.

It will be observed that the literature section is the longest in the book. This does not imply that it is the most important, but merely that it is the most difficult subject to treat briefly. Science and technology form a section which has every claim to equal treatment with it, especially in view of past neglect, but being less unfamiliar they can be discussed more economically. Certain important fields of human achievement have not been given separate chapters at all. Language, for example, was omitted because it does not represent a civilizatory achievement in the same sense as, say, art or literature. Music also could not quite demand a separate chapter, for it would have been impossible to treat in isolation from drama and poetry, and difficult to discuss and illustrate in a general work of this kind. Religion has not been thoroughly surveyed, but its nobler manifestations find mention in various places, while its more popular and superstitious elements, interesting though they are, do not merit much attention in the present volume. For this is an attempt, not to give an exhaustive survey of Chinese culture, but to concentrate on those elements in it which are of lasting value. Although much is said incidentally about these less important topics, to have devoted separate chapters to them would have been to deprive the other contributors of much-needed space.

Indeed, even with the book's present plan all the contributors could have done with much more space. A book of this kind should primarily be concerned, not with the imparting of information, but with the evaluation of achievements. The contributors to *The Legacy of Greece* were free to do this, assuming in their readers some knowledge of the civilization they were discussing. Our contributors have not been able to assume that all their readers will be similarly well equipped, so they have had to interlard their evaluations with some elementary information, which we hope will not prove indigestible to those whose appetites are for more sophisticated fare. I am grateful to them, both for the courage with which they responded to my invitation to try to say much about many things in few words, and for the patience and self-effacement with which they have submitted to my editorship throughout the preparation of this book.

No attempt has been made to mould these essays into a unity. The book should therefore be viewed as a collection of individual paintings rather than as a mural worked on by several artists; and it is hoped that the various styles in which the contributors have worked and the different outlooks which their contributions reflect will illumine the reality of China's legacy as no product of a single hand could do. But there is one great unity which the book has. It is imbued by a uniform respect for the achievements of the Chinese spirit, and a desire which is shared by Western Sinologists of whatever creed, nationality, or political persuasion to pay tribute to them.

RAYMOND DAWSON

December 1963

I

WESTERN CONCEPTIONS OF CHINESE CIVILIZATION

A T the close of the eighteenth century, when the embassy of Earl Macartney went to Peking to try to establish more satisfactory commercial arrangements with the Chinese, not a single Englishman could be found who knew anything of the Chinese language; so that, in the words of John Francis Davis, members of the mission 'were somewhat discreditably reduced to the necessity of engaging the services of two Romish priests to aid the important objects of the mission in the quality of interpreters'.[1] This is a measure of how short a time there has existed in the English-speaking world people with that linguistic qualification which is a necessary aid to a thorough understanding of Chinese civilization. During the nineteenth century some missionaries and diplomats gained reputations as scholars of the language, but its study was very slow to take root in academic soil. Although the first chair of Chinese in Britain was founded as long ago as 1838, at University College, London, it was not until after the Second World War that the language and the unsurpassed cultural achievements of the most populous country on earth ceased to be the concern mainly of occasional students taught by isolated professors, who had generally completed careers in consular or missionary service before taking to academic life. Although the scholars of the Jesuit mission who were active in China during the seventeenth and eighteenth centuries gave continental Europe an earlier start and although American centres of learning now pay much higher regard to these studies

[1] *Chinese Miscellanies* (London, 1865), p. 50.

than do British universities, it is nevertheless true to say that Sinology is one of the newest sciences.

It follows therefore that the average reader of this book will have an image of China which owes remarkably little to the work of serious scholarship. It will owe much ultimately to the accounts of travellers and missionaries, to the influence of Chinese art and art inspired by China, and to the products of the imaginations of literary men; while among its more immediate creators will be the press, radio, cinema, and other modern means of communication, which both process the available information and supply such further material as suits their own purposes. Although these media have in recent decades given many people a more sophisticated awareness of remote civilizations, I am sure that for many more the name China is still mainly associated with such trivialities as pigtails, slant eyes, lanterns, laundries, pidgin English, chopsticks, and bird's-nest soup. Whimsical notions of a quaint civilization in a setting which resembles the design on a willow-pattern plate must be discarded at the outset if a true understanding of Chinese culture is to be attempted.

Even those readers who have drunk largely from the purer springs of serious scholarship are not necessarily much nearer the truth. The springs trickle but slowly, and there is a vast reservoir of information which can only be tapped by a far larger labour force of scholars than is at present engaged on these studies. One must also remember that, in the present century, there has developed a greater awareness of the difficulties and complications of historical study. The historian now recognizes that, while his intellect is focused on one minute problem, his mind is stocked with unquestioned presuppositions about a whole range of much more important historical problems which he has never had time to examine. Like the photographer, however much he may perfect his skill, he can only take a picture from one viewpoint at a time. Philosophers, too, with their increasing awareness of the non-significative elements in language have encouraged him not to take words at their face value; while psychologists with their analyses of the complicated factors underlying men's actions have increased his appreciation of the difficulty of interpreting their deeds. The powerful success of such techniques of deception as political propaganda and mass advertising has given us a heightened scepticism towards the study of the past. At the same time anthropologists, economists, sociologists, and representatives of a host of new disciplines have clamoured for a recognition of their contribution to the study of history. But the main dilemma is expressed with humorous exaggeration by Professor Butterfield: 'When I recall how much more easy it is for a camel to go through the eye of a needle than for the most excellent trained historian to repeat a piece of gossip or an anecdote at the dinner-table without adding a little varnish . . . I have wondered sometimes how such a thing as ancient history . . . could be taken seriously at all.'[1]

It need hardly be added that those who have had the good fortune to visit China are in little better position to form sound judgements about its civilization. The impression that any visitor to China forms of that country is very far from being a simple response to objective fact. His interpretation is partly moulded by his reading of accounts which, even if they lack other demerits, inevitably have the defect of representing partial and out-of-date views; it is a response to a comparison between conditions in his own country and conditions in China, and is thus bound to vary somewhat in accordance with the country of his origin; it is coloured by whatever the Chinese want him to believe about their country and by what they themselves, perhaps mistakenly, believe to be true of their country; and it is distorted by a compulsion to satisfy what the visitor subconsciously needs to believe. With the world split in two these distortions have been intensified, and all but the most well-informed and level-headed

[1] H. Butterfield, *Christianity and History* (London, 1949), p. 28.

observers have leaned heavily towards either unadulterated praise or unqualified condemnation of the People's Republic of China.

A healthy scepticism must therefore inform our attitude towards what we read about China. Old misconceptions of her civilization live long and die hard, for there is a certain inertia in our historical beliefs, so that they tend to be retained until they are ruthlessly questioned by original minds perhaps centuries after they have ceased to be true. In order that the reader may clear his mind of such misconceptions at the outset, I propose to draw his attention to certain features of the West's understanding of China which have proved persistent and often misleading.

I shall start with a conception of China which, although most persuasive and misleading in its day, has not been of much consequence in recent times—the conception of China as a land of great material prosperity. It owes its origin to the accounts of Marco Polo and other overland travellers who were able to reach the court of the Great Khan in the thirteenth century, when much of the Euro-Asian land-mass was under Mongol sway.

These accounts were truly epoch-making: the European's horizons, previously restricted to his own continent and the Mediterranean area, were now immeasurably extended. Yet by a common trick of historical distortion the names of William of Rubruck and other medieval travellers to the Mongol court are unknown to all but a few, while the name of Marco Polo has become a household word and his story a part of our folk-lore. Though greeted with incredulity by his contemporaries, who might have been expected to stretch their imaginations more readily than modern man to accommodate some of his strange stories, his account has had a powerful influence on European impressions of China.[1]

---

[1] Since China was identified with Polo's Cathay as early as the sixteenth century by Martin de Rada, it will be satisfactory for the purpose of this essay to use the term 'China' throughout.

One of the most characteristic features of Polo's account is his obvious love of exaggeration. This is repeatedly exemplified in his famous description of Hangchow, with its 'twelve thousand bridges of stone, for the most part so lofty that a great fleet could pass beneath them'. Another natural subject for such treatment was the magnificence of the Great Khan's establishment. Among the presents the ruler customarily received at the New Year were, according to Polo, 100,000 white horses richly caparisoned; and the 360,000 horsemen gathered for an expedition were merely 'the falconers and whippers-in that were about the court'. It is not surprising that Polo was given the nickname Il Milione and asked on his deathbed to recant and to expunge all the exaggeration from his account. Even Sir Henry Yule, who devoted much of his life to the study of Polo and had so remarkable an affection for him that he used the pen-name Marcus Paulus Venetus when writing to the press, was under no illusions about his veracity; and as late as the nineteenth century a German scholar was prepared to argue that the whole book was an elaborately constructed fabrication. Indeed, one does not even have to take into consideration either the tedious sameness of many of the descriptions of the places he visits, or the characteristic fantasies of medieval travel accounts, such as the story of the dog-headed men, to sympathize with Yule, who, despite his affection for Marco, writes that William of Rubruck's narrative forms 'a book of travels of much higher claims than *any one series* of Polo's chapters'.[1] For, in spite of his long sojourn in China, he failed to mention many of the most obvious peculiarities of Chinese civilization, notwithstanding their complete novelty. He even says nothing about the Chinese script, printing, footbinding, tea, and the Great Wall, all of which are recorded by near-contemporary travellers. Nevertheless, because of the

---

[1] I quote from the famous Sir Henry Yule translation, edited by H. Cordier (London, 1903), the products of more recent scholarship being obviously irrelevant for my present purposes. See vol. ii, p. 185; vol. i, pp. 335, 105.

romantic nature of his personal history, he has captured the imagination of the West as other medieval travellers failed to do and is regarded as pre-eminent among them. Thus the medievalist Eileen Power regarded him as 'incomparably the greatest traveller and the most magnificent observer of the whole Middle Ages'.[1]

The dominant theme of Polo's description is the size and splendour of Chinese cities and the material prosperity of the country. Its impact was not immediate and widespread, for in the days before printing reached Europe ideas spread more slowly; and there were also many who accepted his narrative with caution. But gradually it caught the imagination of adventurous Europeans. Columbus, for example, had in his possession a copy of the work, which he had carefully annotated. Eventually the great period of exploration by sea brought Spanish and Portuguese navigators to the coasts of South China, and from the third quarter of the sixteenth century date interesting accounts of this area from Galeote Pereira, Gaspar da Cruz, and Martin de Rada.[2] They too were mostly impressed by the material prosperity of the country: indeed, they were so uninformed in matters of the intellect and of the spirit that, like the medieval travellers, they did not even mention the name of Confucius. And, when one remembers what sixteenth-century Europe was like, it is not surprising that these travellers were struck by the material superiority of the country. The roads, for example, are praised by Pereira. This may surprise those who are familiar with descriptions of the condition of Chinese roads in more recent times, but at that time highways in Europe were notoriously bad. He praises too the great cleanliness of the towns by comparison with the squalor of Lisbon and other European cities. The wholesomeness of the climate, the richness of the soil,

---

[1] A. P. Newton, ed., *Travel and Travellers of the Middle Ages* (London, 1926), p. 132.

[2] Cf. C. R. Boxer, *South China in the 16th Century* (London, 1953).

and the plenty enjoyed by a happy and hardworking peasant population were other aspects of this material prosperity which were emphasized by all these writers, the conditions of the poor being compared very favourably with their plight in Europe.

When the obvious exaggerations have been discounted, these descriptions were relatively true at the time they were written; but the rapid improvement of conditions in Europe, which was later matched by some undoubted decline in conditions in China, meant that the perpetuation of this conception of China was the creation of a myth rather than the handing down of the truth. With that inertia which characterizes conceptions of alien civilizations the belief in the opulence of the Orient lingered on. As late as 1798 Malthus declared that China was the richest country in the world; and in a description of the Macartney Embassy published in the previous year Sir George Staunton, despite the many frustrations endured by the mission, indulges in occasional eulogies of the country which clearly owe more to his reading and to a hang-over from the sinophilism of the early part of the century than to direct observation. Perhaps the most remarkable of these is the passage in which he says that 'in respect to its natural and artificial productions, the policy and uniformity of its government, the language, manners, and opinions of the people, their moral maxims, and civil institutions, and the general economy and tranquillity of the state, it is the grandest collective object that can be presented for human contemplation or research'.[1]

Within a generation the scales had tilted the other way. With the arrival of Protestant missionaries China became a second-class country peopled by those who, lacking the light of God, must inevitably be regarded as inferior beings. But these descriptions of material prosperity have still had their influence

[1] T. R. Malthus, *First Essay on Population*, Royal Economic Society reprint, with notes by James Bonar (London, 1926), p. 335; Sir George Staunton, *Macartney's Embassy to China* . . . (London, 1797), vol. i, p. 27.

even into the present century, notably in that genre of writing which exploits an idyllic picture of a Utopian China to point a comparison with unsatisfactory conditions in the writer's country. Goldsmith's *The Citizen of the World* and Landor's *Imaginary Conversation between the Emperor of China and Tsing Ti* are earlier examples of this idiom, but in more modern times we have had Lowes Dickinson in *Letters from John Chinaman* contrasting the sordidness of England with a China peopled by 'prosperous peasants, owning and tilling the fields their fathers owned and tilled before them'.[1]

Over-enthusiastic descriptions of China's prosperity have inevitably provoked a reaction from those who have found the place to be not quite the paradise they expected. This dates back even to the time when sinophilism was at its height, for in the widely read *Robinson Crusoe*, published in 1719, Defoe puts this outburst into his hero's mouth: 'I must confess it seemed strange to me, when I came home, and heard our people say such fine things of the power, glory, magnificence, and trade of the Chinese; because as far as I saw, they appeared to be a contemptible herd or crowd of ignorant sordid slaves, subjected to a government qualified only to rule such people.' Such disappointment has been shared by many a traveller since then who has gone out to China with visions of a flowery land dotted with stately pleasure-domes, and inhabited by a permanently smiling and prosperous population.

Though the image of the material prosperity of China has undoubtedly faded in modern times, the next conception which I propose to discuss seems to have survived with almost undiminished vigour until the Communist revolution. This is the belief that China was a monolithic Confucian state, a myth which was mainly the product of descriptions of the country and translations of Chinese books sent home to Europe by Jesuit

[1] G. Lowes Dickinson, *Letters from John Chinaman* (London, 1902), p. 18.

missionaries in the seventeenth and eighteenth centuries. Their conception of the country was entirely new. Before this there had been very little information available in Europe about intellectual life in China. Now there developed a new vision of the country as a strong, united, and self-sufficient state, which owed much to traditions handed down from wise rulers of remote antiquity, and was ruled by a benevolent despot in accordance with moral and political maxims enshrined in the Confucian Classics, and with the aid of administrators chosen because of the knowledge of those works which they displayed in the literary examinations.

Just as the vision of China's fabulous prosperity was mainly conjured up by the reports of Marco Polo, so this new view of China owes much to Matteo Ricci, the first great Jesuit missionary in China. He it was who first introduced Confucius to Europe. Of his journal covering the years 1583–1610, which he spent in China, it has been written: 'It probably had more effect on the literary and scientific, the philosophical and the religious, phases of life in Europe than any other historical volume in the 17th century.'[1] Such success as the Jesuit mission enjoyed owed much to the methods established by Ricci; and many of his successors followed the example of his scholarly interest in Chinese thought, so that for the rest of the life of the mission a stream of books, pamphlets, and letters poured into Europe, deeply influencing thinkers of the Enlightenment with their descriptions of the Confucian state.

The consequent favourable impression of China was due partly to the historical accident that there were features of Chinese society likely to have a special appeal in Europe at that point of time. Wearied by the doctrinal disputes and religious wars which had marred the course of Christianity, some thinkers advocated 'natural religion' as a means to an agreement which seemed

[1] L. J. Gallagher, S.J., tr., *China in the Sixteenth Century* (New York, 1953), p. xix.

impossible between the jealous defenders of different 'revealed religions'. The Jesuits' description of the purified essence of Confucianism suggested that such a solution had been found practicable in China. Politically, too, at a time when democracy was not on the cards at all, the ace of trumps was just such a benevolent despotism as seemed to exist in China. Moreover, at a time when the *philosophe* was gaining influence in Europe, there must have been an enthusiastic reception for such passages as Ricci's: 'The entire kingdom is administered by the order of the Learned, commonly known as the philosophers. The responsibility for orderly management of the entire realm is wholly and completely committed to their care and charge.'[1] It would not have occurred to the reader that the Chinese word corresponding to philosopher denoted group attachment to tradition rather than individual love of wisdom. The perils of translation do indeed help to foster the growth of myths. Thus evolved the image of the moral and political superiority of the Chinese, which made their country an exemplar for many of those in the West who were eager for change.

This image corresponded perfectly with, and indeed derived from, the Chinese conception of the nature of their own civilization, which was automatically absorbed by the Jesuits. The dogma of the monolithic Confucian state was an established part of their code and of their outlook on life. Moreover, in response to the challenge of the spiritual values of Christianity, they were bound to emphasize the spiritual values of their own civilization. This same emphasis has continued and even been intensified in modern times, serving as a prop to Chinese self-esteem when they have had to acknowledge the material superiority of Europe. Hence some writers have found it possible to fit the Chinese into a crude and false antithesis between the materialistic West and an East mainly concerned with the needs of the spirit.

Finally, the development of this conception of China owed

[1] Gallagher, op. cit., p. 55.

much to the needs of the Jesuits who were the agency through which it was transmitted to Europe. Faced with the task of converting the population of a vast country at a great distance from home, they naturally emphasized the more hopeful aspects of their experience in China. They had to give an account of themselves which would ensure continued support for their work. They also had to have a plan of campaign which bolstered their morale by giving some promise of success. In the early stages methods had been adopted which were more suitable for missionizing in backward countries. Then Ricci, after a period when he mistakenly assumed the garb of the despised Buddhist priesthood, later made himself more acceptable by adopting the dress of the scholars and familiarizing himself with the traditions they respected. Thus he acquired the knowledge of their philosophy which he and his successors sent back to their home countries.

Finding the materialistic agnosticism of contemporary Confucianism uncongenial, the Jesuits went back to what they regarded as the pure and undefiled religious tradition of ancient China, wherein they discovered a monotheism similar to that of ancient Judaism. This fitted in perfectly with the belief in the dispersal after the Flood, and was taken as a firm guarantee that China would be fruitful ground for the propagation of the Gospel. Thus the Jesuits came to interpret the Chinese religious system as a dualism between Confucianism, representing the remains of these ancient beliefs, and Taoism and Buddhism, the false sects which had corrupted the old tradition. This is why the Jesuits were able to have such a high regard for the Chinese in spite of the fact that they lacked the light of God. As Ricci wrote:

Of all the pagan sects known to Europe, I know of no people who fell into fewer errors in the early ages of their antiquity than did the Chinese. From the very beginning of their history it is recorded in their writings that they recognized and worshipped one supreme being whom they called the King of Heaven. . . . One can confidently hope that in the mercy of God, many of the ancient Chinese found salvation in the natural law, assisted as they must have been by that special help which, as the theologians teach, is denied to no-one who does what he can towards salvation, according to the light of his conscience. That they endeavoured to do this is readily determined from their history of more than four thousand years, which really is a record of good deeds done on behalf of their country and for the common good.[1]

Thus the Jesuits, in comforting themselves that the Chinese were in a high state of readiness to receive the Gospel, gave Europe an impression of a country of high moral standards. But in a country so vast piecemeal conversion was a formidable task, and the obvious short cut was the conversion of the monarch. Some attempt seems to have been made to this end, and the conversion of some of the imperial concubines fairly early in the mission was doubtless viewed as a step in the right direction. The Chinese court had a long-standing tradition of eclecticism in religious and philosophical matters, and in consequence some of the Jesuits attained positions of remarkable influence with the emperors. Not surprisingly some very laudatory descriptions of their royal masters were in turn expressed by Jesuit courtiers. K'ang-hsi, for example, was described by Parennin as 'one of the most extraordinary of men, such as one finds only once in several centuries', praise which is reminiscent of hagiological descriptions of Confucius from Chinese antiquity. There is no need to dwell on the profound influence this favourable picture of China had on Europe of the Enlightenment.[2] It is perhaps best summed up in this enthusiastic outburst of Poivre: 'China offers an enchanting picture of what the whole world might become, if the laws of that empire were to become the laws of all nations.

[1] Gallagher, op. cit., p. 93.
[2] This important topic is also treated by Professor Kracke and Mr. Hudson. See pp. 335–7, 356–60.

Go to Peking! Gaze upon the mightiest of mortals; he is the true and perfect image of Heaven!'[1]

This image of China faded as the Jesuit mission declined. The Jesuits had overreached themselves in two ways. By claiming that all Confucian rites were innocuous and permissible for a Christian they had antagonized their opponents within the Church; and by praising the moral qualities of the Chinese they had played into the hands of the advocates of natural religion. Eventually the French Revolution stopped the flow of funds to the mission and Christianity in China went into eclipse. With the nineteenth century came a more hard-headed scientific approach to the Confucian texts, typified by that of Max Müller, who, in introducing his *Sacred Books of the East* series in 1879, made it quite clear that he regarded them as of interest as historical source material, rather than as treasure-houses of wisdom.

Nevertheless the concept of the monolithic Confucian state has continued to have a very strong influence. In modern times it has even been boosted by disgust with the follies of the materialistic West, which has stimulated a new interest in the wisdom of the East. In the world of scholarship the myth has continued to be the source of many misunderstandings, through failure to appreciate that it papered over many ugly cracks. For this idyllic and oversimplified view of China ignored or played down the bitterness of the Ming–Manchu conflict in the seventeenth century, the clash of different schools of thought within Confucianism, the wicked influence at court of powerful eunuchs, the pervasiveness of Buddhism, the evils of religious persecution, the recurrent demonstrations of dissatisfaction afforded by peasant rebellions, the cruel intolerance of the literary inquisitions, the absurdly stereotyped nature of the

[1] Quoted in A. H. Rowbotham, *Missionary and Mandarin* (Berkeley, 1942), p. 223; and G. F. Hudson, *Europe and China* (London, 1931), p. 318.

literary examinations, and the ill-treatment of minority peoples, to mention but a few corrupt and divisive features of Chinese society. It is a concept which is blatantly inaccurate, but which through its neatness, simplicity, and self-consistency has had a very strong appeal. It lurks behind many popular accounts of Chinese civilization. It underlies the predominance which has been given to the Confucian Classics on our bookshelves and in our syllabuses, and it explains why the very name of Confucius still seems to inspire awe. Indeed, as Professor Hawkes has said, 'there is no lack of people even today who believe that the society which perished only a few years ago was just such a harmonious Confucian utopia'.[1]

From a misunderstanding propagated by missionaries I pass to two which have been much cultivated by historians. The first is the view that traditional China was in a state of 'eternal stand-still', as the German historian Ranke called it.[2] This conception was related to the one just discussed, in that it was thought that the changelessness was consequent on the existence of a despotic régime able to secure the timeless perpetuation of the ideals and attitudes upon which the society was based.

This supposed changelessness was not remarked by early travellers to China, and when it does first attract comment this is favourable. In Goldsmith's *The Citizen of the World*, for example, China as 'an Empire which has thus continued invariably the same for such a long succession of ages' is regarded as 'something so peculiarly great that I am naturally led to despise all other nations on the comparison'. Contrast this with a generation later, when the wind of change was blowing strongly across Europe and Condorcet wrote: 'The human mind, given

---

[1] *Chinese: Classical, Modern, and Humane* (inaugural lecture) (Oxford, 1961), p. 10.

[2] Leopold von Ranke, *Weltgeschichte* (Leipzig, 1881), vol. i, p. vi.

up to ignorance and prejudice, was condemned to shameful stagnation in those vast empires whose uninterrupted existence has dishonoured Asia for so long.' One can find equally extreme statements of this view throughout the nineteenth century. 'We have before us the oldest state and yet no past,' wrote Hegel, 'but a state which exists today as we know it to have been in ancient times. To that extent China has no history.' Nor was this a misconception peculiar to those who pontificated about China only from the study, for the quotations may be paralleled in the writings of those who knew the country intimately. 'Her language and her customs remain unaltered,' wrote the missionary Medhurst, 'and the genius and spirit of the people are the same they were in the patriarchal age.'[1]

Many different explanations are given for this changelessness in addition to or instead of the primary reason of political organization which has already been mentioned. John Stuart Mill gives a slight variation on this theme, arguing that lack of 'organized opposition to the ruling power' is responsible. Always in such circumstances, he maintains, 'society has either hardened into Chinese stationariness, or fallen into dissolution'. Economists, who have a tendency to give their subject an unchallenged supremacy, have seen it in economic terms and ascribed it to economic causes. Hegel thought that eastern Asia had been cut off from historical development because it had not 'appropriated that element of civilization which the sea supplies', a curious argument when it is remembered that few countries in the world have longer coastlines than China. With typical missionary over-estimation of the power of ethical ideas, Legge put the blame

[1] O. Goldsmith, *Collected Works*, ed. P. Cunningham (London, 1854), vol. ii, p. 226; Condorcet, *Sketch for a Historical Picture of the Progress of the Human Mind* (first published 1795), tr. J. Barraclough (London, 1955), p. 39; quoted by A. Wright in 'The Study of Chinese Civilization', *Journal of the History of Ideas*, xxi (1960), p. 245; W. H. Medhurst, *China: its State and Prospects, with Especial Reference to the Spread of the Gospel* (London, 1840), p. 7.

on the teachings of Confucius. 'There has been a tendency to
advance,' he wrote, 'and Confucius has all along been trying to
carry the nation back.' His fellow-missionary Medhurst even
made the extraordinary suggestion that the invention of printing
bore some responsibility: 'This stereotyping of their books has
caused the stereotyping of their ideas; and kept them in the
same eternal round of uniform notions, without variety or improvement.' And in modern times we have had Spengler seeing
the whole process in terms of biological metaphor.[1]

Other misconceptions concerning Chinese history are obviously
related to this idea of changelessness. Parallel with it runs that
notion of uniformity in space which is involved in the above-
mentioned concept of the monolithic Confucian state. Another
corollary is the view of China as a country of great antiquity.
This widespread notion may be exemplified by means of a
quotation from De Quincey: 'The mere antiquity of Asiatic
things, of their institutions, histories, modes of faith, &c., is so
impressive, that to me the vast age of the race and name over-
powers the sense of youth in the individual. A young Chinese
seems to me an antediluvian man renewed.' In fact, from a
chronological point of view the development of Chinese civilization shows some remarkable parallels with that of European
civilization, and is not comparable in antiquity with that of
Egypt. A further corollary was the idea that the Chinese always
readily absorbed their conquerors. An uncritical adherence to
this belief, which the Chinese themselves have naturally fostered
with diligence, has blinded people to the extent to which, as
Wittfogel puts it, 'instead of relinquishing their privileges of
power, prestige, and revenue the conquerors invariably sought
to maintain them by all manner of political, military, and legal

---

[1] *Mill on Bentham and Coleridge*, ed. F. R. Leavis (London, 1950), p. 87;
Hegel, *The Philosophy of History*, tr. J. Sibree (New York, 1956), p. 101;
James Legge, *The Chinese Classics*, vol. i (Hong Kong, 1861), p. 108; Medhurst,
op. cit., p. 104; O. Spengler, *Der Untergang des Abendlandes, passim.*

devices'.[1] It has also caused people both to neglect the changes in the Chinese way of life brought about by the impact of the Mongols in the thirteenth and fourteenth centuries, and to underestimate the contrast between the native Ming and foreign Manchu dynasties.

Such misconceptions could not be corrected without a genuine and scientific interest in Chinese history among European historians, but this has been very slow to develop. All too often in the nineteenth century we find people expressing an opinion which is best exemplified by the words of a writer in the *Journal of the Peking Oriental Society* for 1886: 'I do not think that the history of China (with the exception of a few episodes) will ever be considered as forming an essential part of the *general* history of *mankind*.'[2] The development of rapid communications and egalitarian thought in the present century has succeeded in banishing this quaint attitude, but the obstacles to its removal have been very great. There was some attempt, for example by the Göttingen school of German historians, to write 'universal history', paying due attention to the world outside Europe, but all the time a centripetal force pulled them back towards their own continent. They lacked authentic material about Chinese history to enable them to incorporate it into an integrated world-history. They believed, too, that the development of the European state-system was by far the most important topic in modern history. The enormous weight of the tradition of European scholarship and of the history of education in Europe has also tipped the scales heavily against the broadening of our historical horizons. If education is seen as training of the character and of the intellect, the main emphasis is bound to be placed upon the proper appreciation and understanding of a limited quantity of historical source material, preferably of an elevating character, rather than upon polymathy. In modern

[1] K. A. Wittfogel, *Oriental Despotism* (Yale, 1957), p. 326.
[2] C. Arendt. The italics are his own.

times educationists have been kept busy by the need to foster
several urgently required revolutions, such as the introduction
of education for women, the democratization of education, the
expansion of scientific, technological, and vocational education,
and the improvement of teaching methods in response to new
media and fresh understanding of child psychology; so that comparatively little attention has been paid, especially in Britain, to
the obvious need of education for world understanding, which
must surely be one of the next big educational revolutions.

At present therefore, in spite of small and recent signs of
improvement, the study of history, especially in British schools
and universities, is still parochial. So many new and interesting techniques can be brought to bear on what one might call
micro-history that there is much satisfaction to be obtained from
the continued evaluation of European history, and it is still
unfashionable to take a wider view. But in the meantime, unfortunately, old misconceptions about the nature of Chinese
history still survive, and true to the spirit of a belief in China's
changelessness some scholars have posited an unrealistic and
exaggerated continuity and similarity between Confucian and
Communist China.

From the belief that China and other Oriental countries do
not conform to the normal patterns of historical development it
is but a short step to the conviction that there exists a peculiar Asiatic or Oriental type of society. Many misapprehensions
arise from the treatment of the terms Asiatic and Oriental
as meaningful in other than a purely geographical sense. The
polarity between Europe and Asia has been one of the categories
by means of which Europeans have arranged and systematized
history since earliest times. By the fifth century B.C. the term
'Asiatic' already implied despotic authority and lavish splendour,
both of which were anathema to the Greeks; and parallel
antitheses between Greece and Persia, Europe and Asia, and

West and East were already firmly established. The Romans, too, although their empire straddled the border between Europe and Asia and they had nothing quite like Marathon or Salamis to act as a focal point for anti-Asian emotions, absorbed and retained the Greek contempt for Asiatics. Christianity added its support, for in its view Europe as the land of Japheth, the Gentiles, the Greeks, and the Christians was opposed to Asia, the land of the Semitic peoples, whose inferiority was implied in the scriptures: 'God shall enlarge Japheth, and he shall dwell in the tents of Shem.'[1] The Crusades gave further encouragement to the East–West antithesis, while the increasing identification of Europe with Christendom helped to maintain the polarity between Europe and Asia; which was later reinforced by the theories of historians and economists, in whose eyes European progress appeared to form a neat contrast with Asiatic stagnation.

This polarity between Europe and Asia, with which European thought has been obsessed, can be broken down into various components. First of all, there is the polarity between smallness and bigness: Leonidas and his three hundred facing the vast hordes of Xerxes; Polo from the tiny city-state of Venice appearing at the court of the Great Khan, whose realms were unequalled in magnitude—these are examples of the romantic images by means of which we visualize the Europe–Asia antithesis. With bigness, too, we associate slowness and ponderousness, and such cartoon-imagery may well have helped to foster impressions of the changelessness of Asia. Secondly, there is the polarity between the maritime and the continental, typified again by the struggle between the sea-going Greeks and the Persian land power and by the contrast between the maritime city-states of medieval Italy and the mammoth land empire of the Mongols. A passage from Hegel already quoted on p. 15 shows how grossly misleading this antithesis can be; for it has caused people to forget such striking evidence of the Chinese

[1] Genesis ix. 27.

aptitude for the water as is afforded by the great quantity of shipping on Chinese waterways observed with amazement by medieval travellers, and the remarkable long-distance voyages as far as the east coast of Africa during the Ming period; and it has encouraged people to believe that seafaring skill is a peculiarity of the European heritage. A third aspect of this polarity has been the contrast between freedom and slavery. This contrast, felt intensely in the childhood of our civilization by the Greeks under the threat of the Persian yoke, has dominated our world-outlook in its maturity. Condorcet is one of many European thinkers who may provide us with an apt illustration of this point. 'If we compare the legislation,' he writes, 'and especially the form and the rules of judgment in Greece with those existing amongst Eastern races, we shall see that with the latter laws were a yoke under which people were bound into slavery whereas with the former they were the conditions of a common pact between man and man.'[1] Hegel, too, regarded this contrast between Europe and Asia as of central importance, and it has been much emphasized by Western thinkers in so far as they have conceived the process of history in terms of the development of human freedom.

Misled by these large antitheses between Europe and Asia and between West and East, some thinkers have tried to develop theories either to explain or to characterize more precisely the nature of Asiatic or Oriental civilization. The characteristic nature of Asiatic societies has often been attributed to economic reasons. The classical economists developed concepts of an Asiatic or Oriental type of society which were adopted by Marx, who had much to say about a specific 'Asiatic mode of production'; but detailed discussion of such theories would demand more space than the subject justifies. In a modern variant of this theme, with which the general reader may be less familiar, Wittfogel has argued that the key to the type of society

[1] Op. cit., p. 53.

which is characterized by what he calls 'Oriental Despotism' is the need for large-scale water-conservation and flood-control projects, which in turn necessitate a centralized despotic administration able to avail itself of large drafts of corvée labour. Thus he has called this type of society 'Hydraulic society', elevating one factor in the development of Chinese society to a position of supreme importance. Others have tried to get to the root of the distinction between East and West by suggesting that there is a difference of outlook between Oriental and Occidental man which is not to be accounted for by economic, geographical, or other reasons, but is mysteriously fundamental. According to Collingwood, Herder was the first to recognize in a systematic way that human nature is not uniform but diversified and to point out 'that what makes Chinese civilization, for example, what it is, cannot be the geography and climate of China but only the peculiar nature of the Chinese'. A modern illustration of this attitude is afforded by Northrop's book, *The Meeting of East and West*. In it he argues for the unity of Oriental culture and holds that the fundamental difference between East and West consists in the contrast between the aesthetic tendencies of the former and the theoretic tendencies of the latter. The absurdity of generalizations of this kind is shown in high relief by the fact that some writers contrast the down-to-earth West with the impractical East, while others argue that it is the East that is always concerned with practical matters. Charles A. Moore, for example, writes that in the Orient 'all philosophy is ultimately for practical purposes, that ethics or the philosophy of life is the essential phase of philosophy, that the theoretical finds its sole justification in its service as a guide to the practical'.[1]

---

[1] Wittfogel, op. cit., *passim*; R. G. Collingwood, *The Idea of History* (Oxford, 1946), p. 90; F. S. C. Northrop, *The Meeting of East and West* (New York, 1949); *Philosophy—East and West*, ed. Charles A. Moore (Princeton, 1946), p. 266.

This polarity between Europe and Asia and between West and East is one of the important categories by means of which we think of the world and arrange our knowledge of it, so there can be no doubt that it colours the thoughts even of those who have a special interest in Oriental studies. Indeed, the very existence of such a concept as Oriental studies, which Sinologists, in co-operation with colleagues in the field of Arabic, Egyptian, Hebrew, Indian, and many other studies, foster by organizing themselves into Orientalist associations and by arranging Orientalist congresses, helps to perpetuate the strange idea that social, economic, and cultural frontiers coincide exactly with geographical ones and that the whole of the East has some common and exclusive factor which enables its civilizations to share a common label.

All the conceptions of China I have dealt with so far have had their origins in earlier times, but the one I propose to discuss next belongs to the nineteenth century. This is the Protestant view of China as a country whose most important characteristic was that the people were heathen, lacking the light of God. This attitude caused many nineteenth-century Europeans to look upon them at best as a people whose greatest minds were necessarily inferior and whose masses were as lost children hungering for the gift of the Holy Spirit, and at worst as subject to what Wells Williams describes as 'a kind and degree of moral degradation of which an excessive statement can scarcely be made, or an adequate conception be found'.[1] And it is to this view that the darker features of the modern popular image of the villainous Chinese depicted in cinema and comic may doubtless ultimately be ascribed.

The difference between this attitude and that of the Jesuits is striking. The latter had praised the moral and political virtues of Chinese society, and their eulogistic cries had been repeated even

[1] S. Wells Williams, *The Middle Kingdom* (New York, 1848), vol. i, p. 836.

more loudly in Europe by those whose enthusiasm was not tempered by first-hand knowledge. The Protestants, on the other hand, were convinced not only that their religion was the only true one, but that they were representatives of an expanding and progressive civilization which would soon dominate the world. This supreme confidence in the superiority of Christian civilization encouraged the missionaries and other representatives of the West to consider that they were conferring great benefits by introducing not only their religion but also the whole ethos and much of the material paraphernalia of Western civilization; a belief which became the more obstinate when confronted with the proud Confucian attitude that China alone had genuine value, and merely needed to make some ancillary use of barbarian techniques.

Both the Protestant and the Jesuit missions of course shared the belief that the Gospel had spread to China in antiquity. The Jesuits, as we have seen, dwelt on the virtues of the pure and unspoilt monotheism of ancient Chinese religion and the fitness of the Chinese to receive the Word; on the other hand the Protestants, who, with some notable exceptions, lacked the scholarly tradition of the Jesuits, were convinced of the inferiority and eventual supplanting of Chinese culture and paid comparatively little close attention to it. The very title of Medhurst's book, *China: its State and Prospects, with Special Reference to the Spread of the Gospel*, is sufficient indication of this attitude. The large question of the early propagation of the Gospel in China is dismissed with the opinion that 'considering the extent, population, and civilization of China it can hardly be supposed that so important a region was entirely neglected by the first propagators of the Gospel', a remark which epitomizes the author's lack of historical sense. He never seems to have made the effort of imagination necessary to an understanding of the people; instead he contented himself with his faith that they had 'no prospect of amelioration, but in the liberalizing and happy influence of Christianity'. Unfortunately it was not easy for them to grasp some of the loftier notions of the faith, such as a sense of sin. 'The only evils with which they charge themselves', he says by way of explanation, 'are quitting their native land while their parents are alive, being without posterity, treading on an ant, abusing printed paper, eating beef, and leaving hungry ghosts to starve.'[1]

Medhurst may be regarded as representative of the less imaginative type of missionary, but on a higher plane even the scholarly and contemplative James Legge, who spent many years of his life translating the Confucian Classics and later became the first professor of Chinese at Oxford University, was not sufficiently impressed by the greatness of Confucius and the other ancient sages to diverge greatly from the views of his fellow-missionaries. His final judgement on Confucius regretfully consigns him to an inferior position:

I hope I have not done him injustice; but after long study of his character and opinions, I am unable to regard him as a great man. He was not before his age, though he was above the mass of the officers and scholars of his time. He threw no new light on any of the questions which have a world-wide interest. He gave no impulse to religion. He had no sympathy with progress. His influence has been wonderful but it will henceforth wane.

Here too is a sample of the admixture of militant Protestantism:

Of the earth earthy, China was sure to go to pieces when it came into collision with a Christianly-civilized power. Its sage had left it no preservative or restorative elements against such a case. It is a rude awakening from the complacency of centuries which China has now received. . . . Disorganization will go on to destroy it more and more, and yet there is hope for the people . . . if they will look away from all their ancient sages, and turn to Him, who sends them, along with the dissolution of their ancient state, the knowledge of Himself, the only living and true God, and of Jesus Christ whom He hath sent.[2]

---

[1] Op. cit., pp. 221, 455, 358.   [2] Op. cit., vol. i, pp. 113, 109.

Thus Confucianism, which for the Jesuits had seemed a wonderful preparation for the Gospel, was, even for Legge the great interpreter of it, an evil which had to be swept away.

Yet Legge was too humane a man to condemn Confucianism utterly. His defence of Mencius against the charge that his doctrine of the goodness of human nature was completely antagonistic to the Christian view of man as fallen was one instance of his supporting Confucianism against the attacks of his fellow-missionaries. He was also too humane a man to think of China as being godless throughout her history. 'The mind recoils shuddering from the thought', he wrote, 'that generation after generation has descended to the grave, without one individual ever having had the thought of God in his mind, or the name of God on his lips.' Nor could he reconcile the viability and populousness of a godless China with the fate of Sodom and Gomorrah, destroyed for their godlessness. Hence in a book which is an interesting example of the difficult psychological conflicts inherent in the position of the missionaries, he goes to great lengths to prove that the old Chinese term *Shang Ti* should be equated with God.[1] One cannot help feeling that there is the ring of truth in the love–hate relationship depicted by Somerset Maugham in his portrait of Mr. Wingrove, the missionary who professed to like the Chinese but was in fact disgusted by them.

If the attitude towards Confucianism was somewhat complicated, this is certainly not true in the case of Buddhism, which was deeply despised by the missionaries as a degraded and idolatrous sect. The Jesuits had abhorred it because it had corrupted the pure ancient faith of the Chinese; and what made the Protestants dislike it more than anything was the striking similarities between Buddhism and Popery. This is in strong contrast with the modern Western view of Buddhism as a monastic religion almost too spiritual for the materialistic West.

[1] James Legge, *The Notions of the Chinese Concerning God and Spirits* (Hong Kong, 1852), pp. 58–59.

For those who seek wisdom across the frontiers of race and creed the Buddhist image has been taken out and dusted and placed before the admiring gaze of an increasing number of Westerners. Confucianism, too, has in modern times regained some of the respect in which it was held by eighteenth-century Europe.

Criticism of the treatment of Asiatics as inferior beings because they were heathen was being made before a Protestant missionary ever set foot in China, and more enlightened views have gradually prevailed. It was the First World War which finally dealt the death-blow to the Protestant sense of superiority by plunging the missionizing countries into a ghastly catastrophe, at the same time cutting off the flow of funds and of new blood to the East. Then came the Second World War, bringing in its train a new sense of the importance of international understanding and of equal rights between peoples; so that within a generation the predominant image of the Chinese as a sinister and inscrutable race, relegated to sub-human status by reason of their paganism and the pigmentation of their skins, has given way to greater knowledge and understanding, although he would be a bold man who would claim that nothing of the Protestant attitude lingers on in the minds of many of us.

In the academic sphere the idea of the 'heathen Chinee' has caused serious damage to the proper study of Chinese religion. Until recently much writing on this subject was done by missionaries whose main purpose was to describe obstacles to the progress of Christianity for the benefit of future missionaries. They always started with the basic assumption that Confucianism, Taoism, and Buddhism were the same kind of thing as Christianity, though markedly inferior; and this preconception tended to make them ask all the wrong questions about these systems of thought.

In this survey of Western conceptions of China I have dwelt almost entirely on the subject of false and misleading attitudes and have tried to explain the circumstances in which these attitudes have developed. I am absolved from the need to pursue this topic further by the fact that similar misconceptions are discussed elsewhere in this book: the fifth chapter, for example, thoroughly demolishes the belief that the Chinese are an unscientific people; while references to *chinoiserie* in the fourth chapter make it clear how false an impression of China has been obtained by those who have treated it as a serious reflection of the country and its art. Moreover, the powerful contemporary myths engendered by the Cold War equation of Communism with consummate good or evil are too familiar and doubtless too ephemeral to demand treatment in a work of this kind.

In pursuing my purpose of helping the reader to clear his mind of such misconceptions, I have emphasized the errors in the picture of China given to the West by great men like Polo and Ricci. It is time, therefore, to turn to the other side of the coin and recognize that they were the principal purveyors of the legacy of China to their own generation and that, once we have guarded against their inevitable inaccuracies, they deserve our praise and gratitude for their role as pioneers in that interpretation of China to the West to which this book is devoted. Future generations will look back upon the present as the paradoxical age when, with the ties of missionary enterprise and commercial relations almost completely severed, the West got down to the serious business of trying to understand China in depth; thus paying to Polo, Ricci, Legge, and all the other pioneers in their several countries and generations the great tribute of being fascinated by their work and of striving towards a more accurate conception of China than they were able to achieve. This modern conception of the country is not for me to deal with here, but is the subject of the remainder of this book.

RAYMOND DAWSON

2

PHILOSOPHY AND RELIGIOUS THOUGHT

This chapter deals in turn with the two main themes in Chinese philosophy and religious thought, namely the development of the indigenous philosophical tradition and the influence of Buddhism. The reader will find that further information about the philosophical and religious ideas of the Chinese comes in various places later in the book.

(a) THE PLACE OF REASON IN THE CHINESE PHILOSOPHICAL TRADITION

AFTER Chinese philosophy[1] became known in Europe in the seventeenth and eighteenth centuries Confucianism greatly interested the thinkers of the Enlightenment as an example of a humanistic ethic independent of revealed religion. More recently Taoism and Zen Buddhism have attracted a different kind of audience, the connoisseurs of the mystical 'perennial philosophy'. Yet Chinese thought continues to puzzle Western readers, even to leave many of them doubtful as to whether it truly deserves the name of 'Philosophy'. The great Chinese thinkers are moralists, mystics, and political theorists, concerned with the conduct of the individual and the organization of society, but seldom interested in constructing metaphysical systems. By itself this fact may not deter readers today as much as a generation ago, metaphysics being at present rather out of fashion; but it is far from obvious to many people that Chinese

[1] The standard work on this subject in English is Fung Yu-lan, *A History of Chinese Philosophy*, tr. Derk Bodde, 2 vols. (Princeton, 1952–3).

thinkers can be credited with thinking rationally at all. Admittedly they are not religious prophets and do not appeal to divine revelation, but the two most influential documents, the *Analects* of Confucius and the *Tao te ching* ascribed to Lao-tzu, do not appeal to reason either. To what extent was the Greek discovery of rational discourse paralleled in China?

We must consider Chinese thought from two sides, the social situation which gave rise to its problems, and the degree to which thinkers appealed to reason rather than to tradition or intuition as authority for their solutions. The great creative period covered three centuries, from Confucius (551–479 B.C.) to Han Fei (died 233 B.C.). This was a time of rapid and drastic social change without equal in Chinese history before the present century. The emperors of the Chou Dynasty (?1027–256 B.C.) had already by the time of Confucius lost all their power; the great fiefs had become independent states which continued to prey upon each other until the final victory of the state of Ch'in and the reunification of China under the Ch'in Dynasty in 221 B.C. At some time about 600 B.C. bronze, in China as elsewhere a near-monopoly of the nobles, gave way to the more plentiful and easily worked iron. Later merchant and artisan classes developed; within the states bureaucracies of varied social origin began to supersede the old aristocracies; serfs evolved into peasant owners and tenants. Confucius and his successors found themselves in a world in which traditional methods of government and standards of conduct were ceasing to apply. They looked back with regret to the stable feudal order of the early Chou, in which there had been an accepted code of *li*, 'rites', 'manners', regulating on the one hand the relations of lord and vassal, father and son, on the other the service of Heaven, of mountains, rivers, and other natural phenomena, and of ancestral spirits. This traditional way of behaving was the 'Way of the ancient kings', and the recovery of the *Tao* or Way became the central theme of Chinese philosophy.

The Chou tradition survived best in the small state of Lu, originally the fief of the duke of Chou, brother of the king Wu (?1027–?1025 B.C.) who established the dynasty by overthrowing the preceding Shang. Lu was the home of Confucius, the first Chinese known to have gathered disciples and set himself up as a teacher of the Way. Confucius, like Socrates and Jesus, is known to us only by later reports of his sayings, and like them has an individual and impressive voice which sounds through the records even when we are least certain of their authenticity. He conceived his mission as purely conservative, to be the guardian and restorer of the deteriorating culture and manners of Chou, 'a transmitter and not an originator, trusting in and loving the ancients'.[1] His collected sayings, the *Analects*, give us glimpses of him overwhelmed by his first hearing of an ancient piece of ceremonial music on a visit to the state of Ch'i, and scandalized when the governing family of Lu usurps the prerogatives of the Chou emperor by using eight rows of dancers in a rite and by performing the sacrifice on Mount T'ai. A striking illustration of his conservatism is his attitude to the growing tendency of rulers to counter the decay of unwritten custom by codifying laws. In 513 B.C. the state of Chin inscribed its laws on a tripod. 'The people will look to the tripod', Confucius objected. 'What reason will they have to honour the nobles? And what special function will there be for nobles to guard? Without degrees of noble and mean, how can one govern a state?'[2]

But if the decay of the *li* impresses Confucius with the importance of conserving them, it also forces him to reflect on their significance. 'In applying the rites', he says, 'harmony is to be valued most. By the way of the former kings it is this which is most honoured, and followed in all matters great or small. But

---

[1] *Analects* VII. 1. Cf. A. Waley, *The Analects of Confucius* (London, 1938). Although quoted passages are identified through references to published translations, the versions which appear in this chapter are my own.

[2] Cf. J. Legge, *The Chinese Classics*, vol. v (Hong Kong, 1872), p. 732.

it cannot be applied everywhere. It cannot be applied by har-
monizing from a knowledge of harmony, without regulating
according to the rites.' This shows Confucius both clinging to
the traditional manners and seeking a principle behind them
which can be used in the increasingly numerous cases where they
cannot be directly applied. The main work of Confucius, although he did not know it himself, was quite original, the development of a conception of moral goodness (*jen*) and of the
gentleman (*chün-tzu*, literally 'lord's son') which he supposed to
be implicit in the poetry, ceremonies, and music of the early
Chou, and which was to dominate the moral consciousness of
China from the victory of his school in the second century B.C.
down to the present century. 'If a man is not good', he asks,
'what do rites matter? If a man is not good, what does music
matter?' Confucius is the discoverer for China of the Golden
Rule and of the principle that love for others is the basis of
morality:

When Fan Ch'ih asked about the good man, the Master answered:
'He loves others.'

What you do not like yourself do not do to others.

The good man wishing himself to stand helps others to stand, wishing
himself to arrive helps others to arrive; the ability to recognize the
parallel to one's own case may be called the secret of goodness.[1]

This conception of the basis of morality, developed into
a doctrine of universal love, became the central tenet of the
earliest rivals of the Confucians, the Mohist school founded by
Mo-tzu (*c.* 480–*c.* 390 B.C.). Mo-tzu's teaching survives in a
series of treatises on his characteristic doctrines, most of them
preserved in three versions apparently derived from different
branches of his school. 'The sage', the treatise on *Universal Love*
begins, 'is one whose business it is to govern the Empire. He can
govern it only if he knows from what source disorder arises, he

[1] See *Analects* I. 12, III. 3, XII. 22 and 2, and VI. 28 for the above quotations.

cannot govern it if he does not; he is like a physician curing a
man's sickness, who can cure only if he knows from what source
the sickness arises.' If we examine the types of disorder, we find
that all derive from lack of mutual love. 'Disloyalty of minister
to ruler and son to father is what one calls a disorder. Sons love
themselves more than their fathers, and therefore deprive their
fathers to benefit themselves; and younger brothers do the same
to elder brothers and ministers to rulers.' All other disorders,
oppression by rulers and fathers, robbery, sedition, aggressive
war, have the same source, loving oneself more than others, and
the same cure, mutual love. 'If we regard father, elder brother,
and ruler as we regard ourselves, what scope shall we have for
disloyalty? . . . If we regard other men's houses as we regard our
own, who will steal? If we regard other men's persons as we
regard our own, who will do violence?'

Laid down in these uncompromising terms, the principle
which for Confucius gives meaning to the traditional conventions turns into a weapon against these conventions. Confucians
always accused Mo-tzu of outraging filial piety by teaching sons
to love other people's parents as much as their own. It is not likely
that he went as far as this, but certainly he was a fierce critic of
various customs which Confucians counted among the major
duties. The Mohist *Economy in Funerals* points out that defenders and critics of mourning customs both appeal to ancient
authority, and proposes this test for judging between them: 'If
fine funerals and prolonged mourning can really enrich the poor,
increase population, replace peril and disorder by safety and
order, then they are good and right, and a duty for loyal sons',
but otherwise they are not. Since extravagance in mourning
wastes goods, interferes with productive work, and damages the
health of mourners, this test is sufficient to discredit it. It is
objected: 'If fine funerals and prolonged mourning are really not
the Way of the sage kings, why is it that gentlemen throughout the civilized world never fail to perform and uphold them?'

Mo-tzu answers that 'This is what one calls "mistaking the familiar for the suitable and the customary for the right" ', and points out that barbarous peoples are equally convinced of the rightness of customs which horrify the Chinese.

But if a custom is wrong, who is to reform it ? The people with effective power were the rulers of the states, who had progressively won themselves complete independence from the Chou emperor and full authority within their territories, rather in the manner of the despots of sixteenth- and seventeenth-century Europe. For Confucians there was still a traditional Way which the rulers and the emperor himself were morally obliged to follow. But Mo-tzu affirms the independence of rulers from every authority except the will of Heaven, which they can discover by listening to him. In his view people accept a ruler with the purpose of escaping the primitive anarchy in which each man has his own idea of right, and they achieve this purpose only by 'conforming to those above', subjects taking their judgements of right and wrong from the ruler and the ruler from Heaven. Another issue on which Mo-tzu supports the new absolute monarchs against feudal institutions is the question of 'the advancement of worth and employment of ability'. The essay *Advancement of Worth* recommends that men be appointed to high office on grounds of personal worth alone, irrespective of wealth, rank, family, and connexions, even if they are peasants or craftsmen.

The sayings of Confucius never show him defending a position by consecutive argument. This is as one would expect; he is the interpreter of a code not yet openly questioned although increasingly disregarded in practice, and is not aware that there are novelties in his interpretation. But Mo-tzu has opinions of undisguised originality on many political, moral, and practical topics, and the pressure of controversy forces him to give reasons. According to the essay *Against Fatalism*, 'One must set up criteria. Affirming something without criteria is like marking

East and West on a turning potter's wheel.' There are three such standards for judging an opinion: 'On what should one base it? Base it on the past deeds of the ancient sage kings. By what should one test it? Test it by examining what nowadays the eyes and ears of ordinary people find real. What use is it? Apply it in administration and observe whether it benefits the people of the civilized states.'

Applying these criteria, Mo-tzu disproves fatalism by quotations showing that the ancient kings disbelieved in it; by the absence of witnesses who have seen or heard this being called Destiny; and by the moral dangers of supposing that one's conduct will not affect one's fortune. It is the last consideration which counts most with Mo-tzu. He cares only for theories with practical consequences, and his first concern is whether the consequences are beneficial or harmful. He accepts the authority of the ancients without reserve, but he also finds a pretext for ignoring it whenever it conflicts with his utilitarian test. Confucius had appealed to a genuine tradition, that of the Chou Dynasty at its prime, which he considered greater than the earlier Hsia and Shang. Mo-tzu is the first to take advantage of the fact that little was known about the institutions of the earlier dynasties. 'You model yourselves on Chou and not on Hsia', he remarks to the Confucian Kung Meng. 'Your antiquity is not antiquity at all.' The essay *Against the Confucians* defends innovation explicitly: 'The Confucians say: "To be a good man a gentleman must assume the opinions and dress of the ancients." My reply is that what we call ancient opinions and dress were all new once, so that the most ancient of the men who expressed these opinions and wore this dress were not gentlemen. Is it suggested that to be a good man one must assume the opinions and dress of the ungentlemanly?'[1]

[1] The above quotations from the *Mo-tzu* may be compared with Y. P. Mei, *The Ethical and Political Works of Motse* (London, 1929), pp. 78, 80, 124, 132, 183, 233, and 203.

There is a further difference between Confucianism and
Mohism which is surprising at first sight. Mo-tzu's ultimate
sanction for moral conduct is reward and punishment by
Heaven and the spirits. He therefore insists on the personality of
Heaven and the existence of spirits. Confucius had always put
aside such topics, as irrelevant to the conduct of ordinary life;
he recommended 'respect for the spirits while keeping them at
a distance', and dismissed an inquiry about death with the
question: 'Until you understand life, how can you expect to
understand death?'[1] Throughout most of its history Confucianism has combined dogmatism concerning rules of government and conduct, and meticulousness in dress and manners,
with the utmost latitude on such trivial questions as whether we
survive death and whether Heaven is a personal God or impersonal power or, in neo-Confucianism, a principle of order
running through all things. Mo-tzu, arguing with a certain
Ch'eng-tzu, accuses the Confucians of calling down the wrath
of Heaven and the spirits by maintaining that 'Heaven is without
consciousness and the spirits are not divine'; and he indicts Kung
Meng for the contradiction of holding both that spirits do not
exist and that it is a duty to sacrifice to them.[2] The latter position, held for example by Hsün-tzu in the third century B.C.,
has never seemed self-contradictory to Confucians. My father's
spirit may or may not exist; the important point is that my performance of the rite should fully express the reverence due to
him. Confucius himself is described in the *Analects* as 'sacrificing
to the spirits *as though* the spirits were present'.[3]

Why is it the traditionalists who on this issue take the side
of scepticism? Part of the answer is that Confucianism, being
a refinement of the accepted aristocratic code, needs no sanction except the self-respect of the man who does not wish to
be shamed before his peers. The aristocrat's sense of fitness is

[1] *Analects* VI. 20 and XI. 11.   [2] Cf. Mei, op. cit., pp. 236-7.
[3] *Analects* III. 12.

independent of religion and may clash with it, as happened in Christian Europe over such issues as duelling and amorous intrigue. Mo-tzu, preacher of a new morality, threatens offenders, not with the contempt of neighbours who are more likely to agree with the Confucians, but with the anger of invisible beings whom he presumes to agree with himself. Psychologically, this is the shift from shame to guilt. Mo-tzu's attitude, rare in China, resembles that of the great religions of Western Asia, Judaism, Christianity, and Islam. But unlike the prophets of these religions he does not claim any personal mission or revelation from the spirits. The essay *Explaining the Spirits* is a rational demonstration using Mo-tzu's three criteria; spirits exist because the ancient sages said they do, because many people have seen them, and because people behave better if they think that the spirits will punish their sins. It is interesting that the Chinese Communists, coping with the same task of converting the masses to a new and rationalistic moral code, have resorted to the apparatus of guilt, confession, repentance, and forgiveness which successive generations of Christian missionaries had failed to implant in the 'shame culture' of traditional China.

Mo-tzu's method of criticizing accepted morality in terms of the resulting benefit and harm was a weapon which could be used in other hands for other purposes. In the fourth century B.C. we find people beginning to use it to defend the claims of private against public life. The struggle for power, as war between the states increased in frequency and savagery, was becoming murderously competitive; just why, people were beginning to ask, do we take it for granted that wealth and power are worth the perils of contending for them? The conviction grew that external possessions, which are replaceable, are less important than the safety and health of one's body, which is not. The individualists flattered themselves that they had risen above the vulgar infatuation with wealth and power to a truer understanding of benefit and harm; but both Confucians and Mohists treated them as shirkers too selfish to serve the community by taking office. The most famous individualist, Yang Chu (*c.* 350 B.C.), has left no authentic writings. He seems to have held that no one should injure his body, even by the loss of a hair, for the sake of any possession, even the whole empire; but his enemies seized on the implication that he would not take the opportunity to benefit the whole empire by good government at the least cost to himself. A fragment surviving in a late book, *Lieh-tzu* (*c.* A.D. 300), shows us Yang Chu debating with Mo-tzu's disciple Ch'in Ku-li, who embarrasses him by pressing him to say whether he would give a hair to benefit the whole world. A disciple recovers the offensive by forcing Ch'in Ku-li to admit that, in spite of the chance to do good, he would not accept a state in exchange for the loss of an arm.

The corrosion of traditional morality by the utilitarian test provoked a Confucian counter-attack from Mencius (*c.* 390–*c.* 305 B.C.). Mencius, like Confucius, is a conservative who expects a restoration of the institutions of Chou to cure all ills; he remains a believer in hereditary rank, and approves of promoting social inferiors only in cases of exceptional merit. He abhors the utilitarian test, and in the very first episode of his book we find him protesting when a king asks him for something which will profit his country: 'Why must Your Majesty speak of profit? I have nothing for you but goodness and right.' In the context of his time this amounts to a refusal to expose Confucian morality to any rational test whatever. Yet the rival schools were pulling Confucians into controversies which gave them no choice but to prove themselves better reasoners than their opponents. When, for example, a certain Hsü Hsing asserts that rulers should plough the land with their subjects, Mencius argues in detail that division of labour and exchange of products is to the good of all, and that those who work with their minds deserve to be fed by those who work with their hands. However much Mencius hates appeals to utility, he cannot escape the necessity of showing that the restoration of Chou institutions will indeed benefit the community. Confucius, when asked how to rule a state, advised the use of the Hsia calendar, the Shang coach, and the Chou ceremonial cap; in the same position, Mencius recommends lenient punishments, low taxes, and no forced labour at times when workers are needed on the land.

The type of Mohist argument which condemns wasting on one's father's funeral goods which could be better used in the service of the community merely convinced Confucians that utility is one thing and morality quite another, and so opened the way to a kind of moral intuitionism. Mencius, with his contemporary and rival Kao-tzu, is among the first Chinese to turn attention inwards, to consider moral feelings as well as moral conduct, and to raise the question whether morality is internal or external, the product of nature or of training. Kao-tzu defined human nature as 'the inborn', identified it with hunger and sexual desire, and pronounced it morally neutral. But the Confucian view that everything outside our control is the work of Heaven, a benevolent even if impersonal power, leads Mencius to the conclusion that human nature is good, and that we can discover whether a course of action is good by looking inside ourselves. He insists that the feelings developed by moral education are present in us without our being taught them. 'Now if anyone suddenly notices a child about to fall into a well, he will have a feeling of alarm and distress. It is not that he expects it to win him favour with the child's parents, or praise from friends or neighbours; nor does it come about because he dislikes a bad reputation.'[1]

Towards the end of the fourth century B.C. the virtuosity of debaters of the rival schools began to breed sophists interested in argument for its own sake. The only surviving writings of the sophists are some essays ascribed to Kung-sun Lung (*c.* 320–*c.* 250 B.C.), of which all but one are of doubtful authenticity or

[1] *Mencius*, Ia. 1, and IIa. 6. Cf. J. Legge, *The Chinese Classics*, vol. ii.

interpretation. The exception is a demonstration in dialogue form that 'A white horse is not a horse', a piece of pure sophistry which assumes that 'A white horse is a horse' affirms identity and not class membership. Among sayings known by quotation the most interesting are a set of ten ascribed to Hui Shih (late fourth century B.C.), of which the last is: 'Love the myriad things indiscriminately; heaven and earth are one body.' The preceding nine are paradoxes evidently designed, like Zeno's, to prove that the universe is one body by showing that it is self-contradictory to make divisions. We can make guesses of varying plausibility as to the nature of Hui Shih's arguments. Spatial divisions lead to the paradoxes that the universe both must be and cannot be infinite ('The South has a limit and has no limit') and that a quantity is an aggregate of its smallest parts, which however being infinitely small will add up to nothing ('What has no bulk cannot be accumulated, but its size is a thousand miles'). Temporal divisions imply moments at which the sun is both at noon and declining and at which the dying are both still alive and already dead ('The sun is declining when it is at noon, a creature is dead when it is alive'), and entitle me, if I cross the frontier between two countries at the moment between one day and the next, to say both that I left there today and that I reached here yesterday ('I go to Yüeh today and arrived yesterday').

Philosophers reacted in opposite ways to the sophists, by a total disillusionment with reason or by a new logical rigour. The greatest Chinese anti-rationalist is the Taoist Chuang-tzu (*c.* 365–*c.* 290 B.C.), a friend and critic of Hui Shih. The argument of Hui Shih that all distinctions involve self-contradiction comes dangerously near to discrediting analytic reasoning altogether, and Chuang-tzu takes this further step. His *Treating Things as Equal* denies the consistency of affirming even that all things are one, with an argument used at almost the same time by Plato in the *Sophist*: ' "The myriad things and I make one"— With them already making one, can I still say something? But having called them one, have I avoided saying something? One and the words make two, two and one make three. . . .'

The fruitless debates of Confucians and Mohists, each side starting from its own unproved premises, lead Chuang-tzu to an uncompromising relativism. Every doctrine is right from one standpoint and wrong from another, just as 'this' at one position is 'that' from another position. If you and I disagree, no third party can judge between us because he will have authority only for one side, will need another judge to judge himself, and so on indefinitely. Chuang-tzu's scepticism arises from disputed questions of value, but makes no distinction between these and questions of fact. *Treating Things as Equal* shows throughout the shock of the discovery, stupefying to those who first made it, that a name has only a conventional relation with a thing. 'Speech is not blowing wind,' says Chuang-tzu, 'it is about something; it is simply that what it is about is not fixed. Is it really about something or never about anything? If you think it is different from the twittering of chicks can you or can't you show the difference?' There is no need of sophistry to prove that a horse is not a horse; it is a horse if you choose to name it so, not if you give the name to something else. A curious dialogue between Hui Shih and Chuang-tzu shows the latter's extreme relativism, gives an interesting glimpse of Hui Shih proving a point, and illustrates how the Chinese language sometimes gives an argument a twist difficult to catch in English translation:

Chuang-tzu and Hui Shih were strolling on the bridge above the Hao. 'The dace swim out in their free and easy way,' said Chuang-tzu, 'you can tell that the fish are happy.'

'You are not a fish. How [literally "From where"] do you know the fish are happy?'

'You are not me. How do you know that I do not know that the fish are happy?'

'Not being you, admittedly I do not know you; all the more obvious then that you, who are admittedly no fish, do not know whether the fish are happy.'

'Let us go back to where we started. You said: *"From where* do you know the fish are happy?" You questioned me already knowing that I knew it. I knew it from up above the Hao.'[1]

Hui Shih plays according to the rules, Chuang-tzu kicks over the board. But his last reply is more than a stupid pun. He sees in the use of the word 'where' an admission that a request for reasons is merely a request to define the standpoint from which a judgement is the right one. The stroke of wit at the end is a way of saying that an intellectual position is as arbitrary as a position in space from which some things are 'this' and others 'that'.

Chuang-tzu's relativism commits him to rejecting tradition without any of the Mohists' reservations. Times change, what was good for our ancestors is not good for us. But this contempt both for reason and for ancient authority does not imply despair of finding the Way; on the contrary his destructive criticism is inspired by the conviction that it is self-consciousness, analysis, and conformity with conventions which separate us from the Way. Chuang-tzu is deeply interested in types of ordinary behaviour which thinking inhibits and types of knowledge which cannot be verbally expressed. A player winning while the stakes were low pauses to think when the stakes are raised, and loses his knack; a woman discovers she is beautiful and ceases to be beautiful. Hitting on the Way is a skill like swimming or handling a boat or catching insects with a rod and line. We can no more put it into words than an old carpenter can explain to his son how to use a chisel neither too fast nor too slow. Chuang-tzu guides us towards the development of this dexterity by humour,

---

[1] For the above quotations from the *Chuang-tzu* cf. H. A. Giles, *Chuang Tzu, Mystic, Moralist, and Social Reformer*, second ed., rev. (London, 1926), pp. 451, 24, 16, 218.

poetry, aphorism, and parable, using reason only to discredit reason.

In taking this position, Chuang-tzu is among the originators of the new conception of the Way or *Tao* which has come to be known specifically as 'Taoism'. This conception implies insight from another direction into the distinction which a European might describe as that between laws of nature and moral laws. Heaven and Earth pursue a consistent course through the cycles of the seasons and of the heavenly bodies, a Way which earlier thought had never distinguished from that prescribed for man, and which later Confucianism was to moralize even more explicitly, seeing Heaven's kindness in the growth of spring and justice in the destruction of autumn. But the Taoist sees this order as indifferent both to our morality and to our selfish ambitions, although he still conceives it as in some way prescriptive, obliging us to side with it against morality and ambition. The author of the *Tao te ching*, who wrote perhaps a little earlier in the fourth century B.C., shared Chuang-tzu's assumptions about the Way but drew different practical conclusions. His brief collection of aphorisms expresses in bald paradoxes a complicated pattern of insights into the contradictions between the aims and results of action. One of its focal points is the thesis that 'Reversion is the movement of the Way'; whatever grows stronger arrives at a point from which it declines into weakness. The ordinary ruler strives to perpetuate strength, and to force other things out of their courses into his own. 'The Way of Heaven takes from those with too much and adds to those with too little. The way of man is otherwise; it takes from those with too little in order to make a present to those with too much.' The sage ruler on the other hand 'does nothing' (*wu-wei*), takes the side of weakness instead of strength, acts against a rising power only at the earliest stage before it gathers strength, and otherwise yields until the trend turns in his favour. This is a strategy of government like that of Japanese *judō* wrestling, which it later inspired. It implies that the Way is outside the ruler, whose relation to it, as explicitly paradoxical as every other aspect of the book's many-sided thought, is to use it for his own ends by renouncing those ends: 'It is because he has no selfishness that he can make his selfishness succeed.'[1] What Chuang-tzu teaches, on the other hand, is the ordered spontaneity of the mystic and poet, in the perfection of which human action accords with the Way like the natural processes of Heaven and Earth, because it is itself a natural process undisturbed by reflection. His audience, like Yang Chu's, consists of those who wish to live their own lives free from the cares of office, and he offers a *mystique* where Yang Chu could offer only reasons for thinking that the behaviour he advocated was sensible.

The threat of sophistry on the one hand and irrationalism on the other excited the Mohists of the third century B.C. to a closer examination of the definitions of words and the validity of arguments. Earlier thinkers had defined moral terms and such controversial terms as 'human nature'; the later Mohists defined 'all' ('none not so') and 'some' ('not all'), 'duration' ('filling different times') and 'extension' ('filling different places'). One section of the *Mohist canons* distinguishes different senses of ambiguous words, observing for example that 'same', a word which had been used treacherously by philosophers who denied the validity of all distinctions, can mean 'identical' or 'belonging to one body' or 'associated in place' or 'of a kind'. The same section distinguishes three kinds of names, 'all-inclusive', 'classifying', and 'proper':

'Thing' is all-inclusive; any object must get this name. The naming 'horse' is classifying; for what is like the object one must use this name. The naming 'Tsang' is proper; this name is confined to this object.

The answers of the later Mohists to the arguments of other

[1] *Tao te ching*, chs. 40, 77, and 7. Cf. A. Waley, *The Way and its Power* (London, 1934).

schools have a subtlety and precision no doubt anticipated in the lost writings of the sophists, but unprecedented in the extant literature. To the argument that it cannot be a duty to love all men since the number may be infinite, they reply:

If men do not fill the infinite the number of men is finite, and there is no difficulty about exhausting the finite; if they do fill the infinite the infinite is exhaustible, and there is no difficulty about exhausting the infinite.

In passages which seem to be concerned with Chuang-tzu's thesis that from one point of view all statements are right and from another all wrong, they object that 'treating all statements as mistaken' and 'rejecting rejection' are both untenable, since in the first case 'If this man's statement is admissible it is not mistaken, so there are admissible statements', and in the second case 'If "rejection is to be rejected" cannot be rejected, he is not rejecting rejection.'

One late Mohist essay, the *Hsiao-ch'ü*, is entirely devoted to distinguishing between types of sound and unsound argument. Its theme is that statements can look perfectly parallel and yet not be. 'Inquiring about a man's illness is inquiring about the man; disliking the man's illness is not disliking the man. A man's ghost is not a man; your elder brother's ghost is your elder brother.' This deceptive parallelism often leads us into fallacies. Thus it is common to confuse sequences of these three kinds:

  (i) 'A white horse is a horse; riding a white horse is riding a horse.'
 (ii) 'Her younger brother is a handsome man; loving her younger brother is not loving a handsome man.'
(iii) 'Cockfights are not cocks; liking cockfights is liking cocks.'

Mohists are wrongly derided as sophists for claiming that, although robbers are men, killing robbers is not killing men. (Their motive was no doubt to reconcile execution of robbers with universal love; we could make the point differently by saying that one can kill someone as a robber while loving him as a man.) The claim seems self-contradictory because people assume that it belongs to the first class. But it belongs to the second:

Having too many robbers is not having too many men, having no robbers is not having no men. . . . The world agrees on this. But if so, there is no more doubt that although robbers are men, loving robbers is not loving men, not loving robbers is not not loving men, killing robbers is not killing men.[1]

The pressure of competition with other schools, which had forced Mencius into public debate, drove Hsün-tzu (?298–?238 B.C.) to a much more thorough rationalization of the Confucian position. Although still defending Chou institutions and the prime importance of *li*, 'rites', 'manners', he no longer follows Mencius in insisting, for example, on hereditary privilege. He freely uses the phrase 'advancement of worth and employment of ability' as though forgetting its Mohist origin, and explicitly favours degrading unworthy men of high birth and promoting worthy commoners. A more basic point is that he tacitly accepts what Mencius denied, the Mohist principle that the value of institutions is subject to the test of utility. Hsün-tzu's case for traditional forms and ceremonies is that they do benefit the people. All men desire more than they can get, and are protected from destroying each other only by rules which lay down clearly who is to defer to whom, subject to ruler, wife to husband, younger to elder. His objection to Mo-tzu is simply that he overlooks the utility of degree.

Hsün-tzu is the first and last Confucian to accept the Taoist thesis that Heaven and Earth follow a Way which is indifferent to the desires and the ideals of men. But he sees that this Way imposes no obligation on us to follow it; it is a neutral order which the sage studies for the sake of ordering society in the way

[1] These passages from the *Mo-tzu* are not included in Mei's translation, but the chapters from which they are taken are discussed in H. Maspero, 'Notes sur la logique de Mo-tseu et de son école', *T'oung Pao* (1928), pp. 1–65.

which will take most advantage of the seasons of Heaven and the resources of Earth. The 'Way of the ancient kings', he says, consists of 'rites and duties', and 'is not the Way of Heaven nor the Way of Earth; it is what man takes as his Way, what the gentleman takes as his Way'. One consequence of this is that Hsün-tzu can no longer accept the faith of Mencius that the nature implanted in us by Heaven must be good. 'Man's nature is bad,' he declares, 'and the good in him is artificial.' His opinion is that our nature consists of desires which lead to contention if given free play; it is not quite that they are evil, as understood in the Christian doctrine of Original Sin, but that they share the amorality of all the natural forces which the sage manipulates for the benefit of man. 'Someone asks: "If man's nature is bad, from what were rites and duties born?" The answer is that all rites and duties were born from the sage's artifice and were not originally born from man's nature. . . . The sages thought them out step by step, drilled themselves in artificial habits, and so brought forth rites and duties and established laws and measures.'

Hsün-tzu's *Correct Use of Names* considers the relation between names and objects already discussed by the later Mohists. If a thing keeps the same place although changing in appearance there is one object, more than one if there is similarity of appearance but difference of place. The mind, which knows the passions directly, knows objects through the five senses, and finds them similar or different in varying degrees. Similar objects are given the same name, which may be of any degree of generality; we may distinguish 'animal' and 'bird' or call both 'thing'. Names are conventional, appropriate if 'the convention is fixed and the usage becomes settled'. (The shock of this discovery had by now worn off.) Sentences are complex names: 'The sentence puts together the names of different objects in order to convey one idea.' Errors fall into three types:

(i) 'Confusing names by misuse of names', refuted by showing that a name does not fulfil its purpose of distinguishing the similar from the different. (Among his examples: 'Being insulted does not disgrace', 'Killing robbers is not killing men.')

(ii) 'Confusing names by misuse of objects', refuted by examining the facts. (Example: 'There are few genuine [not artificial] desires.')

(iii) 'Confusing objects by misuse of names', refuted by arguing from something acknowledged. (Example: 'A [white] horse is not a horse.')[1]

An attack on a certain Sung Hsing (fourth century B.C.) in another essay, the *Treatise of Corrections*, refutes in detail errors of the first two classes, although unfortunately not of the third. It rejects 'Being insulted does not disgrace' on the grounds that the sages used 'disgrace' in two senses, social and moral, and that Sung Hsing has no right to use it only in the latter sense; it rejects 'There are few genuine desires' on factual grounds.

Down to the third century B.C. many rulers continued, with remarkable patience, to listen to philosophers who travelled from state to state teaching them how to become emperor of a reunited China—Confucians who recommended reversion to an irrecoverable past, Mohists and other moralists who, although more alive to changed conditions, persisted in preaching universal love and the wickedness of aggression against neighbour states. But at the very end of the great period of Chinese philosophy a school appeared which advised rulers to pursue power undistracted by moral considerations. This was the Legalist school which culminated in Han Fei (died 233 B.C.), a former disciple of Hsün-tzu. Han Fei argues that moral considerations can outweigh self-interest only for a minority, and lead to good government only under the occasional sage; on the other hand a consistent code of rewards and punishments, acting directly on men's interests, will ensure good government except

[1] The above quotations from the *Hsün-tzu* may be compared with H. H. Dubs, *The Works of Hsüntze* (London, 1928), pp. 96, 301, 305, 286, and 290.

under the occasional tyrant. His explicitly amoral reasoning brings him, remarkably enough, to a conception of law which accords closely with Western ideas of justice. The ruler should reward and punish, promote and dismiss, by comparing his subjects' deeds with his own commands and prohibitions as objectively as though he were weighing on a balance, without favouring or sparing even those closest to himself. It is a system which, although it left a deeper mark on Chinese institutions than could ever be officially acknowledged, offended the Confucians' conviction that duties are primarily to those connected with oneself by family, office, or friendship, as well as their dislike of using the harsh methods of law for anything which can be settled by custom and precedent. The Legalists are new also in sometimes, although not always, plainly acknowledging that their teaching is *not* that of the ancient sages. They have advanced from Chuang-tzu's general observation that times change to noticing connexions between social forms and social changes. Han Fei notes that a man can have five children and live to see twenty-five grandchildren, and that the moral appeals of the ancient sages, which may have been effective in a smaller community, no longer work with a large population competing for limited natural resources. The Legalist *Book of Lord Shang* distinguishes three phases of organization as population has increased, a primitive anarchy, growth of moral conventions to control increasing competition, and finally division of land and goods and separation of the sexes, requiring the development of government to ensure that each keeps his place.

The state of Ch'in, which patronized Legalism, completed the conquest of all other states and the reunification of China in 221 B.C. Under the Ch'in Dynasty and the succeeding Han (206 B.C.–A.D. 220) a new and stable social system consolidated itself, the old hunting and fighting aristocracy with hereditary fiefs giving way by degrees to a centralized bureaucracy, sedentary and bookish, recruited to an increasing extent by public examinations which in later centuries were gradually opened to almost the whole population. In spite of the practical success of Legalism its ruthless amorality made it unsuitable as a public ideology, and from the second century B.C. the Han Dynasty earned itself the blessing of the ancient sages by patronizing the Confucian school. Confucianism remained for two thousand years the official philosophy, adapting with remarkable success the old forms to new realities. The great creative period of Chinese thought was now over. Taoism was the only survivor among the rival schools, becoming, until it was overshadowed by Indian Buddhism, the favoured philosophy of those who preferred private to public life. For the next two thousand years nearly all new developments outside Buddhism occurred within these two schools, culminating in the neo-Taoism of the third and fourth centuries A.D. and the neo-Confucianism of the Sung Dynasty.

The Han Confucians, led by Tung Chung-shu (?179–?104 B.C.), pursued the new ideal of rooting Confucian moral and social categories in a cosmology developed by seeking symmetries in natural phenomena. One basis for such speculation was the concept of active and passive agencies, the Yang and Yin, which underlie all pairs of opposites, movement and rest, light and darkness, male and female. Another was the theory of the five elements, earth, wood, metal, fire, water, each with a counterpart in other schemes, the five colours, five sounds, five smells, five tastes. A third was the system of divination by broken and unbroken lines arranged in eight trigrams and sixty-four hexagrams, preserved in the *Book of Changes*, an early Chou manual of divination which the Confucians expanded with appendices. (The numerical calculations used in constructing these diagrams by the sorting of milfoil stalks inspired a number mysticism of the kind which the Pythagoreans derived from music.) This kind of thinking had very ancient origins; its most famous early practitioner, Tsou Yen (*c.* 305–*c.* 240 B.C.), had explained the

rise and fall of dynasties by a cycle in which each element yields
in turn to another, and predicted that the Chou, activated by
the element fire, would have a successor activated by water, the
element which extinguishes fire. The later Mohists rejected this
cycle, protesting that 'there are no regular ascendancies among
the five elements. . . . Fire melts metal when there is more fire,
metal uses up the charcoal when there is more metal.'[1] Unlike
the earliest Greek philosophers, the pre-Han thinkers of China
took little interest in cosmology, although such concepts as the
Yin and Yang were circulating in some of the schools by the
third century B.C. The basic motive of the Han interest in cosmology was perhaps to reunite the cosmic and the moral orders
severed by the Taoists and Hsün-tzu; they were able to con-
nect the five Confucian virtues with the five elements, and the
mutual duties of ruler and minister, father and son, husband and
wife, with the relation between Yang and Yin.

Some have suggested that it is characteristic of the West to
think abstractly and analytically and of China to think con-
cretely in symmetrical patterns.[2] But the kind of thinking which
arranges elements and colours in schemes of five, relates fire
plausibly to red, earth to yellow, and wood to green, and fills the
spaces by fitting metal to white and water to black, however
important it may be in astronomy, alchemy, and medicine, is
rare in philosophy of the classical period, and later is quite
secondary in neo-Confucianism; on the other hand it has been
common in the proto-science of Europe and elsewhere. The
artificiality of such constructions derives of course from the
thinker imposing by his own classifications the symmetry which
he seems to discover; when precautions are taken against this
danger it is still respectable to think in the same way, for example, to infer the properties of an unknown element from its
place in the atomic series. It may be noticed that by this test

[1] Cf. Maspero, op. cit.
[2] Cf. M. Granet, *La Pensée chinoise* (Paris, 1934).

the Yin and Yang make a sounder concept than the five elements. No one could discover that elements, colours, sounds,
smells, and tastes each amount to exactly five without having
strong preconceptions about the appropriate number to find,
and such a connexion as between water and black is quite
arbitrary; but in the presence of a new pair of opposites, above
and below, hot and cold, hard and soft, even a Westerner can
often guess that the former should be Yang and the latter Yin.

A thousand years after the Han Confucians the competition
of the Indian metaphysics introduced by Buddhism excited
Confucians to build systems of a new kind, metaphysical rather
than proto-scientific. This was the work of the neo-Confucian
movement which culminated in Chu Hsi (A.D. 1130–1200). In
the new systems the basic stuff of the universe is *ch'i*, 'breath',
'air'. The *ch'i* is continually expanding and contracting, like
breathing out and in; in its active outgoing phase it is the Yang,
in its passive ingoing phase the Yin. Things condense out of the
ch'i and dissolve back into it; and life depends on activation by
the breath inside us, which is purer, free-moving *ch'i* inside the
dense, inert *ch'i* of the body.

Neo-Confucianism took over from Mahāyāna Buddhism the
Indian assumption that behind the multiplicity of the universe
there is a unifying principle present within man as his innermost nature. (Taoism, it must be noted, had never identified
the Way with the innermost self.) According to Chou Tun-yi
(1017–73) this is the Supreme Pole (*T'ai-chi*), from which the
Yin and Yang are continually growing. According to Chang
Tsai (1020–77) it is the Supreme Void (*T'ai-hsü*, more literally
'Supremely tenuous'), the perfectly tenuous *ch'i* out of which
concrete things condense. According to the brothers Ch'eng
Hao (1032–85) and Ch'eng Yi (1033–1107) it is *li*, 'arrangement', 'organization', 'ordering' (a word distinct from although
probably related to *li*, 'rites', 'manners'). This last is the conception which triumphed, although Chu Hsi incorporated Chou

Tun-yi's system into that of the Ch'engs by identifying the Supreme Pole with *li*. Fully developed neo-Confucianism is a dualist system, positing on the one hand the primal breath out of which things solidify, on the other hand a structural principle which organizes each thing down to the minutest detail and at the same time unites all in one order—in the words of Ch'eng Yi, 'the myriad *li* go back to one *li*'. From the point of view of man, *li* is moral principle, which he can discern inside himself to the extent that the density and impurity of his *ch'i* do not obscure his vision. Thinking in these terms, Ch'eng Yi arrived at a new and for Confucians final solution of the problem of human nature, good according to Mencius, bad according to Hsün-tzu, mixed, neutral, or varying with human types according to nearly all thinkers of the intermediate thousand years. The basic nature of man is his *li*, which is good. Mencius was therefore right; the philosophers who disagreed with him were confusing the basic nature with the endowment of *ch'i* at birth, which gives a man his personal characteristics and which varies in quality from person to person.

Since *li* is both inside and outside us, in which direction shall we look for it? This is the central issue which divides the neo-Confucian schools. According to a secondary tradition which begins with Ch'eng Hao and culminates in Wang Shou-jen (1472–1528), the explorer of *li* has no need to look outside himself. But when neo-Confucians borrowed from Buddhism the form of a metaphysic of the One and the Many, they were extremely anxious to empty it of its mystical content; their goal as Confucians was not release from the deceptions of the senses but moral action within the world perceived by the senses. According to the doctrine of Ch'eng Yi and Chu Hsi, orthodox until the present century, we discover *li* by the 'Investigation of Things'. We arrive at it by pondering over the Confucian Classics, considering historical persons and events, handling practical problems, also perhaps sparing a little time for astronomy or natural history; at first we grasp only disconnected facts and rules, but in due course we discern regularities in the rise and fall of dynasties and in the moral injunctions of the sages, until finally all the *li* reveal themselves in their interrelations. The orthodox school, which saw the taint of Buddhism in any suggestion that *li* are comprehensible in detachment from the external objects, actions, and situations to which they belong, was itself accused of Buddhist tendencies by a later neo-Confucian school led by Tai Chen (1723–77). Tai Chen insisted that since *li* is merely the structure of concrete things, even to treat *li* and *ch'i* as mutually dependent but separate is to fall into the error of postulating another world transcending the one perceived by the senses.

The neo-Confucians conceive *li* as both natural and moral; the difference between these, understood in the third century B.C., had been forgotten since its denial by the Han Confucians. They reconcile their world-order with that of the documents of the sages by identifying *li* with the old concepts of Heaven and the Way. But the novelty of their position is not, as they liked to believe, a matter of terminology. However conscious older thinkers might be of using such words metaphorically, in the last resort they had thought of 'Heaven' as a power which 'decrees' events, and of the 'Way' as a path along which one walks. But *li*, a term already prominent in the neo-Taoism of the third century A.D., is a regularity from which one makes inferences, *t'ui-li* ('extend the *li*'), a phrase which has become the modern compound word for 'deduction'. In redefining the ancient terms in relation to *li*, the Ch'eng brothers and Chu Hsi presented the order of the cosmos as a rational order. But the reasoning which concerned them, it must be emphasized, is moral and practical thinking. For them the orderliness of the cosmos discredits the moral relativism of Taoism and Zen Buddhism; it guarantees that there are fixed moral standards, and constant principles in human affairs by means of which the sage knows how to apply these standards with practical success. The neo-Confucians were quite uninterested either in logical problems or in the detailed working out of their systems as intellectual structures. They ignored the logical inquiries of the third century B.C., as well as the Indian logical treatises translated by the Buddhists. Few of them even left consecutive expositions of their systems, which have to be reconstructed from remarks in commentaries on the Classics and from sayings recorded by their disciples; the textbooks which perpetuated the philosophy are simply anthologies of this material, for the most part quite undigested. They did however take a limited interest in one kind of inquiry outside human affairs, the explanation of natural phenomena. Ch'eng Yi noted that 'there are *li* in every tree and every herb, which must be looked into'. Chu Hsi noticed that fossil shell-fish found in mountains show that places which are now dry land were once under water, and took the resemblance of mountains to waves as proof that the *ch'i* of the earth was once in a fluid state.

If we can make any safe generalization about the whole of Chinese philosophy, it is that interest has always centred in human needs, in the improvement of government, in morals, and in the values of private life. Philosophers have seldom shown much concern for truths which serve no obviously useful purpose. Their thinking, however mysterious it may sometimes seem when we miss its underlying assumptions, impose on it preconceptions of our own, mistake its problems, and grapple with it through corrupt texts or defective translations, is of the same sort as our own moral and practical thinking. It is the kind of thought least conquerable by logicians, too complex to be laid out in all its interrelations even when it concerns the most trivial everyday matters; when we try to convince someone else we can only pick out key phases in our thought in order to guide him in the same direction, and try to fill the gaps when he refuses to make the same leaps, but without hope of achieving full logical rigour. The Chinese, like Europeans who are exclusively interested in action or in contemplative experience, have tended to distrust too logical thinkers who insist on filling all gaps, seeing them as triflers with unimportant questions and gross simplifiers of important ones; even such a considerable abstract thinker as Hsün-tzu often warns his readers against wasting their time on logic-chopping without practical issue. The Chinese have been much more impressed by the opposite extreme of intelligence, the aphoristic genius which guides thought of the maximum complexity with the minimum of words, of which the *Tao te ching* presents one of the world's supreme examples. It seems likely, although no one yet has even clearly identified the elusive problems involved, that this general indifference to logical problems is somehow connected with the structure of the Chinese language. In Indo-European languages word-inflection forces us to think in categories, such as thing, quality, and action, past, present, and future, singular and plural, the muddles and inconsistencies of which show us that the forms of thought present difficulties as well as its content; but in Chinese words are uninflected and their functions marked only by particles and by word-order, so that there is a much more complete illusion of looking through language at reality as though through a perfectly transparent medium.

It was the pressure of public debate after the breakdown of Chou which for some two centuries forced philosophers towards a logical rigour which they quickly abandoned when the crisis passed. This was the single period before the present century in which rapid social change undermined all accepted principles of government and standards of conduct. The competing schools with their contradictory solutions at first shared a nominal allegiance to the ancient sages, an allegiance which soon proved to be empty and was at last openly repudiated. Competition therefore forced them to seek rational tests of indisputable validity, beginning with Mo-tzu's crude formulations at the end of the fifth century, ending with the precise definitions, theories of names, rules of reasoning, and classifications of fallacies of Hsün-tzu and the later Mohists. There can be no question that the Chinese, like the Greeks, and only a little later, did throw open the whole of their fundamental beliefs to the test of reason, although in their case this huge intellectual adventure did not initiate a lasting tradition of rationalism. With the stabilization of Han society a commonly admitted code of standards again took shape. From this time, fundamentals being no longer in dispute, the Confucian and Taoist Classics assumed a nearly scriptural authority for the two surviving traditions, which sometimes clashed and sometimes intermingled, as much complementary as contradictory, one adapted to public and the other to private life.   A. C. GRAHAM

(*b*) BUDDHISM IN CHINA

THE vast field of Chinese Buddhism has long been a *terra incognita* even to the average Sinologue, and the information available to the general public has consequently been scarce and fragmentary. Chinese Buddhism did not share in the general interest aroused by the Western discovery and subsequent popularization of Indian Buddhism which dates from the publication of Sir Edwin Arnold's *Light of Asia* nearly a century ago. Its influence on our culture cannot be compared with that of Confucianism, which stirred the imagination of European thinkers as early as the seventeenth century, or of philosophical Taoism, which in certain Western circles has long been extolled as the quintessence of Oriental wisdom. It is true that one branch of Chinese Buddhist thought—the remarkable doctrine of the Ch'an or 'Meditation' school—has in recent times come to exert a considerable influence on Western intellectual life. But it is symptomatic that it has been popularized in Japanese versions, and hence is generally known by the Sino-Japanese name of *Zen*.

This lack of attention has its historical reasons. In the first place Western observers never had the opportunity to meet Chinese Buddhism as a strong and creative religion. When in the late sixteenth century the first Jesuit missionaries entered China, the interest of the cultured élite had long since shifted from Buddhism to the revived Confucianism, which had obtained its classical formulation in the twelfth century and in Ming times had been elevated to the rank of an official state doctrine. Of all the early Buddhist schools only a few survived; Buddhism as an organized religion had degenerated and had gradually been reduced to the despised creed of the lower classes. At that level it had already merged with countless indigenous cults, the result being a mongrel popular religion in which Buddhist elements had been amalgamated almost to the point of losing their identity. Hence it is not surprising that the first impression of Chinese Buddhism which Europe obtained through the writings of the Jesuit Fathers was highly unfavourable. Their condemnation of the Buddhist creed as superstitious ravings, and of the Buddhist clergy as a pack of ignorant outcasts, was not merely an echo of the contempt expressed by the Confucian literati to whom the missionaries deliberately conformed, but was also inspired by holy indignation.[1] The Buddhist church, with its gorgeous ritual, its clergy, processions, tonsure, celibacy, chanting of scriptures, rosaries, fasting, and masses for the dead, bore such an amazing resemblance to the outward forms of the Roman Catholic church that the early Fathers could not but regard it as a mockery of Christianity itself, devised by Satan in order to delude mankind. In any case these early descriptions

---

[1] See, for example, the description given by Matteo Ricci (1552–1610) in his diary, *Fonti Ricciane* (ed. by Pasquale M. d'Elia), vol. i (Rome, 1942), pp. 125–6; English translation (from Trigault's Latin version) by L. J. Gallagher, *China in the Sixteenth Century* (New York, 1953), pp. 99–101.

served to discredit Chinese Buddhism in Western eyes for centuries, and later observers had little inclination and, in fact, little reason to praise it.

A second factor, which is of the greatest importance, is the fact that Buddhism, in the totality of Chinese culture, has always been a more or less marginal phenomenon. China actually never was a 'Buddhist country' in the proper sense of the words. In China, Buddhism never played the role of a dominating creed, a *central* religious and philosophical tradition, comparable to Christianity or Islam. Even at the time of its greatest vitality and prosperity—in the early T'ang period— Buddhism, both as a doctrine and as a clerical institution, had to bear up against the overwhelming power and prestige of the Confucian tradition. The latter had for centuries dominated the world-conception of the upper class of scholar-officials, and at the same time it had gradually spread, by innumerable channels of indoctrination and oral tradition, throughout the masses of the population. Confucianism was collectivistic, as it regarded the family as the base of state and society. It was paternalistic and authoritarian, since it imposed upon the ruler, the 'father and mother of the people', the duty to control the activities of all his subjects. It was based on the assumption of the absolute superiority of the Chinese way of life, and tended to brand all foreign religions as barbaric, immoral, and even subversive. It was, moreover, an essentially pragmatic and secular doctrine, seeking, in this world and in this life, to fulfil its ideals of stability, hierarchical order, and harmony both in government and in all human relations. It is clear that Buddhism by its very nature was bound to come into conflict with this prevailing ideology. Since Buddhism propagated the ideal of a *personal* salvation, involving celibacy, the monastic life, and the severing of all family ties, it challenged the very foundation of Confucian social ethics. The Buddhist clergy regarded itself as an unworldly body, free from the obligations due to the secular powers (including the duty to perform corvée labour and to pay taxes), and not liable to government supervision. It bore the stigma of its foreign origin, and never quite succeeded in proving its non-subversive nature. Finally, it pursued aims of a metaphysical order—Enlightenment, Nirvāna, Buddhahood—which on account of their abstract and 'impracticable' nature did not rank high in Confucian evaluation.[1]

This conflict between Buddhism and Confucianism, or, at the institutional level, between the Buddhist church and the Confucian state, is a constant and extremely important factor in the whole history of Buddhism in China. At best, there was a kind of coexistence, Buddhism serving as a metaphysical complement to the social and political teachings of Confucianism. Periodically, however, the tension discharged itself in violent persecutions. Buddhism was, generally speaking, tolerated rather than extolled. In order to survive, it had to adapt itself, and it did so in various ways. In the course of time this process of adaptation gave rise to various highly characteristic and distinctively Chinese forms of Buddhism, some of which have flourished for several centuries, producing an amazing wealth of scholastic literature. In this 'digested' form, Buddhism for a certain period (of which the early T'ang is the culminating point) influenced many aspects of Chinese culture, notably in the fields of art, belles-lettres, and popular religion. However, it cannot be doubted that Buddhism in the long run succumbed to the pressure of the secular powers and their ideology. Economically, the power of the church was broken by the great persecutions of the middle of the ninth century. Doctrinally, it was undermined by the powerful Confucian revival of the Sung period. Like Christianity in early Ch'ing times, or like any other foreign

[1] For the early history of the tension between the Buddhist church and the Chinese secular authorities, both at the doctrinal and at the institutional level, see E. Zürcher, *The Buddhist Conquest of China* (Leiden, 1959), especially ch. 5.

religion for that matter, Buddhism was not able to penetrate into the hard core of the central Confucian tradition.

At this point it may be useful to mention a few basic tenets of Buddhism, before turning to the impact of these ideas on Chinese thought, and to the elaboration which they underwent in various schools of Chinese Buddhism.

Buddhism starts from the basic assumptions that suffering is an integral part of all transitory existence; that the motive power of existence (and hence of suffering) is desire in all its forms, including desire *to be*; and that the only way of escaping from suffering is the utter destruction of desire. Various forms of mental and bodily exercise, notably the practice of intense mental absorption known as 'trance' or 'meditation' (*dhyāna*), may prepare the way towards this goal, but final emancipation is actually reached by an act of transcendent understanding, a realization of truth which is beyond rational thought. Unlike other systems of personal salvation, Buddhism most emphatically denies the existence of a permanent 'self', a lasting 'soul', in man. The individual is merely a bundle of visible and invisible elements which is born, suffers, dies, and after death is again integrated into a similar complex of material and psychic elements. It is held together by desire, the most deadly form of which is the desire to exist as an individual, i.e. the desperate belief in the reality of a permanent 'ego'. In fact, nothing exists as a lasting entity: all elements of the pseudo-personality are constantly changing, being subjected to the universal process of causation. This is closely connected with the concept of retribution: each act (*karman*), whether mental, oral, or bodily, produces a seed which moves along with the human compound through successive lives, until it meets an opportunity to develop; then the act is retributed. This process must go on for ever, unless it is broken off by the force of Enlightenment, resulting in the elimination of desire, which is denoted by the word 'extinction' (*nirvāna*). The end of the karmic process does not coincide with physical death; the emancipated one may continue a residual existence in the body for many years, but since he has destroyed the roots of *karman* he can be reborn no more.

The way to salvation is long and difficult. It implies moral training and strenuous exertion, both bodily and mental, which must preferably be practised by leading the ascetic life in the seclusion of the monastery—a life of uninterrupted religious practice, subjected to countless rules of bodily and mental discipline, and shielded from all disturbing influences. The monastery was, in fact, the basic centre of religious life, wherever Buddhism was introduced. There never was a unified Buddhist church under the supervision of one central clerical authority; in China, as in India, it consisted of many different monastic communities, growing up in relative isolation from each other, and dispersed over an enormous and ever-expanding territory. This led to the rise of different schools and sectarian trends, one of which (probably about the first century B.C., perhaps in southern India) developed into a truly revolutionary movement, creating its own pseudo-canonical scriptures, and professing to be the full revelation of Truth, superior to that of the older schools: the 'Great Vehicle' (*mahāyāna*) leading to emancipation. Mahāyāna rejected the 'radical pluralism' of the other schools, which had regarded the individual and the world at large as conglomerations of elements without questioning the reality of these elements themselves. Instead it taught that no element, concept, or phenomenon is either existent or non-existent. By means of a destructive dialectical analysis it showed that nothing can ever arise, remain, or pass away; there is neither cause nor result, neither being nor non-being. Things merely exist at the level of 'conventional truth', in relation to each other. At the level of absolute Truth everything—including even such concepts as Nirvāna and Buddhahood—is 'empty', devoid of identity, homogeneous, and therefore inconceivable and beyond all thought and verbal expression. Emancipation itself is also an illusory process, because at the level of absolute Truth everything is already merged in 'emptiness', and therefore permanently released in Nirvāna. The world of illusion and the Absolute are one and the same, but this supreme fact cannot be understood by rational thought, but must be realized by a kind of mystic self-identification with universal 'emptiness'.[1]

A later (probably fifth century A.D.) development of Mahāyāna thought was the doctrine of 'Consciousness-Only', which taught an extreme form of subjective idealism. All distinctions, all duality, all phenomena, are no more than products of the mind, illusory impressions caused by deluded thought. The whole process of *karman* and causation is mental, being the result of defilement of the fundamental 'Storehouse-Consciousness which in its pure state is identical with the Absolute (Nirvāna, Buddhahood) and therefore impersonal and eternal. By a process of mental training this consciousness has to be purified from all emotions and impressions; then Emancipation is reached. We may conclude that both the school of 'Emptiness' and that of 'Consciousness-Only' had formulated the concept of an all-pervading Absolutum, utterly inexpressible by word or thought, the universal 'Buddha-nature', which is both immanent in, and at the same time somehow identical with, the world of transitory phenomena. Salvation is reached by a mystic insight into this fundamental unity and identity, rather than by the painstaking observance of ascetic discipline.[2]

Another important Mahāyāna concept is that of the Bodhi-

[1] For the scholastic development of the scriptures and treatises of the school of universal 'Emptiness' see Edward Conze, *The Prajñāpāramitā Literature* (The Hague, 1960). For a philosophical treatment of its teachings the reader may be referred to T. R. V. Murti, *The Central Philosophy of Buddhism* (London, 1955).

[2] The development of the doctrine of 'Consciousness-Only', especially in China, is excellently treated by Fung Yu-lan (tr. D. Bodde), *A History of Chinese Philosophy* (Princeton, 1953), vol. ii, pp. 299–338.

sattva, a 'Being destined to Enlightenment', a future Buddha. Mahāyāna affirmed the existence of innumerable Buddhas who are simultaneously active in all parts of the universe, and some of these Buddhas became in the course of time objects of adoration on a par with the historical Buddha Sākyamuni. However, apart from these majestic powers there were innumerable Bodhisattvas, superhuman beings of infinite wisdom and compassion who, even if they could reach Buddhahood and Nirvāna if they wished, voluntarily maintained their existence for the sake of suffering mankind, manifesting themselves on all planes of existence. Since the Bodhisattva fully realizes the illusory nature of all phenomena (including his own self), he is immune to all worldly influences: he knows that he moves in a world of shadows, an imaginary saviour who feigns to save phantoms from non-existing dangers. But such ideas belonged to the realm of philosophy. To the majority of simple believers the Bodhisattvas were great and powerful guides, nearer to mankind than the Buddhas, and therefore fitting objects for worship and devotion. Just as the schools of 'Emptiness' and 'Consciousness-Only' with their penetrating analysis of all phenomena and their huge mass of scholastic elaboration appealed to learned doctors and clerical scholars, so the Bodhisattva-doctrine gave rise to many popular cults, in which we find a striking development of devotionalism.

Although the clerical organization remained roughly the same for most Buddhist schools, in Mahāyāna Buddhism the importance of the monastic way of life was somewhat diminished by the Bodhisattva ideal which allowed even laymen to reach Emancipation. In the Far East this even developed into a kind of self-ordination for laymen, known as 'the Bodhisattva vow'. In general, Mahāyāna is characterized by a more liberal attitude towards the rules of the religious life, less concern for doctrinal purity and dogmatism, and greater pliability and adaptability to other creeds and customs. This has on the whole been beneficial.

It paved the way for its acceptance in China, where, as we said above, adaptation was a primary condition of survival, and its conviction that one should help the world rather than merely abandon it enabled the Buddhist church in China to play a leading role in all kinds of charitable activities and social welfare. On the other hand, the more secular orientation of Mahāyāna has not infrequently resulted in the clergy becoming involved in corrupt practices, such as the acquisition of great material wealth, commercial transactions, financial speculations, and occasionally even military exploits.

According to a famous story, the apocryphal character of which has only been recognized in modern times, the Han emperor Ming (reigned A.D. 58–75) once dreamed that he saw a 'golden man'. When he was informed that this must be the foreign god named Buddha, he sent an embassy to India in order to obtain the sacred texts. After several years the envoys returned together with two Indian masters, for whom the emperor founded the Pai-ma-ssu or 'White Horse Monastery' at the capital Loyang. Thus the Good Law was introduced into China. Although this is no more than a pious legend, it may contain a memory of the existence of Buddhism at the time of the emperor Ming, for the first actual mention of Buddhism in reliable historical sources is connected with the activities of an imperial prince in northern Kiangsu, in the year A.D. 65.

In actual fact it is not known when Buddhism entered China. In any case it did not come directly from India, but mainly from the oasis kingdoms of Central Asia where Buddhism, both of the Mahāyāna variety and of other schools, was flourishing about the beginning of our era. From there is must have filtered in slowly along the continental 'Silk Routes' which connected that region with Northern China. At first it must have lived on as a 'barbarian' creed in the small colonies of foreigners in the capital and other cities: merchants, refugees, envoys, hostages. From there it gradually spread among the Chinese population of the main cities; for in its earliest phase Chinese Buddhism seems to have been a distinctly urban phenomenon. The main centre of Buddhism in Han times was the capital Loyang. From A.D. 148 onwards we find there a number of foreign missionaries: Parthians, Kushans, Sogdians, and also a few Indians. Whatever we know of them is connected with the work of translating Buddhist texts into Chinese—clear proof of the fact that Buddhism had started to spread among the Chinese, although there are certain indications that even in the third century Buddhism was still largely a religion of foreigners. The immense translation activity remained a characteristic aspect of Chinese Buddhism for more than a thousand years. The foreign missionaries seldom had a sufficient command of the Chinese language and script; on the other hand, very few Chinese Buddhists have ever mastered Sanskrit. The solution was found in the 'translation team', the foreign master reciting the Indian text (often from memory) and making, mostly with the help of a bilingual intermediary, a crude preliminary translation, which was noted down and afterwards revised and polished by Chinese assistants. In later times, such a joint enterprise occasionally assumed enormous proportions, involving hundreds of people. The first translations were rather primitive, and the range of subjects treated very limited. Much attention was given to the ancient Buddhist system of mental exercises called *dhyāna*. Some of these practices outwardly resembled certain physical and mental exercises of the Taoists, and this no doubt largely contributed to the popularity of Buddhism in Later Han times, when Taoism was flourishing.

Taoism as an organized religious movement (not to be confused with the philosophical Taoism of the *Tao te ching* and *Chuang-tzu*, the influence of which was limited to the cultured *élite*) probably originated in Later Han times. Its basic aim was to acquire bodily immortality, to become an Immortal who led a life of everlasting bliss in an indestructible 'astral body'.

Among the means to the attainment of this goal were drugs, complicated eubiotic exercises (including respiratory techniques and rules for sexual life), meditation and trance, the confession of sins, the practice of liberality, and frequent ceremonies of an ecstatic or even orgiastic nature. In its earliest phase, Buddhism was probably regarded by the Chinese as another form of Taoism, so that by being grafted on to the Taoist tradition it could reach the Chinese population by indigenous channels; it has, indeed, been argued that in this respect the role of Taoism resembled that of the Jewish communities in the Roman empire through which early Christianity was propagated. In later centuries when Taoism, by appropriating Buddhist elements, had become an elaborate religious system with its own pantheon, a large body of canonical literature, and a monastic organization it became the rival of Buddhism rather than its partner. It even developed the theory that the Buddha had been nobody but a manifestation of Lao-tzu, who had preached to the Indian barbarians a debased form of Taoism which naturally should not have been reintroduced into China! In the course of time the Buddho-Taoist rivalry became another constant feature of Chinese religious history. Several persecutions were at least partly due to Taoist propaganda, and the persistence of the basic issues is shown by the fact this particular theory of 'Lao-tzu converting the Barbarians' can be traced in polemic literature from the earliest period right down to the thirteenth century.

In any case, this kind of Buddhism, deeply influenced by Taoism and other indigenous beliefs, appealed to the masses rather than to the élite; it actually constituted the beginning of popular Buddhism, a mongrel religion which in innumerable local variations maintained itself in the lower strata of society till modern times. Before we turn to the more sophisticated products of Chinese Buddhist thought, let us first pay some attention to this broad undercurrent of popular religion.[1]

[1] For the earliest history of Buddhism in China, and its amalgamation with

At this level Buddhism became associated with all kinds of local cults and ceremonies, often of an exorcistic nature. Both the use of magic formulas and the belief in the superhuman, miraculous powers of the saintly priest were part of the heritage of Indian Buddhism; in China they became amalgamated with existing Taoist practices. In the growing body of Chinese Buddhist folk-lore Indian and Chinese elements were fused together: the identification of the Chinese dragon and the Indian *nāga* is a good example. The Mahāyāna concepts of the existence of many Buddhas, each with his own paradisiacal 'Buddha-field' in a certain part of the universe, and of the great and merciful Bodhisattvas gave rise to various important devotional trends in popular Buddhism. Maitreya was worshipped as the Bodhisattva who will be the next Buddha to appear in this world, and his cult embraces some remarkable eschatological and messianic beliefs concerning the decay of the Buddhist doctrine in the present age of darkness and the glory of a new era under the guidance of Maitreya. It is well known that analogous messianic ideas periodically became prominent in the Taoist religion, and in that context not infrequently formed the 'revolutionary ideology' of peasant uprisings. It is therefore not surprising that, at least from the fifth century onward, the cult of Maitreya sometimes played a role in such popular seditious movements, and therefore came to be regarded by the authorities as highly subversive. Even more popular was the cult of the Bodhisattva Avalokiteśvara, who in China, probably again under the influence of indigenous folk-lore, came to be represented as a female figure, named Kuan-yin. He (or she) was believed to rescue from danger and distress, to preserve from sin, and to bestow all kinds of happiness and prosperity. Kuan-yin was closely associated with Amitābha, the Buddha of the Western Paradise, and was believed to lead the 'souls' of the believers to

the indigenous Taoist religion, see H. Maspero's masterly essays in *Mélanges posthumes sur les religions et l'histoire de la Chine*, vol. i (Paris, 1950).

that region of light at the moment of their death. There, in the 'Land of Bliss' (Sukhāvatī), or, as the Chinese called this branch of devotionalism, 'the Pure Land' (*ch'ing-t'u*), they remain until the moment of their Nirvāna, dwelling in perfect purity and unsullied happiness. The popular cult of Amitābha represents the culminating point of devotionalism and doctrinal simplification: the devotee simply surrenders to the grace of the Buddha, and salvation is not the result of mental and bodily discipline or metaphysical insight, but of faith in Amitābha's miraculous power, expressed by a simple invocation of his holy name.

The performance of 'good works' was held to yield happiness and material prosperity, either in this or in a future life. This simple idea of karmic retribution led to the development of charitable activities, such as the distribution of food in times of famine, and of institutions like hospitals and orphanages. However, the Mahāyāna concept of 'transferring merit'—the performance of pious works for the karmic benefit of other people—made it also possible to reconcile the traditional Chinese family cult with the Buddhist religion. This is most clearly manifested in the field of Buddhist iconography and architecture, where we find innumerable dedicatory inscriptions recording the fact that images were made, or shrines were built, or holy texts were copied 'for the benefit of our departed ancestors'. Even Buddhist monks, who were supposed to have cut off all family relationships, could in this way perform their ceremonial duties towards the family, in accordance with Confucian social ethics. This practice cut across class lines; like other aspects of devotional Buddhism it was a unifying force in the class-ridden society of medieval China. The rulers dedicated temples and monasteries; commoners performed the work of 'transferring merit' on a more modest scale, and those who could not afford to do so individually would join hands and offer a simple votive image dedicated by a group of devotees. Of course these devotional practices were a powerful stimulus to the development of Buddhist art, and to various kinds of technique and craft, one of which is of very great significance. The multiplication of sacred texts was always regarded as a highly meritorious work with favourable karmic consequences, as is testified by numerous colophons on early hand-written copies. The urge to reduce the effort of copying and to increase the number of copies led in the eighth century A.D. to the discovery and rapid development of the art of printing. This Buddhist innovation, which was soon taken over by the secular authorities for other purposes, became a factor of decisive importance in the subsequent history of Chinese culture. Another important by-product of popular Buddhism is found in the field of literature. Literary culture had for centuries been monopolized by the élite of scholar-officials, who used to compose their writings in the highly artificial, formalized, and terse classical language, teeming with rare expressions and cryptic allusions, which was far removed from the normal spoken language, and virtually unintelligible to the uninitiated listener. However, Buddhism, at least in its first phase, addressed itself not to the upper class but to the largely illiterate or semi-literate population; its texts were intended not to be read in the scholar's studio but to be preached— in a more or less vernacular style—to the listening crowd, and its wealth of legend and edifying tales lent itself easily to literary elaboration. Such popular Buddhist stories, sometimes accompanied by pictorial representations and music, actually formed the beginning of Chinese vernacular literature, which was to reach its full maturity in the great novels of Ming times.

The popular and devotional trends of Chinese Buddhism outlined above sometimes attracted members of the cultured élite, but the latter were, generally speaking, more interested in the philosophical side of the doctrine. When, in the early fourth century A.D., Buddhism started to penetrate into these circles, its success was made easier by that fact that Confucianism was temporarily suffering a decline. In the medieval period, from the fall of Han in A.D. 221 to the reunification of the empire in 589, the political unity of China was lost; moreover, from 311 onward China was divided into two parts, the north being occupied by foreign rulers of proto-Turkish, proto-Tibetan, and other origin, whereas the south was governed by a series of feeble Chinese dynasties. The breakdown of the Han empire had been accompanied by changes in the field of thought. We notice a sudden revival of several non-Confucian schools, notably of a new brand of philosophical Taoism based on the *Tao te ching*, *Chuang-tzu*, and the *Book of Changes*, named 'Dark Learning', and a new interest in abstruse metaphysical and ontological speculations. From the early fourth century onward, Buddhism in its more philosophical aspects became closely associated with this 'neo-Taoist' trend, and the amalgamation of the two gave rise to a very remarkable and highly sophisticated philosophy which for centuries influenced the thought of cultured monks and laymen alike. According to neo-Taoism, all phenomena, all change and diversity, in short all 'Being', is manifested and sustained by a principle which is unlimited, unnameable, unmoving, one and undiversified, and which therefore is referred to as 'Non-being'. The basic problem is the relation between this 'fundamental Non-being' and 'final Being'. These do not form a pair of mutually exclusive opposites. In the words of the *Tao te ching*, 'they emerge together, but have different names', and the insight into this fundamental unity of the phenomenal world and 'Non-being' is, again according to the *Tao te ching*, 'the Mystery of Mysteries, the gate of all wonders'.[1] It cannot be expressed in words, but is intuitively realized by the Sage in silent contemplation. It is easy to see that the Mahāyāna doctrine of 'Universal Emptiness', once it was introduced into the inner circle of literati, was almost predestined to merge with this indigenous doctrine of 'Emptiness and Non-being'.[2] In the

[1] *Tao te ching*, ch. 1.
[2] For the impact of Buddhist philosophical concepts on early Chinese

resulting hybrid Buddhist philosophy certain notions were developed which persisted for many centuries, and eventually provided the philosophical background for the most characteristic product of Buddho-Taoist thought: the system of mental exercises and 'shock-therapeutic' techniques named *Ch'an* in Chinese and *Zen* in Japanese. Among such notions we may mention the idea that the Absolute, being inaccessible to rational thought, must be realized in a flash of spontaneous, intuitive insight; the concept of a 'wordless doctrine' as the means to convey the highest truth, all scriptural teachings being regarded as outward trappings or expedient means, useful at a certain stage but to be abandoned later; the use of the paradox, the seemingly nonsensical statement, as a means to adumbrate the Truth; the emphasis on the contact with nature as a source of inspiration. The great scholar-monks Chih Tun (314–66) and Hui-yüan (334–416) were among the first who explained these ideas to the cultured public in terms of traditional Chinese thought.

Another characteristic doctrinal development has been represented since the late Middle Ages by what may be called the Chinese schools of scholastic classification, of which the T'ien-t'ai school, founded by Chih-i (531–97), was the most important (the school is named after the mountain in Chekiang where it had its main centre). Classificatory systems of this type were attempts to solve a problem, which became urgent when by the sustained efforts of several generations a considerable part of Indian Buddhist literature had been translated into Chinese. In India this literature had been the result of organic growth, both temporally, as new texts evolved from or supplanted the old ones, and spatially, since the doctrine was diversified in many

thought, and especially on 'Dark Learning', see P. Demiéville, 'La Pénétration du Bouddhisme dans la tradition philosophique chinoise', in *Journal of World History*, vol. iii (Paris, 1956); W. Liebenthal, *The Book of Chao* (Peking, 1948); E. Zürcher, op. cit., especially ch. 3.

rival schools and sects throughout India and Central Asia. The Chinese, however, were not confronted with the doctrine in this way: to them, the temporal and spatial perspective was lost. They had to base their opinions upon a bewildering variety of Mahāyāna and Hīnayāna scriptures, monastic rules, spells and charms, legends and scholastic treatises of different ages, regions and schools, which not seldom flatly contradicted each other. The integral transplantation of a whole Indian school to China (as happened with the 'Consciousness-Only' doctrine in the seventh century) is a comparatively late phenomenon. Thus the early Chinese Buddhist thinkers were forced to be eclectics by the circumstances under which the doctrine was presented to them, whilst on the other hand they felt the urge to preserve as much of the sacred 'Buddha-word' as possible. In this they were helped by the Mahāyāna concept of 'expediency': the idea that the Buddha in preaching the Law had adapted himself to the level of understanding of his hearers. Hence the scriptures and tenets of the other schools were not regarded as basically untrue or 'heretical', but rather as lower levels of truth, a partial revelation intended for those who were not yet ripe for the higher teachings of the Great Vehicle.

As a result of these factors the various Chinese schools of this scholastic type concentrated upon the elaboration of complicated schemes in which all known scriptures were arranged in an allegedly chronological order, corresponding with various 'phases' or periods in the Buddha's teaching. They held one particular scripture to contain the final and complete revelation of truth, and arranged all other canonical texts in ascending order of doctrinal 'purity' around this central scripture, as 'preliminary teachings' which had merely served to prepare the minds of less advanced hearers. Thus the very important T'ient'ai sect classified the canon according to a scheme of five phases of teaching, the whole culminating in the doctrine of the *Lotus sūtra*, which, according to this school, contained the ultimate truth. In spite of their immense literary production, these schools have produced little of lasting value.

The same tendency towards immense scholastic elaboration and theological hair-splitting characterized the idealistic 'Consciousness-Only' school, which was propagated by the famous scholar and pilgrim Hsüan-tsang (602–64) and his disciples. This period—that of the Sui and T'ang Dynasties, 589–907—was the golden age of Buddhism in China. Materially, the large monasteries flourished as never before, and the church's economic power, based on large landownership and various forms of commercial and financial activity, gradually assumed dangerous proportions.[1] Temples and pagodas dotted the landscape. Chinese Buddhist pilgrims travelled to the ends of the known world; Chinese Buddhism had some influence in Tibet, and several of its sects were transferred to Japan. Buddhism profoundly influenced contemporary art and literature; Chinese Buddhist sculpture, now fully emancipated from its foreign prototypes, followed its own lines of evolution. But in the realm of thought the most startling development did not take place in the powerful monasteries of the leading sects, but in the small groups of masters and disciples belonging to another movement, which, though inspired by many of the ideals of the earlier Buddho-Taoist trend mentioned above, was unique in the choice of the practical means by which it sought to realize these ideals.

The origin of this Ch'an or 'Meditation' school is obscured by legend.[2] According to later tradition it was introduced into

[1] The economic activities of the Buddhist church in medieval times are brilliantly described by J. Gernet in *Les Aspects économiques du Bouddhisme dans la société chinoise du Ve au Xe siècle* (Saigon, 1956).

[2] The literature on Ch'an (Zen) Buddhism in Western languages is voluminous, but of very unequal quality. For the historical development of this school one may consult H. Dumoulin and R. F. Sasaki, *The Development of Chinese Zen* (New York, 1953); J. Gernet, 'La Biographie du Maître Chen-houei de Ho-tsö, in *Journal Asiatique* (1951); H. Dumoulin, 'Bodhidharma

China around 520 by the Indian master Bodhidharma, after having been handed down by a succession of twenty-seven earlier Indian patriarchs, the first of whom was Mahākāśyapa, the disciple of the Buddha. In fact, Ch'an Buddhism was a purely Chinese phenomenon without any Indian counterpart or prototype. The final version of the list of 'Indian patriarchs' dates only from the tenth century, and even the figure of Bodhidharma belongs to the realm of hagiography rather than to that of history. Such pseudo-genealogical tables and tales about the prehistory of Ch'an no doubt served to enhance the prestige of the new movement, and to defend it against the attacks of T'ien-t'ai and other sects which not unreasonably regarded it as heretical. On the other hand, Ch'an has always in later times attached the greatest importance to purity of transmission, with the doctrine being directly communicated from master to disciple, and to the codification of this transmission in tables indicating the filiation of masters in the various Ch'an sects. This practice may also have stimulated the attempts to extend the line of transmission into the past, to the time of the Buddha, and even to the Buddhas of past world-periods.

As an organized movement Ch'an appears for the first time in the seventh century A.D., around the time when it was split up into two rival groups: a northern branch led by the master Shen-hsiu (died 706), and a southern branch under Hui-neng (638–713). The northern branch, which was less revolutionary

und die Anfänge des Ch'an Buddhismus', in *Monumenta Nipponica* (1951), vol. vii; for the doctrinal aspects the reader may still be referred to the popularizing and somewhat over-enthusiastic accounts by D. T. Suzuki, especially to his *Studies in Zen* (London, 1955) and his *Studies in the Lankavatara Sutra* (London, 1930). Among the translations from Ch'an literature may be mentioned: J. Gernet, *Entretiens du Maître de Dhyāna Chen-houei de Ho-tsö* (Hanoi, 1949), W. Gundert, *Bi-yän-lu, Meister Yüan-wu's Niederschrift von der smaragdenen Felswand* (Munich, 1960), J. Blofeld, *The Zen Teaching of Huang Po* (London, 1958), and D. T. Suzuki, *Manual of Zen Buddhism* (repr. London, 1950).

and still attached importance to the study of certain canonical scriptures, never became very prominent. The southern branch, which propagated the idea of 'Sudden Enlightenment' and emphatically rejected all scriptural studies, became very popular, and in the course of time developed all those techniques and practices which are now commonly regarded as characteristic of Ch'an as a whole. It attained great prosperity in the eighth century, notably through the activities of the famous masters Ma-tsu (died 788) and Shih-t'ou (700–90). Around that time the southern branch was already becoming diversified into various schools or sects, often only distinguishable by subtle variations in doctrinal matters or teaching techniques. Two of these early schools, the Ts'ao-tung (Jap. Sōtō) sect founded by Hsing-ssu (died 788) and the Lin-chi (Jap. Rinzai) sect of Huai-jang (677–744), still form the main divisions in Japanese Zen. In the following centuries Ch'an became ever more diversified into countless ramifications of sects and sub-sects.

Ch'an survived the great persecution of Buddhism in the mid-ninth century, which dealt a heavy blow even to non-Buddhist religious communities in China. That it could do so may have been mainly due to material reasons. As long as the T'ang state was strong, it had been able to bear the enormous pressure exerted upon the national economy by the great monasteries, with their large tax-free domains and their expensive ceremonies. But from the middle of the eighth century the power of the dynasty had rapidly waned, and its attitude became less tolerant. Anti-clericalism became stronger than ever, and in 845 led to a persecution on an unprecedented scale. More than 40,000 temples and shrines were confiscated and in most cases demolished, and 260,500 monks and nuns were secularized. Later the clergy was allowed to grow again, but most schools, and the economic power of the Buddhist church as a whole, had suffered a blow from which they never recovered.

Ch'an could survive because, not only doctrinally but also

institutionally, it stood outside the main stream of Chinese Buddhism. Around A.D. 800—some fifty years before the persecution—the Ch'an master Huai-hai had created the first monastic rules for the new creed, which thereby obtained its own characteristic form of organization. Unlike the large monasteries of the traditional schools with their hundreds of monks, loosely bound together according to non-hierarchical principles, the typical Ch'an community was small and strictly hierarchical. It consisted of a master surrounded by a number of disciples, whom he instructed personally and individually, and who led a life of extreme simplicity, strenuous mental exercises and equally exhausting manual labour, and strict discipline.

Ch'an consciously departs from all other schools of Buddhism; it claims to contain the essential truth of Buddhahood and Enlightenment, and to provide the right method to reach that highest goal here and now; it justifies its claim by asserting that this 'wordless doctrine' of Ch'an has been separately handed down, outside the normal scriptural tradition, from the Buddha himself via an unbroken succession of patriarchs down to the time of Hung-jen, and from then on to the present. Its basic doctrine is that the 'Buddha-nature', the principle of absolute Truth and Enlightenment, and hence of Emancipation in the Buddhist sense, is immanent in ourselves and can be realized by meditation and introspection under the guidance of an enlightened master. It does not attach importance to scriptural studies or scholastic reasonings, since the essence of Truth can neither be expressed in words nor reached by rational means. All this is aptly summarized by the four 'slogans' which are traditionally attributed to Bodhidharma himself: 'A direct reference to the mind of man'; 'Realization of Buddhahood by looking into [one's own] nature'; 'A separate tradition outside the [normal] doctrine'; 'No reliance on [scriptural] texts'.

Two fundamental attitudes play an important role in Ch'an

Buddhism: the irrational and the iconoclastic. Both had their roots in the indigenous tradition of philosophical Taoism and neo-Taoism, the amalgamation of which with Mahāyāna Buddhism had, as we said above, given rise to a hybrid Buddho-Taoist trend of thought since medieval times. In Ch'an Buddhism, however, the irrational and iconoclastic tendencies, which have always been clearly observable in Taoism and potentially present in Mahāyāna Buddhism, have been driven to extremes. Mahāyāna Buddhism had indeed taught that rational thought is unable to perceive the Absolute, but it had never propagated the use of the irrational, the seemingly nonsensical or bizarre, as a preparation for Enlightenment. Mahāyāna Buddhism had stressed the relativity of all scriptural teachings as 'expedient means' or inadequate expressions of Truth, but it never advocated that they be discarded altogether. In these respects Ch'an is much nearer to the spirit of Taoism with its anti-ritualism, its cult of the bizarre, and its outspoken aversion from all book-learning and literary culture. It is therefore understandable that Ch'an has sometimes been characterized as 'the Chinese reaction to Buddhism' rather than as a part of it. If we prefer to treat it as an integral part of Chinese Buddhism—in fact, as the most typically *Chinese* expression of Buddhism—it is mainly because the basic aim of Ch'an, as of Mahāyāna Buddhism as a whole, is the experience of Enlightenment and Emancipation, concepts which even in their Chinese formulation are definitely not inspired by any Chinese creed.

Another concept of the greatest importance is that of 'Sudden Enlightenment', which was the object of discussions of learned monks and laymen as early as the fifth (or perhaps even fourth) century A.D., long before it became the basic assumption of Ch'an Buddhism. If, as is taught by the Mahāyāna doctrine of 'Universal Emptiness', at the level of the highest Truth all phenomena, all duality, all distinctions are effaced, including the distinctions between the world of suffering and Nirvāna, or between delusion and Emancipation—then one must conclude that the traditional Buddhist path of gradual training and mental discipline loses its *raison d'être*. In actual fact everybody is already emancipated and identical with Nirvāna and the Buddha-nature, and has been so since the beginning of time. And for the same reason this fact is not something that will slowly dawn upon one in the course of a long mental development, but is realized in a sudden revelation of unity and totality, a flash of insight, an explosion. With these earlier thinkers, Ch'an agrees that Enlightenment cannot be obtained gradually, by deliberate intellectual effort, but that it breaks out in a single moment, 'like the bottom of the tub falling out'.

If in these respects the Ch'an doctrine is not original at all, it is unique in its choice of the means employed to evoke the experience of Enlightenment (*wu*, Jap. *satori*) in the disciple: perplexing subjects for meditation, paradoxes, nonsensical questions and baffling answers, even yelling and beating. It seems that in the earliest period the masters used the method of free improvisation in applying this 'shock-therapy' to their disciples. When the disciple, probably exhausted by mental and physical exertion and consequently in a state of extreme nervous tension, appeared to be ripe for the decisive step, it was the master's task, by means of a well-chosen word, an exclamation, or anything fitting the occasion, to break the last barrier of the intellect and to plunge the disciple into the undifferentiated state of 'no-mind', in which Enlightenment is experienced.

From the early Sung onward such 'explosive' sayings were compiled into collections of *logia* (*yü-lu*). Ch'an became formalized into a system, in which the spontaneous utterances of the great T'ang masters were used as themes for meditation, named 'cases' (*kung-an*, Jap. *kōan*). Paradoxically, the 'wordless doctrine' of Ch'an thus gave rise to an extensive doctrinary literature, with commentaries and sub-commentaries that generally explain the cryptic sayings of the masters in even more cryptic terms. In this somewhat fossilized form Ch'an Buddhism continued to be influential until well into Ming times, although it cannot be denied that in many cases it functioned as the intellectual game of a refined leisure class rather than as a serious quest for Enlightenment. But even so, Ch'an Buddhism became one of the great creative forces in Far Eastern culture. Its influence upon art and literature was enormous at the time of its greatest vitality, and remained considerable for centuries afterwards, both in China and in Korea, whereas in Japan, where the first Zen sects were introduced in the twelfth century, it has flourished down to the present day.

In recent times some aspects of Ch'an have become popular in the West, notably its anti-rational and iconoclastic attitude and its ideal of direct and intuitional perception of Truth. The importance of this influence cannot be denied; it is, in fact, one of the major phenomena of present-day cultural life in the West. It should, however, never be forgotten that this is only one part of Ch'an—its necessary counterpart, the Ch'an *discipline* with its characteristic meditation techniques, the personal contact between master and disciple, and the quest for Enlightenment with all its specifically Buddhist or Buddho-Taoist associations are left out of the picture. There are also Western Buddhists who sincerely strive to study and practise the Good Law. But in general, neo-Buddhism—including the activities of Western 'Zen Societies'—all too often results in a diluted pseudo-Buddhism mixed with occultism. In all essentials Ch'an is a product of a great but archaic and alien civilization—it remains to be seen to what extent this tender exotic plant will survive a transplantation into foreign soil.   E. ZÜRCHER

3

LITERATURE

(a) AN INTRODUCTORY NOTE

It would be idle to pretend that our own culture has been noticeably influenced by the legacy of Chinese literature. Indeed, since the 'literary revolution', initiated in 1917 by the manifestoes of Hu Shih and Ch'en Tu-hsiu and consummated in 1922 when the Chinese Ministry of Education substituted vernacular for classical textbooks in the schools, literary influences have all been in the opposite direction. In fiction, in poetry, in drama, traditional forms have been jettisoned and Western models pursued.

As citizens of the world we are entitled to look on Chinese literature as part of our heritage, but before we do so we should do well to inquire why the Chinese themselves have rejected it, and whether their rejection has in fact been a total one.

There are two grounds on which the Chinese rejected their traditional literature, one ideological and one linguistic. Let us consider the ideological one first.

When in the middle years of the nineteenth century the Chinese sustained a series of humiliations at the hands of the Western powers, having previously regarded themselves as the greatest power on earth and all other nations as their inferiors both in culture and in might, it did not occur to them that anything was wrong with their fundamental beliefs, or with what we might call the Chinese way of life. They saw the Western superiority as a purely technological one. There was something vulgar and ungentlemanly about the mechanical skills which gave foreigners their superior power; however, if needs be these skills must be mastered. And so an attempt was made to learn the industrial, military, financial, and diplomatic techniques of the West whilst retaining and even strengthening the traditional Confucian patterns of government and society. Woolsey's *International Law* and Fawcett's *Political Economy* were translated into Chinese, but not Homer or Shakespeare.

The 'self-strengthening' movement, as it was styled, proved a dismal failure; already discredited by 1871, it was finally and totally wrecked in the disastrous Sino-Japanese War of 1894. China's faith in herself thereupon collapsed entirely. The old system of education and the civil service examinations, both founded upon the Confucian Classics, were steadily eroded, and enlightened Chinese began a wholesale and unreserved study of Western civilization in all its aspects. Now not only sciences and skills were studied; the philosophy and literature of the West were also scanned in the hope that therein might be discovered the sources of that dynamic which had led to the conquest of nature's secrets and of so much of the earth's surface.

It must not be thought that the literature which translators made available was always the best. The voluminous output of the great translator Lin Shu included a good deal of modish trash. But the people who read his elegant classical renderings of Rider Haggard and Conan Doyle were not in search merely of entertainment. They were in conscious pursuit of the Occident, and were constantly reminded in the prefaces to these translations of the morals they might be expected to draw from them. In introducing *Allan Quatermain* Lin Shu lectures his readers on the white man's love of adventure and innovation; and in his preface to *People of the Mist* he reflects that if an Englishman would endure the sufferings and hardships that its hero underwent for the sake of a bag of rubies, the outlook for China with her vast resources of gold, silver, silk, and tea was very poor indeed.

From whole-heartedly embracing Western culture it was only

a step to repudiating outright the traditional Confucian culture. Nearly all the intellectual *avant-garde* of the 1920's were noisily anti-Confucian, and sometimes not only Confucianism but the whole literature of the past came under their attack.

Traditional Chinese literature, the Confucian Classics in particular, was identified in the popular mind with the old examination system of bureaucratic recruitment and hence, by association, with the bureaucracy itself and all the corruption and ineptitude it had acquired in the period of dynastic decline. There was no doubt an element of irrationalism in this, but no more so than in the attitude to Greek and Latin literature of those like Bernard Shaw who believed that the educational system which taught them was effete.

This brings us to the linguistic grounds for rejection. In a country of China's great size, where for centuries literacy was confined to a small educated *élite*, it was inevitable not only that there should be considerable regional variation of dialect but also that the difference between the spoken and written languages should gradually widen. Even in the first and second centuries A.D. one can already observe an archaizing tendency among certain writers; though it seems probable that the written word was as a rule still intelligible when read aloud. Six centuries later the very much wider divergence between written and spoken Chinese was accentuated by an extremely artificial and elaborate prose style, and in the ninth century an attempt was made to introduce greater simplicity by imitating the models of the ancients. Unfortunately the success of this archaizing movement had the effect of divorcing written Chinese finally and irreversibly from the language of speech. The following examples, in the pronunciation of Peking, will give some idea of the gap between them:

English	Classical Chinese	Modern Colloquial Chinese
What man is this?	*Tz'u ho jen yeh?*	*Che shih shen-ma jen?*

I cannot see his head.	*Wu pu chien ch'i shou.*	*Wo k'an pu chien t'a ti t'ou.*
These things are not enough.	*Shih wu pu tsu.*	*Che-hsieh tung-hsi pu kou.*
The sun is about to come out.	*Jih yü ch'u.*	*T'ai-yang yao ch'u-lai.*

After the revolution of 1911 which overthrew the Manchu dynasty and what remained of its bureaucratic machine, Chinese radicals increasingly came to feel that regeneration of China's corrupt, demoralized, and dispirited society would only be possible by means of education, and that education on the scale and of the kind they envisaged would only be possible in a medium less restricted than the difficult and archaic Classical Chinese.

Once the vernacular was adopted as the normal literary medium, a great part of the literary heritage of the past became irrelevant from the point of view of the Chinese writer in quest of a style. Lu Hsün (1881–1936), the greatest twentieth-century writer in the vernacular language, made much use, as did most writers of the twenties and thirties, of his classical education, but only for garnishing—rather in the way that some people have of interlarding their conversation with scraps of Latin or French. He neither wrote in the language of his predecessors nor developed the forms they had used. His models were foreign, mainly Russian—Gogol, Chekhov, Gorky, Andreyev, &c.

Since the middle years of the twentieth century the Chinese have continued to read and translate Western literature in ever greater volume, but at the same time they have begun a reassessment of their traditional literature; and though few of them still write either prose or verse in the traditional forms except as an academic exercise, there has been a growing tendency to restore the 'literary heritage' to its former level of esteem— higher, indeed, in the case of the vernacular literature, which in the past seldom enjoyed the prestige it has today. But whereas at the beginning of the century men of letters could feel that what they read and wrote formed part of a tradition which extended backwards without a break to Confucius and the sages of antiquity, the modern Chinese looks back at the bulk of his country's literature across a linguistic gulf almost as great as that which separates us from our own classical antiquity.

If we cannot point to Chinese influences in our own literature—a few diverting pages could no doubt be written on Crusoe's travels in China and Lamb's *Dissertation upon Roast Pig* but they would have little to do with Chinese literature—we can at least point to the importance of Chinese studies to Comparative Literature.

Although it was already old when Rome fell, Comparative Literature was until recently little esteemed as a 'serious' academic subject. It has taken the authority of scholars like Bowra in Britain and Levin in America to remove some of the suspicions which have mysteriously hung about it for so long. The value of Chinese literature to its study is that it forms a complete literary 'world' of its own, which is wholly removed from that of the West.

The student of Comparative Literature, after examining certain themes or genres or ways of organizing words and ideas in a number of different European literatures, may feel tempted to conclude that what emerges is truths about some abstract entity called Literature, or a set of natural laws unconsciously obeyed by all who use language as an art. In fact, no guarantee of universality ever attaches to generalizations about European literature. We are all, as it were, Children of the Book; all have passed through the winepress of Aristotle.

But if we test our assumptions about the novel, or the ballad, or drama, or poetry against what can be observed of Chinese literature, we find ourselves very soon raising quite fundamental questions of a kind which might not otherwise get asked, but which it is important that we should ask from time to time.

Take the question of genre. It is conventional and extremely useful when dealing with literature to speak of 'form' and 'content' and to assume—as did the early Chinese critics—that a certain form is appropriate to a certain content. The marriage of a certain kind of form with a certain kind of content is what we mean by a genre. This *sounds* fairly reasonable. For example, it seems to us obvious that a sequence of ten limericks would make an unsuitable dirge for ten people killed in an accident. But can we be sure that the unsuitability is inherent in the form and is not simply conventional?

Of course, a morphology of literature would show that the theme or subject evolves its own form as it is developed. The genres are not Platonic ideas that have existed from the beginning of time which are selected by the writer according to their appropriateness for the job in hand, as clubs are selected by a golfer. But there are many, many factors other than the nature of the theme which contribute to the evolution of a literary form, some of them possibly fortuitous or even trivial.

The problem is not of merely academic interest. For example, it is widely affirmed, and rightly, that China has no epic poetry. When we are talking about 'the epic', however, we often include the Icelandic prose sagas for consideration. In that case are we to take another look at *The Romance of the Three Kingdoms* and *The Water Margin*, which grew out of popular tale-cycles? They are usually called 'novels' and dismissed contemptuously by people looking for the Chinese Proust. Of course, if we call *Paradise Lost* an epic, we are implying that the epic must have something to do not necessarily with heroes but with myth. In that case the Ossianic poems and the Chinese epic novels are romances.

At this point we perhaps begin to feel that our categories are impossibly large and call in Form to the rescue by talking of heroic poetry, prose epic, prose romance, and so on. But the formal categories are soon discovered to be far too arbitrary. We cannot discuss epic without discussing prose epic.

It may be argued that we do not have to bother in any case. We can either stop using the categories altogether and deal only with the individual works, like so many islands in a vast archipelago called Literature; or else we can invent temporary *ad hoc* groupings and arrangements to last for as long as the fancy takes us or the need remains.

Alternatively we might decide that Chinese literature is a literature *sui generis*, in which it is pointless to look for the genres with which we are familiar in our own. We might try to do so, but we should soon discover ourselves attempting to explain away the fact that *War and Peace* and *A la recherche du temps perdu* have far more in common with *Hung-lou meng* than with *Gil Blas* or *Don Quixote*, and Chinese folk-songs with our own ballad tradition than either with the *Satires* of Juvenal.

In fact, we are in a situation somewhat similar to that of a linguist asked to make a descriptive analysis of a hitherto unrecorded language. We shall expect to find some of the things we are familiar with and not others, and some which are new and not paralleled in our past experience.

If we begin looking for features of our own literature which are not paralleled in Chinese literature, we shall find the most striking instance in the absence of religious inspiration. Our drama began in pagan ritual and developed in medieval mystery. Chinese drama is secular for as far back as we can trace it—to the masques and buffooneries with which Han emperors were entertained two thousand years ago. Our greatest poets sing of Juno's jealousy and Apollo's rage, of journeys through Heaven and Hell, of Satan's fall, and Paradise Lost and Regained. Chinese literature is in the main a secular literature. When one considers the intense devotionalism which swept through China during the 'Buddhist centuries' from the fifth to the ninth centuries A.D., one is startled to find how comparatively little of it is manifested in contemporary literature. The monks used popular literature as a proselytizing vehicle, and they played a leading part in the development of printing, which gave China a half-educated urban reading public for cheap popular fiction centuries before the same phenomenon appeared in Europe; but few people could name any religious poetry other than the deservedly famous but not outstandingly important verses of the 'Master of the Cold Mountain'.[1]

The word 'secular' tends to recur when one speaks in general terms about Chinese literature—or, for that matter, about Chinese society. Imperial China may be likened to a medieval European society without Christianity in which all, not only half, the ruling class were clerks. The immense esteem in which literacy and education were held meant that a great deal of literary activity was patronized and institutionalized by the state. Notable among the products of this activity were the great dynastic histories and the enormous encyclopedias commissioned by emperors in order to survey the sum of the country's learning. Indeed, the encyclopedia could well be regarded as a Chinese invention, and certainly no other country can have produced encyclopedias so numerous and so vast.

Let us now—as we should have done long before—consider what the Chinese themselves say about their literature. Chinese literary criticism is of venerable antiquity and has had some brilliant exponents.

The scholar class—the clerks—were Confucians, and their views on literature were coloured by their Confucian training and their belief that the Confucian Classics were the repository of all Truth and consequently represented, among other things, the ultimate perfection of literary merit. The Confucian Classics always were, and still generally are, the first section in a Chinese library; they always come first in bibliographies; and essays about them frequently appear as the first section of a writer's collected works. For centuries they were the central part of Chinese

---

[1] Cf. *Cold Mountain, 100 poems by Han-shan,* tr. Burton Watson (New York, 1962).

education, knowledge of them was required in the civil service examinations, and until comparatively recently most educated Chinese could recite at least the most important sections by heart.

The Confucian Classics are not religious texts, but they resemble our own scriptures in being extremely heterogeneous. An ancient manual of divination with philosophical commentaries, a collection of documents purporting to be the conversations and speeches of the earliest kings, a book of songs, hymns, and ballads apparently dating from the eleventh to the seventh centuries B.C., the annals of an ancient feudal state and the historical commentaries accompanying them, three collections of writings on ritual and etiquette, the collected sayings of Confucius, the writings of the philosopher Mencius, a schoolbook of short essays on the virtue of filial piety, and a glossary of the difficult words in the other books of the canon—a glance at this catalogue does not suggest a likely receptacle for the sum of human wisdom. It had to be assumed that Truth was concealed in these books, or expounded by them in some allegorical manner. Literature, then, must imitate the Classics in expounding Truth; it must exalt virtue and dispraise vice; in short, it must be didactic. This was the earliest Confucian view and continued, with some variations and modifications, to be the most commonly held view until comparatively recent times.[1]

Some writers—Po Chü-i is a good example—took their duties as moral censors very seriously indeed; some did not, but conformed by making extravagant claims for the effectiveness of such perfunctory statements of social conscience as their works contained; very few indeed felt able to reject the didactic position outright.

Liu Hsieh (465–522), perhaps the greatest of all Chinese

---

[1] Owing to the heterogeneous nature of the Confucian Classics, passages which give further information about them are scattered throughout the book. They may be traced by referring to the pages listed in the Index under 'Confucian Classics'. [Ed.]

literary critics, lived at a time when literary artistry was far more highly esteemed than moral fervour. It is interesting to observe the way in which he deals with the problem of explaining how the uncouth, archaic writings of the Confucian canon could come to be the well-head and exemplar of the elegant and sophisticated art which is the subject of his book. He is able to solve the problem thanks largely to an etymological coincidence.

The word *wen*, which is Liu Hsieh's word for 'literature', has a wide range of meanings. From the basic sense of 'pattern'—the natural markings on the bodies of birds, beasts, and fishes, the tattooing on a human body, the design painted on a shield, and so on—two separate subsidiary meanings developed:

(1) pattern→device→written symbol→writing→script→literature;
(2) pattern→embellishment→adornment→refinement→culture→ civilization.

To Liu Hsieh, *pattern* is therefore the principle which underlies the universe; the rugged canonical books *expound* the principle, and literature, which is the noblest and most comprehensive of the patterns made by man, *exemplifies* it. He sets forth this view in a passage of great beauty and magnificence in the very first chapter of his book,[1] in which he points to the patterns of the stars above, the patterns in cloud and in flower, the patterns of sound that make music, and lastly to man's wonderful invention of the patterns that we call writing. For 'if even insentient things are so beautifully adorned, it would be strange indeed if those possessing minds were to lack a pattern of their own'.

This almost mystical conception of literature is perhaps not really so very far removed from our own when we talk of literary 'creation', thereby in a sense likening the writer to God. Be that as it may, it certainly explains the great importance which Chinese critics attached to *form* (in which the patterns of literature are most apparent), and may serve as justification for the

[1] The *Wen-hsin tiao-lung*, tr. Vincent Yu-chung Shih, *The Literary Mind and the Carving of Dragons* (New York, 1959).

relatively large amount of attention paid to form in the sections
which follow. DAVID HAWKES

(b) CHINESE POETRY AND THE ENGLISH READER

ONE does not—in spite of Lucretius, and the *Georgics*, and the
Essay on Criticism—read poetry for information or instruction,
but for a kind of experience, part emotional, part intellectual,
which can only be described tautologically as the experience of
reading poetry. The demands which different kinds of poetry
make on the reader vary infinitely; but in general it is true to
say that all poetry requires a fairly high degree of sensitivity to
language and an ability to respond, if only unconsciously, to the
images and archetypes employed by the poet.

For this reason the poetry of an alien culture is likely to be
appreciated much later than the more functional parts of its
literature. Its historical, philosophical, religious, technological
writings will begin to yield up some of their content of fact and
opinion after only a quite rudimentary level of linguistic facility
has been attained. The terms used in such writings are often
limited in reference and narrowly defined, and a translator's task
consists mainly in identifying them. But the language of poetry
is essentially evocative, pregnant, and ambiguous, and a prolonged linguistic and cultural immersion is needed before the
foreign reader can even begin to be aware of its implications.

It is not surprising, then, that in the West the study of
Chinese poetry lagged far behind, for example, the study of
Chinese philosophy. The Jesuits of the seventeenth century and
the Protestant missionaries of the nineteenth sought China's
contribution to world culture in her political institutions and
secular philosophy; Chinese poetry they generally ignored or
dismissed, encouraged to do so, no doubt, by the views of such
educated Chinese as they were able to meet.

To be sure, a few translations from Chinese verse did from time to time appear, but nothing which could conceivably have interested a Western poet until the publication of the *Livre de jade* by Théophile Gautier's daughter in 1867. This book was probably not much known about in England and America until the turn of the century; and it is the reception of Chinese poetry in English-speaking countries rather than its influence on the West as a whole to which we must confine ourselves here in the interest of coherence. In fact, it is most unlikely that Chinese poetry had any influence, however slight, upon English literature earlier than the 1920's, when Ezra Pound and Arthur Waley, one a distinguished poet and one a scholar of great literary sensibility, began publishing their translations.

I suspect that the influence of twentieth-century translations from Chinese poetry upon twentieth-century English-speaking poets has been less insignificant than might be supposed, but that the task of tracing it would prove oppressively great and depressingly unrewarding.

Assuming that some scholar of the future will undertake this labour, we can most usefully prepare the ground for such a study by examining here the relationship which the translations from Chinese poetry bear to the originals. It might, after all, turn out that the kinds of things believed to be most typical of Chinese poetry and therefore most likely to have made some sort of impression on English-speaking poets are not really characteristic of Chinese poetry at all, but are simply atmospherics produced by the translator. And of course if we are going to carry out this examination at a general level, eschewing the mere enumeration of particular instances and particular translators, we shall in fact find ourselves mainly concerned with an examination of the problems which the translation of Chinese poetry poses.

It may seem wilful in writing an essay on Chinese poetry to limit oneself at the outset to a consideration of the problems of translation; but what is the alternative? To write the poetics of a poetry which few people have read would be insane; whilst an historical outline of China's two and a half millennia of prolific poetic output would, if condensed to essay proportions, read like an auctioneer's catalogue. The logical alternative would be a beginner's lesson in the Chinese language;[1] but that, after all, would belong to a different part of this book.

At the very threshold of any discussion of Chinese poetry one stumbles on the problem of definition. The problem is twofold, in that we need to consider both what we mean by 'poetry' in an English context and what we mean by it in a Chinese one. What we mean by the one will obviously to some extent condition what we mean by the other.

As regards the definition of 'poetry' in an English context, I propose not to bother with the sort of value-judgement that bestows this term as an award of merit on certain kinds of verse of which it approves, but to use 'poetry' as the name of all verse literature, leaving to others the task of defining what literature is. Ambiguous 'prose-poem' forms, provided that we are quite sure they are not in some odd kind of verse, can only be called 'poetry' in a metaphorical sense.[2]

The definition of 'poetry' in a Chinese context involves in the first place the clearing up of a certain amount of semantic muddle. The customary modern Chinese equivalent of 'poetry' is *shih*, a word which sounds like *shr* in *shrub* as pronounced by most Londoners, or *sure* as pronounced by some Americans. Unfortunately in traditional Chinese criticism *shih* is ordinarily used as the name of a literary class from which large sections of verse literature are excluded.

---

[1] James Liu, in *The Art of Chinese Poetry* (London, 1962), does in fact devote the first part of his excellent book to explaining the Chinese language to the common reader.

[2] This definition automatically excludes various bits of Whitman and Rimbaud; but it is impossible to generalize at this level without smashing a certain amount of china.

In the excluded categories there are *tz'u*, a type of lyric verse; *ch'ü*, another type of lyric verse which conventionally includes drama; and *fu*, a sort of verse essay which is sometimes all in verse but more often in a mixture of verse and prose.

Very little *tz'u* and *fu* and hardly any *ch'ü* verse has been translated into other languages; and this circumstance, coupled with the confusing modern use of *shih* as an equivalent of our word 'poetry', occasionally betrays Western scholars into talking about the *shih* category as though it represented the whole of Chinese verse literature. And even the conscientious ones who avoid this pitfall can seldom make up their minds about *fu*; so that a basic uncertainty remains about the definition of Chinese poetry.

All this really amounts to saying that the Chinese did not, until modern times, have any word or concept exactly corresponding to our 'poetry'; and the unsatisfactory consequence of this is that the terms of reference in any study of Chinese poetry have to be imposed arbitrarily. The definition already proposed for 'poetry' in an English context seems impracticably broad in a Chinese one when it is remembered that there was a time in the history of Chinese literature when nearly *all* artistic writing bore the main prosodic features of verse—regular, recurring, rhythmic patterns and rhyme—and it would clearly be absurd to have to classify treatises, letters, obituaries, and chancery documents as poetry. It seems safest to set the limit somewhere within a broad class of literature containing *shih*, *tz'u*, *ch'ü*, and *fu*, excluding anything outside it and including at least everything inside it which is wholly in verse.

To ask, as people often do, whether Chinese poetry is translatable is strictly speaking meaningless. The correct answer is, yes, quite a lot of Chinese poetry has in fact been translated. 'Translation' is the name of a process which can be done well or badly, skilfully or clumsily, successfully or unsuccessfully. It is the process of making a substitute in one language for something which was at first written in another. The question really is, how close can the substitute be to the original, and what does 'close' mean?

Some people would say that 'close' means having as many elements as possible in the translation as are to be found in the original. But who is to decide what is *in* the original? It is perfectly legitimate to consider association as a part of meaning, albeit a peripheral, unstable, easily detachable part. And that is one of the reasons why there can never be a single definitive statement of the total meaning of a poem. The personal, subjective element in association is too strong. If you asked several people to enumerate all the significant features they could find in a poem, they would be sure to come up with different lists. This is the situation which exists before the process of translation has even started. Once that begins, the already existing differences of interpretation will be intensified by such factors as the relative skill and expressiveness of different translators, and the different ways in which they evaluate what they conceive to be the constituent elements of the poem.

In trying to assess the translation of a poem we need to ask three quite separate questions about it:

(1) What was the translator's understanding of the original poem?

(2) To what extent did he succeed in communicating his experience of the original poem by means of the translated substitute?

(3) In so far as the substitute falls short of the original in effectiveness, how much is this due to inhibiting factors beyond the translator's control—i.e. to what extent, and why, was his experience of the original simply incommunicable?

It is the last sort of question which chiefly interests me here; and it is really this question that people have in mind when they inquire whether Chinese poetry is translatable.

The least communicable aspect of Chinese poetry is the formal or prosodic one. Some elements of Chinese prosody are totally incommunicable; others are theoretically communicable but are virtually incommunicable in practice.

Chinese is a tonal language. This means that the tonality of a word is semantically, not, as with us, grammatically, significant. If we pronounce 'jam' with a rising tone, it becomes a query: 'Jam?' ('or would you prefer honey?'). If a Chinese pronounces *ma* with a rising tone, it becomes a word meaning 'hemp'. If he pronounces it with a falling tone ('Jam! How ghastly!'), it becomes another word meaning 'curse'. Since about the sixth century there have been a number of verse-forms in common use which prescribe a fixed tonal pattern as part of their prosodic structure. It would not, of course, be even theoretically possible to reproduce this feature in English.

If tonal pattern is totally incommunicable, metre must be counted as one of the features which are theoretically communicable but incommunicable in practice. The Chinese language consists very largely of monosyllabic and bisyllabic words and most Chinese metres are therefore syllabic ones. The *shih* type of verse, which is characterized by lines of equal length, is in fact formally classified into pentasyllabics, heptasyllabics, tetrasyllabics, &c. Now once in a while it is possible to hit on a Chinese poem which just could, with a little contriving, be rendered in an equal number of syllables. Miss Louise Hammond attempted this in some of her translations, though readily admitting that the ensuing loss of meaning was very considerable:

Chung feng ch'ieh pao	O cruel Wind,
Ku wo tse hsiao	With smile too kind,
Nieh lang hsiao ao	I know thy mind;
Chung hsin shih tao	No peace I find.[1]

But as a rule it is simply not possible to reproduce the Chinese

[1] 'The Tunes of Chinese Poetry', *The Year Book of Oriental Art and Culture*, vol. i (London, 1925), p. 122.

metre, because of the necessity of using articles, prepositions, and grammatical inflections in the English, and because English frequently has only a polysyllabic equivalent for the monosyllabic Chinese word:

> *Chu yeh hsiang nan ch'uang*
> *Yüeh kuang chao tung pi*
>
> Bamboo leaves rustle by the south window;
> The moon's light shines on the eastern wall.[1]

Even if you substitute 'sound' for 'rustle' and 'east' for 'eastern' and decide to omit everything except the nouns, verbs, and adjectives, 'bamboo' and 'window' remain intractable. Your fanatic might achieve pentasyllabicity by further omissions:

> Leaves sound by window
> Moonlight shines on wall.

But this is to prune away so much that what is left is scarcely worth having. And in any case the sacrifice is unavailing, since once you get beyond four syllables, a line of English verse begins to develop stress patterns. In the distich above each line contains three stresses:

> Leáves soúnd by wíndow
> Moónlight shínes on wáll.

This is wholly unlike the Chinese metre, which, in so far as it contains stress at all, puts it on the third and fifth syllables in each line. Inversion in the first line would bring you very close to the Chinese metre:

> Leáves by wíndow soúnd
> Moónlight shínes on wáll.

But in the original the antithesis of 'window' and 'wall', 'sound' and 'shine' is deliberate; so you would only have maimed even further an already hopelessly crippled translation.

Waley's solution is to use what, borrowing the term invented

[1] Except where otherwise indicated, all the translations in this essay are my own.

by Gerard Manley Hopkins, he calls 'sprung rhythm'. He employs it in such a way that each line of the translation, regardless of the number of syllables it contains, has as many stresses as there are syllables in the Chinese line:

> Bámboo leáves rústle by the soúthern wíndow
> The moón's líght shínes on the eástern wáll.

It is hard to think of a more satisfactory solution than this. Yet it has its drawbacks, one of which is that it tends to obscure the sharp differences existing in the Chinese between one kind of metre and another. For example, the *fu* type of verse differs categorically from *shih* in using stress metres:

Ti Káo Yáng chih miáo i hsi *chén huáng k'áo yüeh Pó Yúng*
Shé-t'i chén yü méng-tsóu hsi *wéi kéng-yin wu i chiáng*

The Lord Kao Yang's descendant My father's name was Po Yung
When She-t'i was in Meng-tsou On keng-yin I was born.

Ch'ü metres, also, can be thought of as containing an element of stress; though in a kind of verse primarily intended for singing it is not always easy to distinguish prosodic features from musical ones. Many of the songs in Shakespeare's plays—for example, *Where the bee sucks there suck I* or *Take O take those lips away*— are in four-stress trochaic metres when read, but when set to music become metrically indistinguishable from the heptasyllabics of French verse (e.g. *J'ai perdu ma tourterelle*) or Chinese verse (e.g. *Han huang chung se ssu ch'ing kuo*).

The Chinese explain the prosody of *ch'ü* verse by saying that it contains 'padding words' which do not count in the metre. The effect is not quite what we mean by stress in our poetry, but comes very near it. The following three lines from the sixteenth-century *Peony Pavilion* are of unequal syllabic length but contain an equal number of stresses in each line:

> *Méng ch'ü chih t'á shih shih shúi?*
> *Ping lái chih súng ti ko hsǔ hsǔ ti ni.*
> *Tso hsing yǔn hsien k'ó táo tsai Wú yáng húi*

The dream gone, who knows this 'so true, substantial' he ?
But, sickness come, we soon shall lose an all too insubstantial thee—
Dead of love's thirst, poor thing, before the fertilizing cloud ever
rained its showers upon her!

One feels that so radical a distinction as that separating stressed
from syllabic metres ought somehow to be reflected in translation. Yet in 'sprung rhythm' translations *shih* and *fu* come out
pretty much the same, whilst *tz'u* and *ch'ü* become metrically
indistinguishable.

When translating French, German, or Italian verse into English, it is often possible to find a satisfactory metrical equivalent
which somehow 'feels' right even though it is perhaps struc-
turally quite different from the original. For example, French
alexandrines translate naturally into English iambic pentameter,
although these are quite different metres. Unfortunately the
only obvious correspondence between an English and a Chinese
metre occurs at an extremely humble level. The '3–3–7' nursery
jingle found in *Hot Cross Buns* and *One two three, Mother caught
a flea* exactly parallels a metre, very popular in China but not
much favoured by serious poets except in ballads, which is found
as early as the third century B.C. in the works of Hsün-tzu and as
recently as the most recent set of *shu-lai-pao* extemporized by
some Peking comedian. It represents one of the basic rhythms
common to people all over the world, and is probably older than
language itself, being in fact the simplest rhythm that can be
beaten in 4-time :

But it must be avoided, even when translating Chinese folk-
songs and ballads, because the English associations are so much
more vulgar than the Chinese ones. So it remains broadly true
that metre is one of the formal elements which are lost sight of
when Chinese poetry is translated into English.

Another prosodic feature which can seldom be reproduced in

English translation is the Chinese use of rhyme. Chinese has comparatively few word-endings and therefore rhymes easily, like Italian. Not only is all Chinese verse without exception rhymed, but it customarily sustains the rhyme in quite long runs. In the eight-line *lü-shih*, which has for centuries been an extremely popular Chinese verse-form comparable to the European sonnet, the same rhyme *must* be used throughout the poem. In longer poems a sequence of thirty instances of the same rhyme is by no means uncommon and can be achieved fairly effortlessly.

Clearly it is impossible to use the same rhyme for very long in English without running into serious difficulties, and at the same time introducing a heavy emphasis into the rhyming word which is not present in the Chinese. Moreover the effort of sustaining a rhyme in English verse generates a tension which often finds relief in laughter. It is no accident that most English examples of this use of rhyme are to be found in comic or humorous verse.

Modern translators of Chinese verse generally avoid rhyme altogether. In some ways this is more logical than the earlier practice of rendering everything into rhyming couplets, since the consequence of that is to introduce a prosodic unit into the English which did not exist in the Chinese, with possibly harmful effects on the unity of the poem.

So general has been the abandonment of rhymed translation that many Western readers are under the impression that Chinese verse is itself a kind of rhymeless *vers libre*, and the scholar who knows better may sometimes develop a hankering for rhyme. A brief glance at some of the atrocities perpetrated in the cause of rhyme by an earlier generation of translators is usually sufficiently deterrent in such cases. Herbert Giles began his translation of a simple little poem by Chang Chi as follows:

> Knowing, fair sir, my matrimonial thrall,
> Two pearls thou sentest me, costly withal[1]

[1] *A History of Chinese Literature* (London, 1901), p. 176.

when all the chaste wife said in the original poem was:

> Knowing that I have a husband, sir,
> You sent me a pair of pearls.

Fortunately it is not a very good poem. But hundreds of much better ones were subjected to the same maltreatment.

The only notably successful use of rhyme by a modern translator is Ezra Pound's *The Classic Anthology Defined by Confucius*; but it must be admitted that this delightful book communicates an extremely idiosyncratic impression of the Chinese *Book of Songs*; also that the *Songs* are extremely ancient, and present a rather different problem, prosodically, from the great mass of Chinese verse.

Arthur Waley once used rhyme with great effect to translate a *tz'u* poem:

> Immeasurable pain!
> My dreaming soul last night was king again,
> As in past days
> I wandered through the Palace of Delight,
> And in my dream
> Down grassy garden-ways
> Glided my chariot, smoother than a summer stream.
> There was moonlight,
> The trees were blossoming,
> And a faint wind softened the air of night,
> For it was Spring.[1]

This very beautiful rendering admirably conveys the combination of irregularity and strictly formal pattern which is a great part of the charm of *tz'u* verse. A rhymeless translation would have had no observable formal pattern at all.

One reason why there is a better chance of using rhyme successfully in the translation of *tz'u* and *ch'ü* verse is that the translator is liberated from the strain of trying to rhyme in a line

---

[1] From *The Temple* (London, 1923), pp. 144–5.

of fixed prosodic length. But in the case of *shih*, certainly, he will as a rule regretfully decide to abandon rhyme. There is too much of it in the Chinese for his frail bark to carry.

One of the formal aspects of Chinese verse which should be mentioned here is strictly speaking a rhetorical rather than a prosodic feature, but has prosodic implications owing to the monosyllabic nature of the language. I refer to the use of antithesis or verbal parallelism, which I have already briefly touched on in the discussion of metre.

Antithesis can be used in poetry either to make a contrast, when it acts as a sort of inverted simile (How unlike each other these two things are! How poignantly we feel the one when we consider the other!), or as a kind of hendiadys—the expression of a single statement in two complementary parts.

> And bonny sang the mavis
> Out o' the thorny brake;
> But sairer grat the nourice
> When she was tied to the stake

would be an example of the first kind;

> The sun, as common, went abroad,
> The flowers, accustomed, blew

would be an example of the second kind.

On the one hand the cheerful, unconcerned song of the innocent bird is in sharp contrast to the screams of the woman who is about to be burnt; on the other hand the shining sun and blowing flowers are complementary parts in the description of a summer's day.

If we examine these two examples prosodically, we observe that in the first one 'And bonny sang the mavis' parallels 'But sairer grat the nourice' syllable for syllable. 'And' parallels 'But', 'bonny' parallels 'sairer', 'sang' parallels 'grat', and 'mavis' parallels 'nourice'. In the two lines taken from Emily Dickinson's poem the verbal parallelism is logical but not prosodic, or even, in the strictest sense, grammatical. 'Sun' is a monosyllable, 'flowers' is bisyllabic; 'as common' and 'accustomed' are both adverbial, and 'went abroad' and 'blew' are both verbal; but they are not exact equivalents grammatically, and 'went abroad' is two syllables longer than 'blew'.

In Chinese literature, which shows an immense partiality for antithesis, the verbal parallelism is always prosodic as well as semantic and grammatical because of the nature of the language. Moreover, as a rhetorical device it is much more forceful and effective in Chinese than in English, because it is much more condensed. In the two contrasting lines from *Lamkin* there are only four correspondences in seven syllables:

| And | bonny | sang | mavis |
| But | sairer | grat | nourice |

In Chinese rhetoric it would be thought intolerably feeble not to obtain a separate correspondence for each of the seven syllables in the line. Po Chü-i's *Spring walk by Lake Ch'ien-t'ang* contains the following two lines. There is a slight caesura between the fourth and fifth syllables of each line:

	1	2	3	4	5	6	7
A	chi	ch'u	tsao	ying	cheng	nuan	shu
B	shui	chia	hsin	yen	cho	ch'un	ni

The word-by-word sense of this is as follows:

	1	2	3	4	5	6	7
A	several	places	early	orioles	dispute	warm	trees
B	someone's	house	new	swallows	carry	spring	mud

It will be observed that A1 parallels B1, A2 parallels B2, and so on, syllable by syllable throughout the line, and that syntactically the lines are constructed on the same pattern: 1–2 adverb of place; 3–4 subject; 5 verb; 6–7 object.

In *lü-shih* poems this sort of parallelism is compulsory in the two middle couplets (lines 3–6), but so exuberant is the Chinese talent for antithesis that often the first couplet will be accorded the same treatment for good measure.

You might think that if any single formal feature of Chinese verse must be carried over into the English translation in order to convey some impression of the original, it is surely this. Yet any attempt at reproducing in English the antitheses of Chinese poetry leads at once to orotundity—diffuse verbosity infinitely removed from the neat conciseness which is a central quality of Chinese verse. There are simply too many syllables in English. The ingeniously compressed epigrams and conceits of the original unpack into those flaccid orientalisms so familiar to readers of translations.

The fifth-century poet Wu Mai-yüan put the following conceit into the mouth of a young wife parted from her husband:

1	2	3	4	5
jung	*fa*	*ts'ao*	*mu*	*huan*
ts'ui	*chi*	*shuang*	*lu*	*pei*

which means:

1	2	3	4	5
flowering	lacks	plant	tree	gladness
affliction	exhausts	frost	dew	sadness

i e.

My flowering prime is deprived even of the vegetable happiness of
trees and flowers;
Yet in my bitterness I taste all the hardships of blighting frost.

The thought underlying this is surprisingly complex. The wife compares herself with a flower. She likens her prime to the blossoming time of the flower, and the hardship of separation from her husband to the effect on it of the first frosts of autumn. At the same time she supposes, by a familiar use of the Pathetic

Fallacy, that flowers take a quasi-human pleasure in the warmth, light, and colours of summer, and experience a quasi-human grief at the approach of the frosts. From this she goes on to reflect that although she is *really* a human being, she is actually worse off even than a mere flower, since she experiences all the hardships that plants and trees are subject to without enjoying any of their compensating pleasures.

It has taken approximately a hundred words of polysyllabic English to explain these ten syllables of Chinese verse. English is simply not susceptible of the same degree of condensation as Chinese. The languages have different specific gravities.

No doubt it is fallacious to think of poetry as so many notions and images called 'content' poured into so many moulds called 'form'. Nevertheless, provided we are clear that these are only two different types of analysis and not two separate entities, it is perfectly legitimate to use these terms in our examination of Chinese poetry.

Having, then, investigated the main formal aspects of Chinese verse which resist successful communication by the translator, let us now consider some features of its content which can prove equally refractory.

A notable one is the Chinese poet's preference for impersonal statement. The Chinese verb can be, and often is, left uncommitted as to number and tense. When, in addition to this, the personal pronoun is omitted, the effect is a timeless, universal quality comparable to that of the statement made by a painting. Significantly, Keats had to use three or four different forms of the verb in describing the figures on the Grecian urn, even while he was stressing the timelessness of the scene. When the Chinese poet is describing anything his statements are invariably and automatically timeless.

Of course, the poet's presence may often be inferred even when it is not explicit. Yet even so there is an objectiveness in the Chinese which cannot quite be paralleled in English. The following poem by the eleventh-century Sung poet K'ou Chun demonstrates the translator's dilemma:

> *Feng k'uo ch'iang hsi p'o miao mang*
> *Tu p'ing wei chien ssu ho ch'ang*
> *Hsiao hsiao yüan shu su lin wai*
> *I pan ch'iu shan tai hsi yang*

Widely separated peaks, a few scattered masts, a great blank of water;
All alone, leaning on vertiginously high-up railings, far lost in thought;
Forlorn, leafless trees in the distance beyond the sparse woods;
One half of the mountains wearing the colours of sunset.

This is not a finished translation but the intermediate draft from which a translation is made. When we come to make the final draft, what do we do with line 2? When did the leaning occur, and who is its subject? I? You? She?

In this particular case we know that the poem was one of four written by K'ou Chun on the wall of a riverside pavilion, each describing the view from the pavilion at a different season of the year. This poem is the one for autumn. So K'ou Chun's presence in the scene can be assumed.

But this still does not entirely dispose of our problem. Is the verb 'I am leaning'? 'I have been leaning'? 'I leaned (last autumn)'? 'I often lean'? Or is it 'One might lean'? Or 'When you lean'?

In fact, it is impossible to say. It could be all or none of these. The Chinese poet does not really care, and to tell the truth would probably not understand the question. He is describing a picture which includes a little figure in a pavilion looking at the view. He is not interested in the history or identity of the little figure or the date of the painting, even if the little figure is himself and the time is now.

The problem of allusion, regarded by many Western students as the greatest bugbear of all in interpreting Chinese poetry—

or indeed Chinese literature of any kind—is a product less of Chinese obscurantism than of our own cultural alienation. Our literature, even our daily speech, teems with allusions of every kind. 'Look at Hercules!' said of a muscular man on the beach lifting a heavy object above his head is not a remark indicative of profound classical learning. It is, nevertheless, an allusion, and would mystify an Asiatic visitor who knew our language but nothing of what we call our cultural heritage. When we speak of universal themes, having in mind psychologically interesting stories like the myth of Oedipus, we ought to remind ourselves that although we and our European cousins were reared on Bible stories and the tales of Greece and Rome, a large part of the human race knows nothing of either.

I do not know whether poetry is necessarily 'better' poetry if its appeal is universal, though critics sometimes speak as though they thought it was. I suspect that it is the emotions evoked rather than the themes which evoke them that are universal in the case of those poems which travel most easily. Po Chü-i's *Song of Everlasting Regret* is perhaps the single most famous Chinese poem outside China. It swings along in a fairly simple narrative, and it strongly evokes that cheerful-tearful, slightly self-indulgent feeling of pity which the spectacle of Love triumphant in Death inspires in us.[1] *Tristan* inspires the same sort of feeling. Yet 'Love in Death' is much too vague a formula to describe the *themes* of those two very different poems. *Tristan* is about a peculiarly Western type of adulterous love; the *Song of Everlasting Regret* is about the infatuation of an ageing emperor for a concubine, and his inconsolable grief after he has consented under duress to her death. Tristan and Isolde triumph over death by producing trees from their graves (like the suicides in a

---

[1] This may seem unduly scornful of what is usually felt to be an ennobling sentiment; but one has only to think of the sadism of *Little Musgrave* or Flecker's *Hassan* to realize that some of the emotions surrounding it are very unpleasant indeed.

famous Chinese ballad); Yang Kuei-fei and the emperor triumph by being able to communicate from one world to the other.

What happens, I believe, in the case of the most easily exportable poetry is that strong emotions or an interesting narrative permit the foreign reader to make what he likes of the rest of the poem—which may be something very odd indeed—while still feeling that he has obtained from it something of value.

But translators should not worry themselves about naïve or facile judgements. A great many people do not read or enjoy poetry in their own language, and it is of the utmost inconsequence if they do not enjoy Latin or French or Russian or Chinese poetry either. This is as true if they are great scholars with international reputations as it is if they are semi-literates.

On the other hand, the degree of cultural empathy which a scholar may attain after many years of reading and study is of little use in determining the extent to which Chinese or any other poetry is communicable in another language. A poem which makes him cry in the original may turn out jejune or ridiculous in translation because of factors beyond the control of the translator.

Some degree of empathy is needed for the appreciation of any poem, and this must be attained by deliberate effort. If we expect to have to *learn* the symbols used by our own poets, to accustom ourselves to their imagery, to trace, if we do not already know, their allusions, we must be prepared to make at least an equivalent effort in order to understand Chinese poetry.

But clearly there is a point beyond which a translation would disappear entirely into a quagmire of footnotes. Consider the following poem by the ninth-century poet Li Shang-yin. Its title is *Peony*:

1 *Chin wei ch'u chüan Wei fu jen*
   Brocade curtain just unrolled, Lady of Wei
2 *Hsiu pei yu tui Yüeh ngo chün*
   Embroidered coverlet still heaped, Lord of Yüeh-ngo

3 *Ch'ui shou luan fan tiao yü p'ei*
  'Hanging hands' wildly dangle carved jade girdle
4 *Che yao cheng wu yü chin ch'ün*
  'Bending waist' energetically flutter saffron coloured skirt
5 *Shih chia la chu ho ts'eng chien*
  Shih household wax candles have not trimmed
6 *Hsün ling hsiang lu k'o tai hsün*
  Hsün secretary's incense burner no need perfume
7 *Wo shih meng chung ch'uan ts'ai pi*
  I am in dream handed coloured brush
8 *Yü shu hua yeh chi chao yün*
  Want write flowers leaves send morning cloud

Before one can even begin to understand this poem, it is necessary to familiarize oneself with the following stories. (The figures represent the numbers of the lines in which the allusions occur.)

1. Confucius once dismayed his disciples by accepting an invitation from Nan-tzu, the wicked concubine of Duke Ling of Wei. She received him concealed behind a screen, so that he did not see her, but could hear the tinkling of her jade ornaments when she bowed to him.

2. The sixth-century-B.C. prince of Ngo once, while being rowed in his state barge, was moved by the barcarolle a Yüeh boatman was singing and asked his interpreter to translate it. On hearing what it meant, he embraced the boatman and covered him with his embroidered coverlet.

5. Shih Ch'ung, a third-century millionaire, was popularly believed to use wax candles (then a luxury commodity) as kindling.

6. Hsün Yü was a statesman and courtier of the third century of whom it was said that when he visited a house the place where he had sat remained fragrant for three days afterwards. Chinese perfumes were worn in the clothes, which were scented by being hung on racks over incense-burning braziers.

7. The fifth-century poet Chiang Yen once dreamed that the

poet Kuo P'u (who lived a century and a half before his time) stood before him, pointing to his chest and demanding the return of his writing-brush. Feeling in his heart, he took out a multi-coloured brush and handed it to him. Thereafter he never wrote another good line of verse.

8. In the fourth century B.C. the goddess of Witch Mountain appeared to King Huai of Ch'u in a dream and lay with him. She told him that the morning clouds and evening rainfall on the mountain were her manifestations.

It is also necessary to know that *ch'ui shou* ('hanging hands') in line 3 and *che yao* ('bending waist') in line 4 were the names of dances.

It can now be seen that line 1 refers to the peony's newly opened flowers, line 2 to its leaves, lines 3–4 to the graceful movement of the whole plant in a light breeze, line 5 to its blazing colour, and line 6 to its fragrant smell.

Li Shang-yin's first patron was Ling-hu Ch'u, who lived in a quarter of Changan famous for its peonies. It is thought that he composed this poem while flirting with a singing-girl at a feast given by his patron. We can now see that lines 7–8 mean, 'I, who owe all my skill to an older poet (i.e. Ling-hu Ch'u), want to write a poem about peonies to give to a beautiful girl.'

At the time and place in which this poem was written peonies were considered exotic, expensive flowers. The imagery in all these allusions is therefore suggestive of richness and splendour. It also, as a secondary function, serves to hint at the lavishness and aristocratic magnificence of the poet's patron, who is openly flattered for his literary genius in line 7. Thirdly, it serves to describe the girl, who was no doubt magnificently dressed, and had probably been dancing for them. There is more than a hint that the poet intends to sleep with her, since 'morning cloud' has strong sexual overtones. Jumpiness is avoided, although there are so many allusions, by making use of associations: for example, the tinkling jades of the dancer's girdle in line 3 recall the jade tinklings of the invisible Nan-tzu in line 1, and the undulating skirts in line 4 recall the undulations of the brocade counterpane covering the amorous prince and his handsome boatman in line 2. The quite unconnected stories in lines 5 and 6 are both about some kind of combustion, and the quite unconnected stories of lines 7 and 8 are both about dreams.

Without pursuing the analysis any further, it can be seen at once how the Chinese poet is able to use allusions so as to suggest a number of widely differing meanings, where a more direct, less complex imagery would be incapable of carrying so heavy a charge. At the same time it can at once be seen that so great a degree of allusiveness renders successful translation impossible.

Literary allusions are even more difficult to deal with; for whereas the allusions in Li Shang-yin's poem presuppose only the sort of general knowledge we require to understand a line like Milton's 'Atropos for Lucina came' (of a woman dying in childbirth), or the lovers' dialogue at the beginning of Act V in the *Merchant of Venice*, the literary allusion presupposes memory of some particular text. When an anonymous Han poet says:

> Hawk harbours bitter thoughts
> Cricket at constrictions chafes,

he expects you to realize that he is not really talking about wild life at all, but alluding to two poems from the *Book of Songs*, one called *The Hawk* and one called *The Cricket*—the first about the disquiet of a lady waiting to meet her lord, and thought to be allegorical of wise ministers dismissed by a foolish prince; the second about the fleetingness of time and the need to enjoy oneself while one can.

As for conventional symbols—willows for parting, cypresses for death, wild geese for letters from afar, thoughts of home in exile, or solitariness, the pine-tree for constancy in adversity, spring wind for youth, love, desire, &c., &c.—these can easily be learned by those who enjoy reading Chinese poetry and would like to enjoy it more. Translators should be readier to point them out when they occur, so that they may be learned the sooner.

So far we have been examining the various opacities which lie between a Chinese poem and the Western reader of Chinese poetry in translation. Perhaps it is time to begin considering those elements which survive the hazards of translation and cause him such enjoyment as he is able to derive from it.

I think it will at once strike anyone who comes fresh to the study of Chinese verse that it relies on a heavy preponderance of natural imagery. The characteristically Chinese way of dealing with natural imagery is in part a product of Chinese poetic theory, and derives ultimately from the way in which natural imagery is used in the *Book of Songs*. This ancient collection of anonymous poems (composed between 1000 and 600 B.C.) early attained the status of a canonical scripture, and Chinese poetics were, in theory at any rate, founded upon it.

One of the commonest features of the poems in the *Book of Songs* is the *hsing*, a piece of imagery, almost invariably taken from nature, which begins the stanza. It can be in antithetical contrast with the rest of the stanza, or a mere refrain, or—and this applies to the great majority of cases—it can imply comparison with what follows it:

> Unsteady is that cypress boat
> In the middle of the river.
> His two locks looped on his brow
> He swore to me that he was my comrade
> And till death would love no other.
> Oh, mother, ah, Heaven,
> That a man could be so false![1]

Here there is obviously an implied comparison between the unsteadiness of the boat and the inconstancy of the fickle lover. The comparison is all the more forceful for being expressed

[1] Arthur Waley, *The Book of Songs* (London, 1937), p. 53.

elliptically. This can easily be demonstrated. Take the following English poem which uses implied comparison in the same way as the Chinese one:

> Western wind, when wilt thou blow,
> The small rain down can rain?
> Christ, if my love were in my arms,
> And I in my bed again!

In epic poetry this would become an extended simile:

Even as in time of drought, when the shoots of corn are parched, men long for the west wind to blow, bringing the rain that falls in a fine shower upon the earth, gladdening man and beast, even so did he long to hold the bright-eyed maiden in his arms, lying upon his couch in honey-sweet dalliance.

The long simile, by gloating much more over the comparison, only succeeds in enfeebling it; the stark juxtaposition of images challenges the mind and compels it to take their relationship more seriously.

Chinese poetry, habituated from its infancy to this method of using natural imagery, developed it in the course of centuries to a wonderful degree of suppleness. In the following *tz'u* poem the exiled poet Wei Chuang gives poignant expression to his homesickness while scarcely bringing himself into the poem at all:

> *Ch'un yü mu*
> *Man ti lo hua hung tai yü*
> *Ch'ou ch'ang yü lung ying wu*
> *Tan hsi wu pan lü*
> *Nan wang ch'ü ch'eng ho hsü*
> *Wen hua hua pu yü*
> *Tsao wan te t'ung kuei ch'ü*
> *Hen wu shuang ts'ui yü*

> The spring begins to die
> And all around on the ground, rain-sodden, the fallen red flowers
> lie.

Dejected in his jade cage, the cockatoo,
Perching companionless, nothing to do,
Speculating (where is the road home?), on the South fastens his
eye:
Asking the flowers, but the flowers will give no reply.
We must return together, you and I.
Had I only your painted wings with which to fly!

Wei Chuang died a great minister, but in a strange land in which he had settled under constraint—a bird in a gilded cage, like the cockatoo. The fallen splendour of the blossoms may or may not symbolize the fall of the T'ang Dynasty which Wei Chuang had served. In any case the whole poem reeks of overpowering nostalgia and a melancholy sense of decline. Yet all this is done by the use of natural images: a garden in late spring and a parrot in a cage.

To say that the Chinese poet habitually uses natural imagery heavily charged with emotion is not to say that he is a passionate poet. Chinese verse generally strikes the Western reader as somehow quieter and more detached than his own poetry. There are a number of reasons for this. In the first place, verse writing in China was always very much a social activity. Verse composition was for centuries a required subject in the civil service examinations; almost any kind of party or outing could be the occasion for co-operative or competitive versification; and the exchange of verses was a common means of communication between men of letters. In China, therefore, the poet was seldom an outsider, as he so often has been in Europe, and very few Chinese poets felt that they had to be mad or bad in order to assert their individualism and *épater le bourgeois*. This in itself was enough to make Chinese poetry on the whole more restful than ours.

But there is another reason. If we consider the history of poetic inspiration in the West, we find that in the early stages it was thought of as a kind of demonic possession in which the poet abandoned himself to the Muse. Something of the feeling that the poet is a man set apart from others and as a consequence slightly crazed persists even into modern times. Certainly the nineteenth-century Romantic poets frequently showed demonic, self-destructive tendencies.

If we look for the supernatural origins of Chinese poetry, we find that Ch'ü Yüan and the Ch'u poets of the third century B.C. write poetry which is only at a very short remove from the trance utterances of shamans. Ch'ü Yüan, for example, sings of aerial travel in a chariot drawn by flying dragons through the marvels of a magical, animistic universe. But it is important to note that the shaman and the ancient poet were alike *controllers* of this magical universe. Ch'ü Yüan does not surrender himself to divine possession; on the contrary, he commands the gods of earth and sky to wait upon him and do his bidding.

The spirit journey became for a time a stock-in-trade of the Chinese poet. But long after the theme had gone out of fashion it survived in other forms. Most often it survived in a kind of escapist travel: the journey of the dreamer's soul in Li Po's *Dreaming of T'ien-mu*, or the fisherman's journey into the pastoral paradise of the Lost Valley in T'ao Yüan-ming's *Peach-flower Stream*. But always, even when he is most inspired and even when he is in retreat from human society, the Chinese poet remains very much in control of things.[1]

Western readers are sometimes struck by what they do *not* find in Chinese poetry—epic and tragedy, for instance, or religious themes, or the elevation of love to a central position. But I do not propose to deal with these topics here.[2] It has been my intention to do no more than touch on some of the problems

[1] I have gone into this subject at somewhat greater length in an article entitled 'The Supernatural in Chinese Poetry' published in *The Far East: China and Japan*, a *University of Toronto Quarterly* supplement (Toronto, 1961), pp. 311–24.

[2] In my 'Introductory note' to this chapter there is some reference to the lack of epic and religious poetry.

which begin to emerge when a Western reader becomes interested in Chinese poetry. I hope I have at least made it clear that his understanding and pleasure can be very greatly increased by only a little knowledge of the methods and materials of the Chinese poet. And it is not impossible that a greater understanding of the 'samenesses and differences', to use the Chinese expression, may even lead us to reassess some of the views we hold about our own poetry.   DAVID HAWKES

(c) THE DEVELOPMENT OF FICTION AND DRAMA

I

ALTHOUGH Western dramatists and novelists have from time to time made use of Chinese themes or settings, it cannot be claimed that Western literature owes very much to Chinese fiction or drama. If we were to restrict ourselves to a search for influences, we should have to explore the literatures of other Far Eastern countries, a journey which would take us far outside the proper confines of this book. Instead, the real value for us of Chinese fiction and drama lies elsewhere, in the very fact of their separateness. They should possess a special interest precisely because they are the products of a highly developed, but unrelated, literature.

Their isolation is one cause of our present lack of knowledge about them. Another more important cause is the low esteem in which they were traditionally held by Chinese scholars. In contrast with other genres, to which a vast amount of scholarly energy was devoted, the novel in particular remained largely unstudied and unvalued as late as the first decades of this century. Since then, detailed research on both fiction and drama has had some impressive achievements to its credit, but in the main these have not yet been made accessible to the Western reader.[1] All he has at his disposal is some successful translations, mostly of fiction, a few specialist studies, and not much besides. Small wonder if he cannot form any complete picture of the nature or development of either genre.

This essay offers a brief account of the principal stages in the development of Chinese fiction and a brief description of the main features of the Chinese drama. It is concerned solely with the period beginning about the eighth century A.D. and ending in the second decade of the twentieth century, when influences from abroad transformed the situation entirely. The Chinese literature of the period is too complex a matter to discuss as a whole. It is necessary instead to speak of more than one distinct 'literature' existing in China at the same time.[2] If we think of a literature in terms of the composition of the public for which it was intended, or in terms of the kind of author who created it, we can quite easily distinguish two, and even three, separate but concurrent Chinese literatures. Or, alternatively, we may reach a roughly similar conclusion by defining a literature in terms of the means of communication which it employed.[3]

The first of these means of communication was the classical (literary) language, an obsolete form so far as ordinary speech went, but a form none the less in which all literature—in the qualitative sense of the word—had to be composed. (Since fiction and drama are largely outside the province of this literature

---

[1] Almost the only general work to be translated from Chinese is Lu Hsün's *A Brief History of Chinese Fiction*, of which an English translation was published in Peking in 1959. It is a pioneer work of literary history, which gives an account of the stage which the study had reached—in large measure due to the efforts of Lu Hsün himself—by the middle of the 1920's. In the translated version some additional notes and corrections are included.

[2] For the sake of brevity the distinctions introduced here are stated bluntly and dogmatically. They ought properly, of course, to be subjected to countless modifications.

[3] China was not unique in this complexity. See H. M. and N. K. Chadwick, *The Growth of Literature*, vol. iii (Cambridge, 1940), pp. 697–8.

we are not much concerned with it here.) The other two media were the spoken language, addressed to a listening public, and the written vernacular, addressed to a wide reading public. The literary language was remote enough from the speech of the day to allow a flourishing oral literature not only to develop, but to develop along its own lines; its listening public consisted of the great majority of people, cut off from written literature by their inability to read. Between its beginnings and the time of its fullest development in the thirteenth century, this literature showed many of the familiar features of oral literatures in other parts of the world. From the fourteenth century onward, written works were made out of the existing oral literature; they used a language which, to put it at its lowest, made some concession to the vernacular, and they were clearly intended for a wide, but not highly lettered, readership. From the sixteenth century, an increasing number of original works were composed in the same medium and for a similar readership. However, a strong demand persisted for the oral literature. It continued to exist, and indeed flourishes still at the present time, although hardly with the creative vigour that it showed in its heyday.

Thus during the whole of the period covered by this essay there existed a literature, written in the literary language, which constituted the sole recognized literature. An oral literature developed in the early part of the period—or well before it, depending on one's definition—which, although sometimes written down, was primarily intended for a listening public. And in the fourteenth century there came into existence a third literature, intended for a wider reading public than the recognized literature and composed in a different language, the written vernacular.[1]

These distinctions enable us to deal comprehensibly with Chinese fiction, but not with the drama, which cuts across

[1] It is referred to below as the vernacular literature, rather than as the written vernacular literature.

almost all such boundaries. There are, for example, certain forms of the drama which comprehend nearly the whole range of Chinese authorship and the whole range of the Chinese public. Nevertheless, within the drama there is a distinction of a less explicit kind—yet still dependent on the criterion of authorship and even to some extent on that of public—which has to be made. It is a distinction commonly drawn in European literature—that between the popular and the literary theatre. It was from the oral literature in the first place that the Chinese drama emerged, and the greater part of it from that day to this has belonged within the sphere of the oral literature. This is the popular theatre, the player's theatre, in which emphasis is placed on the performer to the virtual exclusion of the author. In addition to it, however, there is an important body of drama written by men equipped to write within the sphere of the recognized literature; most of them did indeed contribute to it. This is the literary theatre which, while it uses the same kind of language as the other—the vernacular, though with a far greater dash of classical—nevertheless makes on the spectator at least some of the demands which the recognized literature makes on its readers. The popular theatre was the first to develop, and it was in the popular theatre that the main innovations first occurred; the literary theatre was built on a foundation that had already been laid. As the principal means through which change in the drama has taken place, the popular theatre has ramified in the course of centuries into a multitude of musically distinct forms. The literati chose only a few of these forms within which to write, but the forms that they chose became the high forms of the drama.

Existing in such proximity, the three literatures inevitably had a deep effect upon one another. This is naturally most marked in regard to subject-matter. Here no single pattern of influence is to be discerned; each literature borrowed freely from the other two. Sometimes a story from the recognized literature, for example the Western Chamber love story, received its most famous treatment in the oral literature or the drama; sometimes the opposite process occurred. It is significant that when a story was translated—for translation is what it amounts to—from one literature to another, it was seldom translated direct. Instead it was rendered into a literary form already current in that literature. This is not to deny, of course, that literary forms were copied in different literatures, but merely to assert that compared with subject-matter they proved less imitable. And when they were copied, moreover, the process was one-way. The move was almost always 'upward', from the oral to the vernacular literature, or from the oral to the recognized.

It will be obvious that the publics for the three literatures corresponded, very roughly, to divisions in Chinese society. In the nature of its authorship and of its audience, the oral literature was mainly a plebeian art. In this respect it has to be sharply distinguished from the oral literatures of those countries where, because there was not the same plurality of medium that existed in China, the court minstrel or the court story-teller played the most formative role. It is true that some Chinese performers received royal patronage, but they were a relatively small number, and they do not seem—admittedly with certain exceptions—to have had a special influence upon their art. The typical Chinese performer carried on his profession as a branch of entertainment, in public and before a paying audience. The practical impetus behind most of the oral literature and most of the vernacular literature is an immediate commercial one; it is this motive, as much as anything, which sets these two apart from the recognized literature.

Chinese fiction is the preserve of the oral and vernacular literatures. The one important exception is a kind of prose tale, usually fairly short, which belongs to the recognized literature. (It was in this form that the first version of the Western Chamber story was written.) The drama, as we have seen, cuts across these boundaries; nevertheless, if only because of its popular origins and its preponderant use of the vernacular language, it also deserves to be considered together with the two non-recognized literatures. Thus it is with these two that this essay is chiefly concerned.

Our knowledge of oral fiction in its early phase is almost entirely due to the discovery at the beginning of this century of a cache of manuscripts. They were found in caves at Tunhuang in the far west of China, and had presumably been taken there centuries earlier from the libraries of local monasteries. Apart from numerous manuscripts of Buddhist scriptures and a variety of other documents, they contained several score pieces of narrative which were clearly intended for oral performance.[1] Some were ballads, others were prose, others again were in alternate verse and prose (for singing or chanting and speaking, respectively), a form which, allowing for countless variations, a great part of Chinese oral literature takes even today.[2] In technique, although they do not bear comparison with later stories, they are far from rudimentary. Their characters are mostly named, and they include a liberal amount of speech and dialogue. The familiar division[3] into heroic and non-heroic can be applied to them, although, perhaps because of the circumstances of their preservation, the non-heroic stories far outweigh the heroic ones. Most of the former kind are stories of Buddhist hagiology, remoulded by the popular imagination. There are folk-tales, as well as one or two items, such as a cursing, which remind us of the early stages of oral literature in other countries.[4] There are stories taken from history; some are heroic, but others, although concerned with the matter of heroic fiction, stress miraculous intervention above the qualities of personal prowess and valour.

---

[1] A. Waley (tr.), *Ballads and Stories from Tun-huang* (London, 1960).
[2] For similar forms in other languages see Chadwick, op. cit., p. 716.
[3] Ibid., pp. 727 ff.   [4] Ibid., pp. 841–4.

There are two stories about local campaigns in the ninth century which are in the heroic vein; they seem to show that there was a contemporary tradition of heroic narrative.

The only dated manuscripts—the dates refer to their copying and not to their composition—are of the tenth century, but we know from other records that this kind of oral literature was already current as early as the eighth. It is clear that at that time one use of the oral tale or ballad was as an instrument of evangelizing Buddhism. But monks were by no means the only singers and narrators of the early literature; they were merely its best-documented kind of performer.

II

The decisive stage in the growth of Chinese fiction and drama was brought about by a physical development of the Chinese city—the establishing, on a large scale, of centres of public entertainment. It was in these centres that story-telling flourished as never before, and that the drama emerged for the first time. The close conjunction of the two arts, as well as the nature of the place in which they were practised, explains a great deal about each of them.

The capital cities of the Northern and Southern Sung (tenth to thirteenth centuries) enjoyed, in the eyes of people living at that time, a remarkable affluence.[1] Contemporary accounts catalogue in wonderment, as part of the prosperous city life of those days, all their multitude of varied entertainments. The form that the centres took was of a number of areas within which, in booths and enclosures, every conceivable art and spectacle was

[1] For a description of the Southern Sung capital of Lin-an (modern Hangchow) see Jacques Gernet, *Daily Life in China on the Eve of the Mongol Invasion 1250–1276*, translated by H. M. Wright (London, 1962), especially the section on amusements, pp. 222–7. This was the city of Quinsai where Marco Polo lived for some time at the end of the same century and of which he has left a lengthy description. See A. C. Moule and Paul Pelliot (tr.), *Marco Polo: The Description of the World*, 2 vols. (London, 1938).

offered to the public. The largest of the booths in the Northern Sung capital, so we are told, was able to accommodate several thousand spectators; and apparently the Southern Sung capital outdid its predecessor. The relative prosperity of the cities gave to the performer a stable living and a chance to perfect his art.

The performer was a professional, specialized to a high degree. Among the story-tellers, for example, were men who narrowed their special fields down to a span more restricted than that of the modern scholar—the fifty years of the Five Dynasties period, say, or the Three Kingdoms. There is a general division among the story-tellers which springs from the nature of their source material as well as from their narrative technique. First, there were the tellers of religious and miraculous stories; they used an alternate prose and verse form. Second, there were the 'historians', who narrated chronicle history with a strong admixture of legend. Third, there were the narrators of a species of story for which it is hard to find an English label, although its most important single constituent was the story of everyday life.[1]

In this environment the Chinese drama developed. The art of the drama in China has so many dimensions that the origins of the genre, depending on the element one selects, can be placed at almost any time within a space of a thousand years. As a date, the beginning of the twelfth century is, it must be admitted, only a degree or two less arbitrary than any other. Yet it is the first time that the performance of a named play is recorded. It is mentioned in an account of the Northern Sung capital, and the play, *Mu-lien Rescues his Mother*, was a Buddhist miracle-play of which the subject-matter is familiar from the Tunhuang stories. It was performed just before a religious festival to which its theme was related. Significantly, it was performed by professionals within the centres of public entertainment.[2]

---

[1] The whole category is loosely referred to in this essay as 'stories of everyday life'.

[2] Meng Yüan-lao, *Tung-ching meng-hua lu*, chüan 8.

We can gain an idea of the close relationship between the narrative and dramatic arts from a passage in the heroic novel, the *Shui-hu chuan*,[1] for although the novel itself was put together about the fourteenth century, there is good reason to believe that this passage refers to a much earlier time. It describes the performance of a 'medley'—a narrative form of which the parts are alternately sung and spoken—which takes place in a Shantung market-town. The singer-narrator is a girl from the capital 'as outstanding in her beauty as in her art'. The girl's father evidently stage-manages her performance, and comes forward to appeal for donations when it has reached a height of interest. In the interval, while the money is being gathered in from the audience, some actors come on and play a comic interlude. Thus, in these circumstances at least, a form of story-telling and an early form of play make up the same programme.

Apart from the performers, who are well documented, even to the names and specialities of scores of them, there were other contributors to these arts of whom very little is known. These were the writers, who worked collectively in small groups to compile, adapt, embellish, and conceivably even create, the story-teller's or actor's material. They must have been men with a certain amount of literary education, but without enough to qualify for a civil service post, who turned to this trade to make a living. Some of their texts, initially compiled perhaps as prompt-books for the story-teller, have survived, although it is impossible to know what changes they may have undergone at the hands of later editors. Such writers were in the service of the oral literature; their function needs to be distinguished from that of the long line of men from many different positions in Chinese society, sometimes from commercial motives and sometimes not, who have prepared the oral texts for publication, and have thus served as middlemen between the oral and vernacular literatures.

Only within the last decade have the first steps been taken to

[1] Chapter 51

record something of the fecund tradition of oral narrative. One contemporary example may suffice to illustrate the transmission of the art and to show how specialized it is. Wang Shao-t'ang is the most famous exponent of a special style of saga which has been current in the city of Yangchow and thereabouts for at least two centuries. His speciality, the saga of Wu Sung, one of the *Shui-hu chuan* heroes, is of prodigious length; it came to about a million characters when it was recorded, and it lasts him for seventy-five days of story-telling, with a two-hour stint each day. He can trace the descent of this material, his stock-in-trade, from father to son, master to pupil, for at least a hundred years, and it probably goes back much farther still. Each man has added something to it; it has trebled in length in those hundred years. Apparently there are still thirty performers practising this art in Yangchow alone.[1]

III

The texts based on the early prompt-books, as well as the novels that writers fashioned out of the existing story-cycles, belong at the same time to both the oral and vernacular literatures; they are the culmination of the one and the starting-point of the other.

The *Hsi-yu chi*, parts of which have been translated by Arthur Waley under the title of *Monkey*, is the most famous of the novels fashioned out of the magical or miraculous kind of story-cycle. The cycle was given its definitive treatment by Wu Ch'eng-en, an official and minor poet of the sixteenth century. Like the other story-cycles, it has a nucleus of historical fact, the overland journey made by Hsüan-tsang to India in the seventh century A.D. Such a journey, undertaken for the pious purpose of fetching back some Buddhist scriptures to China, proved a convenient peg on which to hang adventure after adventure, without too much need for co-ordination. At an early date, the

[1] See *Wu Sung* (Nanking, 1959), vol. i, pp. 1-3; vol. ii, pp. 1111-31.

fantastic tale of a monkey possessed of miraculous powers was added to the cycle; he becomes Hsüan-tsang's helper on his long and perilous journey. This is the stage reached in the earliest surviving form of the cycle, a text which may date from as early as the thirteenth century.[1] The gulf between it and the stage represented by the sixteenth-century *Hsi-yu chi* is a huge one. The earlier work contains no other named disciple besides Monkey, nor any account of how Monkey acquired his miraculous powers, or of his tumultuous rebellion against the gods of the Taoist and Buddhist pantheons. And its record of the dangers that beset the pilgrims on their way to India is short of interest and humour, a mere catalogue of perils endured. Consider for a moment the treatment the two works give to an episode which they have in common—the visit to the Country of Women. In the earlier work, when the queen proposes that Hsüan-tsang, a Buddhist priest, should take the place at her side and reign as king, he refuses, and that is the end of the matter; she acquiesces tearfully in his decision. There is no hint whatever of that hectic tussle on the royal couch by means of which, in the later work, the priest so narrowly contrives to honour his monastic vows.

The origins of the cycle were, in part at least, a religious tale, a saint's life; and if we bear in mind the history of the word 'legend', we shall not be surprised at its transformation into something fantastic. Nor, if we consider the medieval miracle-plays, shall we be surprised at the infusion of the comic and the grotesque into a religious story. The cycle had a long career in the popular theatre before the *Hsi-yu chi* was ever compiled, and even if the novel owes no direct influence to the drama, it may well have been affected by that comic spirit in which its saints and deities, priests and nuns are commonly conceived.

The *Hsi-yu chi* is a comic novel of vast and varied subtlety. Fantastic though its characters are, they nevertheless have both a consistency and a shape. Thus, although they clearly have an

[1] *Ta T'ang san-tsang ch'ü-ching shih-hua.*

allegorical reference, to say as much is by no means to dismiss them. Monkey is subversive wit, perspicacity, arrogance, mischief. Pigsy represents the fleshly appetites, plus a cumbrous animal cunning; he plays a kind of comic Caliban to Monkey's Ariel. The action of the novel springs from the byplay between these two grotesque disciples, and from the interplay between them and the priest Hsüan-tsang, and between all three of them and the assorted ogres, magicians, temptresses, &c., that they meet *en route*. Part of the comedy is produced by disparity, disparity between what we expect and what turns out to be the case, and the deliberate disparity between the tone of the author's narrative and the event he describes. Irony is piled on irony; among all the spiritual creatures—and they include Monkey and Pigsy, who are really fallen angels trying, by escorting Hsüan-tsang to India, to work their passage back to heavenly favour—it is the human being, Hsüan-tsang, who alone shows any trace of moral behaviour. And yet by a further twist this only lands him in absurdity and ineffectiveness. By turns cautious and credulous, law-abiding, anxious to do the right thing, he is lost in a world of amoral creatures who exhibit nothing but the most venal of human instincts. The spiritual beings are brought down to the mundane level where comedy is possible; the tone of the book is almost wholly ribald. Magnificent fun is had with all the established mysteries of religion, and, through them, with the whole human set-up.

The two great novels of the heroic kind both passed through the hands of the same remarkable writer, Lo Kuan-chung. Otherwise known as a playwright, and living in the fourteenth century, he is said to have compiled one of them himself (*San-kuo yen-i*)[1] but merely to have revised the manuscript of a contemporary, Shih Nai-an, in the case of the other (*Shui-hu chuan*).[2]

[1] C. H. Brewitt-Taylor (tr.), *San kuo or Romance of the Three Kingdoms*, 2 vols. (Shanghai, 1925).

[2] Pearl Buck (tr.), *All Men are Brothers* (New York, 1937). See also

The two novels differ vastly in style and language. The former is terse, and written in a language that tends always toward, but never quite reaches, a simple form of the literary, while the other is full, expressive, working out the issues minutely in terms of the individual, and written, with the exception of the formulaic passages, in the current vernacular. The two works are, in fact, the product of two different techniques of story-telling. The *San-kuo* represents, at one remove, the tradition of historical narrative; the *Shui-hu* belongs, in point of its technique, to the stories of everyday life. However, different though they are in technique, from the thematic point of view they must be considered together. Both make similar assumptions about human character, and both share the same scale of values. As works in the heroic mould, they need to be discussed together just as one might discuss epic poetry and saga in the same context.

The *San-kuo* has as background the history of the Three Kingdoms, that half-century of intermittent civil war which followed the collapse of the Han Dynasty, and which ended only when China was reunited under the Chin. Like one or two similar periods, this one has a special force of fascination for the story-teller; because the emperor's power is derisory, the natural leaders are able to aim at the greatest of earthly prizes. But simply because no limits are set to ambition, the dangers in the way of the ambitious are sharp and real. The leader feels impelled to grasp the prize, but, like Shakespeare's Henry IV, he may find that grasping it is merely the beginning of his troubles. The novel is about men in pursuit of power and the means that they use, political and military skill, daring, intrigue. As it narrows down from a horde of characters to the three great protagonists, so it opens out spatially, from the confines of the royal palace with its dying emperor, with his empress, concubines, princes,

R. G. Irwin, *The Evolution of a Chinese Novel: Shui-hu chuan* (Cambridge, Mass., 1953).

ministers, eunuchs, and so forth, to the three men each ensconced in his third of China. At the first, because of the book's laconic treatment, its many characters are dehumanized, so that one has the same impression as when watching Eisenstein's *Ivan* series; later, the fewer characters are described more amply, and a good deal of the novel's tension arises from the interplay among them.

The two novels share a familiar heroic ethic, although it is not unmixed with Confucian precept. The crucial bond is that between leader and led, or between sworn-brother and sworn-brother. All other relationships are depreciated in comparison. Righteous mothers in the *San-kuo* pour scorn on sons who, for their sake, have committed some act of mild disloyalty. More than once are a hero's downfall and disgrace attributed directly to his uxoriousness. A father's feeling for his son is consciously placed below his love for his sworn-brother. This is not to say that the hero's ethic, even when observed, does not issue forth in tragedy. It is because Liu Pei cannot put aside his obsessional desire for revenge for his sworn-brother's death that he is impelled into the fatal strategic blunder which puts an end to his ambition.

It is from Liu Pei's viewpoint that we see most of the action. Chang Fei, one of his sworn-brothers, is the kind of impetuous, hot-tempered, brutal-in-his-cups hero that is so common in all the heroic stories. Kuan Yü, the other one, is the epitome of a soldier's honour; accordingly, he is continually inveigled by the author into tense situations in which there is no straightforwardly honourable mode of action. Chu-ko Liang, the strategist, is a compound of scholar-hermit and magician, mesmerizing the opposition with the simplicity and audacity of his campaigns. Later in the book the magical element in the Chu-ko Liang stories grows; the seven surrenders of the King of the Man, for instance, have the symmetry of pure fairy-tale. Yet all of these men are dwarfed by their arch-enemy, Ts'ao Ts'ao, a character

of a complexity that is rarely even attempted in heroic literature.[1]
He is ambitious in a vaunting, accursed way, morbidly suspicious
of all those about him, ruthless to the ultimate degree yet not
begrudging honour where honour is due. He has moments of
self-awareness which set him apart from the other characters.
Yet over his deepest motives there hangs a fog of ambiguity
which the author has deliberately contrived to place there.

The *Shui-hu* is equally concerned with the working out of the
heroic ethic in terms of behaviour. Its nucleus was a real rebellion in the province of Shantung early in the twelfth century.
And although few of its people and events can be traced to
historical fact, it does adhere with remarkable fidelity to the
character of those popular uprisings which have been endemic in
Chinese history, especially as regards the nature of their leader-
ship and the note of messianic prophecy which clings to them.
Most of the book is concerned with the careers of individual
heroes before—often for no fault of their own—they have to flee
from the law's condemnation. Some at least of these individual
sagas are known to have been in existence before the novel itself
was compiled, while some of them, as we have seen, are still being
narrated in that form today, influenced though they no doubt
are by the novel's treatment. For a while the outlaws operate as
a band, repulsing the forces sent against them, until they receive
an Imperial pardon and are enlisted as a corps in the army to
help in suppressing other enemies of state. (The incident of the
pardon is an interesting example of the way popular legend
works. The suggestion that they be pardoned was actually made,
but never taken up; they were crushed by force.) The novel ends

[1] Cf. C. M. Bowra, *Heroic Poetry* (London, 1952), p. 306. The following description would apply equally well to the method of portrayal in the
San-kuo: 'The poet solves this problem [i.e. of describing complexity of
character] by presenting not a complex situation in a hero's soul at a given
moment but a series of psychological states which may look inconsistent, as
they appear in succession, but are actually consistent enough if we see that
this is a way of treating what is really a single problem.'

on a note of muted tragedy, as the heroes die one by one, ill-fitted for the role they find themselves in, ignored by their patrons or betrayed by their enemies.

The focus on events of the *Shui-hu* is altogether different from that of the *San-kuo*. The novel is restricted, in terms of the time and space of its action, to a small part of the other work. No empire hangs in the balance. Instead it is concerned with personal prowess, with tactics rather than strategy. Its characteristic hero is the outlaw-adventurer rather than the warrior; as a type, it is a later development in heroic literature. In keeping with its concentration on the minutiae of heroic action, the language of the *Shui-hu* is outstanding for its precise evocation of the physical; some of its fights, sieges, and trials of strength—Wu Sung's fight with the tiger, for example—have become classics of their kind of prose. The novel has, of course, its set pieces of description, balanced and hyperbolic, expressed in formulae. These, together with the occasional long passages of verse which resume the prose account of some action, are equivalent to the stock elements of epic poetry. It has, too, a power which is rarely found in early Chinese fiction, the power of original, or seemingly original, imagery. Thus when Wu Sung has beaten the tiger into a lifeless mass, it is described as lying on the ground 'like a great brocaded bag'. But the characteristic excellence of the style is its seizure of some accurately observed detail which opens up before the reader's eyes the vision of a whole scene.

In the three novels we have dealt with the chief concern has always been with larger-than-life character. However stirring the adventures that befall a hero, it is always the hero himself who is of paramount interest. Although the character of the heroes in the three novels is relatively static, and develops hardly at all, the hero is still infinitely more important than any one of his actions. It may be true to say that when a hero appears who is greater than the circumstances that give him birth, we have the beginnings of a story-cycle. At any rate, the Chinese story-teller was not solely concerned with such men or such creatures. Among the stories of everyday life, in particular, there are many whose interest lies in a carefully turned plot.

It is so long now since criticism paid any attention to so humble a thing as plot, which is thought of, if at all, as being one of the mere mechanics of the writer's craft, one degree higher than his ability to type, that to make such a statement may seem to condemn these stories to the level of second-class literature. But that would be to forget that the first function of the story-teller—not necessarily the first function of the novelist—is to make an interesting narrative pattern of men and events. It would be to ignore, too, the pitch to which the fashioning of such plots can be brought in the hands of the virtuoso; some of the Chinese stories, *Fifteen Strings of Cash*,[1] for example, or the *Pearl-sewn Shirt*,[2] have the inevitability and symmetry of those stories acquired by Chaucer which, because of their inherent perfection, had already gone the rounds of medieval Europe. Such stories represent the art of story-making carried to its highest level, which is to say, the manipulation of men and events into an aesthetically pleasing form. Their characters, although carefully observed and seemingly authentic, are nevertheless worth no more than their position in the story warrants.

It is tempting to see some of the special features of the short story as instances of the same virtuosity. The prologue which every story possesses is one example. It may consist of no more than a few lines of verse, with a few general comments to point the moral. Or it may be a whole story in miniature, which either anticipates the main story—occasionally with a twist at the end—or else runs directly counter to it. The humdrum function of the prologue, so it is supposed, was that it kept the audience

[1] Yang Hsien-yi and Gladys Yang (tr.), *The Courtesan's Jewel Box* (Peking, 1957), pp. 42–63. For a study of this kind of story see J. L. Bishop, *The Colloquial Short Story in China* (Cambridge, Mass., 1956).

[2] Cyril Birch (tr.), *Stories from a Ming Collection* (London, 1958), pp. 37–96.

happy while a few late-comers were inveigled in. But it is surely possible to see in it, in the most skilful hands, a further exercise of the story-teller's art. As such it would hardly be the first element of a literary form to serve both a practical and an aesthetic end.

For all this, there is a danger in thinking of these stories in the light of those of Chaucer and Boccaccio. That would be to miss what is, I suppose, their unique characteristic, their penchant for documentation, for hard, irreducible, business-like fact. It was one of the story-teller's main concerns to make his material seem authentic. Hence he never glosses over the details of daily life, but gives them fully and accurately, and even goes out of his way to augment them. And the narrator projects himself as constantly on guard against the incredulity of his audience.

IV

The *Chin P'ing Mei*,[1] written at the end of the sixteenth century, may not be the first novel expressly composed as part of the vernacular literature, but it illustrates admirably the change from what was, essentially, an act of compiling to one of individual creation. The story which provides its framework is taken from the *Shui-hu chuan*, where it occupies four or five chapters: it is one of the adventures—the most famous, as it happens—which befall Wu Sung. But the story is altered; Wu Sung, whose very participation justified the inclusion of the episode in the other novel, is thrust on one side, and his vengeance on his sister-in-law and her paramour postponed until near the end of the work. There is nothing heroic about the *Chin P'ing Mei*; it is an unbelievably detailed account of a few years in the life of a single household. Wu Sung, when he returns to take his vengeance, even seems a little incongruous in this settled commercial world.

Despite the author's eclectic borrowing—passages from half a dozen stories, a play or two, as well as scores of popular songs are

[1] Clement Egerton (tr.), *The Golden Lotus*, 4 vols. (London, 1939).

actually woven into the narrative—the work is essentially a new creation. The borrowing of material on so wide, if not so very lavish, a scale merely exemplifies the current conditions of writing in the vernacular literature. The borrowed passages fulfil little or no function; if anything, they weaken the sense of unity with which the book elsewhere impresses the reader. They show the author, without any precedent for a novel of this kind, casting about among all the available methods of writing. His most striking experiment is the use of popular song for a dramatic purpose, a spasmodic attempt, based on the drama, to add a new dimension to a novel-form which had always been inept at expressing the thoughts and passions of its characters.

It is true that in its subject-matter the *Chin P'ing Mei* does bear some resemblance to the stories of everyday life. The most significant new figures in those stories were those of the merchant and artisan, in contrast to the warrior or the outlaw of the heroic sagas. But in the *Chin P'ing Mei* the corrupt world of business and politics in sixteenth-century China is explored in infinitely greater detail than ever the earlier stories explored their environment. Furthermore, in the novel, plot is no longer paramount; a shift of emphasis has taken place to character rather than plot, to lifesize character, that is to say, and not to the larger-than-life character of the earlier novels. The characters of the *Chin P'ing Mei* are new in more than one respect; they are more complex, and they are more varied, especially among the women, than characters in earlier fiction. Even more important, they show the notion of character development applied for the first time in the Chinese novel.

The work is famous, and justifiably so, for its detailed erotic descriptions, and it is obviously related to a Chinese tradition of erotic writing. But its central preoccupation lies elsewhere, in its perception of people as engaged, willy-nilly, consciously or unconsciously, in a struggle for social status. Its women are creatures of a complexity the earlier novel had never sought to attain,

and the book documents to the last detail their fierce, if intermittent, competition within the household. And in this competition the erotic scenes have, to some degree at least, a functional
part to play. But that is only half of the matter. The master of
the household is also a shopkeeper turned businessman and
moneylender, who dabbles in politics. He is evidently a representative of a newly emerging social group in a world in which
everything, save the very highest office, seems to depend on
money. If one defines the novel as in some way concerned with
depicting social change or conflict by the careful documentation
of the texture of a society, then the *Chin P'ing Mei* is the first
true Chinese novel.

We do not know the author's identity, and we can only
speculate about the circumstances in which his novel was written.
Yet there are historical reasons which make it especially appropriate that it should have been written at this time. The climate
of thinking among a section of established writers seems to have
been changing with regard to the oral and vernacular literatures.
The causes of this change, speculative at best, need not concern
us here, but its effects are obvious; they are seen in the collecting
and editing of songs, stories, novels, and plays, as well as in the
maintenance by great patrons of their own private dramatic
troupes. This was the time when the literary theatre flourished
again, using a form of the Southern Drama. Connected with
the change was another development of equal or greater importance—the discovery by publishers of a wider reading public for
works written in the vernacular or in a simple form of the literary
language. This development in itself, which can be paralleled
easily enough in the early history of the English novel, had a great
effect upon the number and nature of the works that were written, as well as on the kind of people who wrote them.

From the seventeenth century until it petered out in the early
years of the twentieth, the Chinese novel defies the simple
generalization. Alongside a copious fiction which repeats the

themes and treatment of the great early models, there are other works which are practically new in form and feeling. The most famous of these latter novels were written by men who were well fitted by training and social position to write within the tradition of the recognized literature. So, no doubt, they would have done, had that choice not limited them intolerably with regard to form and language. Ts'ao Chan, author of the greatest Chinese novel, that unfinished masterpiece the *Hung-lou meng*,[1] makes the point explicitly in his first chapter. He defends, in effect, his choice of the novel-form on the grounds of the naturalness of its language, while at the same time sharply differentiating his novel from other currently popular kinds by reason of its truth to life. It was natural that men such as he carried over into the novel the whole world of feeling inculcated by the recognized literature. The *Hung-lou meng*, in which the elements of plot, character, character development, and the author's feelings about his characters merge into one dramatic whole, shows a far greater sensibility than is met with elsewhere in Chinese fiction. This is not merely the sensibility of feeling expressed by one highly articulate character to another, but that produced by means of the author's narrative style with its subtly emotive symbols. Another effect of the entry of men-of-letters into vernacular literature was the surrendering of the narrator's old external vantage-point and the intrusion of the author into the novel. In the *Ju-lin wai-shih*,[2] this seems merely to take the form of the author's representing himself as one of the characters in the book, against whose behaviour other characters are mirrored. But this is a trivial change; essentially the author retains the narrator's vantage-point because the nature of his work favours it; it is an arrangement of case-histories of official

[1] Chi-chen Wang (tr.), *Dream of the Red Chamber* (London, 1959). For a study of the scholarly problems presented by this novel see Wu Shih-ch'ang, *On the Red Chamber Dream* (Oxford, 1961).

[2] Yang Hsien-yi and Gladys Yang (tr.), *The Scholars* (Peking, 1957).

careers, presented with low-pitched, but deadly, satire. With the *Hung-lou meng* it is different; the novel is created out of the author's direct and imagined experience in a way which in our modern literature has become a commonplace. There are countless points of correspondence between the author's experiences—including things reported to him—and the events of the novel. It is a picture of a great and noble house in its days of decline—set against an objectively described background of eighteenth-century life—when the prop of Imperial patronage, which has long sustained it, begins to be withdrawn. So it was with Ts'ao Chan's own family. In part at least, the novel is his 'recherche du temps perdu'.

v

The drama, like the novel, is stamped with the die of the performer. The novel never finally rid itself of the last vestiges of the story-teller's manner; even those works which, in treatment and insight, are at the farthest possible remove from the story-teller still retain, in some slight degree, the mark of his trade. Similarly, in the theatre, it is the common player, his professionalism and his mode of organization, which have determined the nature of dramatic convention. The formation and development of the drama have been largely in the hands of the acting troupes of the popular theatre. Hence the most instructive comparison is with the popular theatre of other countries, in particular, perhaps, with that best-documented professional popular theatre of Europe, the *commedia dell'arte*.

Both theatres are concerned with a mixture of arts—acting, singing, tumbling, pantomime among them. The Chinese troupes, like the Italians, who often based their scenarios on existing literary plays, took their material from wherever they found it, freely adapting from earlier drama. Both theatres are dominated by the notion of the role or stock character-type, a fairly sure sign of the supremacy of the professional actor. In

China this is even today still the case; the long and arduous training, at least as long and at least as arduous as that of the ballet-dancer, is directed towards a single speciality in which, once he has made his mark, an actor may play during the whole of his working life, so exacting are the standards of singing and movement required of him. Perhaps it is not entirely fanciful to see some resemblance even between the nature of the individual roles. There are roles in the Chinese theatre not so very dissimilar to that of the *zanni*,[1] and as for *Fantesca*,[2] her doubles can be seen in a hundred Chinese plays. In both theatres each role has its appropriate kind of costume. And we can easily equate the masks of the *commedia* with the heavy, caricaturing make-up of the Chinese stage. Finally, anyone who has seen Chinese comedy will be able to visualize the *lazzi*,[3] that pantomime stock-in-trade of the Italian comedian.

But a comparison with the *commedia dell'arte* can be taken too far. The Chinese drama is not, as the Italian was, mere improvization upon a scenario. And although the latter's repertory did extend on occasion to serious drama, it would be absurd to compare it in terms of range or value to the Chinese theatre. The reason is one that serves as the motif for this essay: like some forms of the oral literature, the Chinese popular theatre was established, institutionalized almost, and hence brought to a transcendent pitch of excellence, such as no popular theatre in Europe, because of constant competition from the literary theatre, has ever attained.

Furthermore, comparison with the *commedia* will never do justice to the place of singing and music in the Chinese drama. Of all its elements, including speech, declamation, balletic dance, mock-combat, tumbling, symbolic gesture and action, make-up and costume, unquestionably song and music are the

---

[1] See Allardyce Nicoll, *Masks, Mimes and Miracles* (London, 1931), pp. 267–82.

[2] Ibid., pp. 242–5.   [3] Ibid., pp. 219–21.

most important. The Chinese drama has a musical structure as well as a dramatic structure, and the single most valued art of the performer is his singing. The whole of the traditional Chinese drama can quite reasonably be described as a species of opera. Yet, having made this statement, one is compelled immediately to qualify it. The composer, as such, does not exist. Instead, for any single form of drama there is a stock repertory of tunes, from amongst which the librettist makes his choice. (A choice, one must add, which proves to be governed by fairly strict conventions.) If we can speak of a composer in the modern sense at all, then he is the one who helps to establish the repertory in the first place. The musician Wei Liang-fu, for example, in the sixteenth century, is credited with so arranging and enlarging the music of the opera of his own locality that it came to serve as the vehicle for the second great literary drama of China. For this reason, the parallel that comes to mind, the European ballad opera of the eighteenth century, must also be rejected. Although many of the tunes of the Chinese drama were originally derived from popular song, by the time they came to be widely used in drama they had already been classified as part of a stock repertory; they were not pressed into service *ad hoc*. Nor did the ballad opera, at least as represented by the work of Gay, show anything like the degree of musical organization which characterizes the Chinese drama.

Music and song are the main elements of change in the Chinese drama. Changes in other elements, such as the allocation of the singing parts, there have certainly been, but it is predominantly the music and style of singing which differentiate one kind of drama from another. If we consider the hundreds of different kinds of drama at present being played in China— including all the local varieties—they differ most of all in respect of music and singing, less in respect of dramatic convention, and least of all as regards subject-matter.

The author of a play was primarily a librettist. The copious dramatic criticism of the literary theatre does deal with the art of libretto-writing, but it concentrates above all on the kind of criteria which are properly applied to poetry. And poetic drama is indeed what the literary drama amounted to. It is, for example, in lyrics and lyric sequences of the *kind* used in the drama that much of the freshest and most original poetry from the thirteenth century onward is preserved. It is not far-fetched to compare the literary drama, in respect of its language, with the poetic drama of the Elizabethans. At its best, when the musical structure and the dramatic structure complement each other, and the songs with their highly charged poetic language fit the moments of real passion in the play, it provides as complete a theatrical experience as one can imagine.

There were two periods during which poets were especially attracted into the theatre. In the thirteenth and fourteenth centuries—including the time when China was under Mongol occupation—the chosen form was that of the Northern Drama. In the sixteenth and seventeenth centuries, it was a variety of the Southern Drama. For a time the Mongol rulers of China suspended the examination system—virtually the only respectable road to worldly success—which had long been one of the main supports of the recognized literature. This is one of the reasons which may have caused writers to enter the theatre who otherwise would not have considered doing so. As to the recrudescence of the poetic drama in the sixteenth century, it was probably related to the shift of opinion we mentioned earlier, and in particular to the growing practice among great patrons of keeping their own acting troupes.

The Northern Drama was short, restrictive in form, concentrated in effect. Nevertheless, by the device of radical foreshortening which the Chinese drama possesses—a character on entering utters what is in effect an explanatory prologue to the audience—it could cope with a complicated action widely extended in time. The Southern Drama, by contrast, was several times as long, meandering its way through plot and sub-plot. The poets of the earlier period were more likely to have had experience of actually working in the theatre, but it would not be fair to describe the plays of the later poets as 'closet drama'; mostly they were written to be performed. Broad differences do exist, however, between the two kinds of drama. A comparison between their most famous respective treatments of the theme of clandestine love will give some idea of such differences at their most extreme. In the *Western Chamber*,[1] which is Northern Drama, the lovers, for all their emotion, still belong to the ordinary credible world. In the *Return of the Soul*,[2] which is Southern Drama, the lineaments of ordinary life have been half-dissolved in the poet's fancy; it resembles a medieval romance of courtly love.

Most Chinese plays belong to the category of the serious comedy, a kind of play containing comic elements which poses problems, induces tensions, and finally resolves them. By the side of it, tragedy occupies a fairly small place in the Chinese theatre. Indeed, if we were to adopt a rigorous definition of tragedy, we should not find more than a few plays capable of satisfying it. Yet it is undeniable, I think, that whatever our private gauge of tragic feeling may be, there are many Chinese plays which will produce in us a tragic effect at some point or other. It seems that the Chinese dramatist was more concerned with the intensity of the great tragic moment itself than with the inexorable process which that moment consummates, or with the long articulate struggle with conscience.

The range of experience admitted into the drama is even wider than that of fiction, although most stories have indeed been treated in both the oral and the vernacular literatures as well as in the drama, and many have been treated over and over again, in dozens of different forms, within each medium. To

[1] S. I. Hsiung (tr.), *The Romance of the Western Chamber* (London, 1935).
[2] *Huan-hun chi*. Also known by the title of *Mu-tan t'ing*.

categorize this range of experience within a short space is an impossible task; all one can do is to make out a rough list of some obvious kinds. First, there are the supernatural plays, hagiography or mythology, with their frequent resort to laughter. Second, there are the historical plays, often with heroic themes, far more numerous than the chronicle-plays of Elizabethan England; where a tragic outcome occurs, it is most often among these plays of past kings and queens. Third, there is a great variety of plays with a range even wider than that of the stories of everyday life. Among them are the heroic-outlaw plays, for example those based on the *Shui-hu* story-cycle; in the theatre, the characters with comic potentialities loom somewhat larger than they do in fiction. There is also the crime-case play, which makes one think of that solitary, anonymous English play, *Arden of Faversham*. But the most numerous kind is the play that deals with love, either the clandestine love we have mentioned, or that love between student and singing-girl which, for good reasons, obsessed the Chinese imagination. The student was at the outset of what proved to be a brilliant career, and his affair with a singing-girl prostitute was his first taste of free choice in love. And she, for her part, seems sometimes to have had, paradoxically enough, a semblance of free choice herself, a thing denied to the rest of Chinese womanhood.

There is a further kind of play with which this survey may fittingly end, since it is concerned both with women, who only come into their own outside the recognized literature, and with the ever-present Chinese morality of family obligation. These are the plays of good women. They have at their centre a testing or an ordeal; and they too sometimes rise to the level of tragedy. Famous examples are *Tou O yüan*,[1] superficially a crime-case play, which has a tragic outcome, and the *P'i-p'a chi*, which has not. It is too simple to describe them merely as plays about

---

[1] Yang Hsien-yi and Gladys Yang (tr.), *Selected Plays of Kuan Han-ch'ing* (Peking, 1958), pp. 21–47, *Snow in Midsummer*.

women of transcendent virtue; what they show is the heroic theme applied in a woman's context. Their tension is due to the fact that their heroines are martyrs to the ethical code in its most extreme instance, where, one feels, there is the least possible natural sanction for it. Both heroines are stretched cruelly on the rack of family obligation. Tou O, for example, makes a false confession of murder to save her mother-in-law—who has done everything to forfeit any loyalty she might have deserved—from suffering judicial examination and torture. As an act of self-sacrifice, it is so excessive as to be almost gratuitous. To its nature, however, we owe the terrifying pathos that attends her execution.

VI

In the second decade of this century a generation of young Chinese writers, all of them open to influence from abroad, consciously set about the creation of a new literature in the vernacular. From that time on the criteria we have used so far in this essay become less and less applicable. The recognized literature of the old kind soon ceased to be recognized, and has now almost ceased to be written. The old indigenous Chinese novel is practically extinct; the symptoms of its senility are obvious—it has failed to adapt to modern themes, or even to modern people or places. Oral narrative still flourishes, and is patronized by a large section of Chinese society, but it seems no longer to be the creative medium it once was; it functions mainly as a secondary form, adapting themes from elsewhere, or else merely telling and re-telling the old stories. The drama is as popular as ever; despite the competition of the cinema, it is still the most widely enjoyed kind of entertainment in China. (A modern, non-operatic drama of the sort we are familiar with is now well established, but is not anything like so popular.) So vigorous indeed is the drama that it is quite impossible to predict what course it may take, or to guess which variety may be confined for ever to the performance of a classical repertoire, and which may be successfully developed into a form in which future original creation is possible.

This is a good point in time from which to sum up the history and achievement of the indigenous Chinese fiction and drama. Here I can only repeat the truism which has been the central theme of this essay: that both of them sprang from the art of the performer or entertainer. Immune at first to the literary critic, they recognized in their audience their only final judge. Their history consists on the one hand of an advancement towards an extraordinary level of technical accomplishment, and on the other of a continual interaction with written literature, with its personal authorship, its literary pretensions, and its totally different standards.   PATRICK HANAN

(d) THE HISTORIOGRAPHICAL TRADITION[1]

INTEREST in the past, the real and not the legendary past that is, is not a universal characteristic of mankind or even of civilized mankind. It seems to have been largely absent in ancient India, where the timeless verities of religion were what attracted men's minds. It was pre-eminently present in China. When we look for reasons to explain this, we find them intimately connected with the ideology of the scholar-bureaucrats who wrote and read this history, in a word, Confucianism. Pragmatic, social, this-worldly, rationalistic, yet finding its profoundest emotional basis in the desire to ensure the continuity of family and race and in attachment to the traditional 'rites' which distinguished civilized men from barbarians, the Confucian ethic naturally looked for its

[1] Further information about many of the topics discussed in this section may be found in Charles S. Gardner, *Chinese Traditional Historiography*, first published in 1938, second printing with additions and corrections by L. S. Yang (Cambridge, Mass., 1961); and in the collection of essays *Historians of China and Japan*, edited by W. G. Beasley and E. G. Pulleyblank (London, 1961).

sanctions to the precedents of the past rather than to the inspired utterances of prophets or mystics.

Ancestor-worship, which antedated Confucianism and provided one of its principal ingredients, in itself necessarily led to a certain regard for recording the past, at least to the extent of preserving genealogies. The traditional list of kings of the Shang Dynasty handed down to us in the *Shih-chi* has been proved remarkably accurate by recent archaeology. It is probable that we owe its preservation to its connexion with the ancestral rites of the state of Sung, which claimed descent from the Shang royal house. Moreover the cult of the royal ancestors, to whom important events had to be formally announced, was no doubt one of the motives behind the keeping of chronicles which we find in the various states in the so-called feudal period before the unification by Ch'in in 221 B.C.

The officers of state who had charge of these chronicles were called *shih*. This word, which is etymologically related to *li*, 'clerk', 'official', originally meant no more than 'scribe'. Indeed, it survived in its original sense in bureaucratic usage long after it had also acquired the special senses of 'historian' and 'history' from the name of the first comprehensive history of China, the *Shih-chi* (the 'Records of the Scribe' or 'Records of the Historian'). The authors of this work were Ssu-ma T'an and his son Ssu-ma Ch'ien (see below), who held the hereditary office of Grand Scribe (*T'ai shih*), the duties of which in their day were particularly concerned with the calendar and other astronomical matters. Long before their time, however, scribes in the feudal states were fulfilling the functions at least of archivists, even if it would be anachronistic to speak yet of history.

There are many references to them in early texts and there is good evidence that the records which they kept were looked upon as having a peculiar importance, even sanctity. Two old stories which are quoted innumerable times in later centuries illustrate this One tells how when a certain nobleman of Ch'i murdered the ruler, the Grand Scribe recorded it as 'murder of a ruler' in his tablets. For this he was put to death. Two younger brothers in succession did the same and were also put to death. The Southern Scribe set out with his tablets to take the place of the Grand Scribe in case their family should be exterminated, but a fourth brother was able to make the truthful record and was not executed, so the Southern Scribe returned home.

The other story tells of a member of a hereditary family of scribes in Chin who boldly published in open court the record in his tablets that the chief minister had 'murdered his ruler'. In this case the minister had merely been able to recover his position in the state and avoid exile because of the timely murder of an unrighteous duke by someone else; but he had failed to take steps to punish the malefactor so he was held to be ritually guilty by the scribe. On this occasion the scribe was more fortunate. The conscience of the minister was pricked and the scribe went uninjured. According to the *Tso-chuan* (the 'Tradition of Tso') Confucius praised both the scribe and the minister.

Though the literal historical truth of these stories is open to question, we can at any rate glean from them some idea of the quasi-religious importance of the scribe's 'true record'. It is in the light of this that we may understand how the *Spring and Autumn Annals*, the chronicle of the state of Lu, could become one of the Confucian Classics. The *Spring and Autumn Annals*, like other early chronicles, such as the *Bamboo Annals* of Wei recovered from a tomb in A.D. 281, is little more than an extremely terse, bare record of major events, especially those of ritual importance to the state of Lu. It covers the years 722 to 481 B.C. Taken at face value it seems a most unlikely book to have become a canonical scripture. It owes its importance to its connexion with Confucius. According to the received view, he edited the text, insinuating into it praise and blame through subtleties of wording, mainly the giving or withholding of honorific or depreciatory terminology. In fact it is difficult, if not impossible, to deduce a consistent use of such terminology from the text and a more likely interpretation of the tradition, at least as old as Mencius, which connects the *Spring and Autumn Annals* with Confucius is that he used the chronicle of his native state as a textbook for political ethics, expounding his views orally to his disciples.

However this may be, by the Han period various schools of Confucian philosophy had their traditions for interpreting the *Spring and Autumn Annals*, of which two, the *Kung-yang chuan* and the *Ku-liang chuan*, still survive. In both cases it is evident that they were not written down until several centuries after Confucius's day and are probably the products of long oral tradition. They are as dull and unappetizing in their scholastic moralizing as the *Spring and Autumn Annals* is as a narrative. Nevertheless they cannot be neglected in the history of Chinese historiography. The doctrine that the historian's highest function was distributing praise and blame in order to present uplifting examples and warnings against infringements of the ethical code was something of a millstone around the neck of later historians, who were more interested in narrating and understanding the course of events; but on the positive side, the importance laid on the historical record in Confucianism is no doubt in large part responsible for the unrivalled fullness and continuity of that record in China. In practice the best historians professed themselves unworthy to emulate Confucius in allotting praise and blame, and adopted instead the lesser ideal of the 'true record' which would faithfully and objectively mirror men's conduct.

The third of the so-called commentaries on the *Spring and Autumn Annals*, the *Tradition of Tso*, is far larger and very different in kind from the other two.[1] In its present form it is

---

[1] James Legge's somewhat antiquated translation of the *Spring and Autumn Annals* and the *Tso Tradition* is available in a recent (Hong Kong, 1960) reprint of his *The Chinese Classics*, 5 vols.

arranged as a commentary on the Classic and it contains a certain amount of moralizing interpretation of the same kind as the other two, but the bulk of the text is narrative. It covers a slightly longer period than the *Annals*, extending down to 468 B.C. In some cases its material could be considered as amplification of events recorded in the *Annals*, but often it deals with matters not mentioned there at all. It is a literary masterpiece, the first of Chinese narrative prose, and its sharply vivid and dramatic stories have caught the imagination of many generations of readers. It has inspired some of China's greatest historians. Its compact yet expressive diction has had an incalculable influence on narrative style.

The *Tso Tradition* no doubt existed originally as a work in its own right quite distinct from the *Spring and Autumn Annals*, but we have only internal evidence to guide us as to the date of its composition and the sources on which it may have been based. It seems likely that it drew partly on genuinely historical materials such as the chronicles of the states of Chin and Ch'u, which seem to have been less terse and uninformative than that of Lu, but it also drew largely on what can only be described as historical fiction, though treated as history ever since. Cycles of stories had grown up around major figures, both rulers and ministers, of the feudal period which, though in prose not verse, may be thought of as the Chinese counterparts of the epic poetry of Greece.

The beginnings of this historical fiction are obscure but they may go back as far as the fifth century B.C. A rather primitive example that has accidentally been preserved is the story of the Emperor Mu, which was found along with the official chronicle of Wei in a royal tomb which was opened in A.D. 281. The form of the narrative in this case is a dry, day-by-day chronicle, like the *Spring and Autumn Annals*, but the matter, which deals with two episodes, a journey to the sources of the Yellow River in the west and a hunting expedition in the south, is clearly largely or wholly legendary, though its hero was a real Chou king who reigned from 947 to 928 B.C. The stories about the Five Hegemons and other heroes of the Spring and Autumn period do not survive in their original state, but they must have been freer and ampler in style.[1] Their incorporation into the *Tso Tradition* is what brings the work to life and gives it much of its fascination, even if they detract from its reliability as factual history. Whatever its defects in the latter respect, it can be used as a picture of life in ancient China. As with Homer it is possible that features of a later period are sometimes projected back into earlier times but the time depth is shallower and the possibilities of anachronistic distortion are consequently reduced. Also there is a solid historical framework based on state chronicles.

Material of the same kind as that in the *Tso Tradition* is found in the *Kuo yü* (the 'Speeches of the States') and, for the end of the pre-Imperial period, in the *Chan-kuo ts'e* (the 'Stratagems of the Warring States'). Apart from this, anecdotes of an historical or quasi-historical kind play a large part in the philosophical works of the Late Chou period, being adduced to prove some point in argument or to illustrate a principle. Concrete examples from history or what was believed to be history were felt to be more effective than abstract theorizing. It should be emphasized that, though history was fictionalized, it remained strictly human and there is no tendency to turn heroes into marvellous beings with supernatural powers or to explain events by the intervention of divinities.

Fictionalized history continued to play a major role in Chinese literature and supplied one of the earliest and most important strands in the development of the novel. The *San-kuo yen-i* (the 'Romance of the Three Kingdoms') and the *Shui-hu chuan* (the 'Water Margin') are famous examples. After true historiography had gained its autonomy in the Han period the two genres diverged but in the beginning we find them intimately

[1] On early historical romances see H. Maspero, *La Chine antique*, new ed. (Paris, 1955), pp. 482 ff.

connected and the link was never completely broken. The story element in history was always a potent factor in keeping men's interest in it, however they might talk about moral uplift, and fiction satisfied the desire for the imaginative re-creation of the past which was left unsatisfied by the dry, impersonal works of the historian. Conversely, works of historical fiction were popular just because interest in the past was so lively in Chinese society, not only among the learned but also among the general population.

The works that have been discussed so far are not so much the beginnings of historiography proper in either the Chinese or the Western sense as the ground from which true historiography sprang. The decisive step which created a true historiography was taken at the end of the second century B.C. with the production of Ssu-ma Ch'ien's *Shih-chi* (or 'Records of the Historian').[1] Ssu-ma Ch'ien was completing a work begun by his father Ssu-ma T'an. As mentioned above, father and son held the hereditary office of Grand Scribe (*T'ai-shih*). Living at a time when a new era in history had commenced with the unification of all China under the Han Dynasty, the Ssu-mas in their office as archivists conceived the grand design of combining into a single connected work the existing records of the Chinese people from the earliest times down to their own day.

In so doing they created the model which was imitated and developed in the great series of Dynastic, or Standard, Histories (*cheng shih*) which were continued up to the end of the Imperial period in 1911. Moreover the methods they adopted in dealing with their sources and presenting their material set the basic style for history writing of all kinds quite apart from the standard histories themselves. One of the most important features of

---

[1] Partially translated with an extensive introduction by E. Chavannes as *Les Mémoires historiques de Se-ma Ts'ien*, 5 vols. (Paris, 1898–1905). See also B. Watson, *Ssu-ma Ch'ien, Grand Historian of China* (New York, 1958), and *Records of the Grand Historian of China*, 2 vols. (New York, 1961).

Ssu-ma Ch'ien's work to become a constant principle may be called 'objectivity'. This means that the historian composed his narrative as a patchwork of excerpts, often abridged but otherwise unaltered, from his sources, with any personal comment or judgement kept clearly separate. The work of the historian was to compile a set of documents which would speak for themselves rather than to make an imaginative reconstruction of past events. This did not mean that an historian necessarily became a mere mechanical compiler, since the selection and arrangement of his material called for the exercise of critical judgement, and conclusions about the causes of events or the characters of historical persons could be expressed separately in the appropriate place; but it did easily lead to mechanical compilation in the case of inferior historians. At the same time, from the point of view of the modern historian using Chinese historical works as sources, it has great advantages. Material preserved only in what would otherwise have to be regarded as secondary works can be treated as primary (with of course every care being exercised to determine as far as possible the original source of each statement, and a lively awareness of the errors and misunderstandings that can be introduced by the accidental juxtaposition of originally unconnected material).

The *Shih-chi* is divided into five major sections. First come the Basic Annals (*pen-chi*), which deal with the lives of emperors and the main events in their reigns. They are in annalistic form and are 'basic' in that they establish the chronology—as well, perhaps, as being thought of as somewhat more authoritative than other parts of the work. (The allegedly greater authority of the *pen-chi* is often mentioned by modern scholars, but one does not in fact find that this was used as a criterion of criticism by traditional Chinese scholars.) Next came Tables (*piao*), in which the dynastic chronologies of the separate states in the pre-Han period and the appointments to titles of nobility under the Han were set out. Next came eight Monographs (*shu*), dealing discursively with aspects of traditional Chinese government such as rites, music, the calendar, rivers and canals, &c. This section, which was to be one of the most fruitful in its later developments, is the one for which there is the least evidence of pre-existing models in earlier literature. The fourth section, Hereditary Houses (*shih-chia*), dealt with the history of the separate feudal states of the pre-Han period. Finally came the largest section of all, the *lieh-chuan*. Since these consist mainly of the lives of individuals, they are often referred to as Biographies, but the term itself means 'assembled traditions' and was clearly intended originally to cover additional material of all kinds that did not fall into any of the other categories. Accounts of foreign countries are included in them, for example.

For the earlier part of his work Ssu-ma Ch'ien had necessarily to use a good deal of material which was of doubtful historicity. Nevertheless his work is history in a truer sense than the works which preceded him and on which he drew, since his intention was to establish the most probable account out of conflicting testimony. For the period closest to his own day he was for the most part using first-hand government archives and his work must be regarded as having a high degree of reliability. It is this later part of his work that has remained typical of history writing in China ever since, where archives have always provided the great bulk of the source material. From the Han period onward it is the limitations of the official bureaucratic outlook rather than the inclusion of material of dubious authenticity that one must be most conscious of in assessing the historicity of historical works. (It should be mentioned that doubts have been expressed about the authenticity of large parts of the existing text of the *Shih-chi*, which are supposed to consist of restorations based on the *Han shu*, the originals having been lost. In my opinion there is no justification for this view.)

The next step in the founding of the tradition of the Chinese Standard Histories was taken when Pan Ku (A.D. 32–92), completing a work begun by his father Pan Piao, compiled the *Han shu* ('History of the Former Han Dynasty').[1] This followed the model of the *Shih-chi* in the main but departed from it in a number of points which set the pattern for the future. The most important of these was the definition of the subject of the book as the history of a single, past dynasty instead of all history down to the author's day. Pan Ku incorporated into his own work (with only small alterations or additions) those parts of the *Shih-chi* which dealt with the Han Dynasty and added material up to and including the usurpation of Wang Mang, but stopped short at the beginning of the Eastern Han Dynasty in which he himself was living. This practice had certain conveniences. It meant that the dynastic histories could be regarded as one continuous, definitive, official record, not to be revised but only to be augmented as each new section, uniform with the last, was added. It has meant, however, that the view of history as a continuity has tended to be lost and that the dynastic framework has dominated the conceptualization of Chinese history to an unhealthy degree.

Other modifications introduced into the *Shih-chi* pattern by Pan Ku are of a more technical kind. The section on Hereditary Houses disappeared, since it lacked any *raison d'être* in Imperial China. The number of Monographs (called now *chih* instead of *shu*) was increased and there was some change in the subjects treated. The style of the *Han shu* is more self-consciously formal and literary than that of the *Shih-chi*, which often has an attractive spontaneity of expression.

When it was discovered that Pan Ku was privately writing a history, he was first imprisoned for his temerity and then officially commissioned to complete the work he had begun. This might be looked on as the beginning of officially sponsored

---

[1] The Basic Annals and the chapter on Wang Mang have been translated by H. H. Dubs, *The History of the Former Han Dynasty*, 3 vols. (Baltimore, 1938, 1944, 1955).

history writing (as opposed to archive keeping) in China. It was a long time, however, before it became a regular, bureaucratically organized activity. The work of the government-sponsored historians in the Tung-kuan Library in the second century A.D. provided basic material for the history of the Later Han, but the work which they produced was not considered very satisfactory and there were numerous attempts by private persons to write histories of that dynasty before the *Hou Han shu* (the 'History of the Later Han Dynasty'), that now survives, was composed by Fan Yeh in the first half of the fifth century.[1] Private, or semi-private, history writing flourished during the period of weakness and division that followed the end of Han and many works, short and long, were written, most of which have unfortunately perished.

The multiplication of historical works led to the recognition of history as an autonomous branch of learning and letters. In the fourfold classification of books which came into being in the third century A.D. and has remained standard ever since, history took second place, after Classics and in front of philosophy and *belles-lettres*. The same fourfold division was introduced in the National University in Later Chao (A.D. 319–50) in North China and in the Liu Sung Dynasty (A.D. 420–79) in the South. The *Wen-hsin tiao-lung* of Liu Hsieh (A.D. 465–522),[2] the greatest work of literary criticism of the period, devotes a section to historical writing, criticizing the major historians up to the author's time and making some general remarks about the difficulties in the way of a well-balanced, reliable, unprejudiced record. He stresses the role of the historian as moralist and his heavy responsibility to tell the truth without fear or favour.

[1] On the writing of the history of Later Han see H. Bielenstein, *The Restoration of the Han Dynasty*, vol. i (Stockholm, 1953).

[2] This work has already been discussed in Professor Hawkes's 'Introductory note'.

The establishment of the T'ang Dynasty over a reunited China in 618 gave an impetus to many aspects of intellectual life. Conscious that a new era had dawned, the T'ang government wished to put the seal on its achievement by definitive works such as the new standard commentaries to the Confucian Classics, the *Wu ching cheng-i*, and by definitive histories of the intervening period since the Han Dynasty. A commission was set up, in the first place to write histories for five short-lived dynasties of the previous century for which no histories existed. This was followed by an order for a revised history of Chin (A.D. 317–420) to replace the seven or eight existing works on that period. A natural extension of the work of these commissioners was the setting up of a permanent bureau to prepare materials for the history of T'ang. This became the History Office, which developed and continued through successive dynasties until the end of the empire. From the beginning its principal duty was to gather documentary materials on the immediate past and to compose them at appropriate intervals, which very soon became established as the end of each reign, into chronicles known as *Shih-lu* ('Veritable Records'). From time to time efforts were also made during T'ang to work up these reign chronicles into standard history form and a *T'ang shu* was in fact completed down to around the year 762, which later became the basis for the existing *Old T'ang History*.

From the Sung period onward it came to be the practice for completed Veritable Records to be regarded as secret state documents and the working up of a standard history on the basis of them did not occur until the founding of a new dynasty. It is therefore sometimes said that each dynasty prepared historical materials for the sake of its successor. This is a misconception. The Veritable Records were the National History and, during T'ang, both they and the *T'ang shu* seem to have been quite widely accessible. Even in later times their purpose was to provide a history of the current dynasty which should be available at need to the emperor, and their preparation did not imply a fatalistic anticipation of the inevitable end of the dynasty.

The regular, organized compilation of histories by teams of officials ensured the volume and continuity of the record, which is one of the most immediately impressive features of Chinese historiography. It does not require much imagination to see that it also had drawbacks. Liu Chih-chi (661–721), a sceptical and original scholar, passionately devoted to historical studies, who was employed in the History Office at the beginning of the eighth century when it was still a recent innovation, made some sharp criticisms of officially sponsored collective historiography in a letter appended to his book, *Shih-t'ung* ('Generalities on History').[1] Some of his points have a very modern ring. He complained of the damping of initiative through having so many co-workers involved, the difficulty of getting access to necessary documents, the impossibility of keeping the work secret so that interested parties tried to have statements altered to suit themselves, the contradictory instructions received from different supervisors, the failure of supervisors to make a clear allocation of tasks.

Some of these faults could be remedied by more efficient organization, and in the course of time they were—so that by Ming and Ch'ing times procedures were laid down in a most elaborate and detailed way.[2] The work could proceed smoothly and with a high standard of quality within the limits of its established pattern. The Veritable Records of the last two dynasties form a vast repertory of chronologically arranged official documents, either quoted in full or systematically excerpted. Efficient organization, however, meant a further deadening of individuality and initiative, and we look in vain for the exercise of historical imagination or the effort to explain the

---

[1] See Beasley and Pulleyblank, op. cit., pp. 135 ff.
[2] See Wolfgang Franke, 'The Veritable Records of the Ming Dynasty (1368–1644)', in Beasley and Pulleyblank, op. cit., pp. 60–77.

course of events. This is largely true not only of the Veritable Records but also of the Standard Histories based on them. Even in those sections which had to be composed afresh rather than pieced together by joining quotations, that is, in the prefaces to monographs or the paragraphs at the ends of biographies expressing the historian's judgement, convention is rarely questioned.

An historian who was interested in what we should think of as historical problems had to turn to other genres of history writing in order to express himself.[1] Thus, after T'ang had suffered the

---

[1] The variety and sheer quantity of Chinese historical writing needs to be stressed. One of the four sections of the great compendium of Chinese literature compiled in the eighteenth century, the *Ssu-k'u ch'üan-shu*, is devoted to history, which is classified under fifteen categories: (1) *Cheng-shih*, 'standard histories'; (2) *Pien-nien*—works in chronological form like the *Comprehensive Mirror*; (3) *Chi-shih pen-mo*—a new form of history devised in the Southern Sung Dynasty, in which material for a given period is rearranged under topics; (4) *Pieh-shih*, 'separate histories'—mainly works in standard history form not recognized as official; (5) *Tsa-shih*, 'miscellaneous histories'—mostly short works, often contemporary or near-contemporary accounts of important events; (6) *Chao-ling-tsou-i*—collections of government edicts and of memorials presented to the throne by officials; (7) *Chuan-chi*—biographical works, including private and family biographies of important persons as well as official biographies collected outside the standard histories; (8) *Shih-ch'ao*, 'historical excerpts'; (9) *Tsai-chi*—records of lesser states, not recognized as legitimate, that coexisted from time to time with Imperial dynasties; (10) *Shih-ling*—works on chronology; (11) *Ti-li*, 'geography'—a very large category containing not only compendious summaries of the geography of the empire at various periods (especially but not exclusively in its administrative aspects), but also the countless local histories (*fang-chih*) compiled for each province, prefecture, and sub-prefecture of the empire and often for smaller divisions as well; (12) *Chih-kuan*—works on the evolution of government offices; (13) *Cheng-shu*—institutional histories such as the *T'ung-tien*; (14) *Mu-lu*—bibliographies and library catalogues, also works about inscriptions on metal and stone; (15) *Shih-p'ing*, 'historical criticism'—works such as Liu Chih-chi's *Generalities on History*. Apart from these works formally classified as History, material of essentially the same kind is contained in encyclopedias (*lei-shu*) and the collected works of countless individual writers.

nearly mortal blow of the An Lu-shan rebellion, Tu Yu (735–812) wrote his great institutional history, or historical encyclopedia, the *T'ung-tien* (enlarging the *Cheng-tien* of Liu Chih-chi's son Liu Chih).[1] Though the book is constructed, like the official histories, largely out of excerpts from previous books and documents, it is arranged according to an entirely new plan to show the evolution of governmental institutions; moreover the interlinear notes and the author's prefaces and concluding discussions in each section reveal a man to whom historical studies are important as a means of understanding and dealing with the débâcle of the society in which he lives. Tu Yu was partial to the political philosophy of the Legalists and is refreshingly free of Confucian cant. Later, in the even worse collapse that befell China at the time of the Mongol conquest, Ma Tuan-lin (thirteenth century) used a similar form to a similar purpose. Like the *T'ung-tien*, his *Wen-hsien t'ung-k'ao* is a history in encyclopedic form, covering an even wider range of subjects and showing in the prefaces and discussions written by the author a similar desire to get outside the dynastic compartments of official history and to understand the evolution of Chinese society.[2]

At about the same time as Tu Yu was writing, a new type of critical scholarship was developing in classical studies which came in time to have far-reaching effects on historical scholarship

One must also not forget Buddhist works of history, classified separately under Buddhism in the section on Philosophers (*tzu*). The amount of documentation available for Chinese history, especially in recent periods, is truly enormous, even without taking into account the new material that has come to light in this century through archaeological discoveries and the opening up of government archives at the end of the empire.

[1] See E. G. Pulleyblank, 'Neo-Confucianism and neo-Legalism in T'ang Intellectual Life, 755–805', in *The Confucian Persuasion*, edited by A. F. Wright (Stanford, 1960).

[2] See E. Balazs in 'L'Histoire comme guide de la pratique bureaucratique' (Beasley and Pulleyblank, op. cit., pp. 81–82).

as well. A sceptical attitude to the authority of ancient books was not a new thing in China. Men like Wang Ch'ung (A.D. 27–91) had criticized old stories in the Classics from a rationalistic point of view. Liu Chih-chi, whom we have mentioned above as the author of a famous manual of historiography, gained a scandalous reputation for his willingness to call even Confucius himself into question. But up to his day this kind of scepticism is unsystematic, giving the impression of personal idiosyncrasy rather than of a disciplined search for the truth. A marked change appears in the new school of criticism that grew up in the second half of the eighth century. It began with an attempt to get behind the various schools of commentary and to determine inductively the true meaning of the *Spring and Autumn Annals* by dispassionate analysis. The most interesting results concerned the nature of the *Tso-chuan*. Tan Chu, the founder of the school, concluded from internal evidence that the *Tso-chuan* was compiled from a variety of sources, different for each feudal state. He supposed that Confucius's disciple Tso Ch'iu-ming had taken the histories of the various states and transmitted the material orally to his disciples, and that this had later been re-arranged chronologically and combined with a variety of supplementary materials. Chao K'uang, Tan Chu's disciple, went farther and concluded that the *Tso-chuan* could not have come from Tso Ch'iu-ming at all and moreover that the *Tso-chuan* and the *Kuo yü* could not have been by the same author. The views of this school and, more important, their way of thinking became popular among the young intellectuals at the capital around the year 800 and men like the famous *ku-wen* writer Liu Tsung-yüan called into question the authenticity or the attribution of other early works.[1] This was the start of a type of philology which grew to a high degree of sophistication in Sung and again in Ch'ing.

After T'ang came Sung, less glorious in an imperial sense but

[1] See article cited in n. 1, p. 157.

representing an apogee of traditional Chinese culture. It is impossible in a limited space to do anything like justice to its achievements in historical scholarship. Both in critical re-appraisal of earlier works and in new historical writings it achieved altogether new standards.

Perhaps the greatest synthetic work of history of the period, with some claim to be considered the greatest work of Chinese historiography, is Ssu-ma Kuang's *Tzu-chih t'ung-chien* ('Comprehensive Mirror for Aid in Government'), completed in 1085.[1] This is a history in chronological form of the 1362 years from the end of the Spring and Autumn period to the founding of Sung (403 B.C.–A.D. 959). Ssu-ma Kuang, a leading statesman of his time, had, like Liu Chih-chi before him and other Chinese historians since, been inspired with a lifelong passion for historical studies by an early acquaintance with the *Tso-chuan*. He conceived the idea of continuing that work and, partly through the circumstance of enforced retirement from politics during the ascendancy of the reformer Wang An-shih, was able to bring his grand design to completion. He had official support for his venture but it was not at all official historiography in the usual sense. He chose his own assistants and had personal charge of the whole enterprise. We know in some detail how the work was organized from a letter he wrote to Liu Pin, who was his collaborator for the T'ang section.

First a chronological outline of dates and headings was prepared, based on the Veritable Records. Then passages referring to these headings were copied out from all available sources, not only the Veritable Records and the existing dynastic histories but also from all other available materials—private accounts of important events, family biographies, inscriptions, collections of documents, the literary works of historical personages. This formed the Long Draft, as it was called, a kind of continuous card file—new entries could be easily inserted by cutting the

---

[1] See Beasley and Pulleyblank, op. cit., pp. 151 ff.

manuscript roll and pasting them in. The final stage was to digest the material into a narrative, or rather a string of narratives, for the original annalistic form remained as the underlying structure. The historian's judgement was exercised in choosing among and reconciling conflicting versions of the same event and in choosing what to retain and what to leave out.

One thing that gives Ssu-ma Kuang's work its great distinction and places him above his predecessors is that he was not content to make judgements implicitly but insisted that they be explicitly stated. A series of notes were made of places where the evidence was conflicting or doubtful, the differing versions were quoted, and the reasons for preferring one to another were succinctly argued. These still exist as the *K'ao-i* (or 'Examination of Differences'), usually inserted in the text of the *Mirror* as a commentary.

Like all Confucian historians, Ssu-ma Kuang was a moralist and he inserts from time to time reflections on political morality arising from particular events, but his real purpose was to give a true, unvarnished record which would convey its own moral message. The moralist got the upper hand over the historian in Chu Hsi (1131–1200), the Aquinas of neo-Confucianism, among whose incredibly numerous works is an abridgement of Ssu-ma Kuang's *Mirror* designed to turn it into a new *Spring and Autumn Annals*, expressing moral judgements in the work itself by appropriate terminology and even by distorting the facts. Thus, to Ssu-ma Kuang, a usurper might be deplorable but he had existed and the records of his time had to be put under his reign. To Chu Hsi a usurper's year names were illegitimate and had to be treated as if they had never existed, years being numbered as if the last legitimate ruler had continued to reign.

Unfortunately Chu Hsi's *Kang-mu* and not Ssu-ma Kuang's *Mirror* became the authoritative history read by all but the specialists. This was but one aspect of the dominance of a rigid neo-Confucian orthodoxy which stifled intellectual life in the Ming period (1368–1644), when China turned in on herself after the expulsion of the Mongols. Though many works of history were produced, they are not of great interest in a creative or critical sense. It took the breakdown of the Ming and the Manchu conquest to reawaken the critical spirit that had flourished so vigorously in Sung and give birth to a remarkable last flowering of traditional Chinese scholarship.

The reaction against both neo-Confucian orthodoxy and the intuitional idealism of the Wang Yang-ming school, which had provided the only alternative, led to a renewal of the 'search for evidence' (*k'ao-cheng*) as the way to real knowledge. This spirit, personified in its beginnings by the heroic Ku Yen-wu (1613–82) who stubbornly refused to accommodate himself to the alien rulers of the new dynasty, spread into all fields of intellectual life, not least historiography. Though not remarkable for works of synthetic history, the Ch'ing scholars set high standards in critical reappraisal of the past. Every serious student of Chinese history at the present day must build on the foundations they laid and our task would be immensely greater if we did not have their works.

Ku Yen-wu devoted considerable attention to history. His published notebooks, the *Jih-chih lu*, contain numerous comments based on his reading of historical works. He was not concerned merely with an antiquarian collecting of facts about the past but used history as a means of learning about and understanding the society in which he lived. For example, he writes about the history of the Great Wall, about the differences between North and South China in regard to land tenure and slave-owning, and about the problems of the examination system at different periods.

Of the Ch'ing Dynasty text critics who worked in the field of history Wang Ming-sheng, author of the *Shih-ch'i shih shang-ch'üeh* (the 'Critical Study of the Seventeen Histories'), and

Ch'ien Ta-hsin (1728–1800), author of the *Erh-shih-i shih k'ao-i* (the 'Examination of Differences in the Twenty-one Histories'), were the most notable. Both of them brought a vast scholarship to bear on the detailed textual criticism of the Standard Histories, adducing all sorts of evidence from private works, inscriptions, documentary collections, &c., to correct points of detail. From time to time they would go beyond the limits of criticism of detail to question received judgements about men and events, as when Wang Ming-sheng argued in favour of a group of men, including the famous writer Liu Tsung-yüan, who had had a brief moment of power in the reign of the T'ang emperor Shun-tsung (A.D. 805) and had then fallen into disgrace and ever afterwards been considered as a treacherous and seditious faction. Wang said that they had really been high-minded reformers, traduced by the court eunuchs whom they had tried to curb. This may not seem very remarkable to us now, but it took a good deal of independence of mind in traditional China, where a judicial condemnation, given the stamp of approval in official history and also by Ssu-ma Kuang in his *Comprehensive Mirror*, would have been generally accepted as unquestionable.

Standing a little apart from these text critics is Chao I (1727–1814), author of the *Nien-erh shih cha-chi* (the 'Notes on the Twenty-two Histories'). Whereas they had sought to supplement and correct the standard histories by additional material, his notes arose out of careful reading and re-reading of the histories themselves. In some cases he is concerned to point out inconsistencies between different chapters but he also discusses in a general way the origins of the various histories and, most interesting of all, makes generalizations about institutions, social structure, and secular trends. Many of the ideas which he started have sown seed that has borne fruit in the modern historiography of this century.

But the most original mind of all the Ch'ing historians was

Chang Hsüeh-ch'eng (1738–1801).[1] Chang Hsüeh-ch'eng was not a text critic like the contemporaries we have been discussing. Indeed, he was in conscious opposition to what he considered to be their excessive concern for minutiae and their failure to understand the true purpose of history. Like Liu Chih-chi and Ssu-ma Kuang he was infatuated by history from an early age. To him, history was an all-embracing concept which ought to comprehend the whole of the Chinese literary tradition. 'The sixfold Canon is all history' is his most famous saying. Unfortunately his many ambitious plans for major works, such as a new history of Sung which should break away from the tyranny of the chronicle form, and for local histories, came to nothing. All that we have of his lifetime of brooding on the meaning of history is a few essays and what can be gathered from incidental comments in letters and the like. His ideas had little influence at the time and were largely forgotten after his death. They have been revived in recent times and have provided a fruitful source of inspiration for the new historians of this century. Professor Demiéville likens him justly to the Italian philosopher-historian Giambattista Vico, who was also in advance of his age and has only had real recognition in recent times.

In the long-drawn-out, ever-worsening crisis which China underwent in the nineteenth century with the decline of the Ch'ing Dynasty and the imperialistic encroachments of the West, historical studies ceased to make progress and the next event of importance is the impact of Western ideas which has dominated the present century. Any detailed study of this lies outside the scope of the present work but it is important to stress that acquaintance with Western historiography has not meant simply the introduction of new ideals and techniques to replace an outworn and dead tradition. Rather it has meant the renovation and revival of the best parts of that tradition. There have

[1] See P. Demiéville, 'Chang Hsüeh-ch'eng and his Historiography', in Beasley and Pulleyblank, op. cit., pp. 167–85.

been more freedom and opportunities to escape from the excessively annalistic and scissors-and-paste forms of the past (sometimes, it must be confessed, old habits die hard), and archaeology has revealed wholly new types of source material; but in their critical handling of sources Chinese scholars of today are following in the footsteps of their eighteenth-century predecessors and have little to learn from the West. Increased knowledge of the outside world has chiefly brought liberation from orthodoxies that it was previously inconceivable to question, simply by providing an external standpoint and material for comparison that was formerly almost wholly lacking.

What importance has traditional Chinese historiography for the West? Perhaps it is not different in kind from the contribution which knowledge of Western history has made to Chinese conceptions of the past. The plurality of European civilization has always meant that there was more possibility within its own cultural tradition for points of comparison. Even so, the first knowledge of China, as of other non-European civilizations, had a tremendous liberating effect on the thinking of men of the seventeenth and eighteenth centuries. Even erroneous or vastly oversimplified information about China called into question hallowed prejudices and was used as ammunition by critics of orthodoxy. We are past that stage, and a remotely seen China can no longer serve the function of a Land of Nowhere. But now in the twentieth century, when the world seems fated to be engulfed in a common pattern of 'Western' or 'modern' civilization, it is more important than ever that we should be able to find in a real knowledge of China's independent cultural tradition a point of comparison and criticism. For this purpose China's great and still living historiographical tradition has much to offer.

E. G. Pulleyblank

4

THE HERITAGE OF CHINESE ART

1. *Our Knowledge of Chinese Art*

WHEN barriers of time, distance, or language close all other doors, a civilization may still be approached through its arts; for at least a part of our response to art is direct and immediate. Certainly in the twentieth century, many people in the Western world have derived their chief experience of Chinese culture from Chinese porcelain, bronzes, and paintings in Western collections; while the great Exhibition at Burlington House in 1935–6, the Venice Exhibition of 1954 on the 700th anniversary of the birth of Marco Polo, and the smaller selection of Palace Museum Treasures that toured the United States in 1961–2— these and other exhibitions have left a profound impression on the mind of the Western public. But is it more than an impression? Does it, we must ask, carry with it any understanding of Chinese culture, and has it inspired people to study aspects of Chinese civilization other than art itself?

When we read accounts of Chinese art written by Western scholars and critics who are not themselves students of China, we are often dismayed to find how little light they cast, and how odd the angle often is. So great an authority as Bernard Berenson, who, as he observed, 'had the good fortune to be one of the first to feel the beauty of the exotic arts', and himself built up a small but choice collection of Chinese painting and sculpture, found in it no more than a superficial charm. 'The exotic arts soon weary', he wrote in his *Aesthetics and History*. 'As is the case with Yogi philosophies, Mazdanianism [*sic*] and similar appeals, it is a craving for mere otherness that draws us to them rather than any unique superiority of their own. Nor can we devote ourselves with advantage to intensive study of them.' Berenson could not take Chinese art seriously because it did not accord with his concept of values, of which he gave this definition: 'Human values depend on our physical make-up, on the way our brain, belly, and members act, and on the demands made by the needs, appetites, and impulses they give rise to. It is with these that we treat if we wish to come to any understanding of values.'[1] Berenson saw these values expressed, and these appetites gratified, through the 'tactile values' of the art of classical and Renaissance Europe, and he was unable to appreciate any tradition in which they were not dominant. Roger Fry, on the other hand, though no better informed on Chinese culture in general, was acutely sensitive to what he called the 'linear rhythms' of Chinese art,[2] and he well understood the vitality and stylistic unity that these rhythms give to Chinese art as a whole.

In general, however, Western observers have, like Berenson, been blind to the higher manifestations of Chinese art. Marco Polo, who spent years at the court of Kublai Khan, scarcely seems to have been aware of it. As Eileen Power once pointed out, he must have met the great minister and amateur painter Chao Meng-fu; he would almost certainly have seen him, and his wife, the noted bamboo painter Kuan Tao-sheng, at work with the brush.[3] Yet he never mentions them. When Western writers do refer to Chinese painting, it is as often as not merely to condemn it for failing to achieve the same ends, and employ the same techniques, as those of Western painters. The verdict of Matteo Ricci, whose account of Chinese civilization in general is remarkable for its penetration and accuracy, is severe: Chinese

---

[1] *Aesthetics and History* (New York, 1948), p. 246.

[2] Cf. his essay 'The Significance of Chinese Art', in *Chinese Art* (London, 1935).

[3] 'Marco Polo', in Hsiao Ch'ien, ed., *A Harp with a Thousand Strings* (London, 1944), pp. 307–8.

painters, he comments, 'know nothing of the art of painting in oil or of perspective in their pictures, with the result that their productions are likely to resemble the dead rather than the living'. Alvarez de Semedo, whose account was first published in English in 1641, echoes this view. 'In *painting*', he writes, 'they have more curiositie than perfection. They know not how to make use of either *Oyles* or *Shadowing* in the art. . . .' But, he goes on, 'at present there are some of them, who have been taught by us, that use *Oyles*, and are come to make perfect pictures'. The *Teutsche Akademie* of Joachim von Sandrart, published in 1675, was the first European history of art to devote any space at all to Chinese painting. Beyond describing some paintings that he had seen in Rome (brought back, presumably, by the Jesuits), Sandrart has little praise for it, while he illustrates his account with a portrait of a negro named Higiemondo, whom he calls 'the greatest Chinese painter'.[1] Needless to say, the Chinese, when, rarely, they deigned to take note of Western painting, were equally critical. While Europe accused China of a total lack of perspective, Tsou I-kuei, court artist to Ch'ien-lung, was criticizing the Jesuit painters for a slavish adherence to such technical tricks. 'Even if they attain perfection', he commented, 'it is merely craftsmanship. Thus foreign painting cannot be called art.' These instances, taken at random, show that the mere confrontation with an 'exotic' art does not necessarily break down barriers and open doors. So long as a culture feels itself to be perfectly self-contained and self-sufficient, as did both China and Europe in the eighteenth century, a style may be borrowed, played with, and abandoned, leaving no permanent mark on the culture that borrowed it. A perfect instance of this is the history of *chinoiserie*.

During the first half of the seventeenth century the huge

---

[1] These and other early European accounts of Chinese painting are discussed in my 'Sandrart on Chinese Painting', *Oriental Art*, i. 4 (Spring 1949), pp. 159–61.

quantities of blue and white porcelain imported by the Dutch aroused great enthusiasm in Europe—not for Chinese culture, however, but simply for Chinese blue and white. Pieces changed hands at enormous prices. In 1613, Elizabeth, daughter of Charles I, was given as a wedding present 'a cabinet of China worke' worth £10,000. Soon blue and white was being copied in faience at Delft and Frankfurt, and Chinese lacquered furniture was being cleverly imitated by European cabinet-makers. A second wave of enthusiasm for things Chinese struck Europe in the middle of the eighteenth century; but by this time Chinese exporters had had the opportunity to study their market, and porcelain, often sent out 'in the blank' from Europe, was painted in the European taste. Pseudo-Chinese motifs, inspired by porcelain, gave added charm and gaiety to rococo decoration. Eighteenth-century *chinoiserie* was thus not an imitation of Chinese art, but a purely European style, perfectly suited to the mood of the times.[1] But there was no place for its playful arabesques in the severe neo-Classic art of the Napoleonic era. By 1800 Europe's flirtation with Chinese art (for it was no more than that) was nearly over. Charles Lamb's 'almost feminine partiality to old China', his *Dissertation upon Roast Pig*, and his whimsical description of the decoration on the side of a porcelain jar ('that world before perspective') represent almost the last gestures of affection before the tie was severed.

The Industrial Revolution and the Opium Wars robbed Europe of her old respect for the Middle Kingdom. No longer could her philosophy and institutions be held up as models for Europe to follow, as they had been for the writers of the Enlightenment. Throughout the greater part of the nineteenth century Europe remained indifferent to the higher values of Chinese civilization, if not actively hostile; for how could a nation which the missionaries taught was barbarous and inhuman

---

[1] This point is well brought out in Hugh Honour's excellent survey *Chinoiserie: the Vision of Cathay* (London, 1961).

have produced a great art? Moreover, Europe was forging ahead into the era of the machine, and China could offer her little but tea. Even that precious commodity porcelain was no longer in great demand, except by collectors; for in 1709, after a century of intense efforts in Holland and Germany, true porcelain had been perfected by Johannes Böttger at Dresden, and by now Europe's own factories were producing all she needed.

As the nineteenth century progressed, China and Chinese art sank still lower in European eyes. The new race of art historians, intent on cultivating the virgin soil of Europe, had no time to turn their eyes eastwards. During the first eighty years of the century almost the only significant contribution to the study of Chinese art was Stanislas Julien's translation of the *Ching-te-chen t'ao-lu*, an eighteenth-century description of the great pottery factory, which appeared in 1856. More characteristic of the whimsical antiquarianism of the age is the *Notices of Chinese Seals Found in Ireland*, a paper read before the Belfast Literary Society in 1850, describing a number of Chinese porcelain seals bearing archaic characters which had been picked up in widely scattered places in Ireland during the preceding fifty years. The author, who considered them to be of the highest antiquity, suggested that they might have been brought over by a party of Irish monks from a tour of the Near East in the ninth century. The seals were certainly not ancient, but how they came to be scattered over the Irish bogs is a mystery. Somewhat more serious was P. P. Thoms's *Dissertation on the Ancient Chinese Vases of the Shang Dynasty*, occasioned by the display at the Great Exhibition of 1851 of selected engravings from an edition of the Sung imperial catalogue *Po-ku t'u-lu*. It is noteworthy that both his work and Julien's were translations of Chinese texts, and not original studies of actual objects in Western collections. Europe had to wait almost until the end of the century before the disciplines and techniques of the art historian could be applied to Chinese art itself.

The impetus came primarily from the collectors. The destruction of the Summer Palace in 1861 had released a flood of *objets d'art*, which Chinese dealers lost no time in offering to the new foreign residents of the treaty ports. Thereafter, the increasing pace of modernization of China, the opening up of the interior, the chaos of revolution, war, and civil war, the rapid rise and fall of family fortunes, all combined to create a state of extreme fluidity; family collections were broken up and their treasures scattered, while indiscriminate digging and the pillaging of vast numbers of tombs produced still more. By the nineteen-thirties the great public collections in London, Paris, Berlin, Washington, New York, Boston, Chicago, and Kansas City—to name but a few—contained riches the like of which could not be seen in China outside the Palace Collection. In certain respects, indeed—notably in early ceramics and sculpture—they were far richer.

Parallel to these public collections, and destined eventually still further to augment them, were the great private collections built up, for example, by Grandidier in Paris, Stoclet in Brussels, Von der Heydt in Ascona, Eumorfopoulos, Oppenheim, and Percival David in London, Freer in Detroit. As the collections grew, so did the study of Chinese art and archaeology begin to enter a new phase. An important landmark was M. Paléologue's *L'Art chinois* published in 1887, which contained the first account of Chinese painting based on Chinese literary sources. A more detailed treatment of some aspects was given by Friedrich Hirth in his *Scraps from a Collector's Notebook* (1905). Ernest Fenollosa's *Epochs of Chinese and Japanese Art*, written at the turn of the century (though not published till 1912), was epoch-making in the breadth of its treatment. But Fenollosa saw Chinese art through Japanese eyes; he praised what they admired—notably, of course, romantic landscape-painting of the Southern Sung—and ignored the rest. In the study of Chinese ceramics British scholars have for long held a leading place. In

1904–7 Stephen Bushell published his *Chinese Art* in two volumes, a work which, because it makes such excellent use of Chinese sources, is still consulted on ceramics today, while the later work of Hobson, Honey, and other experts, and the activities of the Oriental Ceramic Society of London, have consolidated Britain's position in this respect. Meanwhile, the explorations of Sir Aurel Stein, Paul Pelliot, and Sven Hedin in Central Asia, and the archaeological discoveries of Édouard Chavannes and J. G. Andersson in China proper, were making it possible for the first time to relate Chinese art to its geographical and archaeological setting.[1]

Western study of Chinese painting has always lagged, partly because until recently very few Chinese paintings of any quality were to be seen outside China and Japan, partly because it demanded a knowledge of Chinese language and literature. It is notable that Arthur Waley's excellent *Introduction to the Study of Chinese Painting* (1923), like the earlier works of Hirth and Herbert Giles, was based on literary sources rather than on actual paintings. The encyclopedic compilations of Osvald Sirén,[2] drawn from collections in China, Japan, and the West, have helped to present some of the vast wealth of material that is available for study, and today a new generation of scholars (chiefly in America), widely travelled and rigorously trained, are beginning to consolidate the study of Chinese painting on a level of scholarship comparable with that expected of historians of Western art.

Nevertheless, it is not possible for Western scholars, however brilliant or well-trained, to outstrip the pace of developments in

[1] Among general Western surveys of Chinese art are the following: Sir Leigh Ashton and Basil Gray, *Chinese Art* (London, 1951); Laurence Sickman and Alexander Soper, *The Art and Architecture of China* (London, 1956); William Willetts, *Chinese Art* (two vols.; London, 1958); and Michael Sullivan, *An Introduction to Chinese Art* (London, 1961).

[2] Most notably his monumental *Chinese Painting: Leading Masters and Principles* (seven vols.; London, 1956 and 1958).

China itself. Since 1950, archaeological excavation and the preservation of ancient monuments have been carried out with a speed and thoroughness that has left both the country's admirers, and her detractors, gasping. To take a few examples: the picture of prehistoric archaeology given by Andersson has been revised and enormously extended; several ancient capitals, including an early Shang city at Chengchow, have been discovered; the palace of the T'ang emperors at Sian has been located and excavated; highly important discoveries of Buddhist cave temples and of ceramic factories have been made;[1] while the paintings that have been brought to light go far towards making up for the losses to foreign collections suffered during the first half of the twentieth century.

This happy situation has brought a significant change in the relationship between Western scholars of Chinese art and archaeology and the subject of their study. Until recently it could be said that the picture which they presented was in part at least based on their own discoveries, explorations, and excavations in China. They knew the material and its sources at first hand. Now, for the time being at least, they must be spectators. Much of their time is taken up with absorbing the published researches of Chinese scholars and in the study of the vast collections already housed in their own museums. This situation is not a matter for regret, however. On the contrary, when we consider that it has been brought about by the energy with which China has taken the study and conservation of her artistic heritage into her own hands, it should rather be a cause for rejoicing.

[1] The results of this intense activity are published in Chinese archaeological journals such as *K'ao-ku hsüeh-pao*, *K'ao-ku t'ung-hsün*, and *Wen wu*; while many separate reports and monographs have also appeared. See also my *Introduction*; and for more detailed accounts William Watson, *Archaeology in China* (London, 1960), and *China Before the Han Dynasty* (London, 1961); and Cheng Te-k'un, *Archaeology in China*, vol. ii: Shang China (Cambridge, 1960).

11. *The Chinese Craftsman*

The remainder of this chapter will be devoted to a short survey of some of the essential qualities in Chinese arts and crafts, and to a consideration of how the Chinese themselves regard their own artistic heritage, and how Chinese art has responded, or failed to respond, to foreign influences. By answering these questions, however sketchily, we will go some way towards defining China's unique contribution to the art of the world.

BRONZE

Chinese civilization can boast of no great ancient monuments comparable with those of Western Asia and the Mediterranean world. Even the Great Wall, as we see it today, is—contrary to popular opinion—largely a creation of the Ming Dynasty. Apart from now shapeless mounds, almost nothing survives above ground of the cities and tombs of Shang, Chou, and Han, while their timber palaces and ancestral shrines have all crumbled to dust. So it is difficult for us to visualize the court ceremonies and sacrificial rites that were performed in them. It would be harder still if the vessels used in these rites had not been interred with the dead, and so preserved for our admiration today.

The archaic bronzes of Shang and Chou have long been treasured both as ritual vessels by the emperors, and as objects of historical study by antiquarians; while at least since the T'ang and Sung Dynasties they have been copied and forged. But it is only in the twentieth century that their chief place of origin has been found. Throughout the later years of the nineteenth century mysterious 'dragon bones' were being brought to the drug-stores of Honan, where they were ground up and sold as restoratives. Some, it was noticed, bore incised markings rather similar to those of inscriptions on the oldest of the bronze vessels. These were in fact the oracle bones used in divination by the Shang rulers. Eventually they were traced to Anyang, where farmers and dealers' agents proceeded to search the ground for more specimens. They were richly rewarded, not only with more oracle bones, but with the contents of the tombs of the late Shang rulers and aristocracy as well. By the mid-twenties, the flow of Shang ritual bronze vessels into the art market had reached such alarming proportions—largely owing to the interest shown in them by foreign museums and collectors—that the government at last took control. In 1927 the Academia Sinica began the protection and excavation of the Shang sites at Anyang, which, but for a break during the Pacific War, has continued ever since. Within the last ten years the picture of Shang culture has been immensely enlarged by the discovery of the still earlier capital at Chengchow, and of scores of less important Shang sites scattered over North China.

While to the Western eye the ritual bronzes of Shang and Chou are admirable chiefly for the power of their forms and the intense vitality of their decoration, to the Chinese antiquarian their value lies mainly in their historical associations, particularly when they are inscribed. Shang vessels bear short inscriptions or none at all, but those of the early and middle centuries of the Chou Dynasty, giving details of the circumstances of their bestowal on a feudal prince, sometimes run into several hundred characters, and thus make the vessel a valuable historical document. The early vessels often bear the injunction to the owner's descendants 'for ever to treasure and use it'. But in fact the vessels were often placed in his tomb, and thus came in time to acquire the infinitely varied patina that is so highly valued by Western connoisseurs. Chinese collectors are not seduced by these accidental effects, and often rub down or even wax their bronzes.

Bronze-casting had been developed in Chaldea at least a thousand years before its first appearance in China, and it is likely, though not certain, that the craft was introduced, and not

PLATE I

Square ritual bronze vessel of type *fang-i*. Ht. 13⅞ in. Beginning of Western Chou
(late eleventh century B.C.)

discovered independently by the Chinese. However, the acquisition of the technique did not involve any artistic dependence upon the Near East, and the ritual bronzes of late Shang and early Chou are not only purely Chinese in form and decoration, but in point of technique far superior to any produced beyond her frontiers. Indeed, they have never been equalled. It was long

FIG. 1. *T'ao-t'ieh* mask decorating a bronze vessel of type *fang-i*. Early Chou Dynasty. Freer Gallery, Washington.

thought that they were cast by the *cire perdue* method: for how, it was argued, could detail of such sharpness and precision have been modelled except in wax? But the recent discovery of thousands of pottery moulds at the sites of ancient foundries makes it clear that most, if not all, of the vessels, weapons, chariot-fittings, and other artefacts were cast in sectional moulds.

Although the zoomorphic motifs that adorn the ritual vessels have been the subject of endless research and speculation, their precise meaning has still not been elucidated. There can be little doubt, however, that the most powerful of them, the monster mask called *t'ao-t'ieh*, which is sometimes feline, sometimes bovine, sometimes composite, had a protective role, though whether it protected the participants in the rite, or the contents

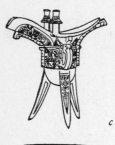

of the vessel itself, is not clear. The cicada, which often appeared on the legs of vessels, is a very ancient symbol for rebirth or long life, the dragon for rain; but again, whether they carried those symbolic meanings in the Shang Dynasty it is impossible to say, and the inscriptions on the vessels never refer to the motifs that adorn them. Today we can only marvel at their beauty, achieved by the marriage of powerful form with those 'linear rhythms' in the decoration which Roger Fry so rightly saw as being uniquely Chinese.

A typical vessel is the powerfully modelled *fang-i* in the Freer Gallery, Washington, illustrated in Plate 1. This is a square container, probably though not certainly for wine, with a deep lid and a large knob. The decoration on the bulging sides consists chiefly of *t'ao-t'ieh*, while below the lip is a two-bodied dragon, and birds adorn the base. The heavy hooked flanges and the long inscription inside the base both help to date this vessel in the first decades of the Chou Dynasty, but in other respects it represents a continuation of the style of the culminating period at Anyang. The blend of strength, vitality, elegance, and fine craftsmanship makes this a masterpiece of the bronze-caster's art.

The detailed researches on the archaic bronzes carried out by Jung Keng, Li Chi, Kuo Mo-jo, and Ch'en Meng-chia in

FIG. 2 (*a–d*). Bronzes of late Shang and early Chou. *a. li; b. ku; c. chüeh; d. hu.* (After Mizuno.)

China, and by Karlgren, Yetts, Wenley, and others in the West, combined with the results of the scientific excavation of the last thirty years, have laid down the main lines of the evolution of the bronze art in China, from its first beginning in the simple, thinly cast vessels of Chengchow.[1] The culmination of the classic phase came in the bronzes of the last century at Anyang, which are unmatched in their co-ordinated power and perfection of technique. The Chou took over the arts and rituals of the conquered Shang, and at first there was only a gradual modification in the bronze style. But by the middle of the ninth century B.C. the expansion of the Chou empire had brought contact with neighbouring cultures, and with it a much more radical change took place. Old shapes disappear, forms become coarser, the hallowed *k'uei* dragon and *t'ao-t'ieh* dissolve in

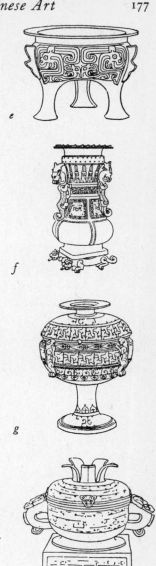

e

f

g

h

[1] For a recent discussion of the evolution of the bronze art in China, see William Watson, *Ancient Chinese Bronzes* (London, 1962). Full details of the bronze ritual vessel illustrated in Plate 1, with a translation of the inscription, are given in J. E. Lodge, A. G. Wenley, and J. A. Pope, *Chinese Bronzes Acquired during the Administration of John Ellerton Lodge* (Washington, 1946).

FIG. 2 (*e–h*). Bronzes of middle and late Chou. *e. li; f. hu; g. tou; h. kuei.* (After Mizuno.)

endless wavelike meanders, chevrons, and scale patterns. Then, as Chou declines and the feudal states gain in power, local stylistic variations become recognizable for the first time. Finally, under the Warring States, a third change occurs. The vessels become elegant and refined, as projecting surfaces are smoothed away; much use is made of geometric decoration inlaid in gold and silver; the *t'ao-t'ieh* returns as a decorative archaism, and there appear new kinds of vessel made as much for domestic delight as for ritual use. Indeed, the very ritual itself has undergone a significant change. Whereas the rites of Shang and Chou were undertaken for the purpose of securing blessing and protection, those of late Chou have become something very different—a means of demonstrating that society is attuned to the workings of nature, and of showing a sense of fitness, of what kind of behaviour is harmonious and appropriate. As the philosopher Hsün-tzu put it in the third century B.C., 'Sacrifice is to express a person's feeling of remembrance and longing. As to the fullness of the sense of loyalty and affection, the richness of ritual and beauty—these none but the sage can understand. Sacrifice is something that the sage clearly understands, the scholar-gentlemen contentedly perform, the officials consider as a duty, and the common people consider as established custom.'[1] Hsün-tzu goes on to say that while gentlemen consider it the 'way of man' the common people still adhere to the old notion that it has to do with the spirits.

What is remarkable, and entirely new, is Hsün-tzu's emphasis upon the aesthetic aspect of the rites, 'the richness of ritual and beauty', a concept which is given visible expression in the new refinement and elegance of the bronze vessels of this period. This concept, moreover, will from this time forward be instinctive in the outlook of the Chinese gentleman. Just as ritual, and its extension through music, poetry, and the shape and decoration

[1] Quoted by Wm. Theodore de Bary, ed., *Sources of Chinese Tradition* (New York and London, 1960), p. 124.

of the objects used in it, was the gentleman's means of demonstrating that he was attuned to the Will of Heaven, so was aesthetic beauty felt to be what results when the artist gives sincere expression to his intuitive awareness of natural order. Beauty, therefore, is what conduces to order, harmony, tranquillity. In later centuries this ideal found its noblest expression in the landscape-painting of the tenth century and Northern Sung. Its roots, as this passage from Hsün-tzu shows, lie in that stage in the development of Chinese civilization when men first conceived of ritual as being 'beautiful'.

JADE

Considered simply as a material, jade has had a ritual significance in Chinese cultural history even greater than that of bronze. Since the dawn of history, and earlier, it has been regarded with special reverence. Excavations of neolithic graves in North China suggest that weapons and ornaments of jade were reserved for chiefs and other important personages. After the coming of bronze, jade weapons and other objects continued to have a purely ritual function as symbols of rank in the complex hierarchy of feudal China. Under the early Chou, for example, the king in audience held a broad perforated sceptre (*chen kuei*); the duke, prince, and earl other forms of sceptres; the viscount and baron a flat perforated *pi* disk decorated with a spiral 'grain pattern'. When proclamations were issued, troops mobilized, or imperial messages carried, the official concerned carried the appropriate jade object as an emblem of his authority. Thus, throughout early Chinese history, jade played its part in maintaining the social order.

The extraordinary hardness of the stone led to the belief, not only that it was itself indestructible, but that it rendered imperishable all that came in contact with it. For this reason the corpse was set about with ritual jades which protected it from harm and decay, and at the same time prevented noxious influences from escaping from the grave. The jade *pi* disk, which by Chou times had come to be looked on as a symbol of Heaven, was placed on the back of the corpse; the *ts'ung*, a tube squared on the outside, symbolizing Earth (Plate 2), was placed under the abdomen; to the east of the body was set a *kuei* sceptre, to the west a *hu* tiger, to the north (at the feet) a *huang* (half sceptre), to the south a *chang* (short stubby *kuei*); while the seven orifices of the body were sealed with jade plugs and caps.

Beside these specific ritual functions, jade has a much wider significance in Chinese eyes, aptly summarized in a well-known definition in the Han dictionary *Shuo-wen chieh-tzu*. 'Jade is the fairest of stones', it runs. 'It is endowed with five virtues. Charity is typified by its lustre, bright yet warm; rectitude by its translucency, revealing the colour and markings within; wisdom by the purity and penetrating quality of its note when the stone is struck; courage, in that it may be broken, but cannot be bent; equity, in that it has sharp angles, which yet injure none.'[1] The Chinese language is rich in words having the jade element as radical. Many carry the meaning precious, pure, beautiful, particularly in regard to women, while the word is also an epithet for the unsullied virtue of the emperor. Thus the word *yü* unites in itself moral and aesthetic beauty, carrying much the same sense as gold to us, as when we speak of 'a heart of gold', or *The Golden Treasury*. Many a scholar would set objects of jade on his desk, not merely as ornaments but also because of their associations, while he would dangle from his belt one or two small jades worn smooth by repeated fondling. It was not essential that the objects themselves be ancient; it was enough that their shapes should be traditional. Thus he could indulge to the full his passion for this beautiful stone, knowing that its moral, ritual, and historical worth would more than justify its purely sensuous appeal.

[1] Quoted by S. Howard Hansford, *Chinese Jade Carving* (London, 1950), p. 31.

PLATE 2

Jade ritual *ts'ung* tube. Ht. 19⅝ in.
Early Chou Dynasty

Part of the value of jade arose from its very hardness, from the patience, industry, and skill needed to fashion this most intractable of stones into objects of such exquisite refinement and beauty. Being harder than steel, jade must be cut with an abrasive mixed with water. In early times this abrasive was quartz sand or crushed garnets, but today corundum (emery) and the even harder synthetic carborundum are generally employed. Using an abrasive, it is possible to cut a hole in a slab of jade even with a bamboo drill. Modern writers have described in detail the evolution of the craft from ancient times, and have shown how the invention of the rotary cutting disk and iron drill enlarged the scope of the carver's art. Already in the Han Dynasty the lapidary was carving animals and figures in the full round, and was learning to exploit the variety of colour in the pebbles, leading eventually to the miraculous craftsmanship of the eighteenth century, when the skilful use of the drill made it possible for the carver to cut a chain from a single slab of jade. After a decline in the nineteenth century, the craft has undergone a vigorous revival in the twentieth, and it has been said that there is no miracle of eighteenth-century craftsmanship that could not be repeated by the carvers of today.

The source of the true jade stone, nephrite, in the mountain slopes and river beds of Khotan in Central Asia has long been known. Chinese authorities have always claimed that jade was also found in China proper. The fifth-century author Huang Chao, for example, wrote a work, now lost, but quoted in the *Pen-ts'ao kang-mu* (1596), in which he enumerated a number of sources of the stone within the confines of the Eighteen Provinces. In the twentieth century the cold light of Western scholarship has been turned on this famous passage, and its testimony discounted on the very reasonable ground that there was no archaeological or geological evidence to support it. An additional reason for scepticism was the fact that the Chinese traditionally class a number of other ornamental stones such as marble and serpentine as *yü*, and it has been assumed that it was to stones of this kind that Huang Chao referred. However, recent discoveries suggest that there are grounds for accepting the traditional view, at least in part. A pure jade discovered near Nanyang in Honan has been geologically identified as nephrite, while a noted jade-carver in Peking, who certainly would not confuse true jade with serpentine, has reported that he was being supplied with jade from Honan. This is but one of many instances of the extent to which the evidence of the archaeologist and explorer in modern China is refuting the sceptics, and confirming traditional Chinese views.

TEXTILES

Europe had first come to learn of the Central Asian sources of Chinese jade through the Jesuit traveller Benedict de Goes (or Bento Göes) who visited the area in 1603. His account of it was incorporated in the journals of Matteo Ricci, published in 1615. The first accurate picture of Chinese bronze, sculpture, and architecture was also presented by Ricci. Europe's familiarity with Chinese textiles has a far longer history.

The great caravan route across Central Asia to the eastern shores of the Mediterranean was already bringing Chinese silks to Rome before the end of the first century A.D. The more the women of Rome craved this gossamer material, the more forcefully did their grave husbands express their disapproval. 'I see silken clothes, if you can call them clothes at all,' wrote Seneca, 'that in no degree afford protection either to the body or to the modesty of the wearer, and clad in which no woman could honestly swear she is not naked.'[1] However, such garments were not worn by the Chinese themselves, who have always shown extreme propriety in matters of dress, but were made from Chinese silks split and rewoven in Syria.

The origins of Chinese sericulture are lost in the mists of

[1] Quoted by Hugh Honour in *Chinoiserie: the Vision of Cathay*, p. 31.

antiquity. Legend has it that it was the wife of the Yellow Emperor herself who first taught the art to her people, and up to modern times the empress has annually sacrificed in her temple in the capital. Evidence of textile weaving has been found in the remains of the large neolithic village of Pan-p'o in Shensi, while under the Shang and Chou, bronze objects were

Fig. 3. Detail of polychrome silk textile discovered at Lou-lan. Han Dynasty.

sometimes wrapped in silk for placing in the tomb. The weave, fossilized as it were in the corroded metal, can still be seen. Under the Han, vast quantities of silk were woven for export. In 16 B.C., for example, the emperor distributed a million rolls along the northern frontier, hoping thereby to sinicize, and soften, China's marauding neighbours. Figured and embroidered silks have been found in Chinese and barbarian graves in Mongolia, Sinkiang, and Southern Siberia. Before the end of the Chou Dynasty fair copies of documents were being written on silk, after rough drafts had been first composed on wooden or bamboo slips; while the earliest Chinese painting yet discovered, depicting a woman with phoenix and dragon, was executed on a silk panel of the fifth or fourth century B.C. unearthed at Changsha.

Silk garments became progressively more gorgeous with the passage of time. The Twelve Symbols which had decorated the robes of the Chou emperors continued to appear on ceremonial robes up to the end of the Ch'ing Dynasty.[1] Under Ming and Ch'ing, robes embroidered with dragons were worn by the emperor and high officials, while from the Yüan Dynasty, civil and military ranks were indicated by the birds and animals set in the so-called 'mandarin squares' on the front and back of the official robes. The best of these were woven in *k'o-ssu* ('cut silk'), a technique that is believed to have been invented by the Sogdians, improved by the Uighurs, and perfected by the Chinese in the eleventh century. Far finer in texture than the finest Gobelins tapestry, *k'o-ssu* was also used decoratively, and for translating paintings with the weaver's art.

Before the end of the Middle Ages panels of *k'o-ssu* were already reaching Europe, and were being incorporated in the cathedral vestments at Danzig, Vienna, Regensburg, and elsewhere, while the weavers of Lucca were imitating Chinese phoenixes and dragons, and adapting them to the grammar of late medieval ornament. This was the final stage in the transplanting of the art which had begun in the sixth century, when the emperor Justinian, disturbed at the drain on the economy that the import of silk was causing, had encouraged the smuggling of silkworms into Byzantium—an event which provoked a characteristic comment from Gibbon: 'I am not insensible of the benefits of elegant luxury,' he wrote, 'yet I reflect with some pain that, if the importers of silk had introduced the art of printing, already practised by the Chinese,'—here Gibbon anticipates the discovery by perhaps two hundred years—'the

[1] For a good general account of this subject see Schuyler Cammann, *China's Dragon Robes* (New York, 1952).

comedies of Menander and the entire decads of Livy would have been perpetuated in the editions of the sixth century.'

LACQUER

The decorative arts of the Han period are remarkable for their variety, vitality, and essential unity of style. Their vitality is an

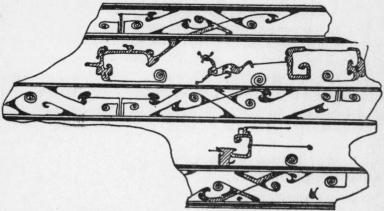

FIG. 4. Painted decoration on fragment of a lacquered toilet box, from Changsha. Third century B.C.

expression of this most vigorous epoch in Chinese history, when China drew strength from all the peoples newly brought within her cultural orbit, and the popular imagination was filled with a richer and more vital folk-lore than ever before or since. The tremendous sense of style which we have seen already in the ritual bronzes now welds all this diverse material into a unified decorative language. The basis of this language is the scroll or volute, which is the product of the natural and spontaneous movement of the craftsman's, or draughtsman's, hand. It lends itself most naturally to the decoration of lacquer-ware, and the most beautiful of Warring States and Han lacquered vessels, boxes, and trays are those adorned with sweeping rhythmic scrolls in light red on a dark reddish-brown ground.[1] On one object the scrolls may take the form of waves, on another hills among which deer are leaping, or scudding clouds where the sky spirits disport themselves. Before the Han, lacquerers were already realizing the potentialities of this fluid medium for figure-painting. A little box of the fourth or third century B.C., found at Changsha, is decorated with a charming processional scene. Under the Han, Chengtu and Kwanghan in modern Szechwan boasted two of the nine official factories of the empire; and their products, bearing the names of their makers, and dates in the first and second centuries A.D., have been found in the tombs of Chinese colonists at Lo-lang in Korea. Even further afield, Chinese lacquer boxes have been excavated from the 'Graeco-Buddhist' city of Begram in Afghanistan.

If we were to gauge the progress of the craft during the Six Dynasties and T'ang from the contents of tombs we would be forced to conclude that it had declined sharply during this long period, if indeed it had not been forgotten altogether. But the lacquer-ware of the eighth century preserved in the Shōsōin repository at Nara in Japan shows that, in the first half of the eighth century, the art had in fact attained a new splendour. Whether the beautiful boxes, arm rests, musical instruments, and other treasures of the emperor Shōmu, many of which are inlaid with mother-of-pearl, were made by Chinese, Japanese, or Korean craftsmen is immaterial, for the style is that of T'ang decorative art at its richest and most magnificent.

Under the Sung, the very few pieces so far excavated point to a much quieter and more restrained taste. The *Ko-ku yao-lun*

---

[1] As yet no useful introductory survey of Chinese lacquer has appeared, but Martin Feddersen's *Chinese Decorative Art* (London, 1961) has a chapter on lacquer, and a full bibliography. See also Sir Harry Garner, 'The Arts of the Ming Dynasty: Introduction', *Transactions of the Oriental Ceramic Society*, 1955–6, 1956–7 (London, 1958); and 'Guri Lacquer of the Ming Dynasty', ibid. 1957–8, 1958–9 (London, 1959).

PLATE 3

a. Cup-stand in red lacquer, carved with phoenixes and peony
scrolls; inside, an inscription by Ch'ien-lung dated equivalent
to 1781. Yung-lo reign-mark. Diam. 6½ in. Ming Dynasty
(fifteenth century)

b. Dish, decorated in underglaze blue with *ch'i-lin* in a landscape
amid fruits and plants, surrounded by a lotus scroll. Diam. 18 in.
Second half of fourteenth century

('Discussion of the Principal Criteria of Antiquities') (1387) tells us that Sung lacquerers were already carving their designs through layers of contrasting colours, but no authentic specimens of this *guri*-lacquer, as the Japanese called it, have yet come to light. Most familiar, however, are the carved red lacquers of Ming and Ch'ing (Plate 3 *a*). The gorgeous colour, the range of their subject-matter, and the variety of techniques employed in carving the designs offer endless satisfaction to the student and collector, while the fact that they were convincingly imitated by Japanese lacquerers adds piquancy to the study of them. Next to porcelain, it was the lacquer-ware imported into Europe in the seventeenth century which inspired the first wave of enthusiasm for things Chinese, and thus gave birth to *chinoiserie*.

ENAMELS

While lacquer-ware and jade-carving were developed independently in China, the art of inlaying enamels was certainly a Western importation, and a late one at that. The earliest true enamelled wares yet discovered are those unearthed in Mycenean sites of the thirteenth to twelfth centuries B.C.[1] At approximately the same time craftsmen at Anyang were inlaying ceremonial bronze weapons with chips of turquoise. Before the end of the Chou Dynasty China had learned the art of glass-making from the West, and glass beads and disks, either as jewels or as substitutes for jade, were being inlaid in bronze garment-hooks and other ornamented objects. But the idea of fusing the molten glass paste into a prepared ground never occurred to the Chinese craftsman.

The *Ko-ku yao-lun* reported that 'inlaid work of the devils' country' (i.e. Arabia) was then being made by Yünnanese craftsmen in Peking, which suggests that the art was introduced from the West in the latter part of the Yüan Dynasty. The Chinese

[1] For a full account see Sir Harry Garner, *Chinese and Japanese Cloisonné Enamels* (London, 1962).

probably based their technique on Islamic rather than Byzantine enamels. Whatever their origin, in point both of beauty and of craftsmanship the Chinese cloisonné enamels of the early Ming are much finer than their Western models. Nor does their subject-matter owe anything to the West. The pictorial themes are borrowed from the popular repertory of Chinese painting, while the lovely flowers and scrolling vines executed in brilliant colours against a background of cobalt blue are very similar to those that decorate blue and white porcelain of the same period. The art remained at a high level throughout the late Ming and early Ch'ing, and the cloisonnés of the reign of Ch'ien-lung almost made up in delicacy and precision for what they lacked of the earlier vitality.

We have not space to dwell upon the many arts and crafts by which the life of the privileged classes was made so agreeable; indeed we need not, for it is precisely with these arts that we in the West are most familiar. Even the most modest collector will have acquired examples of Chinese furniture of recent centuries, or carving in bamboo, ivory, and rhinoceros horn, or jewellery, or the impedimenta of the scholar's desk. Indeed, these charming and exquisite trivia have done much to create in the Western mind the image of Chinese civilization as over-refined. But we may still enjoy these things, and note with pleasure how playfully the Chinese craftsman ignores the limitations of his material; how he will execute a metal shape in porcelain, give a brush-pot of ivory the form and texture of bamboo, an inkstick that of a stone tablet, or a teapot that of a peach.

Much less familiar to Western eyes are the arts of the unprivileged masses. Oblivious of the rise and fall of dynasties and the vagaries of court patronage, the village craftsmen continued to fulfil local needs in a rich and lively craft tradition. One region might specialize in basket-work, another in fan or umbrella making, another in clay toys or in paper-cuts, while the aboriginal tribes of the south-west are famous for their batiks and cross-stitch embroideries. These peasant arts were, of course, completely ignored by Chinese collectors. As China transforms herself into a modern industrialized state, they must inevitably suffer in the long run. In the meantime, however, with active support and encouragement from the government, they are undergoing a vigorous revival.

CERAMICS

Of all the arts of China, that of the potter has exerted the widest influence in the world, and for the longest period. There must be a special magic in a commodity that could soothe the heart of a savage Borneo head-hunter, and convey bouillon to the lips of Louis XIV. All over south-east Asia the native people were buried with Chinese jars, bowls, and dishes of T'ang date and later.[1] A tribe in the Philippines used porcelain bowls in its rain-magic because they rang like a bell when struck, and an early Chinese writer on Luzon reported that the natives of that island could be diverted from attacking a traveller if he left a porcelain bowl on the path; the sultans and caliphs of Western Asia, we are told, believing that Chinese celadon would crack or change colour if poison touched it, would eat off nothing else; the Arab potentates of East Africa decorated their palaces with porcelain dishes inlaid in the walls; and when early in the seventeenth century the Dutch privateers brought ashore at Rotterdam their rich cargoes of porcelain captured from the Portuguese, Europe responded in the same way.

Some of the properties that make Chinese ceramics unique in the world are inherent in the history of the craft, and in the place it has occupied in Chinese life.[2] The shapes range from the

[1] Cf. M. Sullivan, 'Notes on Chinese Export Wares in Southeast Asia', *Trans. O.C.S.*, 1960–1, 1961–2 (London, 1963), pp. 61–77.

[2] For an introduction to the literature of Chinese ceramics, on which so

purely utilitarian to vessels of so exquisite a purity of form and colour that they have no purpose but to gratify the sense of sight and touch. Treasured by emperors and scholars, they have become the subject of poetry, and poems have been written and engraved upon them. Until the growth of the vast factory at Ching-te-chen in the Ming Dynasty imposed a degree of almost mechanical perfection, even the finest wares made for the palace revealed the touch of the potter's hand, giving them a living form utterly different from the static perfection of the Greek vase. This quality is most in evidence in the buoyant shapes of the T'ang stoneware and earthenware, and in the apparently careless way in which the potter allowed the glaze to run down over the body, emphasizing its contour; and even in the more perfectly finished Sung wares this feeling for the living form is never lost.

Fig. 5. Painted pottery vessel from Ma-ch'ang, Kansu. Neolithic period, *c.* 1700–1300 B.C. (After Watson.)

Although the craft is so ancient in China, development has been slow, and not always in a forward direction, reflecting the inability or unwillingness we sometimes encounter in Chinese history to exploit a technical invention. The magnificent painted pottery of the late neolithic period, for example, was followed by the relatively lifeless and uninteresting earthenwares of Shang and Early Chou. Some of the pottery excavated at Anyang is glazed, though it is not certain whether these glazes were deliberate or accidental. Shards from sites of the Western Chou

much has been written in Europe and America, the reader is referred to W. B. Honey, *The Ceramic Art of China and other Countries of the Far East* (London, 1945); Feddersen, *Chinese Decorative Art*; and John A. Pope, *Chinese Porcelains from the Ardebil Shrine* (Washington, 1956).

PLATE 4

Covered jar; pottery, partly covered with three-colour glaze over white slip.
Ht. 9⅝ in. T'ang Dynasty

PLATE 5

Vase of Hangchow *kuan* ware. Ht. 7⅛ in. Southern Sung Dynasty

(ninth to eighth centuries B.C.) have been proved by chemical analysis to be true porcelain—taking that term to mean a hard, fully fused, and vitrified body. But these discoveries, it seems, were not immediately followed up, and it was many centuries before any further important technical advances were made. The next significant steps, the perfecting of pure white porcelain and of coloured glazes, were not taken until the sixth and seventh centuries A.D. (Plate 4). The T'ang also saw the beginning of the art of painting designs under the glaze. For the next six hundred years this technique was confined to the local pottery made for everyday use; it was not employed on imperial wares until the appearance of 'blue and white' in the fourteenth century. Under the Sung the wares reserved for the palace—the five so-called classic wares, Ting, Ju, Ch'ai, *kuan*, and *ko*—were all monochromes of the most exquisite purity of form and colour. The lovely vase illustrated in Plate 5 is a typical example of the *kuan* (official) ware made at Hangchow in the twelfth century for use in the palace.

The traditional view of a small group of factories turning out a limited number of characteristic wares was established by Chinese connoisseurs, and for long uncritically accepted by Western dealers and collectors. But the discoveries and research of recent years have revealed that it by no means presents a true picture of ceramic production in China. It is no longer possible, except in a few outstanding cases, to attribute any ware to a particular factory. It is now becoming clear not only that there were many local kilns which Chinese connoisseurs ignored and of which the literature makes no mention, but also that one district factory often imitated the wares of another: Ting was copied, sometimes very expertly, in other factories in North China, in the Liao Kingdom, and at Chi-chou in Kiangsi; relatively backward Hunan less successfully imitated the Yüeh ware and celadon of Chekiang; kilns in Szechwan copied almost all the important wares that were brought up river; while 'Tz'u-chou' has come to be no more than a convenient name for a tradition of painted stoneware that stretched right across North China, and is still very much alive today.[1]

In later centuries the local traditions continued with little change, but were more and more overshadowed by the industry which grew up at Ching-te-chen in Kiangsi. Kilns making sugary white porcelain had been established there during the T'ang Dynasty and perhaps even earlier. By the Southern Sung, the low hills to the east of the city were already dotted with kilns. When the Mongols established their capital at Peking, they chose as their official ware the white porcelain of Ching-te-chen (the so-called *shu-fu* ware), and the factory thereafter continued to have the monopoly of palace wares until the end of the Ch'ing Dynasty. The white porcelain of the Sung Dynasty had an ivory or bluish tint; but the more perfect materials and techniques of Ching-te-chen now drained all colour out of it, leaving it a pure, dead white that almost demanded to be decorated. Painting in underglaze blue (Plate 3 *b*)—the blue and white which Oscar Wilde found so difficult to live up to—was perfected in the fourteenth century, overglaze enamels in the fifteenth, while the Ming potters also produced monochromes in colours of a new depth and brilliance. In stonewares, Ming potters often turned back beyond what they considered to be the effete aesthetic of Sung to the vigorous coloured wares of the T'ang Dynasty.

The Jesuit father d'Entrecolles has left us, in two letters written in 1712 and 1722, a vivid picture of the factories at Ching-te-chen, which by then had grown to a vast industry employing upwards of a hundred thousand men, with the imperial kilns under the control of a Director sent down from Peking. At these kilns the developments of the Ming potters had been carried to an even higher level of technical perfection. In

[1] Some of these new discoveries are discussed in M. Sullivan, *Chinese Ceramics, Bronzes and Jades in the Collection of Sir Alan and Lady Barlow* (London, 1963).

PLATE 6

Kuan-yin; modelled in white porcelain. From Te-hua, Fukien. Ht. 8⅝ in. Ch'ing
Dynasty (early eighteenth century)

the wares produced under K'ang-hsi, Yung-cheng, and Ch'ien-lung, the range of shapes and glaze colours seems inexhaustible, while Sung and Ming imperial porcelains were being imitated with a skill that has deceived many modern authorities.

Although the imperial kilns fell on hard times after the abdication of Ch'ien-lung in 1796, the commercial factories at Ching-te-chen have continued to produce porcelain of high technical quality, though of less and less originality, up to the present time. Meanwhile, the products of local kilns, notably in Fukien, Szechwan, and Honan, some of which have been hitherto undeservedly neglected both by Chinese and Western connoisseurs, have at last been recognized as the custodians of all that is most vital in the Chinese ceramic tradition; and it is from these that we hope that new life may be put into the porcelain of Ching-te-chen. Te-hua in Fukien, however, has long been noted for its white porcelain. The seated figure of Kuan-yin illustrated in Plate 6 is a very beautiful eighteenth-century example of the Te-hua tradition of ceramic modelling that is still flourishing today.

PAINTING AND CALLIGRAPHY

In China, painting, and more especially landscape-painting, is mistress of the arts. That this should be so seems not unnatural when we consider that one of the aims of Chinese philosophy and religion has always been to discover the workings of the universe and to attune man's actions to them. A Chinese painting, therefore, not only embodies the visible forms and forces of nature, but also displays the painter's understanding of their operation. His purpose is to present the subtle and complex forces of nature as harmoniously interacting, to show man in his true relationship to her, and to convey the life that is in all things by means of the springing vitality of his brushwork. In a sense, therefore, every picture, however slight, is a generalized philosophical, or rather metaphysical, statement, even though it may be inspired by a particular place or memory. For the painter is not concerned with individual events, or with the accidents of time and place.

This generalization, this apparent detachment—so different from the passionate attachment to visible objects that we find in Rembrandt, Chardin, or Van Gogh—makes it difficult for the Western viewer to appreciate Chinese painting at first encounter. He finds it remote, tranquil, or merely decorative, and he is sometimes wearied in the long run by what he takes to be a sameness in style and content. The English critic Eric Newton, for example, finds Chinese painting, for all its charm, ultimately cold and unsatisfying; in its tendency to generalization he sees 'an air of finality' that precludes any possibility of change, or development, or surprise.[1] There is some justification for this view. The restless 'search for form', the experiments with style and technique which give such interest to the study of Western art, play little part in Chinese painting. Like the concert pianist, the Chinese painter must be fully master of his technique and repertoire before he can consider presenting his work to others. He will not hesitate to make use of the vocabulary of 'type-forms' and brush-strokes evolved by his predecessors; and often it is only a highly trained eye that can detect the differences between two painters in the same tradition; between, say, figure studies by Ch'iu Ying and T'ang Yin, or a landscape by Wen Cheng-ming and his nephew Wen Po-jen. And yet, in another sense, the Chinese painter's statement is anything but final; for only a clear statement about something specific can be final—Chardin's bottles, for example, or a Rembrandt self-portrait. On the contrary, he is acutely aware that he is only hinting at the truth; whether he presents a swiftly sketched spray of bamboo, or a vast panorama of mountains and valleys, he is giving us no more than a glimpse of a totality that lies beyond expression.

The apparent lack of perspective in Chinese painting is bound up with this desire to avoid a complete or finite statement. If by

[1] *European Painting and Sculpture* (Harmondsworth, 1941), p. 30.

perspective we mean the delineation of forms on a flat surface as they would appear to a viewer standing at a fixed point, then Chinese painting indeed has no perspective. The eleventh-century critic Shen Kua took the landscapist Li Ch'eng to task for his skill in what he called 'painting his eaves from below'. 'This is absurd', he wrote. 'All landscapes have to be viewed from the angle of totality to behold the part. . . . If we apply his method to the painting of mountains, we are unable to see more than one layer of the mountain at one time. How could we then see the totality of its unending ranges? . . . Li Ch'eng surely does not understand the principle of viewing the part from the angle of totality. His measurement of height and distance is certainly a fine thing. But should one attach paramount importance to the angles and corners of buildings?' Shen Kua objects to Li Ch'eng's application of the principle of one-point perspective because it sets arbitrary limits to the power of the artist to embrace the whole. There are indications that until the end of the Northern Sung Dynasty at least, other painters beside Li Ch'eng were making experiments along these lines, a remarkable example being the long handscroll by Chang Tse-tuan depicting preparations for the Ch'ing-ming festival which has recently been discovered in China. But such experiments ceased after the end of Northern Sung, when the aim of the scholar-painter was no longer to reveal nature but to express himself. Most characteristic of Chinese landscape-painting in all periods is what might be termed a continuous perspective, which shifts horizontally in the handscroll and vertically in the hanging scroll, so that the view of each successive area is correct to the eye directly opposite that point. By thus avoiding a fixed viewpoint, and by the subtle placing in his panorama of a winding mountain path, a ferry, perhaps a tea-house, and a few small figures, the painter not only creates the illusion of an actual landscape, but he also cunningly invites us to explore it.

The Chinese view of what constitutes suitable subject-matter for painting presents another striking contrast with that of Europe. The Chinese painter's aim is always to present a view of the world that is satisfying and spiritually refreshing; consequently only themes which carry this message would he consider worthy of his brush. He would regard with horror the rapes, executions, and massacres which, whether of religious inspiration or not, we are trained to contemplate as works of art; for to him art is indivisible, and our Western ability to admire colour, form, and composition in a picture without being in any way affected by distasteful subject-matter implies, if not a corrupt view of the world, then at least a dangerously fragmented one.

The lofty calm and detachment from worldly things implicit in a Chinese painting suggests that the painter himself lived in a world apart. But this was only partly true. While some of China's greatest painters—Ni Tsan, for example, or Shih-ch'i—have been eccentrics and hermits, many led an active public life, whether as cabinet minister or district magistrate, which brought them face to face with the world and its problems. But when these men returned home at the end of a busy day to paint a landscape or compose verses, they deliberately left the 'dusty world' behind them. The Ming scholar-painter Wen Chengming, for example, was during the middle years of his life too busy with his historical work in the Hanlin Academy to spend his time wandering in the mountains, as he no doubt would have preferred. But he could still take up his brush to paint a landscape panorama that would bring refreshment to himself and pleasure to his friends. To say that such a painting was 'escapist' might suggest that it was insincere. Yet it was in the highest sense escapist because it liberated the mind from material things. To achieve this, a painting had to be tranquil, harmonious, and meaningful. Mere originality counted for little or nothing.[1]

[1] An excellent introduction to Chinese painting from the Chinese point of view is Chiang Yee, *The Chinese Eye* (London, 1935). In addition to the work of Osvald Sirén cited in note 1, p. 198, general surveys include William

To fulfil its role, moreover, it was necessary that a painting conform in its colours and shapes to those of nature, not because realism as such was desirable, but because not to paint things correctly would suggest that the artist did not understand them. Accuracy in depicting the procession of the seasons, for example, with the trees and plants in their appropriate colours and foliage was an outward sign of a deeper understanding. But accuracy alone was never enough. Too meticulous a conformity to nature would rob the painting of the quality essential above all—vitality; for it was through the springing movement of the artist's (and the calligrapher's) brush that he expressed his awareness of the life of nature. Finally, and increasingly as time went on, it was desirable that the painting should contain some reference, in composition or brushwork, or even merely in title, to the work of some great master of the past.

These fundamental requirements of a painting were, so far as we know, first set down in writing by the painter and critic Hsieh Ho (*c.* A.D. 500) in the short preface to his classified list of still earlier masters. His celebrated 'six principles' might be briefly translated as follows: spirit-consonance and life-movement; the 'bone method' in the use of the brush; conformity to the shapes of objects in nature; conformity to their colours; care in placing and arranging the elements in the composition; transmission of the tradition by copying past models. Fidelity to nature and convincing scale relationships were particularly important during this formative period, when painters were still wrestling with elementary problems of proportion and distance; while the last principle enshrines an attitude to tradition which is unique to China, and is discussed further in the next section of this

Cohn, *Chinese Painting* (London, 1957); Sherman E. Lee, *Chinese Landscape Painting* (revised edition, Cleveland, 1962); while James Cahill's *Chinese Painting* (Geneva, 1960) is notable for its fresh outlook and sympathetic treatment of the literary school. Sirén's *Chinese Painting* (7 vols., London, 1956 and 1958) is encyclopedic in its scope.

chapter. Later critics and theorists emphasized one aspect or another, but all were agreed upon the fundamental importance of the first, Hsieh Ho's *ch'i-yün* ('spirit-consonance'). Its precise meaning has been endlessly debated, and every Western historian of Chinese art has produced his own rendering of the term. It may simply be said that it concerns the vital cosmic spirit or breath (*ch'i*) to which the painter must attune himself (*yün*) if he is to be able to express the life and movement, or perhaps life-in-movement, that is manifest in nature. This vitality is conveyed by means of the second principle, the structural strength and tension of the brush-stroke, implied by the apt use of the 'bone' image, that painting and calligraphy share in common.[1]

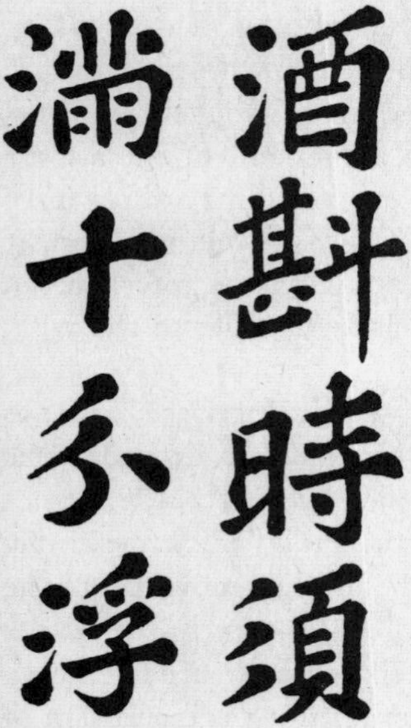

酒 斟 時 須

湍 十 禾 浮

Fig. 6. Part of the *Hsiao-yao fu*; an example of *k'ai-shu* calligraphy by the Sung poet Su Tung-p'o. (After Chiang Yee.)

It was through the practice of calligraphy—whether the square, powerful *li-shu* (clerk's hand) of the Han Dynasty, the elegant standard *k'ai-shu*, the cursive *hsing-shu*, or the still more cursive *ts'ao-shu* (grass writing)—that the scholar-gentleman refined and developed his sense of balance, movement, and form.[2] Calli-

[1] Osvald Sirén's *The Chinese on the Art of Painting* (Peking, 1936), of which a revised edition is in preparation, provides a useful introduction to Chinese critical and theoretical writings, some of which are translated and discussed in more detail in William R. B. Acker, *Some T'ang and Pre-T'ang Texts on Chinese Painting* (Leiden, 1954).

[2] Chiang Yee, *Chinese Calligraphy* (London, 1954), is a good general introduction to this subject.

graphy has often been compared to modern Western abstract expressionism and 'action painting', for both are the product of the controlled nervous energy of the hand that holds the brush. But the comparison is a misleading one. For the Western abstract painter, pure form, divorced from content, is all; form, in fact, is content. But even the most extreme of Chinese expressionists always sought a meaning beyond pure form. The passage of calligraphy would be less admirable if it were totally illegible or its content trivial. In painting, the most outrageous techniques of the modern abstract expressionists were anticipated by Chinese eccentrics in the eighth and ninth centuries: one master would flip his ink-soaked hair at the silk; another splash it with ink while he danced to music, facing in the opposite direction; a third would spread ink in pools on silk laid out on the floor, then drag an assistant round and round sitting on a sheet. But these bizarre methods were never ends in themselves. The records tell us—for unhappily not one of these remarkable pictures has survived—that having thus spilled their ink, the painters then proceeded, by the deft addition of scattered trees, waterfalls, and pavilions, to turn their smears and blotches into landscapes. The Zen ink painters of the twelfth and thirteenth centuries expressed their moment of illumination in brushwork hardly less explosive. Here at least we might expect to find pure abstraction. But Mu-ch'i and Ying Yü-chien conveyed their metaphysical excitement not in empty gestures with the brush, but in the shape of a monk tearing up the sutras, or a mountain village emerging out of the mist (Plate 7). For the painter, as for the calligrapher, mere form was never enough.

The history of Chinese painting can be regarded as the history not, as in the West, of the exploration of the visible world, so much as of the development of a pictorial language. As we trace the evolution of landscape-painting, for example, we can plot the stages in the growth of this language, of which the words, as it were, are rocks and trees, mountains and water, the letters brush-strokes. The first significant steps towards the evolution of landscape-painting as an art in its own right were taken in the Six Dynasties, when painters such as Tai K'uei and Ku K'ai-chih (355–406), liberated from Han orthodoxy and stimulated by the richly descriptive language of contemporary poetry, were striving to create a landscape style.[1] No genuine silk paintings of this period remain, but two of Ku K'ai-chih's scrolls survive in late versions, the famous illustrations to the *Admonitions of the Court Instructress* in the British Museum, one of which shows a mountain scene, being a faithful copy of the ninth or tenth century. Under the T'ang Dynasty the energies of most artists were absorbed in the decoration of Buddhist temples, yet landscape-painting made considerable advance. Later Chinese critics and historians credit Wang Wei (699–759) with having been the first to paint landscapes in monochrome ink, but the evidence suggests that he chiefly worked in the decorative 'green and blue' manner (*ch'ing-lü*) that had been developed by Chang Seng-yu and others in the sixth century. His unique position stems from the fact that he was also a famous poet and scholar, and hence the spiritual ancestor of the 'literary painters' of Yüan, Ming, and Ch'ing.

After a period of relative stagnation during the latter half of the T'ang Dynasty, what would nowadays be called a 'major breakthrough' took place in the tenth century, chiefly under the liberal patronage of Li Hou-chu, ruler of the petty state of Southern T'ang at Nanking, and of the first emperor of Northern Sung. Li Ch'eng and Fan K'uan gave expression to the cold grandeur of the northern scene in landscapes of truly monumental power. The latter's *Travellers amid Mountains and Streams*, in the Palace Collection in Taiwan, combines a noble yet essentially simple composition with great richness and density of texture, achieved by the aid of repeated short dabs

[1] This formative period is discussed in detail in M. Sullivan, *The Birth of Landscape Painting in China* (London, Berkeley, and Los Angeles, 1962).

PLATE 7

Liang K'ai: *The Patriarch Hui-neng tearing up the Sūtras*. Southern Sung Dynasty

PLATE 8

Kuo Hsi: *Early Spring*; dated equivalent to 1072. Hanging scroll; ink and slight colour on silk. Ht. 62¼ in. Northern Sung Dynasty

with the brush which represent the first step in the development of the painter's vocabulary of texture strokes.

The bold, stern style of Li Ch'eng and Fan K'uan, which laid great emphasis upon the calligraphic strength and tension of the brush-stroke, became the basis of the 'Northern' style of later professionals and academicians. In the eleventh century this style was further developed, and its composition made more flexible, by Kuo Hsi, whose superb scroll *Early Spring* is illustrated in Plate 8. At the end of Northern Sung its most influential exponent was the court painter, Li T'ang. Under the Southern Sung, his followers in the Academy, notably Ma Yüan and Hsia Kuei, upheld the new orthodox Li T'ang manner. But the 'Ma–Hsia school', as it came to be called, reflected the very different temper of the court at Hangchow. Though preserving the brilliant, angular brushwork, they abandoned the full composition and dense texture of the earlier masters (Plate 9); in their most characteristic paintings, many of which are fans and album-leaves, rocks and trees are pushed to one side, and a solitary figure gazes out across vast empty distance to where the distant hilltops rise above the mist. It is this kind of painting, delicately evocative and nostalgic in content, somewhat mannered in technique, which has become most familiar to Western admirers, chiefly through the writings of Laurence Binyon and other critics who were influenced by Japanese taste. So highly was it praised, indeed, that all later painting was looked on as a long slow decline from the climax achieved by Ma Yüan and Hsia Kuei. In fact, although this 'Northern' tradition continued to flourish in later centuries, it always remained the special province of court painters and professionals.

The school of landscape-painting which Tung Ch'i-ch'ang and other Ming critics labelled 'Southern', and credited to Wang Wei, was given its first clear formulation in the work of the tenth-century landscapists Tung Yüan and Chü-jan. These and other painters living in the more genial environment of Nanking painted the rounded hills, the dense foliage, and the rain-soaked atmosphere of the South in richer ink and broader, more relaxed brushwork, utterly different from the spectacular contrasts and jerky rhythms of the 'Northern' painters. The style was taken up by Mi Fei and his son Mi Yu-jen, who added their own characteristic ink-blob technique, the 'Mi-dot'. But Hui-tsung would have none of Mi Fei's pictures in the imperial collection, and indeed the Southern style was too personal and informal to find favour at court. Unrecognized during the Southern Sung, it was revived in the Yüan Dynasty by the four great scholar-painters, Huang Kung-wang, Wu Chen, Ni Tsan, and Wang Meng, who refused to take office under the Mongols and lived in retirement in the South. A detail of Huang Kung-wang's masterpiece, a long panorama of the Fu-ch'un mountains in Chekiang, is illustrated in Plate 10. These men and others like them came to be called *yin-shih* ('retired scholars'). Not only their style of painting, but their calligraphy, poetry, scholarship, and indeed their whole way of life became the ideal for all later painters in the 'Southern' tradition, most notably for the Ming masters Shen Chou and Wen Cheng-ming and other members of the 'Wu school' centred round Wuhsien. This part of Chekiang has remained the principal centre of literary painting (*wen-jen-hua*) up to modern times.

Tung Ch'i-ch'ang's division of painters into 'Northern' and 'Southern', based very largely upon whether he despised them as professionals and court painters or admired them as scholars and amateurs, has bedevilled Chinese art criticism since his day. Moreover it is a gross over-simplification. The great Yüan official and court painter Chao Meng-fu, for example, whom he placed in the 'Northern' school largely, it seems, because he was a collaborator, could easily assume the mantle of a *yin-shih* after office hours, so to speak, and thereby become a 'Southern' painter. Under the Ming, certain painters such as T'ang Yin and Ch'iu Ying took up a position midway between the two schools, and

PLATE 9

Hsia Kuei (*c.* 1180–1230): *Pure and Remote View of Rivers and Mountains*. Part of a handscroll; ink on paper. Ht. 18¼ in. Southern Sung Dynasty

PLATE 10

Huang Kung-wang (1269–1354): *Living in the Fu-ch'un Mountains*; dated equivalent to 1350. Part of a handscroll; ink on paper. Ht. 13 in. Yüan Dynasty

their painting contains elements of both. Tung Ch'i-ch'ang's philosophy of art history had a profound influence upon subsequent generations of 'literary' painters, however. For not only did it make them intensely conscious that they, and they alone, were the true custodians of traditional Chinese values, but it also in time made their painting as studied and in its way academic as that of the academicians themselves. Moreover, Tung Ch'i-ch'ang's immense prestige made him an arbiter of taste, almost a censor: the literati could no longer see the painting of Sung, Yüan, and Ming except as he interpreted it. When the 'Four Wangs' of the seventeenth century (Wang Shih-min, the earliest of them, had been his pupil) painted in the manner of Huang Kung-wang or Chü-jan, it was the surviving versions approved by Tung Ch'i-ch'ang which they took as their models. During the last three centuries the rich and subtle language of the brush could still produce landscapes of great beauty and deep poetic feeling, but the attitude of the literati revealed a growing and unhealthy dependence on the past.

Against this dependence, and against the over-intellectualism of Tung Ch'i-ch'ang and his following, some free spirits of the early Ch'ing Dynasty revolted. Shih-t'ao (1641–*c*. 1717), in a celebrated essay, declared that 'the best method is that which has never been a method'; and he and other individualists, such as the monk Shih-ch'i and the eccentric Pa-ta Shan-jen (Chu Ta), proceeded to express themselves with marvellous spontaneity, disregarding all the rules, and generally, though not always, in the intimate framework of the album-leaf. The latter's *Lotus*, illustrated in Plate 11, is a splendid example of their free, unfettered brushwork. They would have perfectly understood John Constable's oft-quoted remark that 'painting is for me but another word for feeling'. But these and other groups of individualists formed a circle within a circle. Even more than the literati as a whole, they spoke only to each other, and their inventiveness was too private a thing to halt the paralysis that was creeping over Chinese painting during the latter half of the Ch'ing Dynasty.

This wide variety in outlook and treatment, equally evident in bird and flower, and in figure-painting, can be partly explained in terms of the position of the artist in society, and the sources of his patronage. Under the Later Han Dynasty the painter belonged to a hierarchy of officials, attendants, and artisans, his status depending on his skill. During the Six Dynasties there were court painters (Ku K'ai-chih was one) but, at least until the time of the emperor Wu of the Liang Dynasty, such was the chaos and uncertainty that imperial patronage counted for little. From this time until the ninth century the greatest patrons were the monasteries, and there was hardly a master who did not do his share of Buddhist wall-painting. The period of most enlightened patronage came in the tenth century and Northern Sung, when the emperors gathered round them a brilliant coterie of painters and poets to whom they gave complete freedom of expression. Hui-tsung, the last emperor of Northern Sung, is generally held to have been the most enlightened of all, but for all his passionate devotion to the arts, he encouraged in his painters an academic realism—or, because the birds and flowers they painted were so flawless and perfect, we should perhaps call it idealism—that boded ill for the future of court painting in China. A beautiful example of the style he both encouraged and practised himself (for he was an excellent painter) is the fan painting of a shrike by the academician Li An-chung, illustrated in Plate 12 *a*. After the fall of the Southern Sung the status of the court artists sharply declined. The Academy was abolished, and court painters to the Ming emperors were seldom more, and sometimes much less, than palace servants. From the time of the Mongol conquest until the reign of K'ang-hsi (1662–1722), talented painters kept well clear of the capital, forming loose groups centred on Soochow, Hangchow, or Nanking, painting for each other's pleasure and that of a few cultivated amateurs.

PLATE II

Chu Ta (Pa-ta Shan-jen, 1625–c. 1705): *Lotus*. Hanging
scroll; ink on paper. Ht. 73¼ in. Ch'ing Dynasty.
(*By courtesy of the Museum of Fine Arts, Boston*)

PLATE 12

a. Attributed to Li An-chung (active 1115–40): *Shrike on a Dry Twig, with Bamboo.* Fan; ink and colour on silk. Diam. 10½ in. Northern Sung Dynasty

b. Yen Li-pen (died 673): The Emperor Hsüan of the Ch'en Dynasty. Part of a handscroll of Thirteen Emperors; ink and slight colour on silk. Ht. 20¼ in. T'ang Dynasty. (*By courtesy of the Museum of Fine Arts, Boston*)

True painting, as opposed to the work of the palace decorators, thus became more and more a private language.

In order not to be taken for professionals, the scholar-painters of Yüan, Ming, and Ch'ing would cultivate a deliberate amateurishness. A celebrated story tells of the Yüan landscape-painter Ni Tsan, who prided himself on his 'awkwardness' (*cho*); when a friend protested that his bamboos didn't look like real bamboo at all, he is said to have answered, 'Ah, but a total lack of resemblance is hard to achieve; not everyone can manage it.' The great statesman Chao Meng-fu was a painter of professional skill, which he found some difficulty in concealing when painting 'scholarly' landscapes in monochrome ink. From this time forward the aim of the scholar-painters was not to depict nature— that could be left to the academicians and professionals—but to express their own thoughts. They spoke of merely 'borrowing' rocks and trees as convenient shapes in which to 'lodge' their feelings, which could as well be conveyed in the language of poetry and calligraphy. Poems, inscriptions, and dedications written on the painting itself, or on its mounting, far from marring it, added to its meaning and value, and strengthened the sense of intimacy between the painter and the viewer.

Poetic, scholarly, intensely personal, the painting of the literary men of Yüan, Ming, and Ch'ing (the *wen-jen-hua*) is the art of an intellectual élite aloof from the world. But it could not remain so indefinitely, and by the nineteenth century its springs of inspiration had run dry. The most significant event of the modern revolution in Chinese art has not been the impact of Western realism, but the breaking down of the social and intellectual barricades behind which the scholar class had entrenched itself.

III. *The Attitude of the Chinese to their Own Art*

The historical sense of the Chinese is nowhere more apparent than in their attitude to their own artistic heritage. We will find no instance in China of the reverent preservation of ancient relics comparable with that of Japan, but neither will we encounter anything like the extreme readiness to abandon or even destroy traditional works of art which the Japanese showed in their first wave of enthusiasm for things Western, late in the nineteenth century. China needed no Fenollosa to reverse the wholesale process of destruction and to point out the value or the legacy to its inheritors, because the Chinese, however careless they might be about the preservation of individual objects, were already imbued with a strong sense of history, and a profound awareness of the value of their cultural heritage.

It is no exaggeration to say that the Chinese gentleman and collector (the terms are often synonymous) is in love with the past, and cherishes any object which by its form or inscription reminds him of it. When his eye falls on the miniature porcelain tripod standing on his desk, not only does he savour the perfection of its form and glaze, but a whole train of associations are set moving in his mind. For him his tripod is treasured not simply for its antiquity or rarity, but because it is a receptacle of ideas, and a visible emblem of the ideals by which he lives. Indeed, although he would be gratified to know that it was the genuine Sung Dynasty piece it purports to be, it would not be robbed of all its value to him if he subsequently found that it was in fact a clever imitation of the Ch'ien-lung period—particularly if it bore an appropriate inscription cut in archaic characters. Even a mere fragment is often enough. The Ch'ing collector Lu Shih-hua notes in his delightful *Shu-hua shuo-ling* ('Scrapbook for Collectors') that members of his circle would be quite content with one or two lines of a rubbing from a Sung autograph, and would not trouble to acquire the rest: 'For as soon as one has come to know the brush technique and the spirit of the work of the ancient artists, one can derive the rest by analogy.'[1]

[1] R. H. van Gulik, *Scrapbook for Chinese Collectors* (Beirut, 1958), p. 50;

A painting, if of high quality, stylistically right, and adorned with the name and seals of a well-known scholar-painter and the laudatory inscriptions of his friends, might well be treasured less for its value as a work of art in itself than for the rich poetic and scholarly association that it evoked. The Chinese collector who, for example, specialized in the landscapes of the 'Four Wangs' or those of the 'Eight Eccentrics of Yangchow' would be more gratified if he had works of high quality attributed to all of them, than if he had incontrovertible proof that any one of them was genuine. Indeed, he would regard the Western passion for mere authenticity as quite inexplicable. It could be said in explanation of this attitude that it is generally much more difficult to detect a fake in Chinese than in Western art, where a case can often be proven by X-ray or chemical tests, and that the Chinese collector is merely bowing to circumstances. But this attitude goes much deeper than can be explained simply in these terms.

In the eyes of the Chinese painter and connoisseur, the art of a great master of the past lives not only in such of his authentic works as have chanced to survive (and who, in any case, can prove that they *are* authentic?), but also in the work of all later masters who have painted in his style. It is extremely unlikely, for example, that any landscape from the hand of the Northern Sung painter, poet, and collector Mi Fei has been in existence during the last four or five centuries. Yet every Chinese painter is familiar with his work, for he is as it were born again each time that one of them paints a picture in his manner. What is chiefly important is not the survival of the actual object (as it is to the Japanese), but the sustaining and constant revitalizing of the tradition. Many a traveller in China has seen the effects of this attitude in the realm of architecture, and has been dismayed to find that the buildings of the T'ang temple that he has journeyed

the same author's *Chinese Pictorial Art as Viewed by the Connoisseur* (Rome, 1958) is an important contribution to the Western literature on Chinese painting.

many miles to see are in fact modern: yet in Chinese eyes it is
still a T'ang temple, and the precise moment in its history when
the present buildings were erected is not considered of much
interest or importance.

The sense of the supreme value of the tradition laid upon the
individual artist the duty to devote at least a part of his time
and energy to copying the works of old masters, in accordance
with the spirit of the sixth principle of Hsieh Ho, which we
have already referred to in an earlier section (p. 197). Copying,
moreover, like the daily exercises of the professional pianist, was
essential for perfecting the artist's technique and for familiarizing him with the stylistic repertory, or 'schema', which he
would draw upon in forming his own style.[1] The traditional
Chinese painter would have heartily echoed Constable's remark
that the artist who is self-taught is taught by a very ignorant
person indeed. Thus Mi Fei copied, or reinterpreted, Tung
Yüan, the Yüan literati copied Mi Fei's version of Tung Yüan,
Shen Chou copied the Yüan masters—and so on down to a
modern literary painter such as Huang Pin-hung. Many of these
copies, or free interpretations, of earlier pictures are works of
the highest quality, not at all to be compared with, say, an
eighteenth-century Italian copy of a Raphael. Tung Ch'i-ch'ang
noted that although Mi Fei, Huang Kung-wang, and Ni Tsan
all followed Tung Yüan, their work was nevertheless entirely
individual. 'But,' he went on, 'when ordinary people make
faithful copies, they do not transmit anything to posterity.'
Confronted with a free copy by a master, where, in the long
unbroken chain from Tung Yüan to Huang Pin-hung, are we to

---

[1] This repertory was finally set down in the manuals of instruction for
painters, of which the first and most notable is *Chieh-tzu-yüan hua-chuan*
('The Painting Manual of the Mustard Seed Garden') first published in five
vols., with woodcuts in colour, in 1679. Before the end of the seventeenth
century *Chieh-tzu-yüan* had reached Japan, where it had a considerable
influence on the early development of the coloured woodcut.

place it? Some Chinese connoisseurs (though not the most discerning) might say that it did not greatly matter. But this situation is the despair of the Western historian and museum curator, who must treat each work of art as a unique historical document, to be pinned down firmly in its proper place.

Admirable in some ways though the attitude of the Chinese *amateur* certainly is, it has opened up a wonderful field for exploitation by the faker. The literature of Chinese art is full of accounts of the skill of famous forgers of antiques.[1] A noted family in Soochow, for example, made archaic bronzes which were buried in specially prepared soil to be dug up and sold by the next generation but one. Bona fide unsigned copies made by reputable painters might pass into the hands of picture forgers, and there acquire a pedigree: title, signature, inscriptions, and seals would be copied, perhaps from those on a painting listed in the catalogue of a former well-known collection, and the picture sold to an unsuspecting enthusiast. He would then consult the catalogue in question, be delighted to find that his painting exactly matched the description, and would conclude, quite erroneously, that he owned the original. The greater and more ancient the name on the picture, of course, the greater the danger of deception, for, as Lu Shih-hua wrote in his *Scrapbook*, 'If one limits his interest strictly to specimens from the Ch'in, T'ang, Sung, and Yüan Dynasties, and then only to those whose paper is still white or whose silk is in perfect condition, then one had better take up his brush and paint them himself.'

The Chinese connoisseur would bear the pleasures and disappointments of collecting with equanimity, and would consider rather vulgar the pride and possessiveness which is shown by the average Western collector. Indeed, as a true Confucian, he would hold too great an attachment to things as unworthy of a

---

[1] This subject is dealt with in some detail in van Gulik's *Chinese Pictorial Art*, part ii; see also E. Zürcher, 'Imitation and Forgery in Ancient Chinese Painting and Calligraphy', *Oriental Art* (N.S.), i. 4 (Winter 1955), pp. 141–6.

gentleman. He would give away, or, as he is generally a practical man, exchange, his treasure with other collectors—a Shen Chou scroll, perhaps, for an album by Shih-t'ao; a Shang bronze for a piece of Sung *kuan* ware. In this way attachment is avoided, his collection is frequently changing, and he is constantly giving new pleasure to himself and his friends. The writer has on occasion recommended this custom to Western collectors of his acquaintance, but with little success.

The collecting of works of art in China has a long history. The Later Han emperors accumulated in the Cloud Terrace of the palace at Loyang a huge hoard of books, paintings, and other *objets d'art*. This was the first of a long series of imperial collections that brought together many precious scrolls which might otherwise have been lost; but it also ensured the eventual destruction of these masterpieces when, as so often happened at the fall of a dynasty, the capital was sacked and the palace looted. The Cloud Terrace and all its contents, for example, went up in flames during the rebellion of A.D. 195. At the fall of Liang in 557, the last emperor, Yüan, crying out 'Learning and culture shall not survive this night!' threw thousands of scrolls of painting and calligraphy into the flames, and was barely prevented from casting himself in after them. The collection of the greatest of all imperial connoisseurs, Sung Hui-tsung, was almost entirely lost when the capital fell to the Tartars in 1127. It is disasters such as these that account for the extreme rarity of ancient Chinese paintings.

The present imperial collection, the bulk of which was taken to Taiwan by the Nationalist Government when they quitted the mainland in 1949, is chiefly the creation of Ch'ien-lung.[1] Among its thousands of scrolls are a few from the Sung imperial

[1] A selection of reproductions, *Three Hundred Masterpieces of Chinese Painting in the Palace Museum* (edited by Wang Shih-chieh, Lo Chia-luen, Chuang Shang-yen, and others), appeared in 1959. James Cahill's *Chinese Painting* (Cleveland, 1960) illustrates a further selection in colour.

collection, rather more from that of the Ming. Slightly augmented by later Ch'ing emperors, it remained virtually intact
until shortly before the fall of the dynasty, when depreda-
tions by palace eunuchs, followed after the revolution by
sales masquerading as lavish 'gifts' made by the last emperor,
P'u-i, began to eat it away. Nevertheless the collection still contains 5,600 scrolls of paintings and calligraphy, 2,382 bronzes,
3,894 jades, and over 17,000 pieces of porcelain. Since 1950 the
People's Government in Peking has rehabilitated the old Palace
Museum and has begun to make good the loss of these treasures.
Some lost paintings have been recovered, and the collection has
been greatly strengthened by gifts and purchases from private
owners.

The palace collection bears all the hallmarks of Ch'ing imperial
taste. There is hardly a painting, genuine or otherwise, which
does not carry the seals and one or more inscriptions from the
brush of Ch'ien-lung, to bear witness to his untiring and indiscriminate enthusiasm. For true connoisseurship we must turn to
the great private collectors down the centuries: to Mi Fei, who
spent a lifetime searching for a genuine work by the tenth-
century master Li Ch'eng; to Tung Ch'i-ch'ang, whose influence on Ch'ing connoisseurship we have already mentioned;
or to the wealthy salt-merchant An I-chou, who built up an
important collection from scrolls scattered at the fall of the
Ming, and whose catalogue *Mo-yüan hui-kuan* is a valuable
source for the study of Ming painting. The latter's seals on a
painting, or those of the great Ming connoisseur Hsiang Yüan-
pien, are often all that a collector requires as proof of its authenticity.

This very sophisticated attitude to painting is also reflected
in the vast amount of critical and historical writing that has
survived. Indeed, for the period up to the end of Northern
Sung, our knowledge of painting is based very largely on later
copies and written sources. We have already referred (p. 197) to

Hsieh Ho's short preface to the *Ku-hua p'in-lu* embodying the Six Principles, and should also mention a brief but significant essay on landscape-painting by the fifth-century painter Tsung Ping, in which he equates the experience and aims of the landscape-painter with those of the Taoist mystic. The first history of Chinese painting, Chang Yen-yüan's *Li-tai ming-hua chi* ('Record of Famous Painters of Successive Dynasties'), preface 847, antedates the earliest comparable European work, Vasari's *Lives of the Painters*, by seven centuries.[1] The remaining years of the T'ang are covered by Chu Ching-hsüan's *T'ang ch'ao ming-hua lu*,[2] the early Sung by the *T'u-hua chien-wen chih* of Kuo Jo-hsü.[3] Thereafter the deepening rift between court and professional painters on the one hand, and scholar-amateurs on the other, made the compiling of a comprehensive record of any given period difficult, if not impossible. The careers of the leading court painters are covered by imperial catalogues such as the *Hsüan-ho hua-p'u* of Hui-tsung and the *Shih-ch'ü pao-chi* of Ch'ien-lung, but to extract a coherent account of the life and work of the scholar-painters, particularly of the last three dynasties, requires an enormous amount of reading in the official biography (if any), collected works, and reminiscences of the painter concerned and of his friends and associates. This is the task upon which modern scholars in China, Japan, and the West are now chiefly engaged.

IV. *Foreign Influences on Chinese Art*

There are two views of China's attitude to foreign influences that are widely current in the West. One sees her as a rock, upon

[1] Annotated translation of the first four chapters by William Acker in *Some T'ang and Pre-T'ang Texts on Chinese Painting* (Leiden, 1954), pp. 59–382.

[2] Revised annotated translation by Alexander Soper in *Artibus Asiae*, xxi. 3/4, 1958.

[3] Annotated translation by Alexander Soper, *Kuo Jo-hsü's Experiences in Painting* (Washington, 1951).

which the waves of foreign invasion and cultural influence have broken in vain; the other, as a kind of vast sponge, implacably soaking up these influences, remaining herself unchanged by them. Like all generalizations, both contain some truth: China has rejected much, and absorbed much. But this could be said of India also, or of any great civilization. By the study of what she has selected and what rejected, and what she has found necessary to remould before she could accept it, and how this was accomplished, we can go some way towards an understanding of China herself.

The cultural diffusionist, when he comes upon a form or style in art appearing in one country appreciably later than in another, is apt to say not only that it was borrowed, but that the borrowing implied some kind of subordinate status in the borrower, or even that the new form was introduced by immigrants. However, we need no longer postulate a *Völkerwanderung* to account for the similarity of designs on the neolithic painted pottery of Kansu to those produced in Western Asia as much as a thousand years earlier. It is now well recognized that, even when contact is relatively brief, cultures freely borrow motifs and techniques from each other without being themselves changed in other respects.

Another instance of this can be seen in the art of the Shang and early Chou Dynasties. The carving of the stylized zoomorphic motifs in bone and wood, of which no trace can be found in the neolithic art of the same region, is

Fig. 7. Carved bone handle from Anyang. Late Shang Dynasty. (After Li Chi.)

also a characteristic of the nomadic people of the steppes and forests of Central and Eastern Siberia, and has survived until modern times in the art of the coastal Indians of North America. This had led to the suggestion that the Shang ruling class were, like the Aryans in India, a northern intrusive stock. But this is not confirmed by anatomical measurements from Shang graves. Nor does the apparently sudden appearance of bronze-casting in Honan in the middle of the second millennium B.C. imply a cultural migration from the West. The recent excavation of stratified Shang sites at Cheng-chow reveals a continuous occupation from late neolithic times onwards, and suggests that there can have been no transfer of culture on a large scale, still less any sudden intrusion of an alien race from beyond China's northern and western frontiers. In fact, the picture we have of Shang and early Chou culture shows that only a very limited number of techniques and weapon types were imported, the latter including the leaf-shaped spearhead and the animal-headed knives of China's South Siberian neighbours in the Minusinsk region. The chariot too was probably copied from that of Western Asia.

The striking change in the bronze art of the middle Chou period, however, was the direct result not merely of foreign pressure, but of the infiltration into the heartland of North China by the Ti barbarians of the north-west. They were expert in the use of leather and skins, in the plaiting of ropes and thongs, and in the art of interlacing animal bodies in decoration—all of which were quite foreign to Chinese tradition. Yet all these features appear on the ritual bronzes of the middle and late Chou period, notably in those from Hsin-cheng and Li-yü; while on garment-hooks, chariot-fittings, and other bronze objects the animal style, or 'Ordos style' as it is often loosely called, persisted into the Han Dynasty. The great expansion of China at this time meant, moreover, that the whole country was no longer under the cultural dominion of the Chou. The newly independent feudal states developed much as they chose, discarded the traditional forms and motifs, adapted them to their own taste, or accepted new ones from their barbarian neighbours, even when these were quite inappropriate to the art of bronze-casting.

But the Chinese craftsman has never shown the least hesitation in borrowing a form and adapting it to whatever material

FIG. 8. Interlaced dragons decorating a bronze *chien* basin. Late Chou Dynasty. Freer Gallery, Washington.

he might be working in. The arts and crafts of the T'ang Dynasty, for example, are full of instances of this. Persian and Sassanian shapes such as the amphora, rhyton, and shell-cup, imported in metal, are turned out in pottery; the repoussé decoration of Western silverware is copied in appliqué relief on the sides of pottery ewers; Arab glass cups are reproduced in white porcelain.[1] T'ang China's unusual readiness to respond to foreign fashions in the arts was greatly helped by the cosmopolitan nature of T'ang society. The foreigners who crowded the streets of Loyang and Changan, carrying on their own trades and practising their own religions, are often portrayed, or caricatured, in lively manner in the pottery tomb-figurines (Plate 13).

---

[1] This aspect of T'ang art is discussed in detail in Willetts, *Chinese Art*, vol. ii, pp. 455–89, and in Bo Gyllensvärd, *T'ang Gold and Silver* (Stockholm, 1957).

Some Chinese were converted to Manichaeism, Zoroastrianism, Christianity, or Islam; while many merely flirted with these foreign cults, on the sound principle that what other nations found helpful was at least worth trying. A striking instance of this in T'ang art is the 'sea-horse and grape' mirror which was widely popular (judging from the number of such mirrors that

FIG. 9. Bird-headed ewers: left, T'ang glazed earthenware; right, Sassanian parcel-gilt, from Kharkov. (After Willetts.)

have survived) for a short period before the proscription of foreign religions in 845. Its symbolism is Manichaean, but it would be quite wrong to conclude from this that all the Chinese who possessed such mirrors were Manichaeans.

T'ang receptiveness to foreign ideas and forms may be explained by the fact that, for all its brilliant achievement, the T'ang Dynasty was not artistically one of the most creative eras in Chinese history. The questioning, the sense of discovery, of infinite possibilities for experience that we find in the poetry and aesthetic theory of the Six Dynasties are not to be found in

PLATE 13

Seated Armenian merchant with bird. Pottery. Ht. $7\frac{1}{4}$ in. T'ang Dynasty

T'ang art. There is grandeur and confidence in the work of a court painter such as Yen Li-pen (Plate 12 *b*), but the wild poetry of the Six Dynasties period, and the profound penetration into nature that we later find in Northern Sung painting, are absent. It would be a gross exaggeration to say that the T'ang produced no original artistic ideas of its own, but it was a prosperous and materialistic age, like imperial Rome living on the fruits of its early expansion and power, and, like Rome, ready to enjoy all the arts brought to its twin capitals by friendly and subject nations beyond its frontiers.

We might be tempted to assume that the situation in the Han Dynasty had been much the same. Han military power reached out into Central Asia, and Han art is full of Western themes. But there is a difference. Han China altogether lacked the sense of prosperous fulfilment that shines out from every aspect of T'ang culture. Although the Han Dynasty saw the establishment of a Confucian system of government and education, and the re-habilitation of the Classics, it was a period of intense imaginative activity. The mission of Chang Ch'ien and the conquests of the emperor Wu did not bring foreigners flocking to the capital; they merely opened a window on a new world beyond China, giving a glimpse through travellers' tales of the vast deserts and great mountain ranges of Central Asia, of K'un-lun, the axis of the world, of the Huns who fought and hunted over the desert, and of India, the home of a strange new religion. Han China, herself vitally alive with the gathered folk-lore and magic of all her united peoples, was awake as never before or since to the stimulus of these distant lands.

Evidence of this receptiveness is everywhere in Han art. Among foreign innovations now introduced we may cite the vaulted or domed stone tomb, approached by an avenue of monumental stone sculpture. Before the tomb of General Ho Ch'ü-ping, who died in 117 B.C. after a lifetime campaigning against the barbarians, were placed life-size figures of horses and other animals. One horse stands triumphant over a fallen barbarian bowman, symbolizing the victory brought to the Chinese by cavalry using techniques learned from the barbarians themselves (Plate 14 *a*). It must be said that as sculpture in the round the figure leaves much to be desired, for the carver merely conceives of the horse as two reliefs placed back to back. It was several centuries before fully modelled stone sculpture on a monumental scale was achieved. Yet even then the emphasis was always upon the linear movement over the surface. Carving in high relief was also a foreign technique adopted by the Han Chinese, but it was one they were never at home in. The most successful examples are the figures of horsemen on the Shen memorial pillars in Szechwan, but they are so Western in form and spirit that their presence there is hard to explain. On stone slabs from tomb shrines in Shantung, notably those of the Wu family (first to second centuries A.D.), there is not even a pretence of modelling, the background being merely cut away from the flat surface of the stone to leave the figures in flat relief.

When we turn from technique to content, we can see how Han art is full of foreign subject-matter: Mount K'un-lun is ubiquitous; the royal hunting parks, stocked with wild animals from beyond the confines of China, and the animal combats and hunts enacted there, are reproduced in relief on the sides of pottery 'hill censers' (Plate 14 *b*). Monsters and demons of the frozen north, serpents and dragons of the tropical south, strange beings and prodigies from foreign lands—such motifs are incorporated with such whole-hearted enthusiasm into Han art that we cannot see them as merely fashionable, as foreign forms and styles were under the T'ang, but as filling the imaginative life of the Han people. Yet strangely little of this survived to become a permanent part of Chinese culture. Many of the Han myths and legends were in time forgotten, and, as China lost her cultural innocence and became sophisticated, her artists could no longer respond to such stimuli. Between the end of Han and modern

PLATE 14

a. Stone horse standing before the tomb of General Ho Ch'ü-ping
(died 117 B.C.), Shensi. Ht. 5 ft. 4 in. Han Dynasty

b. Hill-jar; pottery, covered with green glaze. Ht. 9½ in. Han Dynasty.
(*By courtesy of the Museum of Fine Arts, Boston*)

times the only foreign import to leave a permanent influence on Chinese art was Buddhism.

There is ample evidence that Buddhism had reached China before the end of the first century A.D., and that Buddhist communities were flourishing in North China during the second century. The extreme rarity of examples of Han Buddhist art is therefore hard to account for. Single stone reliefs in Szechwan and Honan, and a handful of mirrors bearing Buddhist figures, are about all we have.[1] Indeed, the pieces that can with confidence be dated earlier than 400 A.D. are extremely few. A possible explanation is that though based on Indian models they must have been very crude, and would have been replaced as techniques improved. Today we can only seriously begin to study Chinese Buddhist art with the sculpture and painting of the fifth century.

FIG. 10. Rubbing of earliest Buddha relief yet discovered in China. From Chia-ting, Szechwan. Second–third century.

Most of the small bronze votive statues of this period appear to be closely modelled on the style developed in Gandhāra as the result of the meeting of the early Buddhist sculpture of Mathura with the ideas and conventions of the late classical art of the Near East. But when, as at Yün-kang, Chinese stone-carvers began to disengage from the cliff-face huge seated Buddha figures in emulation of those in India and Afghanistan, their

---

[1] Good accounts of the development of Chinese Buddhist art are to be found in Sickman and Soper, *The Art and Architecture of China* (Harmondsworth, 1956), and Mizuno Seiichi, *Bronze and Stone Sculpture of China: from the Yin to the T'ang Dynasty* (Tokyo, 1960). See also Alexander Soper, *Literary Evidence for Early Buddhist Art in China* (*Artibus Asiae*, Supplementum xix, Ascona, 1959).

ignorance of the originals, combined with the formidable technical problems imposed by the scale, forced them to modify the style. The head of the seated colossus in Cave XX at Yün-kang, for example, is broad and mask-like, with none of the classical purity of the best Gandhāran work; the proportions are heavy,

FIG. 11. Colossal seated Buddha at Yün-kang, Shansi.
Northern Wei, late fifth century.

and the drapery, indicated by parallel ridges ending in points as it rounds the curve of the arm, suggests that the carvers were working from a model, or perhaps a drawing, which they imperfectly understood. Nevertheless, the faithful who worshipped this figure would have been convinced that it was an exact replica of some particularly holy icon, or even that it had been miraculously transported from India.

The wall-paintings in the early caves at the frontier city of Tunhuang (fifth to sixth centuries) likewise reveal the Chinese craftsman's efforts to copy both the content and the style of

Indian Buddhist art.[1] In the seated Bodhisattva in Cave 254, for example, the artist has achieved a sinuous grace and plasticity that is thoroughly Indian; he even shows some grasp of the 'arbitrary shading' by which the painters at Ajānta had given sculptural volume to their figures. But his treatment of the anatomy is unconvincing. Here he has failed to understand the Indian conventions, and there is nothing in his own schema to which he can refer. It is remarkable that throughout the centuries of wall-painting at Tunhuang the Chinese painter, unless closely following an imported model, never achieves a convincing rendering of the human figure. This reflects a deeply rooted prejudice against the nude in Chinese art, where, as in that of Flanders and North Germany, almost the only nudes are the pitiful figures of the damned undergoing punishment in hell. In Buddhist art China was prepared to accept much that was wholly foreign to her way of self-expression; but in this respect her rejection was complete.

During the early centuries of its expansion, Buddhism was nourished by a constant stream of missionaries and pilgrims flowing back and forth between India and China. Yet even when this movement was at its height, in the fifth and early sixth centuries, Chinese Buddhist art was beginning to acquire a character uniquely its own. In the late sculpture at Yün-kang, and in the caves carved out at Lung-men after the Wei moved

[1] The first pictorial record of the caves was that published by Paul Pelliot in *Mission Pelliot en Asie Centrale: Les Grottes de Touen Houang* (Paris, 1914–24). The most important of the hoard of banners discovered by Sir Aurel Stein are illustrated in his *Serindia* (4 vols., Oxford, 1921), and in F. H. Andrews, *Wall Paintings from Ancient Shrines in Central Asia, Recovered by Sir Aurel Stein* (2 vols., London, 1948). See also Basil Gray and J. B. Vincent, *Buddhist Cave Paintings at Tun-huang* (London, 1959). Since 1942, the caves have been under the care of the National Tunhuang Research Institute, which has carried out a considerable amount of recording, conservation, and research. The latest and so far most valuable of their publications is *Dunhuang Bihua* ('Tunhuang Wall-paintings') (Peking, 1959).

their capital southwards to Loyang in 494, all attempts to copy Western models are abandoned. The proportions of the figures become elongated; the square, staring mask of the Yün-kang colossus is replaced by a long, sensitive face with a withdrawn expression of wonderful sweetness; the body fades to nothing beneath a flat, rhythmic cascade of draperies. One might imagine that this was the expression of some new and more profound or poetic interpretation of Buddhist doctrine; but that is not the case.

Although we associate the change with the Northern Wei because most of the surviving sculpture in this new style was carved under their patronage and in their territory, it has recently been shown that the style originated in the independent South as much as a century before it appeared at Yün-kang. Its roots lay in the religious and artistic climate of Nanking in the fifth and early sixth centuries. Contact with India and Central Asia, so easy for the Toba Wei, was tenuous and intermittent for the Southern courts; moreover, while the Wei had no art of their own, Nanking at this period was the focus of the Chinese tradition, expressed in the abstract, linear style of Ku K'ai-chih and of the painter and sculptor Tai K'uei. Moreover, Southern Buddhism itself was different from that of the North. The great propagator of the faith, Hui-yüan, was steeped in Taoism, expressed Buddhist ideas in Taoist terms, and built his temples in mountain beauty spots already sacred in the Chinese nature cult. These forces were too powerful to surrender completely to Indian ideas and forms, and for nearly a century succeeded in imposing a wholly Chinese style upon Buddhist painting and sculpture. A beautiful example of this style, in gilt bronze, is the Maitreya dated 536 illustrated in Plate 15.

As they observed the effects of this change, were Chinese Buddhists aware how far their new images were departing from the old Indian models? Nowhere in the literature do we find any specific comment to this effect. Nevertheless, it is a remarkable

PLATE 15

Maitreya Buddha, dated equivalent to A.D. 536. Gilt bronze. Ht. 24 in.
Northern Wei Dynasty

fact that when, in the middle of the sixth century, a purer Indian style once more penetrated into China, its effects were felt at once. This time it came not across Central Asia, for that road was blocked by fresh barbarian incursions, but northwards from the hinduized kingdoms of Indo-China. There are many references in the *Liang History* to the arrival of icon-bearing missions from Fu-nan (Cambodia) and Lin-yi (Champa) at the Liang court. In 519, for example, Rudravarman of Fu-nan sent 'an

FIG. 12. Development of the Buddha image. From the left: Yün-kang (*c.* 480–500); Lung-men (*c.* 490–550); Ch'i-chou (*c.* 550–80;) Sui type (*c.* 580–620); T'ang type (*c.* 620–750). (After Mizuno.)

auspicious Indian sandalwood image' to the emperor Wu, and in 503 one of coral. Believing himself a second Aśoka, the sovereign received these images with vast enthusiasm, and had them copied and distributed among scores of temples that he caused to be erected throughout the kingdom. Such was the vigour with which this genuine 'Indian' style was propagated that by the middle of the century it was beginning to influence the art of the northern barbarian kingdoms also. Long before the end of the century the flat, abstract manner of the 'second phase', as it has often been called, had completely disappeared.

It may seem surprising that China, having absorbed the first Buddhist style and moulded it so successfully to her own instinctive preferences, should have been prepared to abandon it so readily in favour of a new foreign style. The explanation is to be found partly in the influence of the emperor Wu as a tireless propagator of Indian ideals; partly, perhaps, in a natural desire for a more robust and plastic rendering of form; partly also in the fact that a renewal of contact with India, first by way of Indo-China and later across Central Asia, not only stimulated the flow of Indian images, but at the same time made the Chinese

FIG. 13. Two Bodhisattva torsos: left, from Sāñchi, India; right, from Lung-yen-shan, Hopei, late seventh century. (After Willetts.)

more conscious of the Indian origins of both the doctrine and its art: Indian ideas must be clothed in Indian forms. The old compromise with the Taoists was forgotten.

This 'reindianization' of Chinese Buddhist art reached its climax in the seventh and in the first half of the eighth century, when Chinese power was at its height, and under the Pax Sinica missionaries and pilgrims could once more move freely back and forth across Central Asia. T'ang Buddhist sculpture is often astonishingly close to Indian models. The grandeur and purity of late Gupta art is recaptured in the great Vairōćana at Lungmen (672–5), and in the reliefs from Hsiang-t'ang-shan now in the Freer Gallery in Washington, while the seated Buddhas and bodhisats in the caves at T'ien-lung-shan, and the hoard of stone figures recently discovered at Chengtu, show how far the Chinese sculptor was now prepared to go in surrendering to Indian aesthetic ideals. The face is full, the lips pouting, the ample fleshy body bends and twists seductively, caressed by its drapery. Yet even here Chinese feeling is not wholly absent. The sweeping lines of both figure and drapery are more fluent than those of India. Whereas in Indian sculpture the rhythm is that of the dance, which suggests the possibility of abrupt changes of tempo and direction, the rhythms of the Chinese figures are suave, liquid, and unbroken.

Chinese Buddhist sculpture, however, was not made to be seen in isolation. In temples, even in most cave temples, the figures generally stood against a wall on which other figures were painted, and together they formed a unified composition. There was thus an intimate stylistic bond between the two arts. Sculpture—except in the hands of a tiny minority of masters whose names are recorded—was a craft, often seen at its best and most vital in the folk tradition of pottery tomb-figurines; painting, on the other hand, was practised by gentlemen, and its influence was nearly always dominant. It is true that in painting foreign techniques were also introduced: under the Liang, for example, Chang Seng-yu was noted for his Buddhist icons adorned with 'flowers in relief' in the Indian manner; the Tocharian Wei-ch'ih Po-chih-na and his son (?) Wei-ch'ih I-seng (active 680–730) 'always worked from foreign prototypes'; their lines were like 'bent iron or coiled wire', and they made use of arbitrary shading in the rendering of both figures and drapery.

The masses admired these foreign techniques enormously, as they always admire realism, but a critic of the period, Yao Tsui, merely remarked that 'since the Chinese and barbarian styles are different, we cannot criticize them on the same basis'. Educated men were, in fact, always conscious that Buddhist painting was a special kind of foreign art, practised by specialists, and not to be judged by the standards applied to their own painting. It was significant that the greatest of all Chinese painters of Buddhist subjects, Wu Tao-tzu (c. 700–60), did not, so far as is known from descriptions of his frescoes, make any use of these foreign techniques after his own style had matured. His was an art of pure line, so broad in conception and so powerful in execution that crowds would gather to watch him as he painted. This Michelangelo of T'ang China executed more than three hundred wall-paintings in the temples of Loyang and Changan, many of which were afterwards coloured by assistants or well-meaning but inept 'improvers'. Perhaps his greatest contribution to Buddhist art lay in his power to transform the essentially sculptured ideals of India into the linear, painterly terms of the Chinese tradition. In achieving this he provided the basis of all later Buddhist art in China, and indeed for almost all large-scale figure painting. Though none of his work survives, the kind of synthesis that he achieved is illustrated in some of the T'ang frescoes at Tunhuang, such as those in Cave 148, of which a detail is illustrated in Plate 16.

In the light of these events can it be said that Chinese artists 'absorbed' Indian art? China, it is clear, was forced to adopt the language of Indian Buddhist sculpture, not only because her own sculptural tradition was unable to meet the challenge, but also because it was essential that 'authentic' imported images be copied as closely as possible if they were to be considered efficacious. Here there was no choice. Nevertheless, without any significant sacrifice of iconographic requirements, China did succeed in imposing her own aesthetic upon the Indian model:

PLATE 16

Bodhisats; detail from wall-painting in Cave 148, Tunhuang. Middle T'ang Dynasty (eighth century)

first in the startlingly flat and linear sculpture of the late fifth and early sixth centuries, and again from the mid-T'ang onwards. While in the first instance the linear flatness proclaims a total victory for the Chinese brush line, in the second the Chinese line is used to convey an Indian feeling of plasticity. In both cases the crucial factor is the influence on sculpture of the ideals and techniques of Chinese painting.

In the realm of architecture China's rejection of Indian ideas was almost complete, because not only the materials and techniques, but the very conceptions of space and planning in the two traditions were too remote from each other to make any fusion possible. India builds in brick and stone, China in timber. The traditional Indian architect is the stonemason, his Chinese counterpart the master carpenter. The Indian shrine is heavily ornamented on the exterior with sculpture in relief, dark and enclosed within; the Chinese temple building is essentially an elaborate roof raised on a forest of columns, its walls no more than thin screens which form ideal surfaces for wall painting. The first Buddhist images were probably worshipped in the houses of rich patrons, and, even at its most complex, the later Chinese temple and monastery always retained the character of a palace or great mansion, composed of a succession of courtyards linked by pavilions and galleries. Some early attempts were made to copy the Indian *stūpa* (relic mound), but China already had her own tall, storied timber towers (*lou*) which fitted more congenially into the Chinese landscape and could easily be adapted to the symbolism of the pagoda; and even when pagodas were built in brick or stone, timber posts, brackets, and half-roofs were imitated in relief on their surface. Although Chinese builders have known the arch and vault for nearly two thousand years, their use has been confined almost entirely to the construction of gateways and tombs.

The sweeping curve and uplifted corners of the roof represent the one successful example in Chinese architecture of a borrowing from abroad. Their introduction was the result of China's southward expansion at the beginning of the T'ang Dynasty, which brought her into contact with the cultures of south-east

FIG. 14. Pagoda at Yakushi-ji, Nara, Japan.
Eighth century.

Asia. By the end of the T'ang, the curving roof had spread to North China. Supported on an increasingly elaborate system of brackets and cantilever arms, it has come to be regarded as the uniquely Chinese mode of expression in architecture, and it is indeed one of the most beautiful forms that man has devised. Chinese architects in the twentieth century, understandably reluctant to modify or abandon it, have tried to superimpose it on a modern brick or concrete structure. While this compromise has never been wholly successful, it was less disastrous than China's flirtation, during the first decade of the People's Republic, with Stalinist wedding-cake architecture. This latter phase has now happily passed, but as yet Chinese architects seem not to have learned the lesson so well mastered by modern Japan, that the basis of their architecture is not the roof, however beautiful, but the timber frame, and that the frame provides the ideal starting-point for an architecture that is modern in form and yet essentially Chinese in spirit.

Any foreign idea, form, or technique reaching China has had to reckon with the formidable strength and unity of the Chinese artistic tradition itself. On a superficial level she has always been ready to borrow from abroad: witness, for example, the 'influence' of the animal art of the border regions in late Chou and Han, and that of Near Eastern metalwork on the pottery of the T'ang Dynasty. But though of relatively long duration, these were merely fashions, and were dropped when people grew tired of them. On a deeper level our brief survey of these influences suggests that elements of foreign art have been appropriated only when they fulfilled a need which could not be supplied by China herself. When that happened, the foreign elements have taken a permanent place, but always in respect of that particular need. Indian techniques of colour, shading, and impasto, for example, have been continuously employed in certain limited categories of figure and flower painting. They have made no impact on landscape or bamboo painting, where their application would have served to distort, rather than to assist, the expression of purely Chinese ideas.

We can find further support for this view if we glance briefly at the impact of Western art on China. When the Jesuits introduced European painting in the seventeenth and eighteenth centuries, court painters and craftsmen admired these new techniques much as they had those of Wei-ch'ih I-seng in the T'ang Dynasty. Yet although the followers of Castiglione applied Western perspective and shading to their paintings with laborious charm, they looked upon these attainments as mere technical tricks. We have already quoted the opinion of the eighteenth-century court painter Tsou I-kuei regarding Western perspective. The literati completely ignored these techniques. Wu Li, one of the six great masters of the Ch'ing Dynasty, was in close touch with the Jesuits and spent the last twenty years of his life as a Catholic missionary; yet his landscape-painting shows not the slightest hint of European influence.

Western art made little impression on the Ch'ing painters because they saw it in isolation. They could not regard it as the expression of anything of which China felt herself to be in need. On the contrary, its impact came at a period when Chinese self-assurance was still at its height. The effect of Western art in the twentieth century has been far greater, precisely because it is the expression of ideas and forms which China has been strenuously adopting.[1] The move towards Westernization in art began just before the Revolution of 1911. By the nineteen-twenties, some painters, trained in Tokyo and Paris, had abandoned traditional art and were working entirely in the modern European idiom.[2]

[1] The period between 1900 and 1950 is covered by my *Chinese Art in the Twentieth Century* (London, Berkeley, and Los Angeles, 1959).

[2] The influence of Chinese art on that of her neighbours throws further light on this point. It had little or no effect on south-east Asia, already deeply penetrated by the culture of India and the Islamic world. Korean art, on the other hand, throughout its history has made the fullest use of Chinese forms, because Korea herself has been continuously fertilized by Chinese culture. Japan offers a more complex picture of the interplay between Chinese influence and nascent, and resurgent, native ideals. The art of Nara and Kyoto in the sixth, seventh, and eighth centuries is very Chinese, for then Japan was modelling her whole way of life on that of China. Later, Chinese influence returned: Ashikaga ink-painting, for example, was inspired by that of the Southern Sung 'idealists' Ma Yüan and Hsia Kuei and the Chinese Zen painters, while the *bun-jin-ga* of the Tokugawa period was derived from the

They returned to set up their *ateliers* in the French Concession of Shanghai, wore their hair long, and affected floppy bow ties: for these things were as much a symbol of their liberation from the shackles of the past as was the style of painting itself. But while some painters surrendered totally to the West, others saw European art as a dangerous threat to the tradition, and continued to paint in the old manner as though nothing had happened. A very few, excited by the new range of expression and technique that Western art presented to them, and yet conscious of their own roots, succeeded, briefly and very tentatively, in creating a new kind of painting that was both modern in style and Chinese in feeling. Western abstract painting, however, has made little or no impression on Chinese art, partly because the abstract element in art has already been so thoroughly explored in calligraphy, and partly because, as we pointed out in discussing the T'ang 'action painters', the Chinese painter is never content with mere form. Western realism found its most powerful expression in the woodcut movement, launched in the late twenties by the great writer and critic Lu Hsün as an instrument of social and political propaganda; though in the work of some later engravers, notably Huang Yung-yü, it has become more lyrical and personal. However, the long war with Japan and its chaotic aftermath discouraged such experiments, while since 1950 a new orthodoxy has been imposed. Today the conventional Chinese and Western styles are both practised with China's age-old skill. There is a tendency to employ the former for more timeless themes and the latter for those with a 'socialist-realist' content. But this distinction is by no means

---

wen-jen-hua of Ming and early Ch'ing. But Ashikaga idealism went out of fashion with the resurgence of the Japanese spirit in the Momoyama period, while the *bun-jin-ga* was seldom more than a *style* which Japanese painters, very few of whom in any case were scholars, freely blended with other styles; to them it was never, as it had been in China, the pure expression of a scholarly outlook.

rigidly maintained, and painters, now more secure in their liveli-
hood than at any previous period, are encouraged to experiment
in adapting the traditional medium to modern themes. Such
experiments, however, are confined to technique; the content
must be 'correct' and unambiguous. Although within these
strict limits there is considerable variety, a true picture of

FIG. 15. Huang Yung-yü. The music lesson. Woodcut (contemporary).

modern China's response to Western art can only emerge after
individual artists have had the opportunity to explore all the
possibilities that the confrontation of the two traditions has
opened up.

And what has the West learned from Chinese art in the twentieth century? Apart from the enthusiastic welcome of a handful
of collectors and abstract painters, and the more incalculable
response of visitors to exhibitions, its influence has so far been
negligible. Europe, much more than America, is still wrapped in
her old cultural self-sufficiency. Can we hope that the influence

of Chinese art will in time go deeper?—that Western art will be enriched not simply by the techniques of the Chinese painter, but also by his all-embracing view of nature, by the sense of harmony, peace, and wholeness that Chinese art expresses, and by the vital linear rhythms of the brush in her painting and calligraphy? Is it possible that the Western collector may cultivate a more detached attitude to his possessions, or that the Western painter might be willing to surrender part of his heroic individualism for the sake of the preservation of the tradition? Fortunately, in this day of the 'museum without walls' this latter sacrifice will not be required of him. But he could certainly benefit from the sense of history which, for all its surface changes, gives such inner strength to the Chinese tradition. Whether such influences as that of China on modern abstract painting are permanent or temporary will depend not only upon the needs of individual artists, but even more upon the extent to which the West feels the necessity to study and acquire some of the values of Chinese civilization as a whole. In the meantime, when we as individuals contemplate the achievements of Chinese art, and as artists and craftsmen are inspired by them, we are taking the first steps in that direction.   MICHAEL SULLIVAN

5

SCIENCE AND CHINA'S INFLUENCE ON THE WORLD

I

In all civilizations it has been customary for those who are departing from this life to designate others as the heirs and inheritors of their worldly goods, and if such an action has the approbation of law we are accustomed to call what is thus transmitted a legacy. For the earlier volumes of this series the term was appropriate enough, because the civilizations and the languages of classical Greece and imperial Rome have indeed long been dead in the historical sense, but difficulties naturally arose when the expression was continued for a civilization which is still living. If it is true that Sanskrit itself is a dead language, Indian culture as a whole is very much alive, and the same is true of the culture to which the present book is devoted. In fact Chinese civilization has never been living more vigorously than it is today. I shall not labour the point, for it has already been discussed in the Introduction; nevertheless, where the history of science and technology is concerned, it raises questions of substance.

Who was supposed to be the 'legatee' in the original conception of this series? Was not the unspoken conception that it was 'modern Western' civilization, rapidly spreading over the world, and destined to supersede all cultures not based on European Christendom? A 'Legacy of Europe' was not thought worth writing, for Europe alone was the repository of immortal truth.[1]

[1] It is still not at all difficult to find expressions of this attitude towards the European inheritance by Western scholars. For example Costa Brochado has

It seems very doubtful now whether this implicit assumption has any validity. Modern science has indeed created a universal and international culture, that of the airman, the engineer, and the biologist, but although modern science originated in Europe and in Europe only, it was built upon a foundation of medieval science and technology much of which was non-European. Thus we must define our terms. The 'testator' here is a civilization with a longer continuous living tradition than any other, with the possible exception of Israel, and one which is in no danger of decay. The 'legatee' is the international world of which every country now inevitably forms a part; not simply a Europe deigning to adopt a few exotic elements from peripheral peoples. Each people enters the modern world with its own offering of thought, discovery, and invention, some richer perhaps than others, but each able and willing to participate in the universal discourse of applied mathematics while yet most faithful to its own inheritance of language and philosophy, an inheritance from which all others have much to learn. Indeed, the metaphor of inheritance is unsatisfactory for our purposes,

written: 'Truly the motive power of the forces which are working against us in Asia and Africa today is a millenary hatred borne by Asiatic orientalism against the last torches of occidental civilization which still burn in those regions. What it cannot abide is the strong and redeeming light of a culture which proclaims the civil and moral liberty of man against that caste tyranny which is at the base of all oriental philosophies. This is the explanation of how it has been possible for the wonderful technology of Western civilization to be completely assimilated, from the frontiers of Asia to the confines of Japan, without any modification of the philosophic-religious conceptions of human life among those peoples. It looks as if China, Russia, India, and Japan, to name only the greater countries, have profited exclusively by the experimental sciences of our civilization in order to arm and equip themselves to destroy in the end all that is profound and essential in it, its spirit and its morality.' (*Henri le Navigateur*, Lisbon, 1960, p. 34.) Let it not be thought that this European chauvinism is confined to the Portuguese or other Europeans; a very similar statement can be found in C. C. Gillispie, *The Edge of Objectivity: an Essay in the History of Scientific Ideas* (Princeton, 1960), p. 8.

for the inheriting process has been a series of mutual transmissions going on for more than twenty centuries. One would rather prefer the image of the great rivers of past science and technology flowing into the ocean of modern natural knowledge, so that all peoples have been testators and all are now inheritors, each in their several ways.

Secondly, the history of science and technology is not to be bounded by Europe and what Europe received of these transmissions. During the first fourteen centuries of the Christian era, as this contribution will have no difficulty in showing,[1] China transmitted to Europe a veritable abundance of discoveries and inventions which were often received by the West with no clear idea of where they had originated. The technical inventions of course travelled faster and further than the scientific thought. But besides all this there were important influences upon nascent modern science during the Renaissance period, and these continued on throughout the eighteenth century. By that time we reach the beginning of the modern period, when science has become a worldwide enterprise in which China is participating along with all other cultures. If we were to interpret the term 'legacy' in what was probably its original sense, we should restrict our attention to those factors which were concerned in the direct historical genesis of modern science, excluding factors which fell into place after the Galilean breakthrough of the early seventeenth century. But if we take the term in the wider sense outlined above, we shall be interested in what China contributed to

[1] It will of course be impossible to give detailed chapter and verse for any of the statements made in this contribution. Abundance of references to both Chinese and Western literatures, together with Chinese characters, will however be found in *Science and Civilisation in China* (7 vols. in 12 parts, Cambridge, 1954–), by J. Needham, with the collaboration of Wang Ling (Wang Ching-ning), Lu Gwei-djen, Ho Ping-yü, Kenneth Robinson, Ts'ao T'ien-ch'in, and others. I am glad to record here my great indebtedness to my Chinese friends and co-workers, without whom the work would have been impossible.

the world at all periods. To explain what this means we must not only consider pre-Renaissance and post-Renaissance transmissions separately, but also distinguish between science and technology.

There can be no doubt that in the opening phases of modern science, when mechanics, dynamics, and celestial and terrestrial physics came into being in their modern form, the Greek contribution had the greatest share.[1] Euclidean deductive geometry and Ptolemaic planetary astronomy, with all that they imply, were certainly the main factors in the birth of the 'new, or experimental, science'—in so far as any antecedents played a part at all, for we must not underrate its basic originality. In spite of Ptolemy and Archimedes, the occidental ancients did not, as a whole, experiment. But Asian contributions were by no means absent from the decisive breakthrough, for apart from algebra and the basic numerational and computational techniques (e.g. the Indian numerals, the Indo-Chinese zero, and Chinese decimal place-value, the most ancient form of the method), China provided all the basic knowledge of magnetical phenomena. This field of study (to which we shall return presently, p. 252) was radically different from those which Greek physics had cultivated, and its effect upon the initial stages of modern science, mediated through Gilbert and Kepler, was of vital importance. There were also significant influences from China in practical astronomy, such as the adoption of the Chinese celestial coordinates by Tycho Brahe.

In technological influences before and during the Renaissance China occupies a quite dominating position. In the body of this contribution we shall mention among other things the efficient equine harness, the technology of iron and steel, the inventions

---

[1] For a discussion of this point see J. Needham, 'Poverties and Triumphs of the Chinese Scientific Tradition', art. in *The Structure of Scientific Change* (Report of History of Science Symposium, Oxford, 1961) (London, 1963), p. 117.

of gunpowder and paper, the mechanical clock, and basic engineering devices such as the driving-belt, the chain-drive, and the standard method of converting rotary to rectilinear motion, together with segmental arch bridges and nautical techniques such as the stern-post rudder. The world owes far more to the relatively silent craftsmen of ancient and medieval China than to the Alexandrian mechanics, articulate theoreticians though they were.

We have next to think of those achievements of Asian and Chinese science which, though not genetically connected with the first rise of modern science, yet deserve close attention. They may or may not be directly related genetically to their corresponding developments in post-Renaissance modern science. Perhaps the most outstanding Chinese discovery which was so related, even though it influenced the West relatively late (the end of the eighteenth and the beginning of the nineteenth centuries), was that of the first successful immunization technique. Variolation, the forerunner of Jennerian vaccination, had been in use in China certainly since the beginning of the sixteenth century, and if tradition is right since the eleventh; it consisted in the inoculation of a minute amount of the contents of the smallpox pustule itself into the nostril of the patient to be immunized, and Chinese physicians had gradually worked out methods of attenuating the virus so as to give greater safety. The origins of the whole science of immunology lie in a practice based on medieval Chinese medical thought. A case of direct theoretical influence which springs to mind concerns cosmology— the old Chinese doctrine of infinite empty space as opposed to the solid crystalline celestial spheres of medieval Europe, but again it did not exert its full effect towards their dissolution until after Galileo's time. Examples of later incorporation would be the development of undulatory theory in eighteenth-century physics, which immensely elaborated characteristically Chinese ideas without knowing anything of them; or the use of ancient and medieval Chinese records of novae and supernovae by modern radio-astronomers. A good case of the probable absence of any stimulus would be the seismograph as used in China from the second to the seventh centuries A.D.; though an outstanding achievement and a permanent legacy to the history of geology, it was almost certainly unknown to any of the scientific men who developed seismographs again in post-Renaissance Europe. Chinese biological and pathological classification systems occupy the same position; they were clearly unknown to Linnaeus and Sydenham, but none the less worthy of study, for only by drawing up the balance-sheet in full shall we ever ascertain what each civilization has contributed to human advancement. Similarly, it is now becoming clear that medieval Chinese anatomy was far more advanced than has generally been thought, for judgements have been based by Western anatomists only on the few remaining block-print illustrations, since they were unable to read the texts themselves and to pursue the complex and elaborate nomenclature. But it exerted no influence on the revival and development of anatomy in Renaissance Europe. Nor did the outstandingly good iconographic tradition of the pharmaceutical compendia of the *Pen-ts'ao* genre, centuries ahead of the West in accurate botanical illustration, which has gained appreciation only in our own time.

Lastly we have to think of technical inventions which only became incorporated, whether or not by re-invention, into the corpus of modern technology after the Renaissance period. A case in point might be the paddle-wheel boat, but it is uncertain, for we do not know whether the first European successes were based on a Byzantine idea never executed, or on a vast fund of practical Chinese achievement during the preceding millennium, or on neither. A clearer example is the iron-chain suspension bridge, for while the first European description came towards the end of the sixteenth century, the first realization occurred only in the eighteenth, and in knowledge of the Chinese antecedents, going back, as we now know, for more than a thousand years previously. Independent invention occurred, no doubt, with the differential gear, for though this was present in the south-pointing carriages of ancient China, their construction has been revealed only by modern historical research and could hardly have inspired the later mechanics of the West who fitted up again this important form of enmeshing wheel-work. So also the Chinese methods of steel-making by the co-fusion process and by the direct oxygenation of cast iron, though of great seniority to the siderurgy of Europe, were not able to exert any influence upon it, if indeed they did, which is still uncertain, until long after the Renaissance. At the same time one must always refrain from being too positive about the absence of influence. In human intercourse there have been innumerable capillary channels which we cannot see, and especially for earlier times we should never be tempted to dogmatism in the denial of transmissions. Sometimes one wonders whether humanity ever forgets anything. The sailing-carriage of early seventeenth-century Europe was consciously modelled on supposed Chinese prototypes which had in fact been rather different, but it is possible that they in their turn derived from the model boats with sails outspread which, supported upon low wooden wagons, conveyed the coffins of ancient Egyptian gods or kings across the deserts to their tombs. Broadly speaking, experience shows that the further one goes back in history the more unlikely independent invention was; we cannot infer it from the conditions of modern science today, where it frequently occurs.

Thus in relation to the 'legacy' of China we have to think of three different values. There is the value of that which helped directly to effect the Galilean breakthrough, the value of that which became incorporated in modern science later on, and last but not least the value of that which had no traceable influence and yet renders Chinese science and technology no less worthy of study and admiration than that of Europe. Everything depends on the definition of the legatee—Europe alone, or modern universal science, or the whole of mankind. I would urge that it is not in fact legitimate to require of every scientific or technological activity that it should have contributed to the advancement of the European culture-area. Nor need it even be shown to have constituted building material for modern universal science. The history of science is not to be written solely in terms of one continuous thread of linked influences. Is there not an oecumenical history of human thought and knowledge of nature, in which every effort can find its place, irrespective of what influences it received or handed on? Is not the history and philosophy of universal science the only true legatee of all human endeavour?

II

So much for indebtedness and its various meanings. Misunderstandings have been corrected, but nothing intrinsically new has emerged. Yet in this contribution I do want to make an important, if paradoxical, point which I do not remember seeing fully brought out anywhere hitherto. The proper title for this chapter ought to be 'The Ten (or the Twenty or Thirty) Discoveries (or Inventions) that Shook the World'. That Chinese discoveries and inventions there were, we have long known; that they were transmitted one after the other to Europe, we can demonstrate or show to be extremely likely; but the extraordinary paradox arises that while many, even most, of them had earth-shaking effects upon occidental society, Chinese society had a strange capacity for absorbing them and remaining relatively unmoved. We shall return to this at the conclusion, having systematically pointed out the social effects of the Chinese novelties as we speak of them; perhaps to offer some tentative explanation of the outstanding contrast. Here I wish only to strike the real keynote of this contribution.

One common misconception which it is desirable to get out of the way before going further is that Chinese achievements were invariably technical rather than scientific. It is true, as has already been said, that ancient and medieval Chinese science was hemmed in within the boundaries of the ideographic language and penetrated little outside it. But because the practical inventions were the only things that the Indian, Arabic, or Western cultures were generally capable of taking over from the Chinese culture-area, this does not mean that the Chinese themselves had always been mere 'sooty empiricks'. On the contrary, there was a large body of naturalistic theory in ancient and medieval China, there was systematic recorded experimentation, and there was a great deal of measurement often quite surprising in its accuracy. Of course, the theories of the Chinese remained to the end of their autochthonous period characteristically medieval in type, for the Renaissance, with its mathematization of hypotheses, did not happen among them.

The point can be illustrated perhaps by a quotation which in any case would only inexcusably be omitted from this chapter.

It is well to observe [said Lord Verulam] the force and virtue and consequences of discoveries. These are to be seen nowhere more conspicuously than in those three which were unknown to the ancients, and of which the origin, though recent, is obscure and inglorious; namely, printing, gunpowder, and the magnet. For these three have changed the whole face and state of things throughout the world, the first in literature, the second in warfare, the third in navigation; whence have followed innumerable changes; insomuch that no empire, no sect, no star, seems to have exerted greater power and influence in human affairs than these mechanical discoveries.[1]

Subsequent scholars, who might have been expected to know better, were content that the origin of the discoveries should remain obscure and inglorious. J. B. Bury, for instance, when

---

[1] Francis Bacon, *Novum Organum*, bk. 1, aphorism 129.

describing the Renaissance controversies between the supporters of the 'Ancients' and those of the 'Moderns', shows that the latter were generally considered to have had the best of it, precisely because of the three great inventions which Bacon described. Yet nowhere in his book is there even a footnote pointing out that none of the three was of European origin.[1] In what follows we shall show not only where their origin was, but how it arose from ancient scientific theorizing.

Bury's book was written forty-five years ago, but the same attitude of 'invincible ignorance' about non-European contributions persists today as strongly as ever. One cannot help noticing it in a recent work, *The Inspiration of Science*, by Sir George Thomson.[2] After emphasizing the twin Greek successes of geometry and planetary astronomy, he goes on to say:

> But with things on earth they were less successful. They knew that amber when rubbed attracted chaff, and that a stone from a place in Asia Minor called Magnesia attracted iron, and they had observed that a pole sticking out of the water seemed bent; but they made no real progress with the corresponding sciences. It is sometimes said that this failure was due to an unwillingness to experiment. No doubt up to a point this is true, but I think that there is something more. . . . [The Greeks] failed to realize the importance of these apparently trivial occurrences. The heavens were impressive and grand, perhaps the abode of gods or even of something greater than the gods. Little bits of chaff and shreds of iron were amusing but hardly of the first importance. This is a very natural attitude.

Yet the greatest discovery in method which science has made is that the apparently trivial, the merely curious, may be clues to an understanding of the deepest principles of Nature. One can hardly blame the Greeks. Even with Newton behind him, Swift could be witty at the expense of the Royal Society in his account of the 'projectors' of Laputa, with their studies of cucumbers as a source of sunlight—and Swift, though an unpleasant creature, was no fool. Just how the discovery came

[1] *The Idea of Progress* (London, 1920), pp. 40 ff., 45, 54, 62, 78 ff., 138.
[2] Oxford, 1962.

about is not clear. It is the great thing that marks off our age from others, and may well have had several independent causes. Among these, probably, was the importance of magnetism for navigation, and of optics for spectacles. Gunnery perhaps added a little, and made Galileo's mechanics sound rather less improbable. But a greater cause was the excitement that came from the discovery of a way round Africa to India and then of the New World. In an age in which the wildest projects of geographical discovery had proved successful it was natural to try others of a different kind, to open the mind and ask more searching questions on matters nearer at hand. The first discovery must always be that there are things worth discovering. So the apparent trivialities of the stone from Magnesia and of amber grew in importance, and since the time of Maxwell it has been clear to the discerning that the ideas behind them are as fundamental as any in the world, not even excluding that of matter.

Much of this is well said, and worth saying; but some of it is surely an example of what Claude Roy has called 'the iron curtain of false enigmas'. Not only is the Chinese origin of magnetical science and of explosives chemistry quietly ignored, but the beginning of curiosity about apparently trivial natural occurrences is made into a mystery. It may possibly be that the Greeks lacked this[1]—if so, they were already infected with that false sense of values which led Thomas Aquinas to say that 'a little knowledge about the highest things is better than the most abundant knowledge about things low and small'.[2] If the secrets of the Magnesian stone were first revealed in China this was perhaps not only due to the organic materialism of her cosmology, but also because all Chinese philosophical tradition lay behind Ch'eng Ming-tao's eleventh-century criticism of the Buddhists: 'When they strive only to "understand the high"

---

[1] But I should be surprised if it were not possible to find statements in the Hippocratic corpus and in Galen about the great importance of very small pathological symptoms or anatomical structures.

[2] *Summa Theologiae*, Ia, i. 5 ad 1.

without "studying the low", how can their understanding of the high be right?"[1]

III

Let us now return to the inventions listed by Bacon. Since everything cannot be discussed, we shall leave the epic of printing on one side,[2] and stay only upon the discovery of chemical explosive force and that of magnetic polarity. It is hard to over-rate either of them, and both developed from Taoist (originally Shamanist) magic, guided into practical reproducibility by the theories of Chinese natural philosophy working within alchemy on the one hand and geomancy on the other. The development of gunpowder weapons was certainly one of the greatest achievements of the medieval Chinese world.[3] One finds

[1] *Honan Ch'eng-shih i-shu*, ch. 13, p. 1b. The quoted phrases are from the *Analects* xiv. 37, where Confucius says that the study of the lowly elucidates the supernal (*hsia hsüeh, erh shang ta*). What a contrast to the theme of 'suspiciendo despicio'!

[2] In order to complete the pattern of this paper it is necessary however to point out that while the spread of printing in Europe has always been recognized as a necessary precursor of the Renaissance, the Reformation, and the rise of capitalism, because of its democratizing of education, its effects in China were far less. From the Sung onwards the ranks of the scholar-gentry were widely increased by the spread of printing, and the mandarinate was recruited from a much wider circle of families, but the basic structure and principle of the non-hereditary civil service remained essentially quite unchanged. The Chinese social organism had already for centuries been 'democratic' (in the sense of the *carrière ouverte aux talents*) and could therefore absorb a new factor which proved explosive in the aristocratic society of the West. As for transmission, I am satisfied that Gutenberg knew of Chinese movable-block printing, at least by hearsay. *The Invention of [Paper and] Printing in China and their Spread Westwards* is the title of the classical book by T. F. Carter (2nd ed., ed. L. C. Goodrich, New York, 1955).

[3] No study of this in a Western language as yet incorporates all the new knowledge brought to light in recent times by Chinese scholars, especially Feng Chia-sheng, but the paper of Wang Ling on 'The Invention and Use of Gunpowder and Firearms in China', *Isis*, vol. xxxvii (1947), p. 160, is still broadly speaking correct in its account. For the wider comparative background

the beginning of it towards the end of the T'ang, in the ninth century A.D., when the first reference to the mixing of charcoal, saltpetre (i.e. potassium nitrate), and sulphur is found. This occurs in a Taoist book which strongly recommends alchemists not to mix these substances, especially with the addition of arsenic, because some of those who have done so have had the mixture deflagrate, singe their beards, and burn down the building in which they were working.

After that things happened rather rapidly. The 'fire drug' (*huo yao*), which is the characteristic term for gunpowder mixtures, occurs as igniter in a flame-thrower in A.D. 919, and by the time we reach the year 1000 the practice of using gunpowder in simple bombs and grenades was coming into use. Its first composition formulae appear in 1044. This is a good deal earlier than the first references to any gunpowder composition in Europe, 1327, at best 1285. These bombs and grenades of the beginning of the eleventh century did not of course contain a brisant explosive like that which became known in the following two centuries when the proportion of nitrate was raised; they were more like rocket compositions which go off with a 'whoosh' rather than anything which gives a destructive explosion. And indeed it was about this time, the early eleventh century, that a new kind of incendiary arrow (*huo chien*), in fact the rocket, developed. Here immediately we see the importance of the availability of a natural form of tubing, the stem of the bamboo, because it was only necessary to attach a bamboo tube to an arrow and fill it with a low-nitrate composition to get the rocket effect. In this day and age it is hardly necessary to expatiate upon what the Chinese started when they first made rockets fly.

Thence there followed the important transition to the barrel gun. It occurred early in the twelfth century, about 1120, when the Sung people were conducting their great def nsive campaign

we now have J. R. Partington's important work: *A History of Greek Fire and Gunpowder* (Cambridge, 1961).

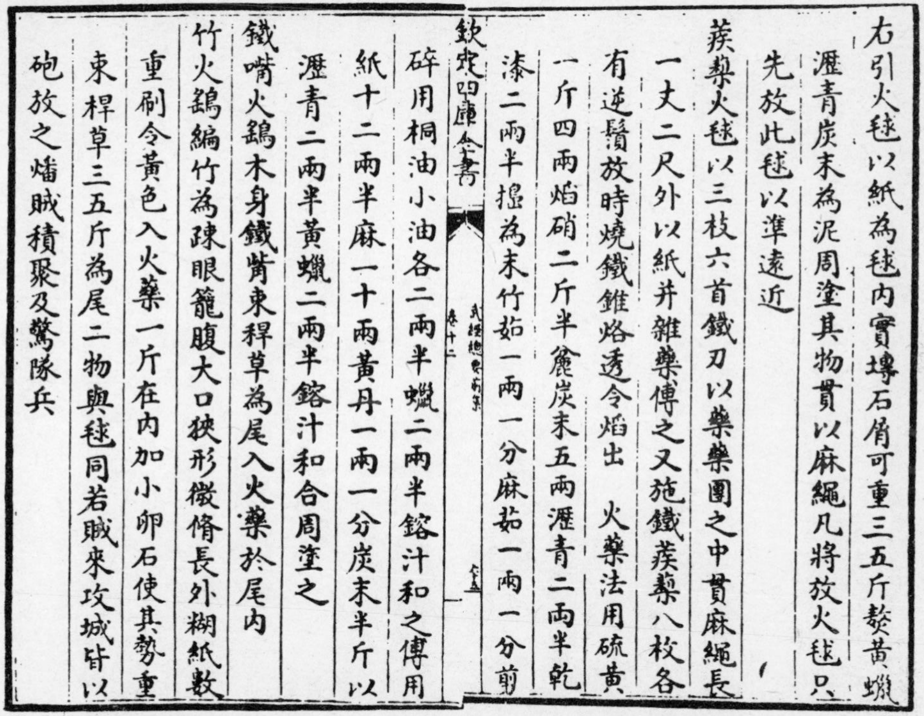

右引火毬以紙為毬內實塼石屑可重三五斤熬黃蠟
瀝青炭末為泥周塗其物貫以麻繩凡將放火毬只
先放此毬以準遠近
蒺藜火毬以三枝六首鐵刃以藥藥團之中貫麻繩長
一丈二尺外以紙并雜藥傅之又施鐵蒺藜八枚各
有逆鬚放時燒鐵錐烙透令焰出　火藥法用硫黃
一斤四兩焰硝二斤半麄炭末五兩瀝青二兩半乾
漆二兩半搗為末竹茹一兩一分麻茹一兩一分剪

欽定四庫全書　武經總要前集　卷十二

碎用桐油小油各二兩半蠟二兩半鎔汁和之傅用
紙十二兩半麻一十兩黃丹一兩一分炭末半斤以
瀝青二兩半黃蠟二兩半鎔汁和合周塗之
鐵嘴火鷂木身鐵嘴束稈草為尾入火藥於尾內
竹火鷂編竹為疎眼籠腹大口狹形微脩長外糊紙數
重刷令黃色入火藥一斤在內加小卵石使其勢重
束稈草三五斤為尾二物與毬同若賊來攻城皆以
砲放之燔賊積聚及驚隊兵

FIG. 16. Two pages from the *Wu-ching tsung-yao* of A.D. 1044 showing the earliest gunpowder formula in any civilization. It begins in the sixth column from the right.

against the Chin Tartars. In a remarkable book by Ch'en Kuei, the *Shou ch'eng lu*, on the defence of a certain city north of Hankow at that time, there is described the first invention and use of the fire-lance (*huo ch'iang*)—a tube filled with rocket composition but not allowed to go loose, held instead upon the end of a spear. An adequate supply of these five-minute flame-throwers, passed on from hand to hand, effectively discouraged enemy troops from storming one's city wall. By about 1230 we begin to have descriptions of really destructive explosions in the later campaigns between the Sung and the Yüan Mongols. Then about 1280 comes the appearance of the metal-barrel gun somewhere in the Old World. As yet we really do not know where it first occurred, whether among the Arabs with their *madfa'a*, whether

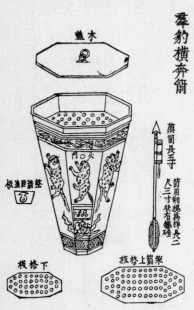

FIG. 17. Rocket-arrow and launching box (*Wu-pei chih*, A.D. 1621).

among the Chinese, as seems most likely from the preceding history, or whether possibly among the Westerners. Between 1280 and 1320 is the key period for the appearance of the metal-barrel cannon. I have no doubt that its real ancestry was the substantial bamboo tube of the Chinese fire-lance.

There are two important points to be made about this Chinese development of the first chemical explosive known to man. Firstly, it is not to be regarded as a purely technological achievement. Gunpowder was not the invention of artisans, farmers, or master-masons; it arose from the systematic if obscure investigations of Taoist alchemists. I say 'systematic' most advisedly, for although in the sixth and eighth centuries they had no theories of modern type to work with, that does not mean that they

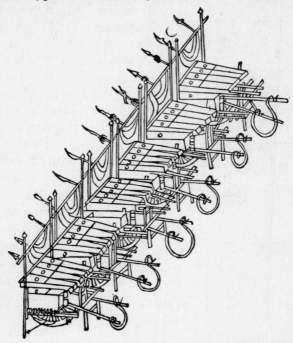

FIG. 18. Battery of rocket launching boxes on wheelbarrows (*Wu-pei chih*, A.D. 1621).

worked with no theories at all; on the contrary it has been shown that an elaborate doctrine of categories of affinities had grown up by the T'ang, reminiscent in some ways of the sympathies and antipathies of the Alexandrian mystical aurificers, but much more developed and much less animistic.[1] I use the term 'mystical

---

[1] See Ho Ping-yü and J. Needham, 'Theories of Categories in Early Mediaeval Chinese Alchemy', *Journ. Warburg & Courtauld Institutes*, vol. xxii (1959), p. 173.

aurificers' here because the first alchemists of Hellenistic times, though very interested in counterfeiting gold, and in all

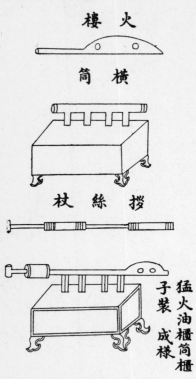

kinds of chemical and metallurgical transformations, were not as yet in pursuit of a 'philosopher's stone' which would give a medicine of immortality or an 'elixir of life'. There is every reason for believing that the basic ideas of Chinese alchemy, which had been 'longevity-conscious' from the beginning, made their way to the West through the Arabic world. Indeed, one cannot really speak of alchemy in the strict sense before the contribution of the Arabs, and it is even claimed that the word itself, and also other alchemical terms, are derived from Chinese originals. Many pieces of chemical apparatus from the Han period have come down to us, such as bronze vessels probably used for the sublimation of mercurous chloride (the making of calomel), vapour rising

Fig. 19. 'Greek Fire' (*meng huo yu*) flame-thrower, with tank for the naphtha, and double-acting pump with two pistons to work continuously (*Wu-ching tsung-yao*, A.D. 1044).

through the two arms and condensing in the centre (Plate 17). Certain forms of distilling apparatus are also typically Chinese, and quite different from those in use in the West. The distillate, condensed by the vessel of cold water above, drips down into a central receiver and flows out through a side-tube.

PLATE 17

A bronze 'rainbow vessel' (*kung teng*) of the Han period (*c.* first century B.C. or A.D.), probably used for sublimation, front view

This is an ancestor of apparatus used in modern chemistry.[1] In sum, the first compounding of an explosive mixture arose in the course of a systematic exploration of the chemical and pharmaceutical properties of a great variety of substances, inspired by the hope of attaining longevity or material immortality.

Secondly, in the gunpowder epic we have another case of the socially devastating discovery which China could somehow take in her stride but which had revolutionary effects in Europe. For decades, indeed for centuries, from Shakespeare's time onwards, European historians have recognized in the first salvoes of the fourteenth-century bombards the death-knell of the castle, and hence of Western military aristocratic feudalism. It would be tedious to enlarge upon this here. In one single year (1449) the artillery train of the king of France, making a tour of the castles still held by the English in Normandy, battered them down one after another at the rate of five a month. Nor were the effects of gunpowder confined to the land; they had profound influence also at sea, for in due time they gave the death-blow to the multi-oared slave-manned galley of the Mediterranean, which was unable to provide gun-platforms sufficiently stable for naval cannonades and broadsides. Less well known, but meriting passing mention here, is the fact that during the century before the appearance of gunpowder in Europe (i.e. the thirteenth) its poliorcetic value had been foreshadowed by another, less lasting development, that of the counterweighted trebuchet, also most dangerous for even the stoutest castle walls. This was an Arabic improvement of the projectile-throwing device (*p'ao*) most characteristic of Chinese military art, not the torsion or spring devices of Alexandrian or Byzantine catapults, but the simpler sw. pe-like lever bearing a sling at the end of its longer arm and operated by manned ropes attached to the end of its shorter one.

Here the contrast with China is particularly noteworthy. The

[1] See Ho Ping-yü and J. Needham, 'The Laboratory Equipment of the Early Mediaeval Chinese Alchemists', *Ambix*, vol. vii (1959), p. 58.

basic structure of bureaucratic feudalism remained after five centuries or so of gunpowder weapons just about the same as it had been before the invention had developed. The birth of chemical warfare had occurred in the T'ang but it did not find wide military use before the Sung, and its real proving-grounds were the wars between the Sung empire, the Chin Tartars, and the Mongols in the eleventh to thirteenth centuries. There are plenty of examples of its use by the forces of agrarian rebellions, and it was employed at sea as well as on land, in siege warfare no less than in the field. But as there was no heavily armoured knightly cavalry in China, nor any aristocratic or manorial feudal castles either, the new weapon simply supplemented those which had been in use before, and produced no perceptible effect upon the age-old civil and military bureaucratic apparatus, which each new foreign conqueror had to take over and use in his turn.

IV

Next let us look at the third of Bacon's great discoveries. If Ptolemaic astronomy was purely Greek, the early study of magnetism was purely Chinese, a point of immense importance. If we go into any place today where nature is under accurate observation or control—into an atomic power-station, the engine-room of an ocean liner, or any scientific laboratory—the walls are covered with dials and pointers, and people are making dial-and-pointer readings. But the first of all dial-and-pointer devices, so classical in the philosophy of science, was the magnetic compass, and in the development of this Europe had no part.

In the Sung period we find as one of its early forms a small piece of lodestone embedded in the body of a wooden fish with a little needle projecting from it; floating in water, it indicates the south.[1] The same thing was done with a dry suspension; a thin

---

[1] We are, of course, accustomed to think of the needle as pointing to the north, but in China the south was always considered to be indicated. In Chinese cosmic symbolism the emperor represented the pole-star, and so faced south on his throne, theoretically doing nothing, yet ruling all things with perfect success.

chopstick cut off and sharpened to a point bore the lodestone inside a little wooden turtle, with again a needle sticking out to add a small amount of extra torque. These designs date from about 1130, but we have a still earlier one, from 1044, described in a book called *Wu-ching tsung-yao* ('Compendium of Important Military Techniques') by Tseng Kung-liang. This is nothing other than the 'floating fish' so often mentioned by Arabic writers later on, the cup-shaped fish of magnetized iron floating on the water. Still more interesting, this compass-fish was not magnetized by being rubbed on the lodestone but by being heated to red heat while held in a north–south position in the earth's magnetic field. Remanent magnetism is a surprise to meet with in the early eleventh century. By its end, the most usual thing was to have a magnetized needle suspended on a single thread of raw silk.

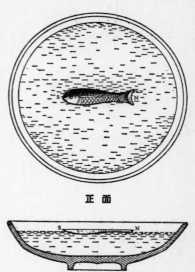

FIG. 20. Floating iron compass using remanent magnetism (*Wu-ching tsung-yao*, A.D. 1044, reconstruction by Wang Chen-to).

To get back to the beginning one has to mention the divination devices called *shih*. Used by the diviners in Han times, they had a square earth-plate surmounted by a discoidal heaven-plate, having the Great Bear carved on its upper surface together with the standard cyclical characters, compass points, lunar mansions, constellation names, and so on. In Wang Ch'ung's *Lun heng* ('Discourses Weighed in the Balance'), written in A.D. 83, there is a text which says that if you take the 'south-controlling spoon' (*ssu-nan chih shao*), and throw it on the ground, it will always point to the south. The accepted view is that to 'throw it on the ground' was not meant literally, but indicated that it was to be placed on the ground-plate of the diviner's board. The spoon itself was an actual piece of lode-stone, carved into the shape of the Northern Dipper (the Great Bear), i.e. into a Chinese spoon. It has been found experimentally that this can in fact be done if the bronze plate is polished as highly as possible; then the torque will rotate the spoon so that it turns to the south. Originally the spoon had been but one of a number of magic models of the heavenly bodies used in techniques of divination allied to board games (Plate 18).

It is true that this device is a reconstruction from a text, and that an actual spoon made of lodestone has not so far been found in any tomb. But during the following thousand years there are constant literary references to a 'south-pointer' which can only be explained if something of this kind existed. Later on there is a firm priority of two or three centuries before the first European mention of magnetic polarity about 1180. Indeed it is true to say that people in China were worrying about the declination[1] before Europeans even knew of the polarity. It is a remarkable fact that past variations of declination can be found embalmed in the Chinese geomantic compass. This has three circles, not only for the astronomical north–south, but another with all the points staggered $7\frac{1}{2}°$ east of it and another similarly $7\frac{1}{2}°$ west. Thus the geomantic compass preserves a record of declinations which at certain times were east of astronomical north–south, and then west.

The priority in knowledge of polarity, induction, remanence, declination, &c., was also maintained in priority of first use in navigation, which must have started at least as early as the tenth century. We have charts of the early fifteenth century which

---

[1] That is to say, the variable deviation of the magnetic needle from astronomical north.

PLATE 18

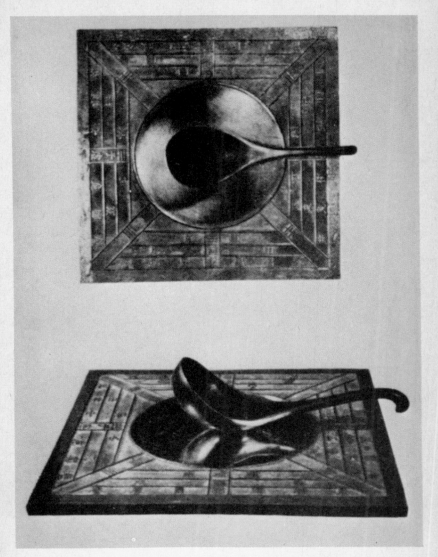

The earliest form of the magnetic compass; the diviner's board (*shih*) of Han times (first century B.C. or A.D.) with the lodestone spoon (*shao*) upon it. (Wang Chen-to)

show itineraries diagrammatically like steamship routes across the oceans, with the compass-bearings marked along them. So many watches on such-and-such a bearing, then change course and carry on again for a prescribed time, &c., &c. Such knowledge came to the West, but how it came remains a mystery. Perhaps some Arabic or Indian text will throw light upon it. Perhaps the knowledge even travelled overland through Tartar kingdoms and not by sea at all.

Magnetical science was indeed an essential component of modern science. All the preparation for Peter of Maricourt, the greatest medieval student of the compass, and hence for the ideas of Gilbert and Kepler on the cosmic role of magnetism, had been Chinese. Gilbert thought that all heavenly motions were due to the magnetic powers of the heavenly bodies, and Kepler had the idea that gravitation must be something like magnetic attraction. The tendency of bodies to fall to the ground was explained by the idea that the earth was like an enormous magnet drawing things unto itself. The conception of a parallelism between gravity and magnetism was a vitally important part of the preparation for Isaac Newton. In the Newtonian synthesis gravitation was axiomatic, one might almost say, and spread throughout all space just as magnetic force would act across space with no obvious intermediation. Thus the ancient Chinese ideas of action at a distance[1] were a very important part of the preparation for Newton through Gilbert and Kepler. The field physics of still later times, established in Clerk Maxwell's classical equations, and more congruent with organic thought than Greek atomic materialism, can again be traced back to the same root. Hence the concluding words, entirely justified, of the passage quoted above on p. 244.

---

[1] A valuable history of this conception in relation to that of continuous contact action (though only so far as Western thought is concerned) has been written by Mary Hesse: *Forces and Fields: the Concept of Action at a Distance in the History of Physics* (London, 1961).

Mutatis mutandis one can make the same two statements about the magnetic compass as were made about gunpowder. It was not a purely empirical or technological achievement because the Taoist geomancers had their theories during its long developmental period, as we know well from many texts that have been preserved. The fact that these theories were not of the modern type does not entitle us to ignore them. The whole discovery had arisen from a divination procedure or cosmical magic, but what carried it forward was the Chinese attachment to a doctrine of action at a distance, or wave-motion through a continuum, rather than direct mechanical impulsion of particles; atomism being foreign to them, this it was which led them on to see nothing impossible in the pole-pointing property of a stone or of iron which had touched it. Secondly, the magnetic compass, or more broadly speaking, the knowledge of magnetic polarity as well as magnetic attraction, had also its sociologically earth-shaking character in the Western world. The part which it played in the nascent phases of modern science would be sufficient justification for this in itself, but there was more; for in the hands of the European sea-captains of the fifteenth century the compass crowned a whole period of navigational science which had been inaugurated in the thirteenth, and made possible not only the circumnavigation of the African, but the discovery of the American, continent. How profoundly this affected the life of Europe, with the influx of vast quantities of silver, the marketing of innumerable new kinds of commodities, and the opening up of colonies and plantations, hardly requires elaborate emphasis here, when even elementary textbooks tell the story. But again there is the other side of the picture. Chinese society was not upset by the knowledge of magnetic phenomena; the geomancers continued to advise families upon the best siting of houses and tombs with ever-increasing refinement of their baseless art,[1] and the sea-captains continued to find their way to the

[1] I say 'baseless', because the idea that good or evil fortune would follow

East Indies or the Persian Gulf in a trade that was peripheral to China's main economic life.[1]

v

We may now leave the thoughts which flood in upon the reader of Francis Bacon's passage, and go on to consider a number of other outstanding scientific and technological gifts of China to the world. The scientific material which I have chosen may be divided into three parts: (*a*) explosives chemistry or proto-chemistry; (*b*) magnetic physics and the mariner's compass; (*c*) astronomical coordinates and instruments, mechanical clockwork, and the 'open' cosmology. Having discussed the first two already, we shall now deal with the third. Afterwards there will follow four technological subjects: (*a*) the use of animal-power, with the inventions of the stirrup, the efficient equine harnesses, and the wheelbarrow; (*b*) the use of water-power, with associated inventions such as the driving-belt, the chain-drive, the crank, and the morphology of the steam-engine; (*c*) iron and steel technology, bridge-building, and deep drilling; (*d*) nautical inventions such as the stern-post rudder, fore-and-aft sailing, the paddle-wheel boat, and watertight compartments. It must be emphasized that these are only a selection from a large variety of choice, and that the selection made is particularly

the proper situation of dwellings or tombs was purely proto-scientific, or as some would say, superstitious. But one must not forget that a very strong aesthetic element entered into medieval Chinese geomancy, as is evidenced still today by the exquisite patterns in which farmhouses, paths, towns, pagodas, and all kinds of human habitations blend with the physiographic scenery.

[1] Even the great period of maritime expansion during the first half of the fifteenth century, when the fleets of the Ming navy under the admiral Cheng Ho repeatedly found their way as far as Madagascar, Medina, and Muscat, to say nothing of the spice islands and the northern fur coasts, had little effect upon Chinese economic life as a whole, and certainly never ran any risk of switching it into some new track.

deficient on the biological side.[1] It will also be worth while to consider the chronological order in which the transmissions to Europe occurred, coming as it were in 'clusters' at particular times rather than one by one over long periods of time. Finally, I shall return to the paradox already adumbrated of European social instability compared with Chinese stability, and link it with that other paradox of the primary Asian success in applying science to human needs, followed by the secondary European success in discovering the method of scientific discovery itself and so inaugurating modern as opposed to medieval science and technology.

There are three ways of measuring the position of any star in the heavens, and modern astronomy uses, not the ecliptic co-ordinates of the Greeks or the altazimuth measurements of the Arabs, but the equatorial system of the Chinese. The measurement of position on the surface of the celestial sphere (the apparent dome of the heavens) was accomplished in all civilizations by building graduated circles into an armillary sphere. The greatest Hellenistic astronomer Ptolemy (second century A.D.) had such an instrument at his disposal, and it lives on in the location gear of the modern telescope, for the latter is simply a sighting-tube of vastly increased size and power, not a finding mechanism. The sighting-tube and the graduated rings were the two essential elements for ascertaining celestial positions.[2]

[1] For example there is no room to say anything of physical meteorology or mineralogy among the inorganic sciences; or of sphygmology, nutritional science, entomology, plant protection, &c., among the biological ones. It is nevertheless certain that the study of the pulse and the empirical discovery of deficiency diseases in China influenced general scientific thinking from the seventeenth down to the end of the nineteenth centuries. As for technology, we have no room to say anything of the ceramics industry or the porcelain which Europeans strove so much to imitate in the eighteenth century, nor of the first plastic, lacquer, nor of mines, nor yet of fisheries.

[2] The Chinese did not use the 360° graduation, but one of 365¼°, based on the number of days in the year. While at first sight this seems very awkward, it had some concrete advantages.

Now the time of the development of the armillary sphere in China and in Greece is about the same, if indeed the Chinese do not have some priority. It is fully present by the time of Chang Heng, that great scholar and scientist of the Later Han whose period of activity was from A.D. 100 to 130, just before Ptolemy. But it is quite likely that it was already complete in most of its details as early as the time of Lohsia Hung, who was repairing the calendar about 100 B.C. in the Former Han period; and rings of some kind must have been used by Shih Shen and Kan Te in about 350 B.C. if the tradition is right that they were the first to give star positions in degrees. Even in these early times measurements were always equatorial. One of the finest Chinese instruments was the armillary sphere of Su Sung, set up in 1088 at Kaifeng, the capital of the Northern Sung Dynasty. This was the first observational instrument in astronomical history to be provided with a clock-drive. The finest extant Chinese instrument is no doubt the bronze armillary

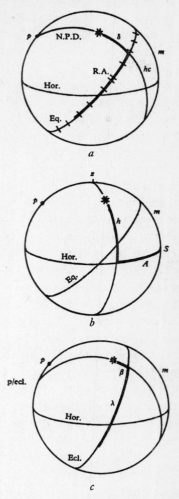

FIG. 21. The three systems of celestial coordinates: *a*. the equatorial Chinese and modern system; *b*. the Arabic altazimuth system; *c*. the Greek ecliptic system (original diagram).

sphere of Kuo Shou-ching, the great Yüan astronomer who re-equipped the observatory at Peking in 1275. It is now at Nanking in the grounds of the Purple Mountain Observatory (Plate 19).

If the sighting-tube was destined to swell and the graduated circles to shrink, the line of progress lay in dissecting the concentric cage of the armillary sphere. The equatorial mounting of the modern telescope was invented in China three and a half centuries before any telescopes existed. If one takes all the concentric circles apart and mounts them non-concentrically in their correct planes suitably connected together, one has an instrument which came later to be called 'Turkish', i.e. the 'torquetum'. Its first inventor, the Spanish Muslim Jābir ibn Aflah, designed it in the twelfth century largely as a kind of computing machine for transferring from one set of coordinates to the others. But when it was introduced to China by the scientific mission of Jamāl al-Dīn in 1267 it quickly led Kuo Shou-ching to the invention of a device called *chien i* or 'simplified instrument'. This was essentially the torquetum with the ecliptic components omitted, and it was indeed the forerunner of the mounting of all modern telescopes.

It is an extraordinary fact in the history of science that the Chinese were able to make such brilliant advances, pushing far ahead of the West (except for the complicated astrolabe), without full knowledge of geometry in its deductive Euclidean form. In any case it was the father of modern observational astronomy, Tycho Brahe, who in the sixteenth century introduced both the Chinese practices, the equatorial mounting and the equatorial coordinates, into modern science, which has never since departed from them.[1] His explicit reason was the greater instrumental

---

[1] Soon after writing this I had the pleasure of viewing Tycho Brahe's subterranean emplacement for his great equatorial armillary at Stjärneborg (Uraniborg) on the island of Ve-en in the Øresund between Denmark and Sweden.

PLATE 19

Kuo Shou-ching's 'equatorial torquetum' (Simplified Instrument, *chien i*) of A.D. 1276, the first equatorial mounting; in the position it now occupies at the Purple Mountain Observatory near Nanking (original photo. 1958)

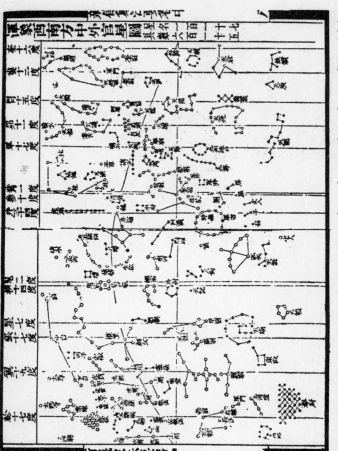

FIG. 22. Star-chart from Su Sung's *Hsin i-hsiang fa-yao* (A.D. 1094) showing 14 of the 28 *hsiu* (lunar mansions), with many of the Chinese constellations contained in them. The equator is marked by the central horizontal line; the ecliptic arches upward above it. The legend on the right-hand side reads: 'Map of the asterisms north and south of the equator in the SW part of the heavens, as shown on our celestial globe; 615 stars in 117 constellations.' The *hsiu*, reading from the right, are: K'uei, Lou, Wei, Mao, Pi, Ts'ui, Shen (Orion), Ching, Kuei, Liu, Hsing, Chang, I, and Chen. The unequal equatorial extensions are well seen.

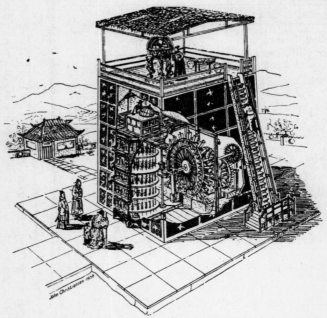

FIG. 23. Reconstruction by John Christiansen of the great astronomical clock erected by Su Sung, Han Kung-lien, and their
collaborators at the Imperial Palace, Kaifeng, Honan province, in
A.D. 1088–92. The water-wheel rotated a celestial globe and an
armillary sphere, and also an elaborate series of jack figures which
announced the time without any dial clock-face. As the sphere was
used for observational purposes, this was the first of all clock-drives
such as are used for modern telescopes. The escapement for hydro-
mechanical clockwork had been invented by I-hsing (a Buddhist
monk) and Liang Ling-tsan in A.D. 725, six centuries before the first
appearance of mechanical clocks in the West. The water-tanks were
replenished by manually operated norias. (After Needham, Wang,
and Price.)

accuracy, but he possessed Arabic astronomical books, and the Arabs knew well what the Chinese usage was.

As has just been mentioned, the Kaifeng armillary sphere of 1088 was provided with a clock-drive. How was this possible? It was because China was responsible for the development of the mechanical clock, not Europe; a story which has only very recently been brought to light.[1] Indeed the mechanical clocks of China built between A.D. 700 and 1300 have revealed at last the missing link between the very ancient water-receiving and water-giving vessels (clepsydras) of Babylonia and ancient Egypt, and the purely mechanical clocks and watches of later ages. From the time of Chang Heng onwards the Chinese were interested in making uranographic models (celestial globes, &c.) revolve by water-power, and it was precisely their equatorial preference which suggested the idea to them. In the earliest form of European mechanical clock (from 1300 onwards), the verge-and-foliot escapement is what dissects the passage of time, the two pallets of the verge alternately arresting the rotation of the crown-wheel, which is powered by a falling weight. In this way the familiar tick-tock movement is achieved, and the whole system is slowed down to the rate of the apparent revolution of the heavens, which is of course man's primary clock. But for six hundred years before this another kind of mechanical clock had been in existence, though only in the Chinese culture-area.

We may take as an example the instrument described in a book entitled *Hsin i-hsiang fa-yao* and written by Su Sung in 1092 about the great clock-tower which had been put up in Kaifeng a few years before. A general reconstruction can be described as follows. The machinery is inside the building on the right, and

---

[1] For a full account see *Heavenly Clockwork* by J. Needham, L. Wang, and D. J. de S. Price (Cambridge, 1960) (Antiquarian Horological Society Monograph, no. 1). More briefly, J. Needham, 'The Missing Link in Horological History: a Chinese Contribution', *Proc. Roy. Soc. A.*, vol. ccl (1959), p. 147 (Wilkins Lecture).

the time-telling apparatus is on the left, with the puppets in their pagoda coming round to announce the hour, and ringing bells and gongs. Above the time-annunciator system one can see the celestial globe which rotated automatically, and lastly on the roof is the armillary sphere which also rotated automatically. The main drive was not a falling weight but a water-wheel. One can see, too, the wheels behind it for getting the water up into the reservoir again. The essential part of the time-keeping was a linkwork escapement quite different from the verge-and-foliot system. Water poured continually from a constant-level tank into the scoops of the water-wheel, but each one could not go down until it was full. As it went down it tripped a couple of levers or weighbridges which by linkwork connexions released a gate at the top of the wheel and let it move on by one scoop. One might say that the machine was arranged so as to dissect time by the accurate and rapid weighing of successive small quantities of a fluid.[1] The main driving-wheel rotated a driving shaft which powered all the puppet wheels, the celestial globe, and also the armillary sphere. In later developments, Mark II and Mark III as one might say, the vertical shaft was replaced by a chain-drive, almost certainly the oldest power-transmitting chain-drive known to history. Working models have been built of the water-wheel linkwork escapement which keep good time.[2]

The Chinese hydro-mechanical clock thus bridges the gap between the clepsydra and the weight- or spring-driven clock. It was not entirely dependent on the constant flow of a liquid, as the clepsydra had been, because its time-keeping properties could be adjusted by varying the counter-weights on the weighbridges. As for its first origin, one finds this in a remarkable

[1] In this case it was water but in some other medieval Chinese clocks it was mercury, which does not freeze.

[2] e.g. by our collaborator Mr. John Combridge, who demonstrated one first at the History of Science Symposium at Worcester College, Oxford, and then at the London Planetarium Reception for the Scientific Delegation of Academia Sinica, in the summer and autumn of 1961.

clock built by the Tantric Buddhist monk I-hsing and an engineer Liang Ling-tsan for the T'ang court at the College of All Sages (one of the imperial institutes of higher learning) about A.D. 725.[1] The tradition lasted on well into the Ming and had still not died out by the time of the Jesuit mission in the seventeenth century, a thousand years later, when it was replaced by the more compact and practical Renaissance clockwork.

What was the significance of all this for Europe? The astronomical achievements had of course no direct social consequences; they were simply incorporated into the body of modern astronomy, with all that that implied for the profound çhanges in world-outlook which have taken place since the seventeenth century. Thus to the break-up of the naïve cosmology of medieval Christendom, seen still in Dante, Chinese influence indirectly contributed. We shall see in a moment how it contributed directly. Clockwork had more obvious and immediate effects. Although the details of any transmission are still obscure there are good grounds for thinking that the Chinese water-wheel linkwork escapement was known and used in thirteenth-century Europe; at the least there was knowledge that the problem of mechanical time-keeping had in principle been solved. From its first European beginnings clockwork generated a type of craftsmanship which together with that of the millwrights was vitally important for the development of mechanical and industrial production in the post-Renaissance period. Moreover the mechanical clock excited Europeans because it embodied the properties of the cosmic models from which it had originated. As Lynn White says in his admirable recent book on the history of technology:

[1] This estimate is based on philological grounds—the similarity of the technical terminology used. But the invention may well go back a good many centuries earlier if the terminology radically changed, since we have numerous descriptions of celestial globes which say that they were accurately rotated by water-power, but do not give details of the mechanism.

Suddenly, towards the middle of the fourteenth century, the mechanical clock seized the imagination of our ancestors. Something of the civic pride which earlier had expended itself in cathedral-building was now diverted to the construction of astronomical clocks of outstanding intricacy and elaboration. No European community felt able to hold up its head unless in its midst the planets wheeled in cycles and epicycles, while angels trumpeted, cocks crew, and apostles, kings and prophets marched and countermarched at the booming of the hours.[1]

Thus the mechanical orreries which had long graced the courts of Chinese emperors and princes entered the service of those European city-states which were soon to burst through the bonds of the feudalism which surrounded them. At the same time the uranographic models succeeded to the inheritance of Ptolemaic planetary astronomy, which constituted a further stimulating challenge to mechanization. Conversely the powered models soon became symbols of the implicit tendencies of the scientific Renaissance. The explanation of nature in terms of the 'analogy of mechanism' was one of the most fundamental concepts which led to the success of modern science, displacing the older analogies derived from organic growth, sympathies and antipathies, or human techniques.[2] Lynn White goes on to point out that just at the time when the problem of mechanical timekeeping was first solved in Europe a new theory of impetus was emerging, transitional between that of Aristotle and the inertial motion of Newton. Now

regularity, mathematically predictable relationships, facts quantitatively measurable, were looming larger in men's picture of the universe. And the great clock, partly because its inexorability was so playfully masked, its mechanism so humanized by its whimsicalities, furnished the picture. It is in the works of the great ecclesiastic and

---

[1] *Medieval Technology and Social Change* (Oxford, 1962), p. 124. I cite this passage with particular pleasure, having just seen the fourteenth-century astronomical clock in the church of St. Nicholas at Stralsund.

[2] For a recent and lucid account of this question see Mary Hesse, op. cit., pp. 30 ff.

mathematician Nicholas Oresmus, who died in 1382 as Bishop of Lisieux, that we first find the metaphor of the universe as a vast mechanical clock created and set running by God so that 'all the wheels move as harmoniously as possible'. It was a notion with a future: eventually the metaphor became a metaphysics.[1]

No more needs to be said, but when to all this one adds the simple fact that the measurement of time is one of the handful of absolutely indispensable tools of modern science, it can be seen that I-hsing and Su Sung started something.

It remains to justify the statement that China provided a direct contribution to the modernization of the world-picture. Passing reference has already been made to this (p. 265). In brief, the medieval cosmology of the Chinese (including Buddhist trends) was far more 'open' than that of medieval Europeans. There were in China three classical astronomical cosmologies: the archaic *kai t'ien* sky-dome (allied to still older Babylonian conceptions), the normal doctrine of the celestial sphere (*hun t'ien*), which did not commit itself to the nature of the phenomena beyond their geometrical relationship, and thirdly the *hsüan yeh* theory, for which the stars and planets were lights of unknown substance floating in infinite empty space. This last view was the one most commonly held by Chinese astronomers in historical times, and it chimed in well enough with the infinities of time and space, both great and small, postulated by Buddhist scientific thinkers. It took untold time for an object thrown from one Buddhist heaven to reach another, or to fall to earth; and T'ang calculations of the eighth century A.D. cheerfully fixed ancient astronomical events a hundred million years before that time—much in contrast with the eighteenth-century European bishop's estimate of the date of creation as 4004 B.C. at 4 o'clock in the morning. Chinese astronomy had always been equatorial and diurnal, not ecliptic and annual, so that it had little of that planetary astronomy for

[1] Lynn White, op. cit., p. 125.

which the Greeks had needed Euclid, but on the other hand this brought some compensating advantages—the Chinese never became enamoured of the circle as the most perfect of all geometrical figures, and hence were never the prisoners of the concentric crystalline celestial spheres which Westerners had found necessary to explain the motion of the planets and the apparent rotation of the fixed stars. Hence their influence was a liberating one when Europeans were breaking forth from this prison. Whether any breath of it reached men such as Giordano Bruno and William Gilbert, who attacked the Ptolemaic–Aristotelian spheres before the end of the sixteenth century, we do not know, but it is quite sure that fifty years later European thinkers who were adopting Copernicanism and abandoning the spheres drew much encouragement from the knowledge that the wise astronomers of China (Europe's sinophile period was just beginning) had never had any use for them.

VI

It is now time to descend from these high celestial regions and to pay attention to some of the more workaday techniques which Chinese ingenuity contributed to the rest of the world—the stirrup, the efficient equine harnesses, and the simple wheelbarrow. About the foot-stirrup there has been a great deal of discussion, and after it had been attributed on what seemed excellent evidence to the Scythians, the Lithuanians, and especially the Avars, recent critical analysis has ruled in favour of China.[1] Tomb-figures from the Chin Dynasty (A.D. 265–420)

---

[1] See the brilliant and well-documented study of Lynn White, op. cit., pp. 2, 14 ff., 28 ff. I cannot accept, however, his cavalier dismissal of the evidence of the Wu Liang tomb-shrines (p. 141) dating from A.D. 147; this date is not contested by Sinologists and everything depends on the credibility of the rubbings made by the Feng brothers in 1821, for much weathering has occurred since their time. In any case this question does not affect the general argument.

PLATE 20

The oldest certain evidence of foot-stirrups; tomb statuettes of the Chin Dynasty (*c.* A.D. 300) from Changsha. (Kao Chih-hsi *et al.*)

show it clearly (Plate 20), and the first textual description comes from very little later (477), after which representations become numerous. The stimulus was no doubt Indian, mediated through Buddhist contacts, rather than nomadic, for the toe-stirrup (only useful for unshod riders in a hot climate) appears in sculptures at Sanchi and elsewhere in the second century B.C. Foot-stirrups did not appear in the West (or Byzantium) until the early eighth century,[1] but their sociological influence there was quite extraordinary. 'Few inventions', says Lynn White, 'have been so simple as the stirrup, but few have had so catalytic an influence on history.'[2] It effected nothing less than the application of animal-power to shock combat. The cavalryman was welded into a unit with his steed in a way which none of the Asian mounted archers had ever been, so that he had only to guide, rather than to deliver, the blow. Horsemen fighting in this new manner with the Carolingian wing-spear, and gradually more and more enveloped in protective metal armour, came in fact to constitute the familiar feudal chivalry of nearly ten European medieval centuries. It may thus be said that just as Chinese gunpowder helped to shatter European feudalism at the end of this period, Chinese stirrups had originally helped to set it up.

A more intractable problem is why nothing of this kind happened in China. Once again we face the astonishing stability of that civilization. So deeply civilian was its ethos that the very conception of aristocratic chivalry was perhaps impossible. Perhaps if the invention had come in the feudal period of the Warring States, before bureaucratism really settled into the saddle,

---

[1] As in so many other cases the means whereby the invention came remain completely unknown. In all such cases the burden of proof clearly lies at the door of those who would wish to maintain independent invention, and the longer the period elapsing between two appearances of an invention the less likely independent invention is.

[2] Op. cit., p. 38.

the story might have been very different. It may be that the tradition of the mounted archer, adopted already in China as early as the fourth century B.C., was too strong to be overcome. Perhaps after all this tradition was fundamentally superior in military science, for when the Mongolian cavalry came at last face to face with the armoured knights of medieval Europe in the thirteenth century, it was not the knights who won the day in any battle; the withdrawal of the Mongols from the West was due to internal political events rather than occidental resistance.

Besides originating the foot-stirrup, China was the only ancient civilization in which the linkwork problem of efficient harness for equine animals was solved.[1] Here again the consequences were almost incalculable. Harnessing the bovine animal is comparatively easy because the ox is of a very convenient anatomical shape. The cervical vertebrae rise in a sort of hump which enables the yoke to bear against them. But this will not work for horses, donkeys, mules, or any equine animal, such vertebral projections being absent. Throughout the centuries there have been only three main ways of dealing with this. The so-called throat-and-girth harness was characteristic of antiquity all over the Old World and lasted in Europe down to as late as the fifth or sixth century A.D. At the other end of the scale is the modern collar harness, a hard part and a soft part being combined in one, and so arranged that the pull comes from the sternal region of the horse. In the throat-and-girth harness, on the contrary, it came from the back of the horse, occluding the trachea and half-choking the animal, which therefore could not exert more than a quarter or a third of its tractive power. With collar harness whether in traces or shafts it can pull thoroughly well. But there is an alternative way of accomplishing this desir-

---

[1] I can never touch upon these problems without paying a tribute to that remarkable man Lefebvre des Noëttes, who in his classical work *L'Attelage et le cheval de selle à travers les âges* (Paris, 1931) first posed the question of the history of harness and its social consequences.

able objective, namely to use the breast-strap harness, where a trace, suspended by a withers strap, surrounds the animal, thus pulling also from the sternum.

The dates of these harness forms are of course vitally important. Ancient Egyptian carvings and Greek vase-paintings always show the typical throat-and-girth harness; Roman sources also.[1] The first representation of the breast-strap harness in Europe occurs on an Irish monument of the eighth century; though there is linguistic evidence that it was known among Slavs and Germans a couple of centuries earlier. But in China we find this very much earlier still. Some time between the Shang period (*c.* 1500–?1027 B.C.) and the Ch'in unification (third century B.C.), probably during the early Warring States period, the breast-strap harness came into universal use, and one sees it invariably in the carvings and moulded bricks of the Han Dynasty (206 B.C.–A.D. 220). The Wu Liang tombshrine reliefs of *c.* A.D. 147 show the breast-strap harness on the chariots of the two secretaries and historians observing the famous incident of the

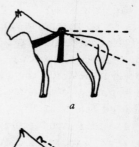

a

b

c

FIG. 24. The three main systems of equine harness: *a.* the throat-and-girth harness characteristic of occidental antiquity; *b.* the efficient breast-strap harness of ancient China; *c.* the collar harness first developed in early medieval China (original diagram).

[1] The Hellenistic and Gallic Romans seem however to have experimented with other forms of harness, most of which did not survive. Ancient Indian harness forms are also obscure. These complicated questions will be found discussed in *Science and Civilisation in China*, vol. 4, pt. 2, sect. 27 f.

Battle on the Bridge. Collar harness in Europe first appears early in the tenth century, as we know from Frankish miniature paintings. But here again China has precedence, for in a magnificent fresco of 851, the triumphal procession of the Exarch of Tunhuang, in the 'Thousand-Buddha Caves', one sees the harness clearly on five horses in the shafts of a series of carts in the train of the exarch's consort (Plate 21). In careful copy enlargements one can see the soft padded collar and a yoke-like cross-bar resting upon it between the shafts. So the collar was essentially a soft cushion devised to replace the 'hump' of the ox and to allow a shaped cross-bar to be placed against it. The oldest pictures of horses and carts at the Ch'ien-fo-tung cave-temples date from *c.* 485 to 520, and although they do not show the collar itself the arrangement is quite clear because the pull is coming from the sternal region, and without a collar the 'yoke' would not have stayed in position at all. Its presence may therefore be inferred with confidence. A throat-and-girth arrangement is out of the question partly because the Chinese had already abandoned it for some eight hundred years, and partly because it never occurs in any civilization combined with shafts.[1] Breast-strap harness is also excluded partly because no such straps are to be seen, while the hard part of the collar is. I consider therefore that these late fifth-century and early sixth-century pictures give unambiguous evidence for collar harness, and between this date and the mid-ninth century there are many more fresco paintings at Ch'ien-fo-tung of the same kind.[2] Particularly interesting is the fact that the collar harness used today in Kansu province and all over North China still consists of two parts, the annular cushion (*tien-tzu*) and a kind of wooden framework in front, the *chia-*

---

[1] Never normally, that is, but it may perhaps have been tried in some of the Roman experiments just mentioned.

[2] The Tunhuang material has been fully discussed and figured by J. Needham and Lu Gwei-djen, 'Efficient Equine Harness: the Chinese Inventions', *Physis*, vol. ii (1960), p. 143.

pan-tzu, which is of course a development of the old cross-bar 'yoke', and is attached by cords to the ends of the shafts. One finds two-part collar harness also in other parts of the world, e.g. in Spain, where perhaps it is a relict form of what was brought by the Arabs. As for the first origin of the annular cushion, philological evidence indicates that it was taken from the pack-saddle of the Bactrian camel.

When we pass from the archaeological origins of efficient equine harness to the panorama of effects which its introduction to the West brought about, we enter a realm already long worked over by occidental historians, and generally regarded by them as of the highest importance for the development of feudal (and ultimately capitalist) institutions. Drawing again from a recent and penetrating study of Western medieval technology, we may say that the general adoption of the heavy plough in northern Europe was only the first stage in the agricultural evolution of the early Middle Ages; the next thing was to acquire such harness as would make the horse an economic as well as a military asset.[1] The horse exerts no greater tractive force than the ox, but its natural speed is so much faster that it produces 50 per cent. more foot-pounds of energy per second; moreover it has greater endurance and can work one or two hours longer each day. But although Chinese breast-strap harness had been available from about 700 (if not by 500 in eastern Europe) and Chinese collar harness from about 900, the harnessing of the horse to the plough was slow in coming. About 860 King Alfred heard with surprise from Ohthere that in Norway what little he ploughed he ploughed with horses, but no pictorial evidence is available until the Bayeux Tapestry (*c.* 1080), by which time a

[1] Lynn White, op. cit., pp. 57 ff., 61 ff., 67 ff. I regret, however, that I cannot accept his earliest datings for the collar harness in Europe, nor his interpretations of the Tunhuang frescoes, the Oseberg tapestry, the Swedish 'horse-collars', and other things. My views are set forth in *Science and Civilisation in China*, loc. cit.

number of texts confirm it. Efficient equine harness was associated with many changes, including crop rotation and a great improvement of the nutritional level of man and beast, but here we can only look at two social effects. One was a marked decrease in the expense of land haulage so that cash-crop produce could travel far more effectively than before; and a considerable technical development in transport vehicles, notably four-wheeled wagons and carriages with improved pivoting front axles, brakes, and eventually springs. The other was more sociological, a proto-urbanization of rural settlement. Since the horse could move so much faster than the ox, the peasant no longer had to live in close proximity to his fields, and thus villages grew at the expense of hamlets, small towns at the expense of villages. Naturally life was more attractive in the larger units; they were more defensible, they could support bigger and better churches, schools, and inns, and commercial facilities penetrated more easily to them. If they grew enough they might hope for a charter. They were in fact the precursors of those urban units later on to be paramount in European culture. Thus by an extraordinary paradox the inventions of a feudal-bureaucratic civilization to which the city-state conception was quite foreign reinforced the intrinsic tendencies within Western feudalism towards a city-state culture which would in time generate an entirely new form of social order.

Why did none of these effects happen in China? In the first place there were no city-state traditions, and any tendency to agglomeration only gave rise to another administrative centre held for the emperor by civil and military authority. More important, in at least half the country neither ox nor horse but the water-buffalo was the essential plough animal, and there was no substitute for it in wet rice cultivation until today's petrol tillers. The entire agricultural picture was so different that horse harness could not affect it in the same way. Transport over land it did affect, but relatively little because China, at any rate since the Han period, had depended for communications primarily on rivers and canals. In military affairs also the canals and irrigation ditches made the Chinese countryside unsuitable for cavalry warfare, as many a nomadic leader from the Tobas to the Mongols found out to his cost. The horse was thus at a disadvantage in Chinese conditions, and though always a factor to be reckoned with, could not affect the life of the culture as profoundly as it did in Europe.

We can dispose of the wheelbarrow in a single paragraph. No pictorial or other evidence of it is known in Europe before the thirteenth century, at which time it doubtless played its part in the building of the great medieval cathedrals. In China, however, it is associated with the famous Shu general of the Three Kingdoms period, Chu-ko Liang (third century A.D.), who used it for supplying his armies; but philological evidence of some weight takes the wheelbarrow back to the middle of the Han period, i.e. the beginning of our era. The replacement of one pair of hands at the end of a hod or stretcher by a wheel would seem to be a piece of mechanization so absurdly simple that all civilizations would have had it from the earliest times, but this is not the case. Nor is the implicit picture of its evolution justified, for the wheel of the Chinese wheelbarrow was not most typically at one end, it was rather in the centre, thus suggesting that the invention was modelled upon the pack animal. Again comes the paradox that China, where labour-power is always supposed to have been so abundant, should have been the region where the invention arose. In Europe it may be counted among the humbler machines of the Renaissance, and it undoubtedly aided the industries then developing, but in China it is difficult to point to any disturbing increase in transportation facilities which it assisted. A subsidiary point is also of interest; at some time as yet undetermined the Chinese fitted wheelbarrows with masts and sails, thus inspiring a famous stanza of John Milton, who spoke of '. . . the barren plaines Of Sericana, where Chineses drive

With sails and wind their canie waggons light'. This embodied
the misunderstanding that four-wheeled sailing-carriages were
involved, an idea which flourished in the ornamentation of many

FIG. 25. Gerard Mercator's representation of a Chinese
land-sailing carriage (A.D. 1613).

sixteenth-century Western atlases, and directly inspired the
Dutch physicist and engineer Simon Stevin to his successful
experiments with sailing-carriages upon the sandy beaches of
northern Holland. These it was which first demonstrated to
Europeans that it was possible for human beings to travel at
forty miles or more an hour without perceptible harm, and thus

PLATE 21

An early example of collar harness; detail copy painting of the lower right cart in the fresco of the Procession of the Exarch's Consort at the Tunhuang cave-temples. (Cave 156, painted A.D. 851; copy painting by Ho Yi)

PLATE 22

Flour-mill on a mountain river; scroll-painting by an unknown artist of the Yüan Dynasty, *c.* A.D. 1300

the sailing wheelbarrows of Kiangsi with their loads of porcelain from Ching-te-chen, though making no particular impression in their own country, struck the imagination of the initiators of that modern science which before long was destined to make aeroplanes fly at four hundred, or rockets (also of Chinese ancestry) at four thousand, miles an hour.

VII

We come now to the second group of technological inventions which deserve attention. A mystery surrounds the origin of rotary milling and the application of water-power to rotary milling, for both these procedures, fundamental in the history of engineering, appear at about the same time in China and the West. One can only assess the fourth to the second century B.C. as the focal period for the former technique, but for the latter we have rather accurate datings. The first water-mill in the West belonged to Mithridates, king of Pontus, about 65 B.C.; the first

---

Description of Plate 22

In the tradition of all Chinese painters, this artist worked not from the life, but in tranquil recollection, hence not being a millwright, he confused paddle-wheels with gear-wheels. Nevertheless, it is clear that a number of different machines were powered in this mill by two large horizontal water-wheels (centre and right lower compartments). The left upper compartment shows right-angle gearing, probably working a battery of trip-hammers. The centre upper compartment has the main mill-stones and an edge-runner mill in front of the staircase. The right upper compartment has a curious contraption almost certainly to be interpreted as an attempt to draw from memory the crank, connecting-rod, and piston-rod combination, i.e. the water-powered reciprocator (cf. Fig. 27), working a flour-sifter, perhaps the latticed cupboard seen at the back of it. The left and centre lower compartments show a number of badly drawn gear-wheels, both horizontally and vertically mounted, the exact purpose and connexion of which is not clear; but in the right lower compartment the artist has drawn a gear-wheel of tub shape, equally isolated but with admirably designed short pinion teeth, thus revealing to us the well-developed technique of the Yüan millwrights.

Chinese water-mills appear about 30 B.C. for working cereal trip-hammer stamp-mills, about A.D. 30 for blowing metallurgical bellows. The difference in date is much too small for direct diffusion in either direction and strongly suggests diffusion in

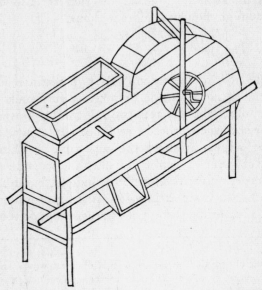

FIG. 26. Rotary winnowing-fan (*yang-shan*) as depicted in the *Nung shu* (A.D. 1313), prototype of the form later widely used in Europe.

both directions from some intermediate source, but we still have no knowledge of what and where this was. Whether the most ancient Western water-mills were vertical (i.e. 'Vitruvian', with right-angle gearing) or horizontal ('Norse') we do not know, nor do we know this for China either, save that the shaft which worked the machinery with its lugs must surely have been horizontal.

Still more fundamental was the invention of the crank or eccentric, and here China's 'legacy' comes in *fortissimo*. For after

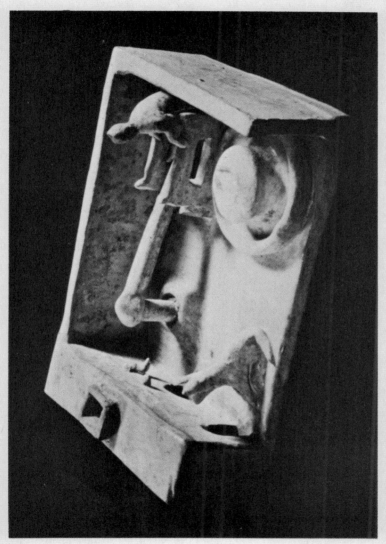

PLATE 23

Han Dynasty (first century B.C. or A.D.) tomb model showing rotary mill, pedal tilt-hammer, and a rotary winnowing-fan worked with a crank handle; the oldest representation of a crank in any civilization

the rather uncertain types of crank descried by some in ancient Egyptian drilling-tools, the oldest sure examples occur on Han Dynasty terracotta models of farmyards which include rotary-fan winnowing-machines worked by crank handles (Plate 23).[1] The oldest European appearance follows after a long period, crank handles for whetstones in the ninth-century Utrecht Psalter.[2] Such an invention is too basic, and at the same time too simple, to leave much trace of its ancient travels, but as a contribution of Chinese technique to that of the Old World as a whole it can hardly be surpassed in importance. In fifteenth-century Europe it generated the crankshaft, a development which in China did not occur, but meanwhile the complete morphology of the reciprocating steam-engine had been perfected there. This requires a little explanation.

Besides the crank, another basic machine had been in use in China since Han times, namely the double-acting piston bellows. There can be little doubt that the very early success of Chinese iron and steel technology had been partly due to this machine, which gave a strong and continuous blast. In addition, the horizontal water-wheel was early in use. These were the components from which one of the most important ancestors of the steam-engine, the hydraulic blower, was constituted. It involved a primary problem of the kinematics of machinery.

For all modern men the most obvious way of converting rotary to longitudinal motion is to use the crank or eccentric,

[1] Critical analysis now dismisses the bailing chain-pump crank handle claimed for the first-century ships of Lake Nemi; and though certain passages in Oribasius and even Archimedes may appear to imply the knowledge and use of it, the philological evidence has not yet been set forth in convincing detail.

[2] The quern with upstanding handle constituted of course a primitive form of crank, but hand-mills of this kind do not antedate the fourth century in Europe, though they are known from the Han period in China (206 B C.–A.D. 220).

the connecting-rod and the piston-rod—a simple geometrical combination which needs only suitable jointing and the maintenance of the piston-rod in a straight line at the end of its back-stroke by means of cross-heads or otherwise. Leonardo da Vinci

Fig. 27. Water-powered blowing-engine (*shui-p'ai*, or water-powered reciprocator) for blast-furnaces and forges as depicted in the *Nung shu* (A.D. 1313). This is the earliest appearance of the conversion of rotary to longitudinal motion by crank, connecting-rod, and piston-rod, hence the inverted predecessor of the reciprocating steam-engine. Motive power is provided by a horizontal water-wheel with a flywheel above it.

used this system in a saw-mill design towards the end of the fifteenth century in the West, but before his time it cannot be found in Europe. Where one must look for it is at the other end of the Old World, in China, for it appears complete already in 1313 in the agricultural engineering treatise

of Wang Chen, who describes it in the form of metallurgical
bellows worked by water-power. A horizontal water-wheel
drives a flywheel on the same shaft above it, and this in turn
rotates by means of a belt-drive a small pulley bearing an

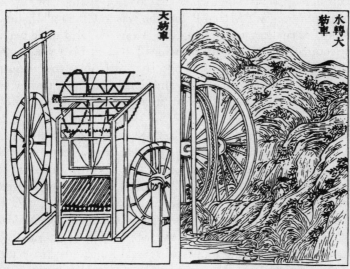

Fig. 28. Water-powered textile machinery (spinning machine, *ta fang
ch'e*) as depicted in the *Nung shu* (A.D. 1313). The picture on the right
illustrates the vertical water-wheel which provides the motive power.

eccentric lug; this then works connecting-rod and piston-
rod, which are joined by means of a bell-crank rocking
lever. Thus the entire structure of the reciprocating steam-
engine is prefigured in advance, but of course in reverse, for
instead of the piston with its rectilinear motion affording the
power-source and driving the wheels, the latter, with their
rotary motion, drive the piston. Since this engine was in common and widespread use when Wang Chen was writing towards
the close of the thirteenth century, it is very unlikely to have
originated less than a century or so beforehand, and one may

therefore confidently say that the crank, the piston-bellows, and the water-wheel met together to produce the steam-engine's anatomy in the Northern Sung. Water-power was also widely used in China at this time for driving textile machinery. I think it can hardly be a coincidence that one of Wang Chen's exact contemporaries was Marco Polo, who was in China while he was writing, or at least meditating, his *Nung shu*; and since we find very soon afterwards at cities such as Lucca in Italy silk filatures using machinery closely similar to that of China, the presumption is that one or other of the European merchants who travelled East in those days brought back the designs in his saddle-bags.

We have just mentioned silk, and we have also just mentioned driving-belts. There is a more than superficial connexion between them. The domestication of the silkworm and the development of the silk industry had taken place at least as early as the Shang period, in the fourteenth century B.C., and this meant that the Chinese alone were in possession of a textile fibre of extremely long staple. The average length of a single continuous strand of silk amounts to several hundred yards, not at all like a short plant fibre such as flax or cotton, with a staple measurable in inches, which has to be pulled out and spun together to form the yarn. The silk is wound off from the cocoons almost by the mile, and its tensile strength (some 65,000 lb. per sq. in.) far exceeds that of any plant fibre, approaching the level of engineering materials. One can thus begin to understand how it was that the Chinese were so successful in the invention of textile machinery long in advance of other parts of the world. Let us consider, for instance, the *sao ch'e* or silk-winding machine. A text of A.D. 1090, the *Ts'an shu*, by Ch'in Kuan, describes it very clearly. The silk is loosened and wound off from the cocoons in the hot water bath; the fibres come up through little guiding rings and are laid down on a great reel. This is worked by a treadle, but its shaft carries also a pulley with a driving-belt which works an eccentric lug on another pulley back and forth, and this in turn operates a ramping-arm to lay down the silk evenly on the reel. We thus have one of the simplest forms of 'flyer'. This is a very important machine from several points of view, partly because it embodies a conversion of rotary to longitudinal motion (though without the piston-rod component) and partly because it is such an early example of the simultaneous combination of motions, one power-source supplying both.[1]

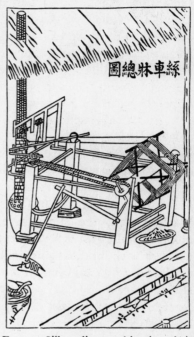

The spinning-wheel is another example, better known, of the driving-belt. We do not yet know whether it took its origin in India, where cotton was indigenous, as is the usual view, or whether it did not rather arise as a quilling-wheel for winding silk on reels in the Chinese culture-area, this apparatus being detectable in literary sources as far back as the Han, and pictured in 1210. The

FIG. 29. Silk-reeling machine (*sao ch'e*), described in the *Ts'an shu* (A.D. 1090). An early form of flyer is worked by eccentric and driving-belt from the main reel shaft, the motive power a treadle crank 'sewing-machine' drive.

___

[1] The example of this usually given (cf. Lynn White, op. cit., p. 119) is the saw-mill of Villard de Honnecourt, *c.* 1235, where the water-wheel not only powered the excursion of the saw but also assured the feed of the wood. The silk-reeling machine is older by at least two centuries but we do not know when it was first worked by animal- or water-power.

latter is more than possible,[1] for our oldest picture of a spinning-wheel from any civilization is in a Sung painting of 1270, some time (though not perhaps very long) before the first European evidence (Plate 24). In many Chinese forms the belt runs over three spindles at one time, and the wheel is driven by a treadle with a strange kind of universal joint. Apart from textual references to spinning-wheels near 1300 the first illustrations of driving-belts in Europe come in the fifteenth-century German military engineering manuscripts. There is thus a considerable priority for this essential form of power transmission in Chinese culture, and as usual no good reason for thinking that it was invented later in Europe independently. If then it is true that driving-belts began among Chinese artisans it would not be at all surprising that power-transmitting chain-drives should also be found early among them. And indeed we have already seen precisely this, the chain-drive in the late eleventh-century monumental astronomical clocks of Su Sung (p. 264), probably not new with him but going back at least as early as the similar clockwork of Chang Ssu-hsün a hundred years before. Endless chains had of course been well known to the Alexandrian mechanicians of the first century B.C., but they were never continuously power-transmitting, and generally more like conveyor-belts.

The effects of all these inventions and engineering solutions on the technology of post-Renaissance Europe are self-evident, and the only question the reader will ask is why they did not lead to a similar upsurge of industrialism in China. Here the answer can only be a part of the general observation that Europe had a capitalist revolution (or rather a series of them) and that China did not. Technical novelty alone could no more bring about a

[1] One must not think that the spinning-wheel necessarily arose in connexion with short-staple textile fibres, for the Chinese, who never wasted anything, used it for spinning silk from wild or broken cocoons, and they may well have done this far back into antiquity.

PLATE 24

The oldest representation of a spinning-wheel in any culture, and hence important evidence on the history of the driving-belt; *A Son taking leave of his Mother*, probably by Ch'ien Hsüan, in any case datable c. A.D. 1270.
(Waley)

fundamental change in the structure of society than mercantile activity alone or social criticism alone. Something beyond that, some complex of prior conditions, not analysable by us here, would have been necessary in China if the inventions of her brilliant technicians were to have exerted their full effects within her borders. As it was they spread out all over the world as part of her 'legacy'.

VIII

The third group of technological advances centres upon the mastery of iron and steel, but leads us into other fields, some rather unexpected, such as bridge-building and deep drilling. Optimistic American writers of the Jules Verne era were fond of referring proudly to the then modern world as the Iron Age, when the 'iron horse' galloped across the prairies and 'ironclads' began to plough the seas. They would have been surprised to learn that there had been a previous iron age, but not in Europe, rather in medieval China.[1] Until the end of the fourteenth century no European had ever seen a pig of cast iron, yet the mastery of the molten metal had already been achieved in Chinese culture some eighteen centuries before. Of all our paradoxes this is perhaps the most extraordinary, namely that advanced iron-working, so deeply characteristic of developing capitalist industrialism in the West, should have existed for so many centuries within Chinese bureaucratic feudalism without upsetting it.[2]

Iron itself was a relatively late introduction to China, datable in the sixth century B.C. or so, a long time after its twelfth-century B.C. discovery by the Hittites in western Asia Minor.

[1] The reader is referred to the monograph by J. Needham, *The Development of Iron and Steel Technology in Ancient and Mediaeval China* (London, 1958, repr. Cambridge, 1964) (Dickinson Lecture).

[2] See a recent interesting paper by R. Hartwell, 'A Revolution in the Chinese Iron and Coal Industries during the Northern Sung Dynasty (960 to 1126)', *Journ. Asian Studies*, vol. xxi (1962), p. 153.

But the remarkable thing is that the Chinese could cast it almost as soon as they knew about it at all. Within two or three centuries the wrought iron of bloomery furnaces was giving place to cast iron. Among the reasons for this rapid advance we must undoubtedly number the double-acting piston-bellows giving its continuous blast (already mentioned), perhaps also the presence of ores with high phosphorus content, which allows the melting of iron at a temperature about 200° less than otherwise. Besides, one must never forget that the Chinese had been perhaps the greatest bronze-founders of all antiquity, so that much furnace experience, drawn not only from them but from their predecessors the potters, lay at the disposal of the first iron-masters.[1] Furthermore, good refractory clay was available, so that a way of reducing iron ore in crucibles stacked in coal was used at an early date, certainly not later than the fourth century A.D. Archaeological excavations have brought to light quantities of cast-iron tools from the fourth century B.C. onwards, and these are now to be found in many museums in China—hoes, ploughshares, picks, axes, swords, and the like. Remarkable cast-iron moulds have also been found in tombs dating from the late Warring States period, though whether they were used to make cast-iron implements or to cast bronze ones is not yet certain. One or two reliefs of Han date (*c.* 100 B.C.–A.D. 100) remain which give an idea of the primitive blast-furnaces and bellows used in those ancient times. Our earliest picture of the characteristic small Chinese blast-furnace comes from the *Ao-p'o t'u-yung*[2] of 1334,

[1] See N. Bernard, *Bronze-Casting and Bronze Alloys in Ancient China* (Canberra and Tokyo, 1961) (*Monumenta Serica*, monograph series no. 14). Bernard doubts the very existence of a bloomery stage of wrought-iron production before the appearance of iron-casting, and it is true that traces of the earlier phase (naturally assumed in parallelism with development elsewhere) are scarce, nevertheless they occur.

[2] 'The Boiling Down of the Sea', a treatise on the salt industry by Ch'en Ch'un. There was always a close connexion between salt and iron, partly because in the ancient world of self-sufficient local communities these were

PLATE 25

The oldest extant cast-iron pagoda (A.D. 1061), at Yü-ch'üan ssu, Tang-yang, in Hupei province. (Boerschmann)

and the best-known one occurs in the *T'ien-kung k'ai-wu*[1] of 1637. These illustrations show the iron flowing out from the blast-furnace and being conducted to the puddling platform for conversion into wrought iron. Such small blast-furnaces lasted down in many rural districts into the present century, and photographs of them, as also of the crucible method, are available.

Many objects both inside and outside museums testify to the great use made of iron in ancient and medieval China. Han statuettes and vessels beautifully cast in iron have long been known. Then there are the famous funerary kitchen stoves of the Three Kingdoms period (the third century A.D.), the material of which first awakened Western archaeologists to the ancient character of the cast iron industry in China. Next come many Buddhist statues cast between the fourth and the eighth centuries, often dated, and showing great skill and artistic taste on the part of the craftsmen who made them. The great lion of Ts'ang-chou, a monument about thrice the height of a man, and one of the largest iron castings in the world, was set up in A.D. 954 by Kuo Jung, one of the Northern Chou emperors, to commemorate his victory over the Liao (Ch'i-tan) Tartars. In the Sung a number of cast-iron pagodas were erected, at least two of which still exist complete today (Plate 25). In the Ming the temples at the top of the sacred mountain T'ai-shan were roofed entirely with cast-iron tiles, to withstand the gales that sweep across the summit. All these were peaceful uses. But iron and steel had of course been the basis of the successes of Chinese arms through the ages, whether in the repulsion of the Huns or the

the two great commodities which could be produced only at particular places and had to be transported, hence their 'nationalization' in Han times; partly also because the evaporation of the concentrated brine needed large cast-iron pans.

[1] 'The Exploitation of the Works of Nature', a general description of technology and industry by China's Diderot, Sung Ying-hsing.

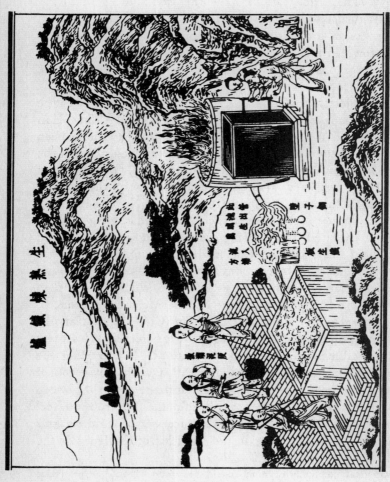

FIG. 30. Traditional blast-furnace in operation, showing the double-action piston-bellows (here manually operated), the tapping of the cast iron, and its conversion to wrought iron, with use of silica, on the fining platform. From the *T'ien-kung k'ai-wu* (A.D. 1637).

Japanese, or the conquests of Sinkiang or Tibet. Protective armour developed more for ships than for men, reaching its apogee in the fleets of armoured vessels under the Korean admiral Yi Sunsin (1585–95). Although it still remains undemonstrated, we can now appreciate better the weight of probability which suggests that the first iron-barrel cannon were Chinese (cf. p. 248 above).

Steel production lagged in no way behind that of iron. In the earliest times steel may have been made by the cementation process of the ancient West, wrought iron being heated in charcoal to gain the necessary carbon; but as soon as cast iron became abundant it proved more convenient to oxygenate the product carefully (refining, as it was called in the West), stopping at the stage of steel, with its intermediate carbon content. Then in the sixth century A.D. came the ingenious invention of the co-fusion process (the ancestor of the Siemens–Martin open hearth of to-day), probably due to a Taoist swordsmith Ch'i-wu Huai-wen; here wrought-iron billets and cast-iron chips were heated together in a special furnace. The cast iron melted and bathed the pasty masses of wrought iron so that an interchange of carbon took place, and, upon forging, good eutectoid steel was obtained. So persistent (indeed because so effective) have been some of the ancient Chinese technical procedures that I myself was able to see in 1958 in Szechwan a closely similar derivative process still successfully at work.

Siderurgical skill had a number of important technical consequences in ancient and medieval China. The availability of excellent wrought-iron chains suggested their use for a fundamental improvement of the suspension bridges of bamboo cables by means of which since ancient times many of the rivers flowing through ravines in western China had been crossed by the main lines of communication. The textual and archaeological evidence available indicates that it was in the Sui Dynasty (A.D. 589–618) that iron-chain suspension bridges first spanned the necessary 200–300 ft. gaps, but there can be no doubt whatever that these bridges were common during the Sung, Yüan, and Ming periods. The first proposal in Europe was made by the engineering bishop Faustus Verantius about 1595, but no successful bridge was built until the middle of the eighteenth century (1741). It is exceedingly likely that Verantius had heard of the Chinese bridges from the early Portuguese travellers, and it is certain that Fischer von Erlach who described and recommended them in 1725 drew from Chinese sources.

Iron entered into bridge construction in yet another manner, also (and still more certainly) attested for the Sui period. This was the time of activity of a very brilliant engineer Li Ch'un, who first threw across a river valley a segmental arch bridge with relieving arches in the spandrels (Plate 26). This superb structure, which still exists at Chao-hsien, and has recently been thoroughly repaired, resembles nothing so much as the bold railway bridges in stone or reinforced concrete constructed since the seventies of the last century; and with its group of similar structures in North China must surely have exerted an influence on the builders of the first segmental arch bridges of Europe, the Ponte Vecchio at Florence (1345) and its successors. Li Ch'un's audacious design was assisted by the use of iron clamps between the stones of the twenty-five parallel arches of which the bridge vault was composed.

The connexion between iron and salt has already been noted; large cast-iron pans were needed for the evaporation of the brine. But there was another more curious link. At an early time it was found that Szechwan province, a couple of thousand miles away from the sea, possessed great stores of natural brine and natural gas in pockets far below the surface of the red-earth basin. The exploitation of this began at least from the beginning of the Han period (second century B.C.), as we know both from textual and archaeological evidence (moulded bricks); and a limiting factor here which soon permitted the drilling of deep bore-holes as far down as 2,000 ft. was the availability of good steel for the bits and drilling tools. The method of drilling has often been described; a group of men jump on and off a beam to give an up-and-down movement, while at the same time the drilling cable is

Fig. 31. The technique of deep drilling practised in Szechwan province from Han times onward for obtaining brine and natural gas. Here the just lengthened bamboo spear or haft of the drilling-tool is being cautiously lowered during drilling operations (*T'ien-kung k'ai-wu*, A.D. 1637).

rotated by another. When the bore-hole is completed, a process that may take several years, a long bamboo tube with a valve is sent down to act as a bucket and bring up the brine.[1] The natural gas, collected from other bore-holes, is used for the evaporation. There can be little doubt that knowledge of these methods spread from China to inspire the drilling of the first artesian well near Lillers in 1126, and there is none at all that the first

[1] Note once again the great value for Chinese technology of the natural tube constituted by the bamboo.

petroleum wells in America's south-western states were drilled by the ancient Chinese method, there known as 'kicking her down'.

Putting these facts together, we have only to add the certainty that cast iron began to flow from the first blast-furnaces in Europe in the neighbourhood of 1380, mostly in Flanders and the Rhineland, and we know also that one of the great urges for the adoption of this new technique was the desire to cast iron cannon. In view of the long prior history of iron, and especially of iron-casting, in China, I am not disposed to entertain any belief in an independent invention in Europe; at the same time we still know little or nothing of the intermediaries through which the knowledge and experience came. One suspects the Turks, with whom some of the earliest European iron-masters had studied, as also the Persians, but nothing very definite can be said. The other outstanding problem of course is how it was possible for Chinese administration to be so stable in the presence of a metal which had such earth-shaking effects in Europe. To begin with we must remember that Chinese iron-working preceded by some time the first unification of the land into a single empire in the third century B.C.; the state of Ch'i had waxed wealthy on iron (as well as salt), but the state of Ch'in, which conquered all the other states, probably had a metallurgical policy more strictly directed to its military use. Iron has been called by ancient historians of the West 'the democratic metal',[1] for its widely distributed ores could be acquired and used by city-states and peasant barbarians alike against the older unified monarchies. Since iron was much superior to bronze for weapons this was a grave matter. But in East Asia the whole city-state conception was quite foreign to Chinese culture, and the unified Ch'in empire simply took over the bureaucratic anti-aristocratic anti-mercantile ethos which had already grown up

[1] Cf. V. Gordon Childe, *What Happened in History* (London, 1942; American ed. 1946), p. 176.

PLATE 26

The earliest segmental arch bridge in any civilization, Li Ch'un's An-chi Bridge at Chao-hsien, Hopei province, built in A.D. 610. (Mao I-sheng)

within the so-called feudal states. At the same time the barbarian tribes both within and without the empire were kept under control, until the fourth century. The 'nationalization' of iron (as well as salt, fermented beverages, &c.) which had been discussed in Ch'i[1] became a reality under the stable dynasty of the Han, and about 120 B.C. all iron production was carried on in forty-nine government factories scattered throughout the empire.[2] Though this was freed in later dynasties, and although doubtless in times of partition certain states benefited from iron and steel supplies which others did not have, individual ironmasters were no more in a position than any other merchant-entrepreneurs to challenge the overwhelmingly bureaucratic domination of the scholar-gentry. And this was just as true after the invention of gunpowder as it had been before. In a word, like the legendary ostrich, Chinese culture could digest cast iron and remain unperturbed thereby; Europe's indigestion amounted to a metamorphosis.

IX

The last group of technical innovations to be considered is connected with the sea. All too unjustly have the Chinese been dubbed a non-maritime people. Their ingenuity manifested itself in nautical matters just as much as elsewhere, the number

---

[1] Cf. T'an Po-fu, Wen Kung-wen, Hsiao Kung-chüan, and L. Maverick, *Economic Dialogues in Ancient China: Selections from the Kuan Tzu Book* (New Haven, 1954).

[2] Everyone should read the *Yen t'ieh lun* ('Discourses on Salt and Iron'), written by Huan K'uan in *c.* 80 A.D., for a partial translation by E. M. Gale has long been available (Leiden, 1931). Additional chapters were translated by E. M. Gale, P. A. Boodberg, and T. C. Lin in *Journ. Roy. Asiat. Soc.* (*North China Branch*), vol. lxv (1934), p. 73. It is the almost verbatim report of a discussion between feudal-minded Confucian scholars and bureaucratic officials concerning the 'nationalized' industries. Some of the problems raised, such as that of standardization of spare parts, have an extraordinarily modern ring. For a further commentary see Chang Chun-ming in *Chinese Social and Political Review*, vol. xviii (1934), p. 1.

of their vessels on the inland waters was found by medieval and Renaissance Western merchants and missionaries almost beyond belief, and their sea-going navy was assuredly the greatest in the world between 1100 and 1450.

It all began with the bamboo, the buoyancy of which was soon found useful for the construction of vessels. The bamboo sailing-raft, still characteristic of the South China and Indo-Chinese coasts and Taiwan, is very ancient in date; indeed it has been important in fishing and trading for nearly three millennia. According to a generally accepted opinion, all ship-building in the Western world derived from the dug-out canoe, strakes being built up on each side of it to obtain the wooden ship (whether carvel or clinker) with keel, stem-post, and stern-post. None of these parts exists in the typical Chinese ship (*ch'uan*, hence the word 'junk'), which seems to have grown up rather in the form of a rectangular box based on the original bamboo raft. The box shape with transom stem and stern is profoundly characteristic of the junk. Hence arose the segmental construction, the hold being divided by transverse bulkheads. These watertight compartments were, we know, adopted in European shipping in the early nineteenth century with full consciousness of the prior Chinese practice. From the square-ended transom stern another remarkable consequence followed. Although there is no stern-post, the aftermost member, or nearly aftermost member, of the bulkhead series, being vertical, permitted the attachment of a 'stern-post' rudder. Some years ago, my collaborators and I built up an elaborate argument from textual sources showing that the stern-post rudder originated in the Chinese culture-area. This conclusion was then strikingly confirmed by the excavation of model ships in terracotta from tombs in Canton belonging to the first century B.C. and the first century A.D., as we saw to our delight when visiting the museum there in 1958 (Plate 27). The stern-post rudder then first appears in Europe about 1180, a time almost exactly identical with the

PLATE 27

Han pottery model of a ship, from a first-century A.D. tomb at Canton; the oldest known example of the stern-post rudder in any culture

Detail of stern of Han ship model showing the rudder

appearance and adoption of the magnetic compass there. Of the obvious importance of the latter for the discovery of the route round Africa and the way to the New World we have already spoken in connexion with Francis Bacon's aphorism (pp. 242, 256), but nautical historians agree that the former can have been no less important.

So far we have spoken of structure and guidance, but propulsion is equally important. It is worth emphasizing that all Chinese history knows nothing of the multi-oared slave-manned galleys of the Mediterranean, so prominent in Renaissance as well as Greek sea history. Though it is true that the hauling or 'tracking' of ships up the great rivers and through the rapids was done in all ages by gangs of pullers (free men, nevertheless, in so far as anyone in feudal-bureaucratic clan-family society could be called free), by and large the universal method of propulsion, from the Tung-t'ing lake to Zanzibar, was sail. Moreover, apart from the sprit-sail, which seems to have been used occasionally in the Hellenistic world, Chinese waters saw the first fore-and-aft sails in the third century, as we know from contemporary textual descriptions. The Chinese were the great proponents of the lug-sail, and great use was made of bamboo up aloft, for the lugs took the form of flat, aerodynamically efficient mat-and-batten sails. The models of the five-masted Shantung trader of fifty years ago in the Science Museum at South Kensington and the National Maritime Museum at Greenwich give one a good idea of what the ships carrying a thousand men or more which sailed in the expeditions of the great admiral Cheng Ho in the early fifteenth century must have been like. Those were the days when the Chinese navy was visiting everywhere from Kamchatka to Madagascar. The physics and mathematics of sails are still imperfectly understood, less well perhaps than those of aeroplane wings, but it is certain that medieval junks could sail well to windward, as the square-sailed cogs of Hanseatic or Catalan Europe could not. Modifications of the Chinese mat-and-batten system have been adopted on many modern racing yachts, notably Hasler's *Jester*, famous for a single-handed Atlantic crossing in 1961. And while speaking of aeroplane wings

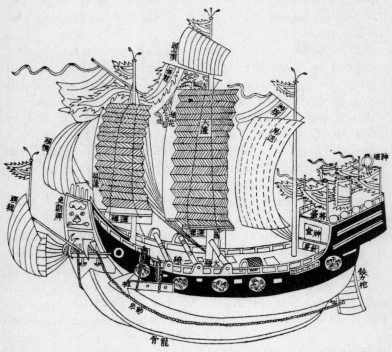

Fig. 32. An eighteenth-century drawing of a three-masted sea-going junk, from the *Liu-ch'iu kuo chih-lüeh* (A.D. 1757).

it may be well to recall that the notable invention of anti-stalling wing-slots is said to have been inspired by the fenestrated rudder of the Chinese junk. For Chinese sea-captains and river-junk masters had long ago found advantage not only in having their rudders balanced (part being forward of the post) but in having them perforated with holes as well.

One last invention must be referred to, that of the paddle-wheel boat. Descriptions of treadmill-operated paddle-wheel boats begin to appear in Chinese literature in the fifth and sixth centuries A.D., and their construction and habitual use for naval combat on lakes and rivers is quite indubitable in the eighth,

FIG. 33. Sketch reconstructing the probable appearance of one of the 23-wheel treadmill-operated naval paddle-boats used in the Southern Sung, as built by Kao Hsüan and others, A.D. 1130. The casing is shown removed from the stern-wheel and from the six forward wheels on the port side. The number of trebuchets and other weapons is only suggested. Sails were mainly for emergency use, and masts carried crow's-nests. Probable dimensions: length 100 ft., beam 15–20 ft. (original drawing).

when a T'ang prince, Li Kao, built and commanded a fleet of them. In the twelfth century, when the Chinese navy began to develop prodigiously after the capture of Kaifeng by the Chin Tartars and the retirement of the Sung Dynasty south of the Yangtze, the paddle-wheel warship came into its own.[1] Since iron wheels were difficult to make, and since no substantial

---

[1] See the interesting paper by Lo Jung-pang entitled 'China's Paddle-Wheel Boats: the Mechanised Craft Used in the Opium Wars, and their Historical Background', *Tsinghua Journ. Chinese Studies*, N.S., vol. ii (1960), p. 189.

power-source was available, the number of wheels was multiplied, and in a campaign against one of the perennial rural rebellions, about 1130 (under Yang Yao), government battle-ships with as many as 23 wheels (11 on each beam and 1 at the stern) were constructed by a naval architect named Kao Hsüan. As he was captured by the rebels soon afterwards and proved willing to build ships for them too, the campaign dragged on for a long time, much use being made of gunpowder bombs and poison-smokes; and it was finally ended by the famous loyalist general Yo Fei, who enticed the rebel ships into an estuary where floating weeds and branches entangled their wheels and boarding action could take place. Paddle-wheel warships continued to be of much importance, however, guarding the Yangtze for a century and a half so well that no further penetration of the Chin Tartars to the south occurred, river-crossings being impossible. Afterwards, with the general conquest of the country by the Mongols, the age of the paddle-wheel ship declined, since they were more interested in sea-fighting (cf. the attempted conquests of Java and Japan), where, without a power-source such as steam, the paddle-wheel was unsuitable. Again we have no knowledge to what extent these traditions influenced the first trials in Europe, which took place in 1543 at Barcelona. They were certainly handed down in China, for during the Opium Wars (1839–42) a considerable number of treadmill-operated paddle-wheel war-junks were sent against the British ships and gave a good account of themselves, though the cause was hopeless. With their usual complacency the Westerners supposed that these ships had been built in imitation of their own paddle-steamers, but study of the contemporary Chinese literature shows that this was not so at all. The whole story has the further interesting feature that there had been a proposal in fourth-century Byzantium for a paddle-wheel ship to be worked by ox whims, but there is no evidence of its ever having been constructed. As the manuscript was only discovered at the Renaissance, it cannot have influenced the Chinese ship-builders. How far it influenced the Barcelona experiment remains uncertain, for there had been proposals for paddle-wheel boats in the German engineering manuscripts of the fifteenth century, and these may have been re-inventions inspired by the omnipresent vertical water-mills. In any case, there is no doubt at all that though the first suggestion was Byzantine the first practical realization was Chinese.

x

This brings us to the term of our survey of China's 'legacy'. Before dwelling upon the principal paradoxes which emerge from it, we must take notice of a curious, and perhaps significant, fact; namely that it is possible to distinguish, at least in the technological field, arrivals of innovations from Asia, mainly China, in particular collocations which I have come to call 'clusters'. Thus for example between the fourth and the sixth centuries A.D. one finds the arrival of the drawloom and the breast-strap harness. By the eighth century the foot-stirrup is exerting extraordinary effects, and soon afterwards the Cardan suspension appears. By the beginning of the tenth century equine collar harness has come, together with the simple trebuchet in the field of artillery. The eleventh century sees the spread of the Indian numerals, place-value, and the zero sign. Towards the end of the twelfth century come in a cluster the magnetic compass, the stern-post rudder, paper-making, and the idea of the windmill, with the wheelbarrow and the counter-weighted trebuchet quickly following; this was the time of the Toledan Tables. Towards the end of the thirteenth century and the beginning of the fourteenth there appear in another cluster gunpowder, silk machinery, the mechanical clock, and the segmental arch bridge; this was the time of the Alfonsine Tables. Rather later, but still forming part of this second inflow, we find the blast-furnace for cast iron, and block-printing, soon followed by movable-type printing. During the fifteenth century the standard method of interconversion of rotary and rectilinear motion establishes itself in Europe, and other East Asian engineering motifs appear, such as the spit vane-wheel, the helicopter top, the horizontal windmill, the ball-and-chain flywheel, and lock-gates in canals. The sixteenth century brings the kite, the equatorial mounting and equatorial coordinates, the doctrine of infinite empty space, the iron-chain suspension bridge, the sailing-carriage, a new emphasis on sphygmology in medical diagnosis, and equal temperament in musical acoustics. In the eighteenth century a rear-guard is formed by variolation (the predecessor of vaccination), porcelain technology, the rotary-fan winnowing-machine, water-tight compartments at sea, and some other late introductions such as medical gymnastics and ultimately the system of civil service examinations.

This list of transmissions, though very incomplete, throws into some relief the historical fluctuations in the reception of East Asian discoveries and inventions by Europe. Though it is generally impossible to trace the course of a 'blue-print', or a stimulating idea, still less the mere conviction that a problem had already been successfully solved somehow, the general circumstances which facilitated flow at particular times present themselves as obvious—for the twelfth-century cluster the Crusades, the Qara-Khitai kingdom in Sinkiang, &c.; for the fourteenth-century cluster the Pax Mongolica; for the fifteenth century the Tartar slaves in Europe; for the sixteenth century onwards the Portuguese travellers and the Jesuit mission, and so on. The earlier periods of transmission are more obscure, and further research will be needed to elucidate them, but an overall picture of the world's indebtedness to East Asia, especially China, is emerging very clearly.

The first of the paradoxes with which I wish to conclude is that according to a common belief there was never any science or technology in China at all. It may seem passing strange in the light of all that has gone before that this should ever have been believed, yet such was the impression of my sinological elders when I began the investigation of these matters, and it has been enshrined in one form or another in many well-known statements. Repeated as it was by generations of superficial observers of Chinese everyday life who knew nothing of the literature, the Chinese ended by believing it themselves. An essay by the great Chinese philosopher, Feng Yu-lan, written more than forty years ago, bore the title 'Why China has no Science'.[1] In this he said:

> I shall venture to draw the conclusion that China has had no science, because according to her own standard of values she has not needed any. . . . The Chinese philosophers had no need of scientific certainty because it was themselves that they wished to know; so in the same way they had no need of the power of science, because it was themselves that they wished to conquer. To them, the content of wisdom was not intellectual knowledge, and its function was not to increase external goods.

There was of course something in this, but only something, and the standpoint may have been influenced by a feeling that what China did not seem to have happened to have was not very much worth having anyway.[2] The converse of Feng Yu-lan's youthful pessimism is to be seen in the equally unjustified optimism of Arnold Toynbee:[3]

[1] *International Journ. Ethics*, vol. xxxii, no. 3 (1922), reprinted (in English) in his collected essays, *Chung-kuo che-hsüeh shih pu* ('Contributions to the History of Chinese Philosophy') (Shanghai, 1936).

[2] A related version of this theme, not infrequently stated, is that in the traditional Asian cultures 'it was felt easier for man to adapt himself to Nature than to adapt Nature to himself'. I quote from Alan Watts, *Nature, Man and Woman* (London, 1958), p. 52, a brilliant and, in other respects, a very perceptive book. This particular thesis is falsified by twenty centuries of Chinese scientific and technological history.

[3] A. J. Toynbee, *A Study of History* (6 vols.; London, 1935–9), vol. iii, p. 386.

However far it may or may not be possible to trace back our Western mechanical trend towards the origins of our Western history, there is no doubt that a mechanical penchant is as characteristic of the Western civilization as an aesthetic penchant was of the Hellenic, or a religious penchant was of the Indic and the Hindu.[1]

Today it has become quite evident that no people has had a monopoly of philosophical mysticism, scientific thought, or technological ability. The Chinese were not so uninterested in external nature as Feng Yu-lan averred, and the Europeans were by no means so ingenious and inventive as Toynbee claimed. The paradox may have arisen partly from a confusion in the meaning of the word 'science'. If one defines science as modern science only, then it is true that it originated only in Western Europe in the sixteenth and seventeenth centuries in the late Renaissance, the life of Galileo marking the turning-point. But that is not the same thing as science as a whole, for in all parts of the world ancient and medieval peoples had been laying the foundations for the great building that was to arise. When we say that modern science developed in Western Europe in the time of Galileo, we mean most of all, I think, that there alone there developed the fundamental principle of the application of mathematized hypotheses to nature, the use of mathematics in putting questions, in a phrase, the combination of mathematics with experiment. But if we agree that at the Renaissance the method of discovery was itself discovered, we must remember that centuries of effort had

---

[1] A related version of this theme has become well known as the thesis of F. S. C. Northrop (see especially his *The Meeting of East and West: an Enquiry concerning Human Understanding* (New York, 1946)). According to him the Greeks developed the way of knowing nature by rational postulation and scientific hypothesis, while the Chinese throughout their history approached nature only by direct observation, empathy, and aesthetic intuition. This is just as untenable as the rest. A cruder, more racialist, formulation of the same ideas occurs in the stimulating, but wholly unreliable, book by L. Abegg, *The Mind of East Asia* (London, 1952), cf. pp. 233 ff., 294 ff., &c.

preceded the breakthrough. Why this happened in Europe alone remains a subject for sociological investigation. We need not here prejudge what such investigations will reveal, but it is already obvious enough that Europe alone underwent the combined transfigurations of the Renaissance, the scientific revolution, the Reformation, and the rise of capitalism. These were the most extraordinary of all the phenomena of Western instability before socialist society and the atomic age.

But here comes the second paradox. From all that has been said it is clear that between the fifth century B.C. and the fifteenth century A.D. Chinese bureaucratic feudalism was much more effective in the useful application of natural knowledge than the slave-owning classical cultures or the serf-based military aristocratic feudal system of Europe. The standard of life was often higher in China; it is well known that Marco Polo thought Hangchow a paradise. If there was on the whole less theory there was certainly more practice. If the scholar-gentry systematically suppressed the occasional sprouts of mercantile capital, it was seemingly not in their interests to suppress innovations which might be put to use in improving the production of the counties or provinces in their charge. If China had an apparently limitless reservoir of labour-power it remains a fact that we have so far met with no single case of the refusal of an invention due to explicit fear of technological unemployment. Indeed the bureaucratic ethos seems to have helped applied science in many ways. One could instance the use of the Han seismograph to signalize and locate calamities before news of them reached the capital, the erection of a network of rain-gauge and snow-gauge stations in the Sung, or the extraordinary expeditions undertaken in the T'ang to measure a meridian arc from Indo-China to Mongolia over 1,500 miles long,[1] and to map the stars from Java to within

[1] Cf. the detailed account by A. Beer, Lu Gwei-djen, J. Needham, E. Pulleyblank, and G. I. Thompson, 'An Eighth-Century Meridian Line . . .', *Vistas in Astronomy*, vol. iv (1961), p. 3.

20° of the south celestial pole. The *li* was keyed to a celestial–terrestrial standard a hundred years before the kilometre. Let us not despise then the mandarins of the celestial empire.

And so we come at last to the paradox of paradoxes—'stagnant' China the donator of so many discoveries and inventions that acted like time-bombs in the social structure of the West. The cliché of stagnation, born of Western misunderstanding, was never truly applicable; China's slow and steady progress was overtaken by the exponential growth of modern science, with all its consequences, after the Renaissance. To the Chinese, could they have known of her metamorphoses, Europe would have seemed a civilization in perpetual upheaval;[1] to Europeans, when they came to know her, China seemed to have been always the same. Perhaps the stereotypic inanity among Western commonplaces is the belief that although the Chinese invented gunpowder they were so foolish—or so wise—that they used it only for fireworks, leaving its full powers to be exploited by the West alone.[2] We may not wish to deny to the West a certain penchant, alas, for *Büchsenmeisterei*, but the idea behind the commonplace is of course that without the West nothing grand or creative would have been done with such inventions. The Chinese made sure that their tombs faced due south, but Columbus discovered America; the Chinese planned the steam-engine's anatomy, but Watt applied steam to the piston; the Chinese used the rotary fan but only for cooling palaces,[3] the Chinese understood selection but confined it to the breeding of fancy goldfish.[4] All such fancied antitheses are demonstrably

[1] It was not that China knew no upheavals of civil strife, dynastic change, and foreign invasion, quite the contrary, but the basic forms of her social life remained relatively constant.

[2] This appears, of course, in the book by L. Abegg previously quoted, as but one exhibit in a museum of similar statements (p. 235).

[3] This they did, but they also used the encased and crank-operated rotary winnowing-fan some eighteen centuries before Europeans got hold of it.

[4] This they did, but far more important was the process of improvement of

historically false. The inventions and discoveries of the Chinese were mostly put to great and widespread use, but under the control of a society which had relatively very stable standards.

There can be no doubt that there was a certain spontaneous homoeostasis about Chinese society and that Europe had a built-in quality of instability. When Tennyson wrote his famous lines about 'the ringing grooves of change' and 'better fifty years of Europe than a cycle of Cathay',[1] he felt impelled to believe that violent technical innovation must always be advantageous; today we might not feel quite so sure. He saw effects only, ignoring causes, and moreover in his time physiologists had not yet come to understand the constancy of the internal environment,[2] nor engineers to build self-regulating machines.[3] Cathay had been self-regulating, like a living organism in slowly changing equilibrium, or a thermostat—indeed the concepts of cybernetics could well be applied to a civilization that had held a steady

rice and other staple crops, which went on for centuries with very conscious imperial supervision and encouragement.

[1] Is it possible that Tennyson knew there was in fact a real Chinese cycle of sixty years? More probably he was thinking of the *kalpa* and the *mahākalpa*. But the mistake, if such it was, illuminates strangely the theme of this paper.

[2] We now know that living organisms maintain a constancy of internal conditions, including the composition of their body-fluids, automatically regulating temperature, pressure, acidity, blood-sugar, &c.; and that they do this the more effectively the higher in the evolutionary scale they are. There is always great danger in applying biological analogies to social phenomena, as I have often in the past pointed out (cf. *Time, the Refreshing River* (London, 1943), pp. 114 ff., 160 ff.; *History is on Our Side* (London, 1946), pp. 192 ff.). Nevertheless in the present case it seems to me that the replacement of the false and meaningless concept of 'stagnation' by the precise and applicable idea of slowly changing 'homoeostasis' brings a definite increase in the clarity of our thought about traditional Chinese culture.

[3] This is not quite true historically, for the fantail gear of the windmill and the governor-balls of the steam-engine had both been long in use by Tennyson's time. But their philosophical significance was hardly noticed, and self-regulating machinery did not impose itself on general thinking until the era of electrical communication-, as opposed to power-, technology.

course through every weather, as if equipped with an automatic pilot, a set of feedback mechanisms, restoring the *status quo* after all perturbations, even those produced by fundamental discoveries and inventions. Struck off continually like sparks from a whirling grindstone, they ignited the tinder of the West while the stone continued on its bearings unshaken and unconsumed. In the light of this, how profoundly symbolic it was that the ancestor of all cybernetic machines, the south-pointing carriage, should have been a Chinese device.[1]

There was no special superiority about the relatively 'steady state' of Chinese society, resembling as it did in many ways ancient Egypt, that age-old continuum which amazed the youthful, changeable Greeks. The constancy of the internal environment is only one function of living organisms, necessary but not as complex for example as the higher activities of the central nervous system. Metamorphosis is also a perfectly physiological process, and in some living things it can go as far as the complete dissolution and re-formation of all the tissues of the body. Perhaps civilizations, like different kinds of living beings, have developmental periods very different in length, and when they metamorphose do so in varying degrees.

There is no special mystery about the relatively 'steady state' of Chinese society either.[2] Social analysis will assuredly point

[1] This invention, which took place in China in the third century if not a little earlier, has been mentioned in passing, above, p. 240. A carriage bore a figure which pointed to the south, and continued to do so in whatever direction the carriage was made to move. It is certain that this was accomplished mechanically, probably by a simple form of differential gear, and it is very likely that the inventor was Ma Chün.

[2] In this contribution I have perhaps overemphasized the continuity and unity of Chinese society. Byzantine society, as Gibbon painted it, seemed similarly 'monolithic', but modern research has revealed great variations of its structure during its different periods. China too will show changes of finer structural detail 'under higher power', as microscopists say, but some simplification was here unavoidable.

to the nature of the agriculture, the early necessity of massive hydraulic engineering works, the centralization of government, the principle of the non-hereditary civil service, &c., &c. But that it was radically different from the patterns of the West is quite unquestionable.

To what then was the instability of Europe due? Some have referred it to the aspirations of the never-satisfied Faustian soul. I would prefer to think in terms of the geography of what was in effect an archipelago, the perennial tradition of independent city-states based on maritime commerce and jostling military aristocrats ruling small areas of land, the exceptional poverty of Europe in the precious metals, the continual desire of Western peoples for commodities which they themselves could not produce (one thinks especially of silk, cotton, spices, tea, porcelain, and lacquer), and the inherently divisive tendencies of alphabetical script, which permitted the growth of numerous warring nations with centrifugal dialects or barbarian languages. By contrast China was a coherent agrarian land-mass, a unified empire since the third century B.C. with an administrative tradition unmatched elsewhere till modern times, endowed with vast riches both mineral, vegetable, and animal, and cemented into one by an infrangible system of ideographic script admirably adapted to her fundamentally monosyllabic language. Europe, a culture of rovers, was always uneasy within her boundaries, nervously sending out probes in all directions to see what could be got—Alexander to Bactria, the Vikings to Vinland, Portugal to the Indian Ocean. The greater population of China was self-sufficient, needing little or nothing from outside until the nineteenth century (hence the Hon. Company's opium policy), and generally content with only occasional exploration, essentially incurious about those far parts of the world which had not received the teachings of the Sage.[1] Europeans suffered from a

[1] This must not be exaggerated. It is well to remember that Europe was discovered by China and not the reverse—when Chang Ch'ien travelled

schizophrenia of the soul, oscillating for ever unhappily between the heavenly host on the one side and the 'atoms and the void' on the other; while the Chinese, wise before their time, worked out an organic theory of the universe which included nature and man, church and state, and all things past, present, and to come.[1] It may well be that here, at this point of tension, lies some of the secret of the specific European creativeness when the time was ripe. In any case it was not until the flood-tide of that modern science and industry so generated washed away her sea-walls that China experienced the necessity of entering the world *oikoumene* which these great forces were forming. And so her legacy joined with those of all the other cultures in a process which is palpably bringing into being the world co-operative commonwealth.   JOSEPH NEEDHAM

through Central Asia from 138 to 126 B.C. and came upon Greek Bactria. Besides, there were periods of great Chinese enterprise in voyaging, for example the exploits of the Ming navy under Cheng Ho in the early fifteenth century (p. 295).

[1] Hence the rather naïve conception of Laws of Nature enacted by a supernatural law-giver did not develop among them. But there is no doubt that this idea had great heuristic value in the initial phases of modern science.

6

THE CHINESE AND THE ART OF GOVERNMENT

THE political life of a modern nation derives distinctive colour from the political tradition that produced it, but it is a fabric interwoven with strands from many, often remote, places. As individual nations come to employ a common technical knowledge, join in the same economic ventures, and enjoy a common cultural life, they face much the same political demands and move towards similar patterns of political life. Two themes from the past are conspicuous in these patterns. One is the concept of democratic political responsibility worked out in the forum, the agora, and the town hall; the other is the technique of personnel management and administrative responsibility first highly systematized in the council chambers of Northern China.

The diverging trends of Chinese and Western political traditions appear soon after the two cultures emerge in history. In the West the tendency towards political fragmentation was evident in Greek city-states, some of whose practices of self-government survived in the Roman empire and gathered new strength in the Middle Ages. The feudal states that grew from the fallen empire transmitted their political diversity to modern Europe. Experiments in self-government were easiest in small, competing political units in an international order without any really dominant power. All the free citizens of sovereign Athens could meet in the market-place and reach some agreement on their common concerns. Group action evolved in guild and medieval corporation, which personified and defended common interests of Ghentish weavers or Lübeck mariners against lord or emperor. Shaken and undermined by Paris and Rome, King John yielded at Runnymede. Foreign rivalries sapped Stuart resources and furthered the cause of Parliament. The weakness of monarchs aided democracy.

In China the twig of political growth was early bent in a different way. The trend towards political unity and central control began early. Despite repeated setbacks, the movement towards empire persisted with a sense of historical inevitability. Irresponsible despotism was most often tamed not by the action of autonomous political units below, but by social and intellectual pressures exerted through a gradually perfected system of bureaucracy. If the checks on Chinese rulers little resembled those on their Western contemporaries, these checks nevertheless made possible a political order whose serenity and justice were long enviable in Western eyes.

When the Chinese appear in history during the second millennium B.C., the scene already seems dominated by a ruler, of the Shang house, whose authority may have been recognized over most of Northern China. Perhaps there existed already a certain sense of a Chinese national entity. Such an entity assumes clearer form at the end of the second millennium, when Chou conquerors established a real authority over the China of their day. But this control was only effectuated through a kind of feudal delegation of power throughout the different regions, and this soon weakened as the feudal governors consolidated hereditary dominions in their several territories. From the eighth century the feudal states were practically independent. A similar process took place within the various fiefs, where feudal subordinates established hereditary claims to offices and lands and commenced to usurp both powers and positions from their lords. At this point, however, a reversal of the process began. Employing a newly rising class of landless knights, the lords replaced hereditary retainers with professional officials, the forerunners of China's bureaucracy, and centralization of power thenceforth proceeded apace. The smaller feudal states maintained for a while a precarious existence, but they lacked both the time and favourable conditions in which their subjects could attempt experiments in oligarchic or popular government.

Political experimentation followed other lines. Towns and commerce were growing; the older social structure was weakening; land could be bought; with the increasing role of the foot-soldier in the armies the plebeian became a greater force in society. Feudalism was on the wane, and the centralized states were the beneficiaries. They fought among themselves for land and power with growing violence. In the competition for survival the rulers sought aid from political theorists among the new officials. The latter, seeking formulas to guarantee security and success, brought political speculation to a high level of sophistication. Shen Pu-hai, a thinker of the fourth century B.C., held that government was an art best practised by controlling with a light hand a carefully balanced administrative machine that would be largely self-operating. He would seem to have urged rulers to use persuasion and the requirement of strict responsibility rather than force and punishment, and to confer office through careful matching of an official's capabilities with the duties of his post. Other theories claiming descent from the contemporary Shang Yang put greater emphasis on fear, punishment, and the exaction of meticulous obedience in minute details. Political thinkers in the following century—Han Fei, Lü Pu-wei, and Li Ssu—combined and developed these power-oriented lines of thought, later to be characterized rather ineptly as Legalist.[1]

The political advice of such thinkers was applied with profit by their patrons. In the forefront were the rulers of Ch'in, who

[1] Cf. H. G. Creel, 'The Fa-chia: "Legalists" or "Administrators" ', *Studies Presented to Tung Tso Pin on his Sixty-Fifth Birthday* (Bull. Inst. Hist. and Philol., Acad. Sin., extra vol. no. 4) (Taipei, 1961), pp. 607–36; J. J. L. Duyvendak, *The Book of Lord Shang* (London, 1928); Derk Bodde, *China's First Unifier* (Leiden, 1938).

employed the last three named, and through power and wile extended their sway to all of China. In 221 B.C. a Ch'in ruler took the newly devised title of emperor (*huang-ti*), abolished all remaining feudal authority, and for the first time brought all Chinese under firm and effective control in a single polity.

One major step remained before the basic concept of Chinese empire was complete. Permanent maintenance of absolute power required at least the compliance of the governed. But extreme regimentation and repression as practised by the Ch'in alienated too many officials and provided willing followers for the disaffected. The second emperor of the first dynasty was overthrown, and after several years of warfare among competing leaders a new house, the Han, was enthroned in 202 B.C. The rebels had numbered among them heirs of the dispossessed noble houses, but the winner in the contest was a commoner of humble origin. He and his successors saw shrewdly the political forces that supported and could unseat them. Their rule was more moderate. For a time they restored some feudal forms. They indulged the most heterogeneous political theorists, among whom followers of Confucius grew increasingly important. Confucius had done much to catalyse political thought in the fifth century, when the feudal states were still disintegrating, but he had found no ruler to apply his remedies seriously. Now men of the Han, disillusioned with unfettered power, took up his ideas with new interest. More will be said of these ideas below. To men weary of Ch'in despotism Confucius offered hope in the dicta that trust by the people is more vital to government than arms or food, and that guidance through virtuous example and an accepted sense of rightness succeeds where rules and punishments are futile. A new turning-point in China's history came when Confucian teachings were declared official state doctrine by the emperor Wu, fifth of the Han line. The new doctrine, substituting government by persuasion and virtue for system, rules, and discipline, conflicted with the old at vital points. Yet a complete departure from the empire's fundamental system was scarcely conceivable. An essential contradiction entered the Chinese political tradition, a perpetual tension between two co-existing but opposite principles, that would remain while the tradition lasted.[1]

The emperor Wu, a prodigy of imaginative energy and far-reaching ambitions, extended in a fifty-four-year reign the centralization and rationalization of power. He founded a school for officials, began to use written examinations somewhat regularly, experimented with nationalization of salt and iron and with price control through state trade agencies, built canals for irrigation and shipping on an unprecedented scale, even while he extended China's borders through military campaigns. His successors and an intervening usurper, Wang Mang, continued some of these experiments and Wang attempted dramatically but vainly to abolish slavery and nationalize land for lifetime allocation to the tillers. The Han house survived four centuries before accumulating economic troubles and administrative laxity brought its fall in A.D. 220. Long periods of disunity and foreign rule followed. But the Han Dynasty in its better years had served China's needs well. China without imperial unity was no longer conceivable. The idea of empire survived and grew with the advance of China's civilization.[2]

A second surge of political development came with the advent of new social forces, reaching its greatest momentum between the eighth century and the eleventh. Peace and reunification, achieved by the Sui Dynasty in 589 and consolidated by the T'ang in 618, prepared the way for commercial transformation that bound the nation in an economic unity of interdependent

[1] Cf. Arthur Waley, tr., *The Analects of Confucius* (London, 1938), pp. 88, 164; H. G. Creel, *Confucius and the Chinese Way* (New York, 1960), pp. 142–72.

[2] Cf. H. H. Dubs, tr., Pan Ku, *The History of the Former Han Dynasty*, 3 vols. (Baltimore, 1938–55).

regions. Slowly at first but with quickening pace, new frontiers were colonized, great cities emerged, and new industries appeared. The age was one of technical innovation and philosophic speculation. Newly prospering classes, attaining the means of education, grew ambitious for the influence and prestige that bureaucratic position alone could offer. Political expediency and dynastic struggles, which led to the courting of the new-risen classes through wider use of public examinations, at times lent support to political reformers. Some decades of disunion in the early tenth century no more than retarded the development. The Sung Dynasty, founded in 960, restored unity and instilled fresh purpose. Within a century a series of administrative innovations brought the imperial system to full maturity.[1]

Later dynasties would experiment and modify, and further perfect certain features. But it is doubtful that any age surpassed the eleventh century in its combined achievement of political stability and free discussion, its recruitment of talented men, and its wealth of innovation. Alone among the great dynasties, the Sung ruled without interruption for more than three centuries and fell at last not through usurpation or internal rebellion but through military defeat. Perhaps no nation dedicated to the arts of peace could have withstood the Mongol armies, which had ravaged unchecked from the Yellow Sea to Silesia and Hungary. The fall of the Sung in 1279—the shock of defeat and the altered conditions that ensued—changed the political climate. Internal control and military strength became overriding considerations. The Mongol (1279–1368) and Manchu (1644–1912) Dynasties lived in danger of Chinese rebellion. The parvenu general who founded the intervening Chinese house of Ming both aspired to inherit the Mongol dominions in Asia and distrusted the scholars who served him. All three dynasties encouraged intellectual orthodoxy. China experienced times of

[1] Cf. E. G. Pulleyblank, *The Background of the Rebellion of An Lu-shan* (London, 1955).

renewed prosperity, political serenity, and cultural brilliance, but never quite the economic, social, and mental ferment of an earlier age. In political life, too, conservatism became the dominant note.

As we view the Chinese political tradition in its centuries of innovation and achievement, and its further centuries of remarkable survival and adaptation to new conditions, we look for a key to its successes. Certainly no single factor holds the answer. But one aspect seems very significant—the co-existence and equilibrium of competing political concepts that began in the Han. The early speculators about ways of operation and control—the 'Legalists'—initiated a train of development that led to pioneering in methods of organization and personnel administration. It led also to expansion of state activity and control that tended to reach all spheres of life, within the bounds imposed by material technology. But Confucian ideology checked and mitigated this trend of thought and action, subordinating it to values beyond those of power and efficiency, and in its way acted to liberate the individual.

Confucian political thought after the Han honoured above all the pithy sayings of Confucius and the interpretations and extensions that Mencius had furnished. It stressed the ruler's obligation to his subjects and their right of criticism and rebellion. Other writings regarded as Confucian also carried weight, however, and could be cited to support views somewhat different in spirit. Writings stigmatized as Legalist survived, and no doubt were read, but were scarcely cited except with disapproval.

The religious sanction of the state was acknowledged, in ritual worship of Heaven and its natural manifestations, by the emperor and his officials at vast altars open to the sky. Similar rites were performed officially in honour of Confucius, Mencius, and their most honoured disciples and followers of later ages. The Mencian writings reiterated plainly that the emperor ruled through the will and favour of Heaven: but only through this will and favour, which would surely be withdrawn from an unworthy ruler and his house. When a ruler erred his ministers should, as Heaven's agents, warn and criticize him; if he persisted his subjects, as Heaven's agents, would dethrone and execute him. His most solemn duties were to exemplify virtue and moderation to his people; to select ministers and officials who would likewise do this; to be to his people a father, ensuring them material necessities, comforts, and leisure for the nurture of virtue, and thereafter providing the means of education. Since man is naturally disposed towards goodness, the ruler who fulfilled these duties perfectly had provided all that was needful for ideal government. But, said T'ang and Sung theorists, ever since the sage rulers of antiquity—the last were the founders of the Chou house—monarchs had fallen short of the requisite virtue. State and society had deteriorated, necessitating regulations and punishments. Hope of progress must lie in a struggle to restore the working of virtue among high and low until the need for force and law should vanish. Every man would then, according to his calling, contribute to the needs of society, receiving in return all that he needed to play his role, enjoy the natural pleasures, and cultivate his moral understanding.[1]

How in practice could the ideal order be regained? Existing organs, conceived for ends so different, were admonished to behave in Confucian ways and lead men back to virtue. Other organs were developed in harmony with the newer state philosophy. But how soon and how fast could a régime of persuasion replace that of law? Perhaps the hope was most immediate in the

---

[1] Cf. James Legge, *The Chinese Classics*, vol. ii, *The Works of Mencius* (Oxford, 1895), especially pp. 143–9, 151–4, 159–61, 167–8, 392; Han Yü, 'Yüan tao', tr. in G. Margouliès, *Le Kou wen* (Paris, 1925), pp. 177–81; Chu Hsi, letter, in Fung Yu-lan, *A History of Chinese Philosophy*, Derk Bodde, tr. (Princeton, 1953), vol. ii, pp. 562–4.

Early Sung, when utopian optimism was in the air. Reformers of many stamps freely decried current practice and called for government reliant on the force of good character. As local administrators they often tried sincerely to practise such government. Other officials, often equally conscientious, believed that both public weal and survival of the state alike required reform of abuses through new regulations. Men like Wang An-shih (1021–86) could support such views by citing later classics such as the *Ritual of Chou*. And even as a majority of the more famed and eloquent argued for a reduction of laws and reliance on virtue, the cautious and hardheaded quietly went on and multiplied safeguards and rules. Doctrinal ambiguity thus allowed scope for experiment and adaptation without fatal damage to ideals that might be unrealizable immediately. Even in later dynasties, when fears of sedition led rulers to stress the duty of obedience above that of criticizing, and utopia seemed more distant, the ideology remained and tempered the exercise of authority. No ruler ever ventured to deny the validity of Confucian principle, the basis for political morality. We meet with many a courageous spokesman for its values and many a humble official who strove to exemplify rectitude, mildness, and forbearance.

In every dynasty realization of good government and dynastic survival itself called for a careful balancing of power among the persons and organs through whom the emperor acted. Isolated by stately pomp within his moated palace, the ruler retained practical freedom of action only through access to varied advice, independent sources of information, and officials of differing interests. Political progress was won through this lesson; the Han and the T'ang fell in learning it and the Ming through ignoring it. Emperors had to exclude from important functions their family and relatives by marriage, who were always prone to intrigue for influence and control of the succession to the throne, and equally the palace eunuchs, so favourably placed to monopolize access to the emperor's person. Within the bureaucracy itself power was divided through balances of several kinds. The highest direction of policy was confided to a Council of State, whose members were heads of several agencies. The Council's views and actions were scrutinized by separate organs of criticism. During the later T'ang and the Sung the emperor could consult also academies of distinguished scholars appointed to provide still another source of advice. To maintain the effectiveness of these structural checks and balances, it was imperative to guard vigilantly against domination of the several policy bodies by any faction or too like-minded a group. (Reformers rarely saw themselves as such a group, and since checks and balances came from the non-Confucian side of the tradition they were less honoured by theorists than they deserved to be.)[1]

The principle of balance was reflected also in collegial organization of the various ministries and other central agencies, commonly headed by two officials similar in rank and authority. In provincial and local government and in military command it was obviously necessary to confide responsibility for a given function in a given area to a single official, but even here structural checks were provided. Under the Sung, the sharing of civilian functions on the provincial level by several intendants provided a degree of mutual surveillance. Boundaries of civil and military jurisdic-

---

[1] The T'ang government and its practices are described in admirable detail in Robert des Rotours, *Le Traité des examens* (Paris, 1932), and in *Traité des fonctionnaires et traité de l'armée* (Leiden, 1947). Sung institutions are considered in E. A. Kracke, Jr., *Civil Service in Early Sung China* (Cambridge, Mass., 1953). Ming governmental organization is considered in C. O. Hucker, 'Governmental Organization of the Ming Dynasty', *Harvard Journal of Asiatic Studies*, vol. xxi (1958), pp. 1–66. For T'ang factions see Pulleyblank, op. cit.; for Sung factions, J. T. C. Liu, *Reform in Sung China* (Cambridge, Mass., 1959); for Ming factions, Hucker, in J. K. Fairbank, ed., *Chinese Thought and Institutions* (Chicago, 1957), pp. 132–62, and Heinrich Busch, S.V.D., 'The Tung-lin Academy and its Political and Philosophical Significance', *Monumenta Serica*, vol. xiv, pp. 1–163.

tions on this level were drawn differently, so that each commander dealt with several groups of civilian intendants and each intendant with several commanders. Further counter-checks existed at still lower levels of local government.

A special problem in China was the relation between policy-forming and executive action. Conceptually, policy was determined not by a preponderance of opinion but by a rational consensus achieved through objective discussion. Both policy suggestions and factual reports often originated with local officials, who were best informed on public needs, and passed through administrative channels to the Imperial Court. Since the Confucian ethos made each official personally responsible for popular welfare and criticism of government, officials at all levels ardently advocated one policy or another. Once policy was decided, each official had the duty of carrying it out in complete and meticulous conformity with the ruler's intention. Here came the difficulty. When an official's opinion conflicted with his duty as obedient executor, his actions and his reports might fall short of the needful co-operative zeal. Habits of over-independence thus justified could encourage a slackness that was likely enough in any case.

The difficulties of control implicit in Confucian responsibility perhaps helped to evoke the remarkable complex of organs for investigation, criticism, advice, and complaint, the perfecting of which took sixteen centuries. The primary organ of independent control was the Censorate, which acted in several ways to maintain proper functioning and health in all parts of the government. Its earliest duty was that of simple investigation, developed under the Ch'in as a natural authoritarian device. With the change of political philosophy in the Han this duty gained new implications. It came to mean not only spying out sedition and indiscipline, but also discovering inadequacies in the provision for public welfare in general. At first one of several duties of a corps of imperial secretaries, the function of surveillance was entrusted in the eighth century to an independent censorial organ of three branches, each charged with investigating specific functions in the capital or local units, including the conduct of penal cases. Some time after the Han, devices for receiving popular petitions, inspired by early legend, were translated into reality and also further developed in the T'ang. Conspicuous among these devices were drums placed before the Imperial Palaces, to be struck by any man with a grievance, and slotted petition boxes which could be opened only by authorized officials. Under the Sung these simple practices were elaborated to provide a group of three complaint offices, administered by the Censorate. Reported users of the petition offices were primarily commoners. Complaints of the illiterate were written for them, and those who felt slighted could appeal to the second office and the third. The Mongols under Kublai Khan reinforced their control by heavy reliance on the Censorate in local administration. They established two dozen regional offices whose staff was required to examine the records and actions of local functionaries in a fixed routine of unprecedented minuteness, so that their visits were anticipated with trepidation. The Ming continued and further refined this system, which was followed also by the Manchus.[1]

Still more significant was the censorial duty of criticizing the policies and actions of imperial ministers and the emperor himself. Such criticism, found already in the Han, expressed explicit Confucian doctrine, and grew without marked encouragement from the criticized. The moral position of the critic was hard to challenge, and his right to criticize with impunity won a secure place in the tradition. To strengthen censorial freedom from inhibiting pressures, T'ang practice provided that any censor could act without the permission of even the Censorate's chiefs. The censors were carefully removed from direct involvement in

    [1] Cf. C. O. Hucker, 'The Traditional Chinese Censorate and the New Peking Régime', *The American Political Science Review*, vol. xlv (1951), pp. 1041–52.

administration, and their action usually extended only to reports, accusations, or the initiation of judicial action, the judgement of which rested in other hands. They need not name the sources of their information. Officials responsible for criticizing policy were also appointed in other parts of the government, and a special officer was empowered to return for reconsideration even edicts bearing imperial approval. The height of critical effectiveness was reached in the eleventh century, when we are told that attacks by the critics agitated even emperors and brought down councillors of state. But censorial courage was still more remarkable in later dynasties when sharp criticism of rulers persisted—as in late Ming times—despite the occasional punishment or even execution of censors. The longevity of China's political system must be credited in significant degree to the power and vigilance of the Censorate.

Many less dramatic aspects of the system must also share credit. Innumerable minutiae of practice and organization added to administrative efficiency, many of them tracing back to the Han and being well developed by the T'ang and Sung. Precision and consistency of action were furthered by habits of conducting business in writing and recording actions carefully (often in duplicate). Objectivity and impartiality gained from the secrecy of ministerial deliberations and the publication of policy decisions and rules of operation. In the central administration the rather haphazard division of duties among early Han offices evolved by the T'ang into a more logical structure, and in the early eleventh century the many specialized bureaux came under three major departments responsible for general, economic, and military matters. In local administration, impelled by multiplying functions and aided by improved communications, the older division of authority by region and locality was modified to one whereby the offices at the capital—especially those with economic concerns—more often maintained direct contact with corresponding agencies on the local level. This trend towards tighter central control was, however, countered under the Mongol and later dynasties by the creation of major regional governments, providing firmer political control within each region but reducing the effectiveness of direction by the central government bureaux.

Most important among administrative methods were those concerned with personnel. Since the ruler depended on professional bureaucrats alike in the formation, implementation, and enforcement of policy, his success was proportional to bureaucratic ability and morale. Personnel policies assumed a major place in state deliberations. We have seen that early Chinese political thinkers evolved interesting concepts in this field; it is not too surprising that China was the first to develop many essential techniques. The primary aim was to improve the civil service proper, an élite group commonly numbering in the developed system some ten thousand or more and filling the key positions of central and local government. To obtain more and better men the emperor Wu of the Han founded a school at the capital which grew into a thriving university. Succeeding dynasties added local schools in all parts of the empire to train promising sons of official or commoner families at state expense.

Men were selected for government employment and advanced in office through varied methods; from the T'ang onwards promotion and recruitment procedures were distinct. Rather primitive methods familiar elsewhere—nomination of officials' younger relatives and the sale of office—were gradually restricted and in later dynasties assumed importance only at moments of dynastic decline. In their place more constructive methods such as competitive examination, controlled sponsorship, and regular merit ratings came to play leading roles.[1]

The earliest to develop was sponsorship. No method suited

---

[1] See note 1, p. 318; also Étienne Zi, S.J., *Pratique des examens littéraires en Chine* (Variétés sinologiques no. 5) (Shanghai, 1894), which provides copious details on examinations in the Manchu Dynasty.

Confucian reform concepts so well as presentation of good men to the ruler by those in a position to judge their character. Tradition asserted that even in feudal times the public recommendation of such men for official position was an act of high merit, and their employment was pleasing to Heaven. By the Han at least the moral obligation assumed by the sponsor was supplemented by a legal responsibility for the acts of his protégé, and the system was widely employed to find men most highly qualified for government service. After the Han, however, recruitment through sponsorship became more and more restricted to rare instances in which exceptionally talented men had failed to seek advancement through normal channels.

In the later T'ang and the Sung, new use was found for the idea of recommendation, in promotion within the service. Here it was valuable as a way of finding proven administrative abilities and probity, complementing the techniques of examination and merit rating (whose inherent limitations are discussed below). It also added inducements to good performance by the receiver of past or prospective recommendations. At first used chiefly to find men for special needs, sponsorship was regularized in the early eleventh century for promotions to all but the highest ranks and functions. When the candidate did well the sponsor was honoured and rewarded. Exact laws governed the legal liability for sponsoring a man who later misbehaved. Penalties were graded according to the demonstrable grounds for the recommendation and the kind of crime or delinquency that occurred. All sponsors of the delinquent man suffered equally. Legislation around 1020 provided that for the most serious offences, including venality, the punishment for sponsors should be identical with that of the man guaranteed (if the latter's penalty were death, the sponsors' would be the severest short of death). In the case of other offences the sponsors would suffer a penalty less than that of the offender's by one degree or two degrees, or go free, according to the gravity of the offence. The number of a candidate's sponsors determined whether or how far he would be promoted. Candidates stationed away from the capital were favoured by rules that allowed more recommendations annually by provincial officials. The utility of the system depended in part on a careful adjustment of penalties; when liability was too onerous few were willing to sponsor, and when too light the practice could encourage factional alliances. On the whole sponsorship proved its worth, and continued in use while the empire lasted.

The examination system, which grew from sponsorship, was destined to occupy a greater place in the history of political institutions. This system served to select men for governmental service through regular written, competitive examinations, open to all candidates of good character, however they came by their training. The system was long in evolving. The earliest applications of examination technique are obscure. At least as early as 165 B.C. men recommended for office were required to answer in writing questions set by the Han emperor Wen. The emperor Wu followed this procedure regularly, placing the candidates in exact order of demonstrated merit. Han state university students were also promoted through written tests. In the early T'ang, competitive written examination of recommended men still produced on average less than ten graduates a year. At the end of the seventh century the empress Wu, usurping power and scheming to found a new dynasty, made competitive examination a tool to recruit supporters from the largely untapped talent of south-east China, and during successive years the number of degrees reached six times or more the earlier average. The T'ang emperor Hsüan-tsung, retrieving the throne, improved and strengthened his government with a series of measures; and examinations grew still more important. The number of graduates diminished with T'ang decline, but Sung rule revived the trend and in the eleventh century the annual average of final degrees passed two hundred and fifty. (In addition, degrees of a lesser order were conferred on many who after persistent effort had failed to pass the final test by the age of fifty or sixty.) The graduates could now supply the greater share of civil service posts.

With growing reliance on examination came contrivance of better methods. The chief of these were in use soon after A.D. 1000. Preliminary local tests and two tests at the capital eliminated some ninety-nine per cent. of the contenders. Those who graduated were classed and numbered in order of ability. All would first hold rather minor offices, but examination ranking went far to determine subsequent promotions. Each examination paper was graded by three independent readers. Fair and objective reading was furthered by concealment of candidates' identities. A number replaced a candidate's name on his paper, which was copied out by clerks lest his handwriting be recognized.

The problems of suiting subject-matter and testing method to needed aptitudes was not so neatly solved. Debates on this were heated. Some premisses were unquestioned: an official should know the principles of government and human conduct; his training should fit him to deal with widely diverse duties and situations; he should be mentally acute and flexible. Classical studies served these ends by showing the foundations of morals and exemplifying historically their bearing on political problems. The Classics also provided a uniform and concise body of knowledge accessible to any scholar. The studies of law, forms of official conduct, literary composition, and later histories provided more directly applicable knowledge. Most minutiae of official duties were left to be learned from practical experience.

Many and ingenious written tests were devised to assess the results of these studies. The candidate proved his memory of classical writings by completing passages from which a few words were given as a clue. Or he was asked to summarize the essential meanings and implications of designated texts from the Classics, histories, formularies, or laws and ordinances, according to his specialization. Or he demonstrated his acumen by proposing solutions to problems posed by seeming conflicts of principle in classical authorities, or to current administrative dilemmas such as those of adjusting commodity supply and demand. He showed his originality and imagination by composing essays on themes presented to him. He displayed his ingenuity by composing pieces of prose or verse for which the themes, rhymes, and complex forms were assigned him.

No one kind of test was felt to be fully adequate. Simple textual familiarity with the Classics did not prove intelligence. Answers to questions on meaning might, with effort enough, be learned by rote. Questions that called for an application of knowledge to conflicts of principle or administrative quandaries might evoke original thinking, but who could grade the answers accurately and objectively? Required compositions on prescribed topics in strictly formulated literary forms might show originality and ability, and could be graded more objectively, but did the studies they encouraged produce the most practical officials? Tests of these many kinds were multiplied and tried in varying versions and combinations. A single examination might last through several day-long sessions. But when any pattern of tests was long in use, clever tutors and assiduous study of past examinations could anticipate questions and supply formulas for glib answers. The best of forms had to change. Some critics decried all forms of written test as lacking the prime requisite—detection of character.

For these reasons, no doubt, competitive examination was applied above all to recruitment. Promotion more often came through other methods. Yet in its prime the examination system brought China's ablest minds into government, and no other device promised equal results. The Mongols, who along with their foreign allies (like Marco Polo) could scarcely compete on a scholarly plane, for a time made official appointments through sponsorship. It would not do; in 1315 the old competitions returned, to continue unbroken until 1905. At first averaging only a score a year, graduate numbers grew under Ming and Manchus. But they never comprised more than half those of the Sung. This was partly compensated by granting lower offices to men who passed the local tests. More serious was the subtle dampening of original thinking. Perhaps inertia, perhaps the later dynasts' instinctive distrust of too much restiveness, took hold. During the last five centuries the famous eight-legged examination essay, treating a given theme in eight different kinds of composition, remained in vogue, and the patterns of questions varied little. Regional quotas made officialdom more representative but limited free competition. Under Mongols and Manchus the ruling races and their allies enjoyed also racial quotas and easier standards. For Chinese, the tests to hurdle on the way to a final *chin-shih* degree were multiplied beyond belief, absorbing mental energies the competitors might have used more profitably. But even so the system brought good men to run the empire, and won respect from Europeans who first met it in these latter days.

Annual merit ratings also grew from sponsorship. Han rulers required that local officials submit, with their annual reports and accounts, the names of those who served well in any capacity, that they might be promoted. Gentlemen of the court were rated on their directness, staunchness, self-abnegation, and performance in office. The T'ang brought the system of promotion by merit to the highest degree of refinement. Each year every official was checked by his superior on his possession or lack of four specified excellences and twenty-seven desirable qualities. One point could be counted for each excellence (renown for uprightness, conspicuous integrity and circumspection, laudable impartiality, or unrelaxing diligence). One point could be added if he had one of the desirable qualities appropriate to his particular office. Five points placed a man in the highest of nine merit categories. No points but fairly good conduct put him in the sixth. A record showing unjustly prejudiced actions put him in the seventh, self-interest and neglect of duty in the eighth, graft in the ninth. According to his category his salary was raised, unchanged, or reduced, and if he fell in the ninth category he was dismissed. Ratings over several years were balanced and, if other than middling, brought promotion or demotion. On paper the system could scarcely be improved. In operation, unbiased objectivity was no easier for the Chinese superior official than for his modern Western confrère who faces a similar task. The system could not be relied on exclusively, but it supplemented other techniques and gained a permanent place among personnel practices.

A government that so stressed suasion could hardly fail to emphasize morale, the first and best promoter of discipline. Fair treatment of officials and *esprit de corps* received attention early, and measures to attain these developed side by side with the techniques already described. Here only their principal features can be enumerated. Honours, titles, and decorations need hardly be mentioned. Positions were carefully classified and pay was determined by exact rules. Severe laws protected the subordinate from arbitrary exactions of his superior. Days of rest were provided at five- or ten-day periods, in addition to longer holidays and leave for family emergencies. Rules for advancement took seniority into account, along with performance in office. At seventy an official could retire on pension. Where inducement failed, penalty lay in reserve. The more humiliating punishments were applied sparingly after the Han, since they tended to damage general morale, and the superior man—the *chün-tzu*—should not need them. Where prestige was so important, threat of fine or demotion was severe, and exile or dismissal from the service was terrible indeed. Officials were bound by social pressures. Those who worked within a single administrative unit shared a joint legal responsibility. But in the end perhaps the most effective sanction was that of public reputation; good or bad, it survived the individual and brought pride or shame to his descendants.

China's political achievement, her success and the bounds of that success, certainly derived from no one political theory or concept, no one administrative device. They stemmed rather from the total energy and imagination directed into political life. Political ideas and systems grew from Chinese culture and unique Chinese experiences. In turn, they shaped the culture and its growth.

Political life both advanced and channelled social change. Prosperity and its social effects had made the expanded examinations possible; the examinations in turn opened the bureaucracy to all the ablest, and made it also representative. Apart from those families of morally tainted origin (professional entertainers, and for a time merchant families), all men could equally compete for a governmental career. Each peasant family cherished a hope of some day winning social distinction this way; folk-embroideries pictured the triumphal homecoming of a son who passed the tests at the top of the list. The hope was sometimes realized. With but one office to a thousand families and more, the chance could not be great. But in the Sung and later, neither high birth nor wealth was essential for graduates. Not a few were poor, and many indeed could count no recent ancestor in office. Many more *novi homines* no doubt entered the civil service and the clerical services through other ways of recruitment. The outlook of government was affected by the bureaucrats' varied origins; their districts, where their family homes remained, benefited also. Freedom of opportunity in traditional China was not that of our modern ideal, or even of modern actualities, but few if any large pre-modern nations could rival it.[1]

---

[1] The extent and significance of social mobility through the Chinese examinations have occasioned much debate. The view here given agrees generally with treatments in Ho Ping-ti, *The Ladder of Success in Imperial*

We saw the high place accorded public welfare, both in theory and in administrative measures. How well was it furthered in practice? The answer of course varies according to the period. Morale and honesty naturally declined when dynasties weakened. The upper ranks of officialdom, normally selected for scholarship and character, at times lacked vigour and wisdom; except in times of eunuch influence they were rarely corrupt. On lower levels, salaries grew inadequate in difficult times, and clerical employees, selected more casually, had poorer *esprit de corps*. When good men supervised them, things went well, as popular petitions to retain such men in office demonstrated. At other times conditions were less happy. Laws were administered according to a carefully formulated code, revised in each dynasty. Legal concepts differed in several respects from those to which we are accustomed. Confucian theory, distrusting laws and advocating persuasion, discouraged litigation and urged the settlement of disputes through voluntary agreement, in which the local official often played a role. Problems of social or business relationship that in Western law might be settled by civil litigation were, when brought to court, often governed by laws of conduct enforced by penalties. Still extremely severe in the Han, the punishments were gradually lightened in later dynasties, those of physical mutilation being largely eliminated and capital crimes greatly reduced in number. Exile, forced labour, and the rod remained, but they were often commuted to fines varying according to a fixed schedule. Legal administration sought a justice that fitted the circumstances of each case. Where no irremediable damage had been done, the law provided that confession in advance of accusation should bring a lightened penalty

China (New York, 1962); Chang Chung-li, *The Chinese Gentry* (Seattle, 1955); and by E. A. Kracke, Jr., in J. K. Fairbank, ed., *Chinese Thought and Institutions*, pp. 251–68. A contrary view is presented in K. A. Wittfögel, *Oriental Despotism* (New Haven, Conn., 1957), which appears to discount the recruitment of new men by means other than examination.

or pardon. Offences were graver when the offended was one, such as a family elder, or official superior, who should command a special respect from the offender. Effort was made also to consider special extenuating circumstances. This called for a broad discretion on the part of the judge. Important cases were, however, regularly reviewed by higher judicial officials, the gravest receiving careful study by high courts at the capital.

How did the individual Chinese citizen fare in actuality? By what standards shall we measure the performance of government in practice, the justice of civil order achieved, the sum of individual freedom and contentment? Today we expect from government a standard made possible through long technical advances and the pooled political experience of the past. Perhaps the most relevant measure of China's success in earlier ages is that of the total impressions made on foreign witnesses, judging in terms of the Europe or the Near East of their times. Such witnesses often criticized certain practices and customs. But their praise of China's polity was almost universal. Arabs remarked the prevalence of literacy among all classes, and the honouring of business obligations. Marco Polo says of the last Sung ruler, whose Mongol successor he served:

He loved peace and strictly maintained his kingdom in so great justice that none was found there who did evil or theft to any there, and the city was so safe that the doors of the houses and shops and stores full of all very dear merchandise often stayed open at night as by day and nothing at all was found missing there. For one could go freely through the whole kingdom safe and unmolested by night also as by day. It would be impossible to tell of the great wealth and the very great goodness which is in this kingdom so that the king was loved by all with very great reason.

Some three centuries later the Jesuit Ricci comments, as a good Christian, that

every public office is therefore fortified with and dependent on the attested science, prudence, and diplomacy of the person assigned to it, whether he be taking office for the first time or is already experienced in the conduct of civil life. This integrity of life is prescribed by the law of [the Ming founder] Humvu, and for the most part it is lived up to, save in the case of such as are prone to violate the dictates of justice from human weakness and from lack of religious training among the gentiles.

By pre-modern Islamic and European political standards, it would seem that China did well.[1]

The relation of political system to economic prosperity was complex. In providing political unity, public order, roads, canals, and a single currency, the state no doubt made possible the private commercial and industrial growth so striking in the Sung. To what extent was the state answerable for the slackening of growth in later dynasties? Bureaucracy, so greatly predominant in society, was also in the accepted philosophy responsible for public welfare. This responsibility it fulfilled by providing granaries for famine relief, and by endeavouring to prevent profiteering in grain through the timing of state purchases and sales (the 'ever-normal granary' system). It also attempted, for extended periods, to replace private land ownership with state allocation of farm lands for life tenure. While these experiments were never wholly successful, they do not seem to have impeded the course of economic change. Governmental action went further than this, however. Increasingly it controlled the greater enterprises, through monopolies and regulations. It drew to itself a growing share of the national income; did it use its resources to the best advantage? It found no full relief for the farmer's hardships, for the problems of

[1] Cf. Jean Sauvaget, *Relation de la Chine et de l'Inde* (Paris, 1948), pp. 17, 19, 21, 26; A. C. Moule and Paul Pelliot, *Marco Polo : The Description of the World*, vol. i (London, 1938), pp. 312–13; L. J. Gallagher, S.J., tr., *China in the Sixteenth Century* (New York, 1953), p. 45; Denis Twitchett, *Land Tenure and the Social Order in T'ang and Sung China* (London, 1962).

growing population, nor finally for those of the state's own finances. These problems might certainly have baffled most pre-modern governments, and some even a state with modern technology at its call. The rise of more effective bureaucracy had paralleled the rise of a new and greater economy. Did the weight of state economic control inhibit a further economic growth that could lead to an eventual solution of these problems? On this we can only conjecture.

China's political character affected profoundly the growth of her sense of values and the nature of her culture. Since force was decried and the military man suspect as a threat to political order, the civilian ideal prevailed. Education and the literary arts were revered; the more as they opened the avenues to mundane success. The invention of printing was prompted by practical needs. Poetry and painting, practised by the able and influential, not surprisingly rose to high sophistication and subtlety. Through more popular arts—the drama, the story, and the novel—the values and tradition of the scholarly affected the outlook of other classes. Most important, the duty of the scholar as political critic led him to habits of freedom in thought that reached to other realms. Individual thinkers were free to interpret the Classics according to their lights. Thinkers of the twelfth century—Chu Hsi, Lu Hsiang-shan, Ch'en Liang—followed divergent paths, and some asserted their independence even of classical authority. The habit of stubborn intellectual independence, surviving the disfavour of the later dynasties, still appeared in reformers like K'ang Yu-wei at the end of the Ch'ing Dynasty.

That Chinese political institutions were sound and serviceable, no fact could testify more convincingly than their striking durability and continuity. The centuries that saw the fall of Rome saw also the wane of the Chinese empire and the founding of barbarian kingdoms in its principal territories. But where Frankish rulers failed to restore the Roman fabric, the Sui and

T'ang in China restored the imperial forms so firmly that unity lasted, despite the fall of dynasties and foreign conquests, for thirteen centuries more. China's circumstances differed from those of Europe. Perhaps her natural boundaries were more forbidding; perhaps internal economic ties were closer; perhaps linguistic unity was stronger. But certainly the Chinese state could never have outlasted these tests without the strength and elasticity of its administrative fabric, the stability of its political organism, and the willing support of its people.

Has China's political achievement meaning for Eastern Asia alone? Could its effects have extended to the Western world? When Chinese institutions reached an advanced stage of development, the growth of modern Europe was beginning. In the six centuries after the battle of Hastings new nations would emerge, transform loose feudal ties into royal régimes, and gradually extend their powers through working out new bureaucratic methods and structures.

During these centuries knowledge of Chinese institutions slowly found its way across the Continent. Arab merchants knew China well as early as the T'ang, dwelling at Canton and following the trade routes that criss-crossed the country. Their observations were recorded in the *Akhbār aṣ-Ṣīn wa'l-Hind* in the ninth century, by al-Mas'ūdī in the tenth, al-Marwazī and Idrīsī in the twelfth. All of these took an interest in details of Chinese administrative practice. Europeans, through increasingly intimate contacts with Arabs from Spain to Egypt, could learn of Chinese ways as they did of Greek philosophy. At the end of the thirteenth century Marco Polo and others saw Chinese government at first hand and, though their accounts of this were somewhat hazy, they conveyed profound respect for the public order and complex organization they witnessed.[1]

[1] Cf. G. F. Hudson, *Europe and China* (London, 1931), especially pp. 154-9.

With the voyages of discovery new sources of information on Chinese institutions began to open, and the full truth began to dawn when in 1582 the Jesuits at last set foot on Chinese soil. Versed in European knowledge and students also of Chinese language and ways, these reporters of Chinese political thought and methods reached new planes of observation and understanding. Europe, which had found Polo's tales incredible, now listened eagerly. From the very arrival of the Jesuits in China, annual volumes of their letters were distributed by their presses in many parts of Europe. Throughout the eighteenth century selected letters and essays were reprinted in sets running to dozens of volumes. De Mailla's history of China, based on standard Chinese works and finally issued in Paris in 1783, filled twelve tomes. Jesuit translations of Chinese Classics had meanwhile appeared. These various writings were commonly issued in Latin, understood in all lettered circles, and reprinted also in many of the vernacular languages.

Perhaps the greatest influence of China's tradition was less through particular notions than through its total impact on European political thought. Chinese ideas were most in vogue in the century preceding the French Revolution, the very time when new theories of government were rife. To the familiar Greco-Roman heritage China added fresh attitudes and theories. And if China was painted in sometimes unduly utopian colours, her prestige did not lose at the time. Leibniz wrote in 1697 with some restraint concerning much of China's culture, but noted with surprise that it still surpassed the European in comprehending the precepts of civil life. 'It is difficult to describe', he said, 'how beautifully the laws of the Chinese, in contrast to those of other peoples, are directed to the achievement of public tranquillity and the establishment of social order.' Voltaire found China the ideal state ruled paternalistically by an enlightened despot. Quesnay and the physiocrats, in the seventeen-sixties, made it their ideal. As the Chinese emperor, in his ceremonial ploughing, honoured farming as the basis of society, the French dauphin and the Austrian emperor performed a similar ceremony. A mid-eighteenth-century Dorset farmer of liberal political views reportedly named his fields after sages, including Confucius, Solon, Lycurgus, and Cicero. Dupont de Nemours chid a lady who carped at his economic views for her ignorance of Confucius.[1]

Chinese political ideas and practices, now common coinage of European thinking, were turned to use more easily. And if they lost their Chinese label in the process, their influence would not be lessened, since partisan use of China's prestige could bring partisan reaction, and instinctive conservatism and national pride resisted foreign importations. Europe's long and repeated encounters with Chinese governmental ideas also helped in practical ways. A political idea was harder to borrow than a product like silk or a technique like printing. Chinese ideas made little sense to feudal Europe. Their full utility came only when the rise of modern states provided institutional trunks on which the new sprouts could be grafted. Strategic situations for their introduction were often long in arriving.

Some perhaps found their way into Western thought quite early. The petitioner's drum is an interesting case. Ninth-century Arab accounts tell of its use in China, but called it a bell. Thereafter Arab writers ascribe petitioners' bells to ancient Persia. Still later chronicles of Europe attribute similar bells to Theodosius the Great and Charlemagne. Islamic and European

[1] Cf. Hudson, op. cit., pp. 298–302, 308–29; D. F. Lach, *The Preface to Leibniz's Novissima Sinica* (Honolulu, 1957), pp. 69–70; idem, 'China and the Era of the Enlightenment', *The Journal of Modern History*, vol. xiv (1942), pp. 209–23; idem, *The Impact of Asia in Europe*, vol. i, *Asia in the Eyes of the West: The Sixteenth Century* (Chicago, 1963); L. A. Maverick, *China a Model for Europe* (San Antonio, Texas, 1946). A thirty-four-volume set of letters published in Paris in 1703–76 emphasized China strongly. Re-editions appeared in 1780–3, 1810, 1819, and 1829–32. A set of Jesuit essays on China, published in 1776–1814, reached sixteen volumes.

versions have similar details; did a Chinese idea find its echo in medieval Western legend? Recent research suggests that Chinese methods, reported by the Arabs, perhaps also found concrete applications in medieval Europe heretofore unsuspected.[1]

From the early eighteenth century methods and practices first evolved in China found use in Europe with great frequency. At times a Chinese origin may be suggested by the appearance of Chinese ideas in association or by the known presence of a special interest in China at the time and place the practice appears. Even as Leibniz praised Chinese examinations, the court of Brandenburg, where he had close contacts, experimented with such a system, and then or soon after with the ever-normal granary also. Ideas already known to the West were sometimes partly or wholly recommunicated later. Chinese contact through the East India Company seemingly played a role in British adoption of a civil service examination system in the nineteenth century.[2] A Chinese scholar contributed towards the conception of the ever-normal granary in the United States under the latter Roosevelt.[3]

Still other political concepts appeared in the West in forms suggesting Chinese prototypes. In most cases we can scarcely hope for evidence to show beyond a doubt whether or not the idea or its application was at some point inspired by Chinese precedent. Organs resembling the Censorate appear more than

---

[1] Cf. Sauvaget, op. cit., p. 18; Aloys Sprenger, tr., Mas'ūdī, *The Meadows of Gold and Mines of Gems*, vol. i, pp. 328–32; Sir Henry Yule, tr., Henri Cordier, ed., *Cathay and the Way Thither* (London, 1915), vol. i, p. 100; Charles Swan, tr., *Gesta Romanorum* (London, n.d.), p. 231; Philip Strauch, *Jansen Enikels Werke* (Hanover, 1891), p. 515. On other Chinese methods in medieval Europe a study by H. G. Creel, Muhsin Mahdi, and Robert Hartwell is in progress.

[2] Cf. Lach, *Leibniz*, pp. 55, 72, &c.; S. Y. Teng, 'Chinese Influence on the Western Examination System', *Harvard Journal of Asiatic Studies*, vol. vii (1942–3), pp. 267–312.

[3] Derk Bodde, *Far Eastern Quarterly*, vol. v (1945–6), pp. 413 ff.

once in the eighteenth century. In modern states we see a trend to copy the Swedish public defenders who inspect local administration, listen to private complaints, defend civil liberties, and bring action against delinquent officials. Such defenders, it seems, existed at least by 1724, and could sue even the king.[1] Events of Chinese legal history, too, are echoed. Han emperors, to weaken feudal power, decreed that properties of all nobles should be divided equally among their heirs. The same expedient served monarchs in Europe to check a troublesome aristocracy, and New World statesmen as a tool for social levelling. The resort to constitutional checks and balances and the merit-rating systems again recall their Chinese analogues. The parallels are striking in their number, and systematic studies on them have only begun. Research will no doubt discover further connecting threads. But the full extent of Western indebtedness must remain obscure.

What further may yet be learned from Chinese political experience? Probably few Chinese administrative methods applicable to modern needs remain untried. But China's political history may still instruct us. Our modern bureaucracies have not been tested very long, and their stores of experience are limited. In China we may examine a bureaucratic history of two thousand years. The records afford us abundant detail on government and its problems. We can trace the play of political, social, and economic forces within a bureaucratic context, and learn where trends and policies have led. Some of what we learn may quicken our minds in meeting problems of our own. China sought a way to join together practical method with the vision of a state that ministered to its citizens' needs, to balance force with an appeal to the good that Confucians found in unfettered human instinct. If their ideal could not be fully realized, their effort helped to

---

[1] Cf. *Dispute Between King and Senate of Sweden 1756* (London, 1756), p. 12; J. E. Maccoll in New Fabian Research Bureau, *Democratic Sweden* (London, 1938), p. 34. The official in question is called the *justitie-ombudsman*.

bring into being a great and lasting civilization. Our study of China's institutions may in the future, as in the past, add to our common political heritage.   E. A. KRACKE, JR.

7

CONCLUSION

This final chapter is intended not merely to add some new material, but also to serve as summary of what has gone before. It deals in turn with two aspects of the legacy of China—her influence on the world and the greatness of her cultural achievements. The first section makes no reference to scientific and technological influences, but is intended as a broad survey of the other intellectual, artistic, and minor cultural influences exerted by China beyond her frontiers. The second section attempts to interrelate some of the book's main themes and draw some general conclusions about the nature of Chinese civilization and the value of its study.

(a) CHINA AND THE WORLD

A SUMMARY OF INTELLECTUAL AND ARTISTIC INFLUENCES

FROM very early times the influence of Chinese civilization has had profound effects on non-Chinese peoples. In Shang and Chou times, in the second and first millennia B.C., for the non-Chinese tribes of what is now central and southern China and for the nomads of the northern steppes, Chinese culture was the sole representative of a way of life based on intensive agriculture, towns, and ordered large-scale government. As such it impressed the uncivilized neighbours of the Chinese, even when they raided and plundered it, and the discovery by the Chinese that their cultural prestige could be used diplomatically to tame barbarians who could not be crushed by military power was certainly one of the sources of the idea, so prominent in traditional Chinese philosophy, that the successful ruler was one who attracted people by his 'virtue' instead of subduing them by force. In those remote centuries the Chinese had the advantage of a monopoly of advanced culture in all the surrounding regions; there was no rival centre of civilization among the peoples with whom they were in contact. It was only with the great development of trade routes westward in the period of the Han Dynasty that influences of Indian and Iranian civilization penetrated into the western borderlands of China and even into China itself. From this time onwards, although Chinese political expansion often reached far into Central Asia, the cultural ascendancy of China was restricted in Burma, Tibet, Turkestan, and Mongolia by the rival cultural forces radiating from India, Persia, and Arabia; it was only to the east and south-east, in Korea, Vietnam, and Japan, that it had an exclusive sphere of influence, and it is today these three countries which have special historic links with China as co-heirs to a common Far Eastern civilization of Chinese origin.

The most important distinguishing feature of this civilization was the use of the Chinese script and the study of Chinese classical literature which went with it. Not only did Korea, Vietnam, and Japan use the Chinese written language as a vehicle of culture much as Latin was used in western Europe in the Middle Ages, but they stocked their own languages with words and phrases borrowed from Chinese, and wrote them either with adapted forms of the Chinese script or with syllabaries derived from it. As a result of their acquisition of Chinese written characters the educated class in these countries had access to Chinese literature and was open to the influence of the ideas which it expressed; thus the Confucian conceptions of society and government, filial piety and the cult of ancestors, classical scholarship and literate bureaucracy were spread abroad beyond the borders of China itself. Even when the main inspiration in these peripheral areas was not Confucian, but Buddhist, it was Buddhism transmitted in its Chinese version, using Chinese and not Sanskrit or Pali as its ecclesiastical language.

Together with this linguistic expansion and the literary and ideological influences which went with it, there were various other elements of Chinese culture which left an indelible imprint on Korea, Vietnam, and Japan. Architecture and the arts in all three countries were profoundly influenced by China; in painting this was partly an effect of the introduction of the Chinese script, for the use of the brush in writing and the art of calligraphy had the same results as in China on the technique of rendering forms on a flat surface. In the sphere of popular custom and usage an extremely important mark of 'sinicization' was the use of chopsticks for eating; for the common man in the Far East no line so definitely divided civilized people from barbarians as that which separated men who consumed their food with chopsticks from those who used their fingers or in later times such inferior instruments as knives and forks.

There was, however, one great difference between Korea and Vietnam on the one hand and Japan on the other with regard to the reception of Chinese civilization. Japan was never politically under Chinese rule, whereas a part of Korea and the whole of the original Vietnam (equivalent to the modern Tongking) were at one time Chinese imperial territory, so that Chinese civilization took root in these areas through actual Chinese settlement and administration. In Korea the Han Dynasty of China subdued the north-western part of the country towards the end of the second century b.c. and created there the province of Lolang with its capital at Pyongyang. Archaeological excavations have shown that this became a rich and flourishing Chinese colony where an upper class of Chinese officials and merchants copied the fashions and luxuries of Changan and Loyang; the mass of the people no doubt continued to speak Korean, but became more or less assimilated to the economic and social order introduced by their conquerors. The north-eastern and southern parts of Korea remained unsubdued by China and relatively primitive, but came under an increasing Chinese influence through trade and tribal diplomatic contacts. Then early in the fourth century A.D. Lo-lang was overrun by the native Korean kingdom of Koguryo, which had had its centre on the upper Yalu and by its expansion became heir to the Chinese civilization of Pyongyang. From this time onwards there was no Chinese colonial rule in Korea, though China under the T'ang Dynasty intervened successfully in the internecine wars of Korean states, and the kingdom of Silla, which unified Korea politically with Chinese aid, acknowledged a tributary relation to China while retaining full independence in internal affairs. This status of Korea as an independent state under a formal Chinese suzerainty became traditional and persisted until China was compelled to renounce the suzerainty after the Sino-Japanese War of 1894.

The history of Vietnam followed a similar course except for the fact that Chinese rule lasted much longer; established under the Han Dynasty about the same time as the founding of Lo-lang, it lasted in Tongking, the lower basin of the Red river, for approximately a thousand years. In the end, however, the Chinese were driven out by a native revolt, and Vietnam became, like Korea, independent, but tributary to China. The Vietnamese were ethnically of the same stock as the Nan-yüeh people who in ancient times inhabited a large part of South China, but were there absorbed by Chinese immigrants from the north; only in Tongking did the race survive and form a distinct nation which achieved its separate existence as a state after being for centuries part of a Chinese-administered society. In later times the Vietnamese themselves became a conquering people, extending their borders towards the south; they subdued and absorbed the Chams, a people of derivative Indian culture in what is now South Vietnam, and took the Mekong delta from the Cambodians. Today the boundary between the traditional spheres of Indian and Chinese civilization coincides with the Vietnamese frontier with Cambodia and Laos.

Both Korea and Vietnam, though geographically secluded by mountain ranges and sea gulfs, were countries of the mainland of Asia and accessible to Chinese armies. Japan, on the other hand, separated by a hundred miles of sea from Korea and by more than four hundred from the east coast of China, was virtually out of reach of continental Asian powers, and the only serious attempt at invasion from the mainland—by the Mongols in the thirteenth century—was a failure. The Japanese received Chinese civilization, not because it was implanted in their country by conquest, but because their contact with it led them to admire and envy it and seek to acquire it. The knowledge of it was obtained partly from Chinese and Koreans who came to Japan as craftsmen, teachers of writing, or Buddhist monks, and partly through Japanese who made the voyage to Korea or China as diplomatic envoys or students. In the seventh and eighth centuries embassies to China became large-scale expeditions; in addition to the crews of the ships hundreds of people sailed with them and returned to Japan full of zeal to transform the customs and institutions of their own country so as to make it worthy of comparison with the T'ang empire. Their enthusiasm for China did not, however, incline them to accept any tributary relation with the Chinese court; the belief in the special divine origin of the Japanese monarchy was incompatible with subordination to any other earthly ruler. For a period in the fourteenth and fifteenth centuries Japanese shoguns—military commanders who governed in the name of powerless emperors—did pay tribute to China in order to obtain trading privileges in Chinese ports, but after 1549 this practice ceased, so that Japan thereafter remained outside the Chinese system of vassal states.

The linguistic ascendancy of Chinese was also greater in Korea and Vietnam than in Japan. In Korea and Vietnam the native languages were culturally smothered by the introduction of Chinese, and although they produced a literature of folk-poetry and ballads, nearly all serious writing by the educated class was in Chinese. In Korea a phonetic system for writing the Korean language was invented in the fifteenth century, but until its adoption as the national script in recent times it never succeeded in making Korean a rival to Chinese as a literary language. In Japan, however, although Chinese established itself as the language of learned writing, a purely Japanese court poetry flourished from the seventh century onwards and a literature of novel and drama in Japanese was afterwards added, so that the national culture was able to express itself without excessive dependence on a foreign tongue. The Japanese language ultimately became one in which words of Japanese and words of Chinese origin were mixed together, and the characters of the Chinese script could usually be read with either a Japanese or a modified Chinese spoken equivalent. The Japanese also developed in the ninth century two phonetic syllabaries for writing their own language, but they did not discard Chinese characters, preferring to use them for the main words in a sentence while inserting signs from the syllabaries to indicate elements of the agglutinative Japanese speech which have no parallel in Chinese; thus modern Japanese writing is a mixture of Chinese characters (*kanji*) and syllabic signs (*kana*). This combination is typical of the mingling of purely Chinese elements with original Japanese traits in the traditional culture of Japan.

Socially and politically also Chinese institutions were modified through being imitated outside China, and much more so in Japan than in Korea or Vietnam. The Chinese system of government through a civil service recruited by competitive examinations went through several phases of development; only by degrees and with many setbacks did it prevail over tendencies towards consolidation of hereditary aristocratic privilege in Chinese society. When the system was transplanted to other countries it was easier to copy its outward forms than to give it the broad social basis which it ultimately acquired in China. It was more or less successfully established, though on a narrower social basis, in Korea and Vietnam, especially the former. In Japan no serious attempt was ever made to introduce the *carrière ouverte aux talents*; although a bureaucratic administration modelled on that of T'ang China was created in the seventh century, its higher offices were confined to a small ring of noble families, and from the twelfth century onwards political development moved away from the Chinese model towards a type of feudalism in many ways similar to that of medieval Europe. By the time Western nations came into contact with East Asia after the opening of the oceanic trade routes there was a wide divergence between the political institutions of China and Japan. The shoguns of the Tokugawa family who governed Japan from 1603 to 1868 were patrons of Chinese scholarship and Confucian philosophy, but the political system they sustained with its numerous hereditary fiefs was far removed from the mandarinate of contemporary China.

In the sphere of the arts the story was much the same, Korea and Vietnam showing a much closer approximation than Japan to the course of their development in China. In Korea a marked creative originality was shown in the great Koryo celadon wares, but on the whole Chinese aesthetic models remained dominant, curbing the growth of a characteristic national art. In Japan, on the other hand, architecture took a turn away from the Chinese tradition in a new direction in the eleventh century, and about the same time the style of painting called *Yamatoe* or 'Japanese pictures' developed on lines for which there were no Chinese precedents. Later on there were two further important infusions of Chinese artistic influence into Japan—that of the ink-painting of the Sung and Yüan periods which conquered Japan in the fifteenth century and that of the *wen-jen-hua* or 'literary man's painting' which created a new fashion in the seventeenth. But after each new wave of Chinese influence there was a revival of *Yamatoe*, and from this background arose in the eighteenth century the school of *Ukiyoe*, the art of the colour-prints of

Harunobu, Sharaku, and Hokusai, which, however 'Far Eastern' to the Western eye, is profoundly un-Chinese.

Japan, nevertheless, whatever the degree of her deviation, belongs historically to the sphere in which Chinese civilization has been dominant. Outside this sphere China's influence in the world has been mainly an effect of trade and occasionally of Chinese emigration and settlement in areas where the prevailing institutions and way of life have not been of Chinese origin. Within the last three centuries moreover there has been an important influence of Chinese thought in the Western world, but this has not been, as in China's traditional sphere of cultural ascendancy, the result of relatively primitive peoples receiving civilization from a country of more advanced development, but the outcome of the intellectual interest of a rival civilization (which has prevailed over China's own) in the Chinese cultural heritage.

Chinese contacts in ancient times with the other main areas of civilization in the Old World—India, Western Asia, and the lands round the Mediterranean—were established almost entirely through an export trade in which the most important commodity was silk. The production of silk was then a Chinese monopoly and the Chinese word for it was the origin of one of the two names by which the Chinese themselves were known to the Romans—Seres or 'the silk people', the other name Sinae being derived from Ch'in (or Ts'in), the name of the great imperial dynasty of the third century B.C., which is also the original of our 'China'. The main route for the silk trade ran overland to the west from North China through the modern Sinkiang across the Pamirs to northern Iran and on to Syria and the Mediterranean, with a branch southward to India from the upper Oxus. There was also a maritime traffic by the South China Sea and the Indian Ocean, and another commodity exported westward by the sea routes was cinnamon bark, which was produced from cultivated trees in Kwangsi. Cinnamon was much in demand and fetched high prices as a spice in the Roman empire, but the Romans did not know where it came from; as it was sold in East African ports, they believed it to be an African product. The Arabs, however, were aware of its source and called it *dār ṣīnī* or 'Chinese bark'.

In both these products the Chinese eventually lost their monopoly of production, but they had been the original suppliers. The technique of rearing silkworms spread gradually from China to south-east Asia and just after the middle of the sixth century eggs of the silkmoth were smuggled to Syria, where a new silk industry grew up within the borders of the Roman empire and was later extended to the Mediterranean lands of Europe. Cinnamon likewise came to be produced commercially outside China, for it was discovered in Ceylon that a local wild variety of the tree could compete with Chinese cinnamon if it was cultivated. In later times Ceylon has been the principal supplier of the world market in this commodity, which has, however, declined in importance among spices, just as spices in general have long since lost the outstanding importance which they had in long-distance international trade in ancient and medieval times.

Although West Asia and Europe were no longer dependent on China for supplies of raw silk after they had developed their own silk industries, the former export trade in the raw material was to some extent replaced during the Middle Ages by exports of decorated Chinese textiles—damasks and brocades—and this had effects which were not merely economic but also aesthetic, for such textiles became a means whereby the specific Chinese feeling for visual form was transmitted to the Islamic world and even to Europe. This influence was reinforced by that of Chinese decorated pottery and porcelain; in particular, Chinese celadon wares had an enormous vogue in Moslem countries and were traded as far west as Morocco. Chinese painting as such was not then appreciated outside the sphere of dominant Chinese civilization, but Chinese pictorial motifs and conventions were reproduced in textiles and ceramics and thus widely diffused through trade in these commodities. Their influence can be traced in the medieval art of Iran. Europe, however, was very little affected by it until after the oceanic routes to East Asia round Africa and across the Pacific had been opened up. But by the seventeenth century substantial quantities of Chinese textiles and porcelain were reaching the European market and to these was added lacquer furniture, also a medium of Chinese decorative design.

In the eighteenth century the vogue of *chinoiserie* in Europe was wide and far-reaching. It had, it is true, only a slight effect on the fine arts in the narrow sense; histories of the major architecture and painting of the period can be written without reference to Far Eastern art, though even here the development of the 'Chinese–English style' of gardens as an adjunct to architecture was important and a subtle Chinese influence can be detected in the painting of Watteau. But throughout the whole range of the decorative and industrial arts of eighteenth-century Europe—in furniture and interior decoration, in porcelain and enamels, in paper-hangings and screens, in costumes and embroideries, and in *Kleinkunst* carvings of all kinds—the factor of *chinoiserie* is of great significance.[1] There were three categories of objects to which the term is applicable as a symptom of eighteenth-century European taste—first, genuine Chinese products made in the first place for the Chinese home market but bought in China by European merchants; second, European imitations of Chinese designs—of which 'willow-pattern china' is a good example; and third, 'Chinese export art' or goods produced in China, mostly in Canton, specially for the European market, often on commission from European trading companies or even from private individuals who sent their instructions to

[1] On this subject Hugh Honour's *Chinoiserie* (London, 1961) is an excellent up-to-date survey with useful bibliographical notes.

China through merchants making the journey there. Only objects in the first category displayed to Europeans the genuine qualities of Chinese art, and then at a relatively low level, since the foreign merchants never concerned themselves with what Chinese scholar-connoisseurs regarded as art; European imitations of Chinese work necessarily transformed the spirit of their originals, and Chinese work done specially for the European market hardly less so, since the producer was catering not for native taste, but for a Western conception of things Chinese. Nevertheless a strong flavour of China penetrated through all these distortions and adaptations, and deeply affected the aesthetic sensibility of Europe in that age, as manifested in the rococo style. It was much more than a mere superficial fashion for the strange and exotic; the rococo, for all its frivolities, was a serious exploration of new possibilities in art, of a new world of feeling and imagination. Above all, it was the new materials of porcelain and lacquer which in themselves opened up new horizons for decorative enterprise and naturally brought with them the forms and colours of their homeland. Porcelain was the Chinese product *par excellence*; it was 'china'. Its fascination for European taste in the early years of the eighteenth century and the corresponding enthusiasm for the country of its origin were well expressed by the lines of a French poet:

Qu'elle a d'attraits, qu'elle est fine!
Elle est native de la Chine.

Brocades, damasks, and embroidered silks and satins—satin probably originally derived its name from the port of Chuanchow in Fukien known to Marco Polo as Zaytun—were also brought back to Europe in large quantities by factors and seamen of the East India trading companies, and made Europe familiar not only with Chinese decorative patterns but also with the Chinese sense of colour. Evelyn notes in his *Diary* for 22 June 1664, of the liveliness of the colours in some Chinese fabrics he had seen, that 'for splendour and vividness we have nothing in

Europe that approaches it'. It became an aristocratic fashion during the eighteenth century to have 'Chinese rooms' in which Chinese silk coverings, porcelain jars, and lacquer cabinets were combined with Chinese wall-papers. The last, though they were seldom on a high artistic level, were most of all an innovation, for the use of painted or printed paper to cover walls had not previously been known in Europe. For some time all wall-papers were imports from China, but European artisans soon began to imitate and compete in the production of these articles of trade, and eventually captured the market for themselves.

Whereas the influence on European taste of Chinese porcelain, lacquer, silk textiles, and wall-papers was exerted through the actual importing of such objects into Europe, the influence of the Chinese garden, which was not physically transportable, was less direct. An attractive idea of Chinese gardens was built up in the European mind by representations of them in scenes depicted in porcelain or lacquer—the 'willow-pattern' designs were ultimately derived from the famous gardens of Soochow—but actual observation of them was confined to Europeans who went to China—either the Jesuit missionaries who had opportunities to see gardens of the imperial palaces or merchants who could view humbler specimens of the art at Canton or other ports. Among the latter was the English architect Chambers, who visited China in his youth in the service of the Swedish East India Company, and later went there a second time for study. Chambers became the pioneer of the 'Chinese–English garden', which had an even greater vogue in France and Germany than in England, where its best-known relic is the pagoda in Kew Gardens. This style contrasted by the asymmetry and irregularity of its compositions with the symmetry and geometrical forms of classical European gardens, yet was differentiated by the artificiality of its rockeries, bridges, and miniature pavilions from the park-like 'natural' gardens which had been developed in opposition to the Italianate tradition.

The Chinese aesthetic influence on Europe in the eighteenth century was limited in its range and to some critics has appeared merely a trivial matter of exotic fashions, but it was certainly one of the main factors in the emergence of the rococo style, and rococo is a not unimportant part of the heritage of European art. That Europe was at that time so receptive to influence from the Far East was due to the fact that contemporary China could furnish so much that was in accord with the mood of aristocratic Europe in the period between *le Roi Soleil* and the French Revolution. It must be repeated that the classical art of China was inaccessible to Europeans in that age; what attracted them was the decorative style of the early Ch'ing Dynasty, and that was part of the culture of a society not unlike their own. The inspiration of rococo was neither the glory of God, nor the heroism of warriors, nor the grandeur of princes and statesmen, but the life of aristocratic leisure in its more relaxed, playful, and sentimental moods, and this outlook as it prevailed in Western Europe in the last epoch of the *ancien régime* had much in common with the spirit of Chinese scholar-gentry in Hangchow or Soochow about the same time. Rococo does not belong to the heights of European art any more than *famille verte* porcelain ranks among the greatest achievements of Chinese civilization, but it created a unique world of the imagination which could claim at least one artist of the first rank. In the words of A. Reichwein:

The delicate tones of porcelain, the vaporous colours of silk, all the things that gave to the rococo world its charm and grace, are, as it were, enshrined in the paintings of Watteau. There is nothing to support the idea that Watteau as a painter really received any inspiration from Chinese landscape painting, but at the same time it is difficult not to believe that something of his technique was borrowed from China. This would not be at all surprising in view of the affinity of feeling, and the superabundance of Oriental models would have provided plenty of opportunity. . . . The fantastic forms of his mountains he had never seen with his own eyes; the Flemings had not shown them to him; but they closely resemble the Chinese forms. The darker tone of the contours is Chinese and so is the curious manner of indicating clouds. The use of monochrome colouring for background landscape, such as Watteau loves, is one of the most prominent characteristics of Chinese landscape painting.[1]

The ascendancy of the rococo style in Europe did not last long, but more enduring was the habit of drinking tea which came from China along with the porcelain pots and cups used for serving it. Tea was introduced into the Western world from the Far East about the same time as coffee, which came from Arabia by way of the Ottoman empire, and the consumption of both beverages went on spreading until today it is difficult to imagine the material life of ages in which they were unknown. Tea became the most important commodity in European trade with China, for the demand continually grew and until the second quarter of the nineteenth century China was the only source of supply. Eventually, however, British enterprise in India succeeded in producing a marketable tea by cultivation of a wild variety of the tea plant growing in Assam, and soon afterwards tea was also successfully cultivated in Ceylon. Thus China lost her monopoly of tea export just as in antiquity she had lost her monopolies of silk and cinnamon, but the trade in 'China tea' continued to be important, as it retained qualities of its own not reproduced in the Indian product. Ginger—though its traffic was never comparable in economic importance with that of tea—was another Chinese product which became prominent in the overseas food supplies of Europe and has traditionally been sold in jars of Chinese manufacture. Finally, the whole practice of Chinese cookery has been exported to the West, and Chinese restaurants have become an established feature of most Western cities. The taste for Chinese cooking was spread partly through

[1] *China and Europe* (London, 1925), pp. 47–48.

the return to their own countries of Europeans and Americans who had lived in China or Far Eastern places of Chinese settlement such as Singapore or Saigon, and partly through 'chinatowns' which sprang up in the seaports of Western countries, and particularly in California, during the later part of the nineteenth century.

The chinatowns of the West were outliers of an emigration the main volume of which went to south-east Asia in the same period and has created the communities collectively known today as the Overseas Chinese. This emigration has come almost entirely from areas of congested population in the provinces of Kwangtung and Fukien on the south coast of China, and neither followed in the wake of Chinese political expansion nor until recent times received any considerable backing or protection from the Chinese government. Chinese merchants were trading round the South China Sea as far as Malaya and Java from medieval times, but the Chinese imperial monarchy took very little interest in the maritime commercial activities of its subjects except when its capital was at Nanking or Hangchow—which has never been the case since 1421 though the series of tribute-collecting voyages in the South Seas and Indian Ocean initiated by the third emperor of the Ming Dynasty went on until 1433. Thereafter the Chinese trading settlements in the South Seas countries were left very much to their own devices; they were established in areas which were already permeated with the influences of non-Chinese civilizations—Indo-Buddhist in Burma, Siam, and Cambodia, Islamic in Malaya and Indonesia, and Catholic European from the sixteenth century in the Philippines—and thus, instead of assimilating the native inhabitants to their own culture and way of life, they tended to form more or less self-contained minority groups. The economic development of south-east Asian countries by European countries in the late nineteenth century brought a new influx of Chinese population, for the most part of a more proletarian character than the earlier settlers; whereas it had been Chinese of the merchant class who established themselves in South Seas ports the better to carry on local trade, it was now landless peasants and unemployed labourers who came south on European steamships to escape from grinding poverty in their over-populated homeland. This kind of emigration, in which hardly any members of the Chinese educated class participated, did not have much effect in spreading Chinese civilization, which was in any case by this time being overwhelmed by the impact of the West on China herself. The Overseas Chinese maintained their ethnic identity in their countries of settlement and, as a result of the Chinese family system preserving close ties with relatives left behind in China, they have also presented a political problem throughout south-east Asia; but they have not had enough demographic or cultural preponderance to create new nations, as have emigrants from Europe in the U.S.A., Canada, or Latin America, and their cultural, as distinct from their economic and political, importance has been small.

It remains to mention an influence of Chinese civilization which has been a consequence neither of Chinese conquests nor of export trade nor of settlements abroad, but of European intellectual interest in China stimulated by observations and studies made by European travellers and residents in China. This interest has been culturally important in two periods separated by an interval of relative indifference; the first began with the mission of the Jesuit Matteo Ricci, who reached Peking in the year 1600, and continued until the third quarter of the eighteenth century, while the second, which still continues, dates from about the beginning of the twentieth century. The Jesuit missions, initiated with the design of converting China to Catholic Christianity, but leading in that context to a scholarly study of Chinese civilization and a flow of information about it to Europe, had the paradoxical result that the Jesuits' revelation of China to the West had more far-reaching effects in Christendom than their own teaching had on the Chinese.[1] This was due to the fact that Chinese civilization in the seventeenth and eighteenth centuries had attained such a degree of intellectual stability and self-sufficiency that it was difficult to make any impression on it except in the limited field of mathematical and natural sciences, whereas in Europe there was an active questioning of traditional religious and philosophical conceptions which rendered the European mind open to the influence of new ideas from any quarter. Confucianism thus came to have a considerable effect on European—or more particularly French— thought in the eighteenth century; this influence went along with a general respect for contemporary China as a powerful empire, more populous than any of the states of Europe and of comparable civilization. In the nineteenth century this attitude was replaced by one of contempt for China; under the political and economic pressures of the West the Chinese empire now appeared pitifully weak and incapable, and the whole Chinese way of life stagnant and degenerate. For the new European liberalism China was a country afflicted with all the evils of despotism, superstition, and scientific ignorance, while the Christian missionaries, whether Catholic or Protestant, were far less tolerant towards 'heathen' China during the nineteenth century than the Jesuits had been. Western 'sinological' studies continued and technically made great advances, but it was not until the last years of the century that there was once more in the West a sympathetic appreciation of Chinese culture, and it then differed significantly from the eighteenth-century enthusiasms for *chinoiserie* or for Confucius; it was directed towards the China of the past rather than the present, and it concentrated on the heritage of Chinese art, particularly on that of the golden age of T'ang and Sung, with much less emphasis on the Confucian virtues and much more on the mystical and

[1] On the Jesuits in China see A. H. Rowbotham, *Missionary and Mandarin* (Berkeley and Los Angeles, 1942).

contemplative side of the Chinese philosophical tradition. This modern angle of interest in Chinese civilization—and it has, of course, to be distinguished from interest in the current modernization of China under the impact of economic, political, and intellectual factors emanating from the West—reflects, as did the European regard for China in the eighteenth century, cultural preoccupations of the time; in the days of Voltaire and Quesnay it seemed that the Europe of the *ancien régime* might have something to learn from the China of K'ang-hsi and Ch'ien-lung, whereas in an age of secular, industrial, and positivist civilization which has invented automation and thermo-nuclear weapons, there is more disposition to consider the wisdom of the *Tao te ching* or Ch'an Buddhism.

In the seventeenth and eighteenth centuries the knowledge of China transmitted to Europe by the Jesuits was quite different from that which was brought home by merchants. The latter had no contact with the world of the Chinese literati or with the imperial court; they did not learn to read and write the Chinese language nor did they study Chinese literature. The Jesuits, on the other side, while commending themselves to Chinese officialdom as indispensable experts in mathematics and astronomy—in which they took advantage of the scientific progress of Europe—sought to qualify themselves also as Chinese scholars so that they could hold their own in the company of the educated élite; at the same time, to facilitate conversion, they tried to minimize the break with tradition involved in acceptance of Christianity by permitting certain Confucian ceremonies, notably those connected with the cult of ancestors, as not incompatible with Christian practice. These tactical compromises were denounced by other Catholic religious orders which took a less tolerant view of non-Christian religions, and the result was the bitter 'Rites Controversy', which was in the end decided by the Papacy against the Jesuits. One consequence of the conflict was that the picture of China drawn by the Jesuits in their writings, which had from the beginning been an indulgent one, became more and more favourable, for the Jesuits under attack by their opponents were concerned to show that the Chinese, moulded by Confucian teaching, were already as wise and virtuous as it was possible for 'natural religion' to make them and thus to justify concessions to their traditional practices. This eulogy of China, however, was carried to the point at which it played into the hands of the 'deists' who in this period in Europe were claiming that natural religion was sufficient for mankind and the Christian revelation superfluous. If the Chinese could do so well without any established and privileged Church distinct from the state and its civil administration, this alleged fact could be used as a handle to attack such an institution in Europe. Nor was it only the deists who invoked the prestige of China in intellectual criticism of the Christian Church in Europe. Some of the interpreters of Confucian philosophy claimed that it dispensed with the notion of deity altogether, and this version was used to show that there was no universal consensus of belief in divine beings and that the highest civilization was compatible with atheism. Even among philosophers who did not dispute the Christian revelation there were those who exalted the Chinese as pre-eminent in natural religion. Thus Leibniz wrote: 'The condition of affairs among us seems to be such that, in view of the inordinate lengths to which the conception of morals has advanced, I almost think it necessary that Chinese missionaries should be sent to us to teach us the aim and practice of natural theology, as we send missionaries to them to instruct them in revealed theology.'[1]

All these discussions were about a China that was very imperfectly known, even with the elaborate accounts of it that were in circulation. The translations of the Confucian Classics which were available were defective and, without relation to their Chinese historical setting, could be highly misleading. There

[1] Quoted in Reichwein, op. cit., p. 80.

was a tendency to contrast an ideal China, which had never existed, with the reality of Europe. Nevertheless the issue at stake was one of vital importance for the development of philosophical thought in Europe and the emergence of what came to be called 'the Enlightenment'. It was the question whether human society could be ordered on a basis of moral principles without a system of religious revelation and other-worldly belief; in China it appeared that it was so ordered and that the results were very satisfactory. The issue was not alto-gether new, for it had arisen with regard to the ancient Greco-Roman world, which had had moral codes based only on human reason, but the historical victory of Christianity over classical paganism had appeared to prove the inadequacy of the latter, whereas Confucian China confronted Christendom as a contem-porary and her challenge did not therefore have the character of a lost cause. Voltaire wrote that the Chinese 'have perfected moral science and that is the first of the sciences';[1] in his *Essai sur les Mœurs* he quotes lines written in praise of Confucius by another French philosopher:

> De la seule raison salutaire interprète,
> Sans éblouir le monde, éclairant les esprits,
> Il ne parla qu'en sage et jamais en prophète;
> Cependant on le crut, et même en son pays.

This verse admirably sums up the attitude to Confucius of which Voltaire was himself a leading exponent. Confucius be-came a kind of patron saint of the thinkers of the Enlighten-ment. The fact that not only was he a great moral teacher but that also the civil servants who governed the Chinese empire were selected for proficiency in a body of learning based on his teachings caused them to regard China as a model of good government. Dissent from this view came increasingly from those who adhered to the principle of popular sovereignty and

---

[1] *Œuvres complètes* (Gotha, 1785), vol. xvi, p. 85.

looked to an elected assembly to remedy the abuses of the *ancien régime*; the pioneers of democratic liberalism naturally could not admire a system of absolute monarchy, however good the theory of its administration might be. But during the greater part of the eighteenth century, and excepting England, progress was expected through the elimination of feudal privileges and the more rational ordering of royal administration—that is, through 'enlightened despotism'—rather than through any revolutionary upheaval of the people or exercise of power by an elected parliament. The ideology of enlightened despotism in eighteenth-century Europe was so decisively overthrown by the French Revolution and later advances of political liberalism that it is hard to realize how seriously it was once taken. But Quesnay and the Physiocrats in their time represented an important body of political and economic thought and they admired China because the imperial authority of Ch'ien-lung was not restricted by the fiscal immunities of a privileged hereditary nobility. For men such as Turgot who had to struggle against the Parlement of Paris and could find no way of legally raising the revenues required by the French State it was the enhancement and not the diminution of the powers of the monarchy that appeared as the cause of reform.

As has already been pointed out, the high prestige of China disappeared in the age that followed the French Revolution and was replaced by disparagement and disdain. Even in the eighteenth century it had been recognized that Europe was ahead of China in the natural sciences; once the compensating pre-eminence in moral science, attributed to the Chinese by Voltaire, had been denied, the former eulogies of the celestial empire gave way to the view that the Chinese were a nation as morally corrupt and as badly governed as they were backward and unprogressive in science and technology. From the last years of the nineteenth century this view was increasingly shared by the younger generation of educated Chinese, who were themselves in revolt against the traditional culture and institutions of their country, and with the fall of the monarchy in 1912 began China's painful movement along the path of modernization which was to lead to Marxism–Leninism and the replacement of Confucius by 'the thought of Mao'.

Meanwhile, however, since the beginning of the twentieth century a new appreciation of historical Chinese civilization has grown up in the West, based on a knowledge of China's past and particularly of her total literary and artistic achievement which was not available in the eighteenth century either to the connoisseurs of *chinoiserie* or to the readers of the *Lettres édifiantes et curieuses*. A more sophisticated approach to Chinese history, assisted by the development of a Chinese archaeology, gave a new perspective to the historical unfolding of Chinese civilization and a setting to the new wealth of works of art which began to come out of China when Western collectors started looking for Sung and Yüan landscape-paintings, T'ang sculpture, and Shang and Chou bronzes, instead of the Ch'ing porcelain and lacquer which had so delighted the European taste of the eighteenth century. The difference between the old and the new *chinoiserie* was similar to that which came about in the appreciation of ancient Greek art when works of Pheidias and Praxiteles, Attic vase paintings, and Minoan and Mycenaean remains were added to that earlier stock of Greco-Roman antiquities among which the Laocoön was long regarded as the greatest achievement of the Hellenic genius. Moreover, since the inspiration of some of the older art of China was specifically religious or philosophical, the study of the history of Chinese art necessarily stimulated interest in the general history of Chinese thought, and particularly the non-Confucian—Taoist and Buddhist—side of the Chinese tradition. The eighteenth century had thought of China as essentially Confucian and therefore rationalist, concerning herself only with practical ethics and social life and entertaining herself with a purely secular and decorative art. Subsequent researches revealed a China of profound religious feeling and mystical contemplation, and certain forms of this made a special appeal to a later Western sensibility because they appeared to be detached from any theistic presuppositions or systematic metaphysical constructions. The most outstanding example of this appeal has been the extraordinary popularity of the *Tao te ching*; by 1957 no fewer than thirty-five translations of it had appeared in the English language alone. More recently Ch'an (Zen) Buddhism, which is essentially a Chinese hybrid of Buddhism and Taoism, has had a remarkable vogue in the West. There has often been an element of affectation and charlatanism in the presentation of doctrines so elusive and obscure to the Western public, but serious study of them has also been pursued, and there can be no doubt that the modern Western mind in moods of disenchantment with its own *Weltanschauung* is strongly attracted by the traditions of Indian and Chinese mysticism.

The great art of China has now been made a common heritage of mankind through the fine museum collections all over the world and innumerable reproductions in art books and prints. Similarly Chinese literature has become accessible to a wide public in the West through translations, which now cover not only the Classics and poetry—whose special quality must perhaps always elude complete rendering in another language—but also the formerly despised Chinese novel, which has enriched the literary inheritance of the world with its marvellously vivid representations of life as it was lived in the old China. We live today in what has become a world civilization, and although this has come into existence through a victorious expansion of the specific culture of a group of Western peoples, the effect of scholarly studies of non-Western cultures combined with modern facilities for travel, the resources of photography and television, museum collections and exhibitions, and the broadening of cultural range in education has made modern man for the first time, if he does not reject his opportunities from national or racial prejudice, culturally a citizen of the world, the heir to all former civilizations and not only his own. In that great inheritance the tradition of China is a major asset.

G. F. HUDSON

(b) THE VALUE OF THE STUDY OF CHINESE CIVILIZATION

THE preceding section of this chapter has surveyed the artistic and intellectual influences exerted by China beyond her frontiers, and the first chapter in this book was also concerned with the impact of Chinese culture on the outside world. Between them came an account of the glories of that culture. It has been demonstrated that China has a philosophical tradition which, although lacking the great intellectual subtlety which is the appeal of much Western philosophy, nevertheless represents a noteworthy attempt to urge rational and humane solutions of the problems of man in society and, furthermore, is a fascinating study for those who are interested in discovering the fundamental ideas of the world and of man which have motivated this civilization. The distinctive contribution of China to Buddhist thought has also been discussed. Something of the richness of the literature, largely concealed from Western readers by formidable language difficulties, has been revealed. The supreme artistic achievements, which have already enjoyed some recognition in the West, have been surveyed; and the no less splendid scientific and technological accomplishments, about which we have until recently been extremely ignorant, have been reviewed. Finally we have been given a glimpse of those outstanding talents in the art of government which seem so incongruous with our conventional impression of the pomp and ceremony of long-gowned mandarins.

In all these fields the Chinese have been responsible for supreme achievements of the human spirit. By some of them our civilization has already been enriched. Others will stand the test of time and contribute permanently to world civilization. All are worthy contributions to the legacy of China.

It is upon these glories of Chinese civilization that this book has deliberately concentrated, avoiding the temptation to try to present an exhaustive survey of Chinese culture. But there is a sense in which a more complete picture ought to be set before the reader as what Staunton called 'the grandest collective object that can be presented for human contemplation or research', as a legacy for the enrichment of the lives of those who come to know and love its many facets. In this sense nothing which adds to our experience and understanding may seem too obscure or too unimportant to be regarded as part of the legacy. It seems appropriate therefore to conclude this book with some consideration of the value of the study of Chinese civilization as a whole. This will have the incidental advantages both of permitting further discussion of topics which have not received very full treatment elsewhere and of drawing together and interrelating some of the major themes which have been developed in this book.

If one is asked to explain the value of the study of Chinese civilization all one really needs to do is to sketch a profile of that civilization; for, however inadequate one's word-picture may be, the explanations will surely speak for themselves. Let us start, then, by thinking of the political structure of Chinese society, which enabled that civilization to endure for many centuries. First we have to think of a distinctive and advanced culture developing among people far removed from other centres of advanced civilization and early imbued with the notion that they formed one society by contrast with the surrounding barbarian tribes. This unity was brought to greater self-consciousness by the pre-Ch'in thinkers, who spoke of the Chinese world as 'all-under-Heaven' and addressed themselves in the main to the problem of how to secure the unification and proper organization of this society. The final unification was secured by Ch'in, a state with economic and military advantages and a more totalitarian ethic than that of the other states; but it was to be perpetuated by the Han and later dynasties, whose political methods were subtle elaborations of the Confucian emphasis on the employment of men of merit, tempered by Legalist regard for impersonal rules and regulations.

This ideological balance has been matched by an institutional balance between the power of the semi-divine monarch and his need to leave the administration of the empire in the hands of Confucian scholar-bureaucrats, who enjoyed the great prestige of handing down and conforming to the wisdom of antiquity. The viability of this system deeply depended on the skilful choice and handling of administrative personnel, and on the emperor's appreciation that the right of Confucian wisdom to govern was as inalienable as his own right to occupy the throne. Oppressiveness was avoided by the fact that, at any rate in more fortunate times, the government appeared to the people in the villages as a superstructure which caused little inconvenience provided that taxes were paid and life pursued an orderly course. Ambition was to some extent satisfied by the system of literary examinations and other devices for securing that men of merit found places in the public service, but was kept within limits by checks against individuals acquiring too much power. Thus China had a political system which provided throughout many centuries, in a country so vast and populous that the idea of democracy could never have taken root, a reasonable opportunity for power to be the prerogative of merit rather than solely of birth; which is in strong contrast with what happened before modern times in Europe, the birthplace of democracy. Moral sanctions and institutional checks and balances guaranteed a tolerable amount of justice and protection to the individual, and not only have China's political methods won respect in the past, but they are also worth attention even now from those who believe that the monopoly of political wisdom belongs to the inheritors of the ideals of Greece and Rome.

Confucian philosophy emphasized not only political duty and responsibility but also duty and responsibility within the smaller social unit, the family; and within this smaller unit there is a pattern as distinctively Chinese as the Confucian model of the state. The importance of the family in Chinese society has become a commonplace, and ancestor-worship is the central feature to which all other aspects of the Chinese family pattern may be related. It was ancestor-worship which from early times gave the family a strong corporate sense. It was ancestor-worship which was an almost certain guarantee of a family's survival through many generations, because of the supreme filial duty of ensuring that there were sons to carry on the sacrifices. It was ancestor-worship which was basically responsible for concubinage undertaken in order to guarantee continuity when the first wife had no son, and for the low status accorded to girl-children because ultimately they could play no part in securing the family line. Such aspects of the Chinese family pattern provide material of particular interest to the sociologist, just as they have also afforded a rich fund of human interest to be exploited by the novelist.

Ancestor-worship, for long of central importance among the religious practices of the Chinese, may be allowed to introduce us to the swarm of deities and the hotchpotch of beliefs which have constituted Chinese religion. It has sometimes been thought that China was a country peopled by the adherents of three religions, Confucianism, Taoism, and Buddhism, all of which were entities similar in kind to Christianity, organized in a similar manner, and demanding a similar unswerving allegiance; and sometimes it has been imagined that individual Chinese were concurrently adherents of all three conflicting religions.

Nothing could be further from the truth than either of these ideas, which spring from mistakenly basing an analysis of the Chinese situation on our Western experience. Until modern times, when a word had to be coined to translate the term 'religion', there was no exact equivalent for it in the Chinese language; nor was there even a general term for gods or supernatural beings. Confucianism, Taoism, and Buddhism were the 'three teachings', and the first two of these were originally quite secular philosophies, the religious aspects of which were later derivatives. Although Taoism had long since degenerated into a corpus of superstitious beliefs, Confucianism was never so much a religion as it was after the death of the Confucian empire meant an end of the outward manifestations of its secular aspects; and it was the ill-fated attempts in the early years of the Republic to reinstate Confucianism as nothing but an organized religion, in addition to the mistaken application of Western categories, that led the West to see it as primarily a religion. The religious practices of the ordinary Chinese were coloured by all of these three systems of thought and by other elements, such as ancestor-worship, which antedated them all, and by a wide range of unsystematized cults. For although there was a state religion, which embraced such important ceremonies as the emperors' worship at the Altar of Heaven in Peking and the cult of Confucius, the essential feature of Chinese religious practice was its unco-ordinated nature. Since there was no body concerned to shape, or even to codify, religion in its totality, its development was random.

To add to the confusion, as the bureaucracy increasingly came to dominate the imaginations of the people, there developed a *reductio ad absurdum* of anthropomorphism, the creation of a celestial bureaucracy to parallel and even to serve as an extension of this terrestrial bureaucracy, with godships being regarded as offices to be filled by worthy human beings after their deaths. The less important divinities were subordinate to higher ranking members of the terrestrial administration. So numerous were the departments of the celestial administration that a vast bureaucracy recruited from the souls of the departed was needed to keep the files. 'People become gods every day in China', wrote Maspero in 1932,[1] and one should certainly not underestimate the influence of religion in Chinese society. Eighteenth-century Europeans formed the impression that the Confucian literati were agnostics for whom philosophy played the part of religion, so it is important not to disregard the extent to which they too were involved in the extravaganza of popular religion. As local magistrates they were the 'proper channels' through whom the City Gods (or 'Gods of Walls and Moats', as they were called) and other deities with local functions were approached. As scholars they were in demand to lend the weight of their prestige and the benefit of their knowledge of ritual for the supervision of funeral and mourning ceremony. As literary men they took part in the worship of Confucius and of the God of Literature. Chinese religion is a subject of infinite variety, as can be seen, for example, in the fourteen volumes of Doré's *Recherches sur les superstitions en Chine*, and much difficult but interesting work remains to be done, particularly in the study of its historical development.

If the bureaucracy with its Confucian ethos was a powerful agent in maintaining the unity of the country, another was the script in which the Confucian literati wrote; for this had the peculiar advantage of ensuring that, however much the spoken language might break up into different dialects, there remained a written medium intelligible throughout the country. It was this aspect of the language—the fact that it was composed of characters which, like numerals, were of universal validity although pronounced differently in different places—that aroused the interest of European pioneers of language planning, notably Bishop Wilkins, who, in his *Essay towards a Real Character and*

---

[1] In J. Hackin *et al.*, *Asiatic Mythology* (London, 1932), p. 262.

a Philosophical Language, published in 1668, tried to devise a written language containing characters to represent things, not words. Starting from the fact that we already possess many symbols of international validity to express mathematical and astronomical notions, he thought that it should not be beyond the ingenuity of man to devise symbols to represent all things and concepts, provided that they could be effectively systematized. One factor which such pioneers have either been unaware of or ignored is the very large phonetic element in Chinese writing; for many characters and elements of which characters are composed are normally used for their pronunciation, not for their original pictographic meaning, rather as in a child's rebus puzzle a picture of a saw may be used to represent the past tense of the verb 'to see'. Only a small proportion of characters are, in fact, the simple ideographs or pictographs which even today are widely considered to be the sole stuff of the Chinese language.

This mistake has been perpetuated by people who have cherished the romantic notion that the character does not simply represent the sound of the word, but also forms an infinitely beautiful stylized picture of the object; so that Chinese poetry, for example, is conceived as having an entirely new dimension, being capable of presenting the reader with a more immediate and fresh awareness of the beauties of nature. Misconceptions of this kind are even fostered by people who have some specialist knowledge of China. Thus Sir John Pratt wrote: 'Every Chinese character calls up a mental picture which is a blend of the meaning of the character as a whole as well as of each of its component parts.'[1] This could only be true of the small proportion of characters which are compounded in this way. Generally speaking, Chinese suffers in this respect by comparison with other languages. Although a person reading English with a lively awareness of the derivations of the words may easily call up a mental picture which is a blend of the meaning of the word as a

[1] *China and Britain* (London, n.d.), p. 56.

whole as well as of each of its component parts, the reader of Classical Chinese can call on no comparable assistance from etymology. Indeed, one of the great difficulties encountered in trying to translate Chinese accurately is that the family relationships between words are not traceable in the same way as they are in Indo-European languages, in which etymological studies give us the root-meaning of a word and its relationship to kindred words in other languages, while devices such as compounding and inflection reveal the word's relationship to a whole family of other words.

The fact that the language has as its basic unit monosyllabic components represented by single characters has meant that its genius has been very different from that of Indo-European languages. Being completely lacking in affixes, it is in strong contrast with Indo-European languages in two ways: firstly, as has already been mentioned, the family relationship between words is obscured; and secondly, grammatical construction is not dependent on the device of inflection, but is a question of word-order, supported by such devices as antithesis and parallelism, further guidance being given by particles whose main function is to serve as signposts indicating the relationship between clauses.

Despite the apparent poverty of the means at the language's disposal, an extremely subtle variety of grammatical nuances is conveyed. An instructive comparison may be made with Latin, which is often praised as a language having supreme educational advantages. The Latin verb has to commit itself as to number, tense, mood, and voice even when these are irrelevant, as in a logical proposition with universal validity such as 'all men are mortal'; but the Chinese verb remains neutral in all these respects except in so far as they are indicated by context when it is strictly relevant to express them. The Latin verb consists of a complicated pattern of different forms: *amo*, for example, appears in nearly three hundred different guises, if one includes

the declension of participial forms, to do what the single character *ai* can do with the most economical assistance from a few
particles and a thorough understanding of context. Latin can
be construed through the operation of grammatical rules and
the mastery of conjugations and declensions, whether or not the
translator really understands what the passage is about; but the
interpretation of Chinese depends much more on a thorough
understanding of the context and a subtle application of all
the clues which may be squeezed from word-order, particles,
parallelisms, antitheses, and the like. As an intellectual exercise
of educational value it would be difficult to justify giving Chinese
lower marks than Latin.

What I have said so far concerns the written language, and
mainly the Classical written language, but one should not forget that it is a common disposition among the highly literate
to over-emphasize written language at the expense of spoken
language. For the great majority of Chinese the language has not
existed as a written language at all, because they have been illiterate. A simple recognition of this fact would have killed the
absurd idea current at one time that it was almost impossible for
the Chinese to communicate without some recourse to the
writing of characters with the fingers on the palm of the hand.[1]
It would also have led people to modify their ideas of a special
relationship between language and thought in China because of
the imagined pictographic nature of the language. In spite of the
fascination of the written character, the important part it has
played in the expression of the Chinese genius, and the contribution it has made to the viability of Chinese society, the spoken

[1] An early-nineteenth-century schoolbook says of the Chinese language that
'only about 350 of its sounds can be marked by our letters; and instead of its
having a system of characters, representing the elements of speech like our
alphabet, it has 80,000 characters, each of which represents not a sound, but a
distinct object, or idea. The obscurity which thence results is so great, that in
talking it is found necessary to express by the finger, the character corresponding with the precise meaning of the sound employed.'

language is of equal interest for an understanding of the nature of Chinese thought.

I have dwelt on the topics of religion and language because they have not been fully treated elsewhere, but it would be both an impertinence and an impossibility to try to summarize those artistic, literary, and scientific achievements to which the bulk of this book has already been devoted. I shall therefore attempt no balanced survey of these subjects, although I shall be referring to them where they are relevant to the discussion of the value of the study of Chinese civilization which follows.

Here then is a civilization which has taken a course remarkably different from our own. How can one summarize its distinctive qualities? One quality which certainly permeates Chinese civilization is what one may describe as 'humanism' and define as the disposition to regard human interests as of paramount importance.

Humanism stands at the very centre of Confucian philosophy. The supreme virtue for Confucius, *jen*, which is often translated as 'goodness' because of its supremacy and generality, could better from the etymological point of view be rendered as 'humaneness' because, in a manner reminiscent of the Latin word 'gentle', it is closely related to a word meaning 'man' or 'people'. In Mencius *jen* has a slightly narrower usage which is even closer to what we mean by 'humane', both in its general sense and in its more particular sense of 'benevolent' or 'merciful'. This conception is the dominant theme in the this-worldly ethic of Confucianism, which regarded concern with problems other than human ones as unjustifiable when human ones remained to be solved. Taoism, the great rival school of thought, was also concerned with human happiness. Although Taoists saw man as a small figure in the vast landscape of the Universe, their concern was to show him how to come to terms with it. Their ideal was that spontaneous conformity with the *Tao* of the

Universe which existed in a bygone Golden Age of happy innocence, and they regretted the unhappiness which mankind
suffered through attempts to impose constant standards of goodness and value on an ever-changing world. They provided com-
fort for man in bereavement by assisting him towards a selfless
acceptance of death as part of inevitable change, and they fortified him in time of disgrace or obscurity by showing that these
were dependent upon arbitrary and relative scales of values.
Thus Taoism provided a philosophy consonant with the mood
of man wishing to escape into his private world, to complement
Confucianism which suited the mood of those who wished to
do what they could to improve the public world. Buddhism, of
course, had some other-worldly content, but, as far as the great
majority of laymen were concerned, it was soon watered down
and mixed with the other ingredients of popular religion; and,
as Maspero wrote, all the gods of the popular religion 'have one
object, and only one, man and his material and moral welfare'.[1]

The basic duties of family affection enjoined by Confucianism
also have this quality of humanism, being founded on natural
relationships rather than on the somewhat desiccated general
principles encountered in much Western moral philosophy;
which one feels would have prompted in many Chinese the kind
of reaction which greeted Mohism in the ancient Chinese world
because of its lack of special concern for those to whom special
concern was due.

Another basic ideal of Confucianism was the principle that
government should be in the hands of those fitted by learning
and experience to provide administration best calculated to
improve the lot of the people. This emphasis on learning and
respect for scholarship, which has soaked through to all levels of
Chinese society to such an extent that the great dream of the
poor was that their sons should pass the state examinations and
become officials, contrasts favourably with the contempt for

[1] Op. cit., p. 267.

learning which has often been encountered in European civilization. Hand in hand with this goes respect for civil values as
opposed to military prowess, for soldiers have traditionally been
accorded a very low status in Chinese society, until the impact of
the West with its reverence for armed might placed a premium
on armed preparedness and fostered the growth of a new type of
military leader like Chiang Kai-shek.[1]

Let us now turn to the humanistic qualities of art and literature in Chinese society. In our own society, as the derivation of
the word shows, civilization has been considered to be primarily
a matter of social and political organization; but the Chinese,
even in antiquity, felt that what separated them from the barbarians was the possession of *wen*, which consisted of literature
and the arts, as well as ceremonial behaviour and indeed anything which added refinement to life. It is often translated
'culture' and, despite the fact that, as Raymond Williams has
emphasized in *Culture and Society*, the word 'culture' has only
recently attained its modern sense and represents a complicated
and elusive conception, it is certainly the nearest equivalent we
have to *wen*. The word *wen* basically meant the patterned, the
ornamental, and hence those things which superimpose variety
and beauty on to the plain background of existence. The idea of
wen or pattern lay at the root of both art and literature, because
it could refer both to the decorative motifs on a bronze or a
pottery vessel and to the ancient pictographic forms of Chinese
characters: hence *wen* came to have the specific meaning of
'literature' in addition to the more general meaning of 'culture'.
It was this *wen*, in the high form in which it had existed at the

[1] This might be the most appropriate place to mention a minor item in
the legacy of China, which has nevertheless interested Western generals and
military historians, as well as having a strong influence on Mao Tse-tung. I
refer to Sun-tzu's essays on the art of war, which are the earliest known treatises
on the subject and probably date from the fourth century B.C., when—as the
term 'Warring States period' implies—civil values were not yet uppermost.
Cf. S. B. Griffith, *Sun Tzu: The Art of War* (Oxford, 1963).

beginning of the Chou Dynasty, that Confucius thought it was his life's work to transmit for the benefit of present and future generations. For the Chinese, therefore, literature and art were not the concern of an élite, nor even a mere embellishment of life; on the contrary they were the fundamental components of that civilized life which separated Chinese from barbarian. Thus it would be hard to conceive of any attempt being made in China to attack literature on rational grounds as harmful to society, as Plato attacked poetry.

Since literature and art were regarded as such essential features of civilized human society, it is not surprising that the Chinese accomplishment in those fields was both impressive and imbued with humanistic values. It is significant that high regard was paid to calligraphy, embodying at the same time the medium for the transmission of *wen*, in the sense of literature, and also the perfection of something which was not grandiose or remote but which all literate men did as a matter of course in their daily lives. Similarly the Chinese artistic genius has been lavished in an unsurpassed manner on the embellishment of objects for daily use and pleasure; whereas in our Christian tradition, which teaches us not to set too much store by worldly goods, much artistic inspiration has been devoted to the building and adornment of churches and to the composition of religious master-pieces, both on canvas and in sound. By contrast, the main achievements of religious art in China were the ancient ritual bronzes, which antedate the Confucian-inspired humanistic ideal, and the great Buddhist statues and cave-paintings, which were the products of a temporary response to a foreign tradi-tion. Similarly religion has played very little part in the inspira-tion of literature. On the other hand one finds in the history of Chinese literature a phenomenon parallel with the great tradi-tion of craftsmanship, and equally illustrating the pervasiveness of culture, namely the great oral literature and story-telling tradition.

The artist, too, is typically not the unhappy genius restlessly searching for a new mode of expression, but often a man of affairs painting in his spare time and, like the craftsman, meticulously following an honoured tradition. Nor has poetry been the concern of the solitary seeker of inspiration from the Muse, but rather the leisure occupation of members of the establishment; not the product of lonely broodings in the garret, but a polite embellishment of social occasions and a delight of the *bon viveur*. It may be argued that China has consequently suffered from the lack of works of great creative originality and of dramatic or rhetorical quality, but the compensating advantages of exquisite craftsmanship, order, and sanity are there in full measure. So too is the humanistic tradition that art and literature are essentials of the civilized life, which for advanced thinkers in our society represents an ideal which they strive to uphold in the face of strong propensities towards treating art and literature as the concern of the few. There is no need to pursue this argument further by calling on detailed evidence from scientific and technological achievements, for it is obvious that any civilization which can boast great successes in this field must have given a high priority to man's material needs.

In a book of this kind, in which writers set out to describe the higher qualities of a civilization, there is a danger that they may appear to be writing in a sentimental and uncritical manner about it. I must therefore make it clear that I am not trying to suggest that traditional Chinese civilization was a thing of unparalleled beauty and nobility. On the contrary, there has been much poverty, squalor, and degradation. But even if it has often not been converted into reality, the Chinese ideal of humanism is surely of value and interest for us today. For in a world in which the lives of millions of people are either shaped by the demands of what many feel to be outmoded religious beliefs, or subjected to the whim of totalitarian political systems, or sometimes even seem to be in thraldom to the great technological advances for which man himself has been responsible, it is surely a good thing to study a civilization which, perhaps more than any other, has given supremacy to the satisfaction of human needs and the problems of human relationships. This I should regard as first and foremost among the values which the study of Chinese civilization holds for us in the twentieth century.

Secondly, this study is valuable because it constitutes an immense and stimulating new field of inquiry. At a time when science reaches out to bring other planets within its embrace and, to the superficial eye, the world seems to have yielded up many of its mysteries, it is good that new vistas should be opening up before the student of the humanities. For the exploration of Chinese culture by the West is only in its initial stages, and much remains to be done before its enormous literature can be thoroughly investigated, and before a scientific achievement as complex as that of Europe can be comprehensively evaluated.

Thirdly, the study of Chinese civilization affords perhaps the best vantage point from which to view and compare our own civilization: in all fields of human activity its development has been virtually separate from our own, and it offers a comparable experience which can supply a valuable corrective to those who are immersed in European studies and who pontificate about them as if their contentions had universal application. For our school syllabuses and university disciplines and our general attitude to learning still largely reflect the time when nothing of value was considered to exist outside the European tradition.

It is only with the breakdown of such parochialism and the widespread growth of respect for alien traditions that there can ever be a serious prospect of a permanent and genuine improvement in international relations. It is difficult to see how one can expect China, with her high regard for learning and a deep pride in her own culture, to be on terms of close friendship with countries which, despite former close ties, remain very ignorant of that culture. This is the fourth and most obvious of the values of the study of Chinese civilization.

Finally, but not least in importance, is the enrichment of experience offered. For those who have the good fortune to visit the country or the perseverance to study its culture there are delights to set beside the greatest which our world has to offer. Some, like the perfection of form and exquisite decoration of a piece of finest porcelain or the spacious grandeur of the Forbidden City, may be appreciated immediately and without special knowledge. To appreciate others, such as the vivid and multiform art of the theatre or the structure, mood, and intricate allusions of a poem, one needs to enter a wholly new world of the imagination.

Although such deep understanding of China is an experience which few foreigners may enjoy, it will have become clear that the influence of her civilization on our own is not so remote as the reader may have thought before he began this book. I should like to conclude by emphasizing this point.

To the superficial eye China may seem to have made little impact on Western culture. Where does she impinge on our literary or philosophical tradition? One may recall some of the great writers and thinkers who have drawn some inspiration from Chinese ideas or used Chinese settings: Voltaire, whose *Orphelin de la Chine* stands out from a host of *chinoiserie* plays and entertainments; Leibniz, whose *Novissima Sinica* proposed a cultural interchange between Europe and China; Tolstoy, who wrote and sponsored several works on Chinese philosophy;[1] Jung, who was also interested in Chinese religion and philosophy;[2] Brecht,

---

[1] Cf. D. Bodde, *Tolstoy and China* (Princeton, 1950).

[2] Cf. R. Wilhelm, tr., *The Secret of the Golden Flower*, English translation by C. F. Baynes, with commentary by C. G. Jung (London, 1931), and id., *I Ching: or Book of Changes* (London, 1951).

with *The Good Woman of Setsuan*; and Pound, with his *Cantos* and Confucian translations. The list is short. Among modern prose-writers one searches vainly for a Chinese equivalent of *A Passage to India* and, although Western society in China was a gift to the satirist, perhaps only Somerset Maugham with his *On a Chinese Screen* has succeeded in transcending the particular and producing a miniature work of art. Similarly, since Chinese film-makers lag behind the Japanese, there has perhaps been only one memorable film set in China, *The Good Earth*, from the book by Pearl Buck, one of the few specialist writers on the Far East to reach a wide audience. Another is the great translator, Arthur Waley, and there has also been a vogue for the gentle philosophy of life purveyed by Lin Yutang and Chiang Yee. A generation ago Ernest Bramah in his Kai Lung books made capital out of the Chinese penchant for involved honorific speech, and in recent years Robert van Gulik with his Judge Dee mysteries has shown the West that the Chinese were first even in the field of detective stories. In the theatre Hsiung's *Lady Precious Stream* interested audiences in the thirties, while in the fifties the tours of the Classical Theatre brought Chinese dramatic art to Western capitals. Chinese entertainment has come into the home in the form of *mah-jong*, while *wei-ch'i* has even had its Western devotees. But if the reader totals all these influences, adds the Zen craze, the vestiges of *chinoiserie* and the budding interest in genuine Chinese art, and fills out this obviously personal list with items of his own choosing, he may still feel that China's effect on our modern culture is slight.

But the big influences are, of course, not the obvious ones. Let the reader remember, as he reads this book, that the very paper and print before his eyes can trace their ancestry back to Chinese origins many centuries ago, and that the wall-paper on his walls stems from a fashion introduced from China. Let him remember that his life is much controlled by a civil service which adopted its modern methods of recruitment by examination only after powerful advocacy of the Chinese system. Let him look out into his garden and reflect upon the number of plants which originated in the Flowery Land and were unknown here before the plant-hunting expeditions of Robert Fortune and others;[1] and let him remember that even the wheelbarrow comes from Chinese stock. Let him remember, when he goes on a sea journey, that the ship's compass is another invention we owe to the Chinese, and that without it the world-wide exploration which opened up the new continents would have been much less feasible.

Let him remember all these and the many other things which owed their origin to Chinese inventiveness, and let him conclude by reflecting on some wise words written in 1886 by W. A. P. Martin, a well-known American friend of the country:

When China, developing the resources of her magnificent domain, and clothing herself with the panoply of modern science, becomes, as she must in the lapse of a century or two, one of the three or four great powers that divide the dominion of the globe, think you that the world will continue to be indifferent to the past of her history? Not only will some knowledge of her history be deemed indispensable to a liberal education; but, while I am in the spirit of prophecy, I may go on to predict that her language and literature will be studied in all our Universities.[2]

RAYMOND DAWSON

[1] The reader who wishes to do this seriously should consult E. H. M. Cox's *Plant Hunting in China* (London, 1945). This history of botanical exploration in China refers to nearly a hundred varieties of rhododendron alone!

[2] *Journal of the Peking Oriental Society*, vol. i (1886), p. 135.

Eastern China, showing principal cities and places of historical interest

INDEX